MAXIMUM RPM

Edward C. Bailey

redhat
press

201 West 103rd Street
Indianapolis, Indiana 46290

For more information on the Linux operating system and
Red Hat Software, Inc., check http://www.redhat.com.

To Deb—My lover, editor, indexer, and friend.

To Matt, who heard, "Daddy can't play right now" far too often.

Copyright © 1997 by Red Hat Software, Inc.

FIRST EDITION

International Standard Book Number: 0-672-31105-4

Library of Congress Catalog Card Number: 97-66201

2000   4   3

Interpretation of the printing code: the rightmost double-digit number is the year of the book's printing; the rightmost single-digit, the number of the book's printing. For example, a printing code of 97-1 shows that the first printing of the book occurred in 1997.

Composed in AGaramond and MCPdigital by Macmillan Computer Publishing

Printed in the United States of America

President, Sams Publishing	*Richard K. Swadley*
Publishing Manager	*Dean Miller*
Managing Editor	*Kitty Wilson Jarrett*
Director of Marketing	*Kelli S. Spencer*
Product Marketing Managers	*Wendy Gilbride*
	Kim Margolius
Associate Product Marketing Manager	*Jennifer Pock*
Marketing Coordinator	*Linda Beckwith*

Acquisitions Editor
Grace M. Buechlein

Development Editor
Jeffrey J. Koch

Production Editor
Kitty Wilson Jarrett

Copy Editor
Kimberly K. Hannel

Indexer
Tina Trettin

Technical Reviewer
William H. Ball

Editorial Coordinators
Mandie Rowell
Katie Wise

Technical Edit Coordinator
Lynette Quinn

Editorial Assistants
Carol Ackerman
Andi Richter
Rhonda Tinch-Mize

Cover Designer
Jay Corpus

Book Designer
Gary Adair

Copy Writer
David Reichwein

Production Team Supervisors
Brad Chinn
Charlotte Clapp

Production
Cynthia Hubler
Chris Livengood
Carl Pierce
Janet Seib

Overview

Introduction   xix

I   RPM and Computer Users: How to Use RPM to Effectively Manage Your Computer

1	An Introduction to Package Management	3
2	Using RPM to Install Packages	17
3	Using RPM to Erase Packages	37
4	Using RPM to Upgrade Packages	45
5	Getting Information About Packages	53
6	Using RPM to Verify Installed Packages	79
7	Using RPM to Verify Package Files	93
8	Miscellanea	101

II   RPM and Developers: How to Distribute Your Software More Easily with RPM

9	The Philosophy Behind RPM	113
10	The Basics of Developing with RPM	119
11	Building Packages: A Simple Example	125
12	rpm -b Command Reference	139
13	Inside the Spec File	163
14	Adding Dependency Information to a Package	205
15	Making a Relocatable Package	215
16	Making a Package That Can Build Anywhere	225
17	Adding PGP Signatures to a Package	237
18	Creating Subpackages	247
19	Building Packages for Multiple Architectures and Operating Systems	263
20	Real-World Package Building	275
21	A Guide to the RPM Library API	305

III   Appendixes

A	The Format of the RPM File	337
B	The rpmrc File	353

C   Concise RPM Command Reference   367
D   Available Tags for --queryformat   375
E   Concise Spec File Reference   387
F   RPM-Related Resources   403
G   An Introduction to PGP   417

    Index   425

Contents

Introduction   xix

Part I   RPM and Computer Users: How to Use RPM to Effectively Manage Your Computer

1   **An Introduction to Package Management**   **3**

1.1. What Are Packages and Why Manage Them? 4
    1.1.1. Enter the Package 5
    1.1.2. Manage Your Packages or They Will Manage You 6
1.2. Package Management: How to Do It 7
    1.2.1. The Ancestors of RPM 8
1.3. RPM Design Goals 11
    1.3.1. Making It Easy to Get Packages on and off the System 11
    1.3.2. Making It Easy to Verify That a Package Was Installed
       Correctly 11
    1.3.3. Making It Easy for the Package Builder 11
    1.3.4. Making It Start with the Original Source Code 12
    1.3.5. Making It Work on Different Computer Architectures 12
1.4. What's in a Package? 12
    1.4.1. RPM's Package Labels 13
    1.4.2. Labels and Names: Similar but Distinct 13
    1.4.3. Packagewide Information 14
    1.4.4. Per-File Information 14
1.5. Summary 15

2   **Using RPM to Install Packages**   **17**

2.1. `rpm -i`—What Does It Do? 18
2.2. Performing an Install 20
    2.2.1. URLs: Another Way to Specify Package Files 20
    2.2.2. A Warning Message You Might Never See 21
2.3. Two Handy Options 22
    2.3.1. Getting a Bit More Feedback with `-v` 22
    2.3.2. `-h`: Perfect for the Impatient 22
2.4. Additional Options to `rpm -i` 23
    2.4.1. Getting a Lot More Information with `-vv` 23
    2.4.2. `--test`: Perform Installation Tests Only 23
    2.4.3. `--replacepkgs`: Install the Package Even if It's
       Already Installed 24
    2.4.4. `--replacefiles`: Install the Package Even if It Replaces
       Another Package's Files 25
    2.4.5. `--nodeps`: Do Not Check Dependencies Before
       Installing Package 29
    2.4.6. `--force`: The Big Hammer 30

2.4.7. `--excludedocs`: Do Not Install Documentation for This
Package 30
2.4.8. `--includedocs`: Install Documentation for This Package 31
2.4.9. `--prefix` *<path>*: Relocate the Package to <path>, if Possible ... 31
2.4.10. `--noscripts`: Do Not Execute Pre- and Postinstall Scripts 32
2.4.11. `--percent`: Not Meant for Human Consumption 33
2.4.12. `--rcfile` *<rcfile>*: Use <rcfile> As an Alternate rpmrc File 33
2.4.13. `--root` *<path>*: Use <path> As an Alternate Root 33
2.4.14. `--dbpath` *<path>*: Use <path> to Find an RPM Database 34
2.4.15. `--ftpport` *<port>*: Use <port> in FTP-Based Installs 34
2.4.16. `--ftpproxy` *<host>*: Use <host> As a Proxy in FTP-Based
Installs 34
2.4.17. `--ignorearch`: Do Not Verify Package Architecture 35
2.4.18. `--ignoreos`: Do Not Verify the Package Operating System 35

3   Using RPM to Erase Packages   37
3.1. `rpm -e`: What Does It Do? 38
3.2. Erasing a Package 38
3.2.1. Getting More Information with `-vv` 39
3.3. Additional Options 40
3.3.1. `--test`: Go Through the Process of Erasing the Package, But
Do Not Erase It 40
3.3.2. `--nodeps`: Do Not Check Dependencies Before Erasing
Package 41
3.3.3. `--noscripts`: Do Not Execute Pre- and Postuninstall Scripts ... 41
3.3.4. `--rcfile` *<rcfile>*: Read *<rcfile>* for RPM Defaults 42
3.3.5. `--root` *<path>*: Use *<path>* As the Root 42
3.3.6. `--dbpath` *<path>*: Use <path> to Find the RPM Database 42
3.4. `rpm -e` and Config Files 43
3.5. Watch Out! 43

4   Using RPM to Upgrade Packages   45
4.1. `rpm -U`: What Does It Do? 47
4.1.1. Config File Magic 47
4.2. Upgrading a Package 50
4.2.1. `rpm -U`'s Dirty Little Secret 50
4.3. They're Nearly Identical 50
4.3.1. `--oldpackage`: Upgrade to an Older Version 50
4.3.2. `--force`: The Big Hammer 51
4.3.3. `--noscripts`: Do Not Execute Install and Uninstall Scripts 51

5   Getting Information About Packages   53
5.1. `rpm -q`: What Does It Do? 55
5.2. The Parts of an RPM Query 55
5.2.1. Query Commands, Part I: Package Selection 55
5.2.2. Querying Commands, Part II: Information Selection 61
5.2.3. Getting a Lot More Information with `-vv` 74

5.2.4. `--root` *<path>*: Use *<path>* As an Alternate Root 74
5.2.5. `--rcfile` *<rcfile>*: Use *<rcfile>* As an Alternate `rpmrc` File ... 75
5.2.6. `--dbpath` *<path>*: Use *<path>* to Find an RPM Database 75
5.3. A Few Handy Queries 75
5.3.1. Finding Config Files Based on a Program Name 75
5.3.2. Learning More About an Uninstalled Package 76
5.3.3. Finding Documentation for a Specific Package 76
5.3.4. Finding Similar Packages 77
5.3.5. Finding Recently Installed Packages, Part I 77
5.3.6. Finding Recently Installed Packages, Part II 77
5.3.7. Finding the Largest Installed Packages 78

6   Using RPM to Verify Installed Packages   79

6.1. `rpm -V`: What Does It Do? 80
6.1.1. What Does It Verify? 81
6.2. When Verification Fails: `rpm -V` Output 83
6.2.1. Other Verification Failure Messages 84
6.3. Selecting What to Verify and How 85
6.3.1. The Package Label: Verify an Installed Package Against the
RPM Database 85
6.3.2. `-a`: Verify All Installed Packages Against the RPM Database 85
6.3.3. `-f` *<file>*: Verify the Package Owning *<file>* Against the
RPM Database 86
6.3.4. `-p` *<file>*: Verify Against a Specific Package File 86
6.3.5. `-g` *<group>*: Verify Packages Belonging to *<group>* 87
6.3.6. `--nodeps`: Do Not Check Dependencies Before Erasing
Package 87
6.3.7.   `noscripts`: Do Not Execute Verification Script 88
6.3.8. `--nofiles`: Do Not Verify File Attributes 88
6.3.9. `-v`: Display Additional Information 89
6.3.10. `-vv`: Display Debugging Information 89
6.3.11. `--dbpath` *<path>*: Use *<path>* to Find an RPM Database 90
6.3.12. `--root` *<path>*: Set Alternate Root to *<path>* 90
6.3.13. `--rcfile` *<rcfile>*: Set Alternate `rpmrc` File to *<rcfile>* 90
6.4. We've Lied to You 90
6.4.1. RPM Controls What Gets Verified 90
6.4.2. The Package Builder Can Also Control What Gets Verified 91

7   Using RPM to Verify Package Files   93

7.1. `rpm -K`: What Does It Do? 94
7.1.1. Pretty Good Privacy: RPM's Assistant 94
7.2. Configuring PGP for U 95
7.3. Using `rpm -K` 95
7.3.1. `-v`: Display Additional Information 96
7.3.2. When the Package Is Not Signed 97
7.3.3. When You Are Missing the Correct Public Key 97
7.3.4. When a Package Just Doesn't Verify 98
7.3.5. `--nopgp`: Do Not Verify Any PGP Signatures 99

      7.3.6. `-vv`: Display Debugging Information 100

      7.3.7. `--rcfile <rcfile>`: Use `<rcfile>` As an Alternate `rpmrc` File . 100

8   Miscellanea   101

   8.1. Other RPM Options 102

      8.1.1. `--rebuilddb`: Rebuild RPM Database 102

      8.1.2. `--initdb`: Create a New RPM Database 103

      8.1.3. `--quiet`: Produce As Little Output As Possible 104

      8.1.4. `--help`: Display a Help Message 104

      8.1.5. `--version`: Display the Current RPM Version 105

   8.2. Using `rpm2cpio` 105

      8.2.1. `rpm2cpio`: What Does It Do? 105

      8.2.2. A More Real-World Example: Listing the Files in a
          Package File 106

      8.2.3. Extracting One or More Files from a Package File 106

   8.3. Source Package Files and How to Use Them 107

      8.3.1. A Gentle Introduction to Source Code 108

      8.3.2. Do You Really Need More Information Than This? 108

      8.3.3. So What Can I Do with It? 108

      8.3.4. Stick with Us! 110

Part II   RPM and Developers: How to Distribute Your Software More Easily with RPM

9   The Philosophy Behind RPM   113

   9.1. Pristine Sources 114

   9.2. Easy Builds 115

      9.2.1. Reproducible Builds 115

      9.2.2. Unattended Builds 116

   9.3. Multiarchitecture/Operating System Support 116

   9.4. Easier for Your Users 116

      9.4.1. Easy Upgrades 116

      9.4.2. Intelligent Configuration File Handling 116

      9.4.3. Powerful Query Capabilities 117

      9.4.4. Easy Package Verification 117

   9.5. To Summarize 117

10   The Basics of Developing with RPM   119

   10.1. The Inputs 120

      10.1.1. The Sources 120

      10.1.2. The Patches 120

      10.1.3. The Spec File 121

   10.2. The Engine: RPM 123

   10.3. The Outputs 123

      10.3.1. The Source Package File 123

      10.3.2. The Binary RPM 123

   10.4. And Now… 124

11   Building Packages: A Simple Example   125
11.1. Creating the Build Directory Structure 126
11.2. Getting the Sources 127
11.3. Creating the Spec File 127
11.3.1. The Preamble 127
11.3.2. The `%prep` Section 129
11.3.3. The `%build` Section 130
11.3.4. The `%install` Section 130
11.3.5. The `%files` Section 131
11.3.6. The Missing Spec File Sections 132
11.4. Starting the Build 132
11.5. When Things Go Wrong 136
11.5.1. Problems During the Build 136
11.5.2. Testing Newly Built Packages 137
11.6. Summary 137

12   `rpm -b` Command Reference   139
12.1. `rpm -b`: What Does It Do? 140
12.1.1. `rpm -bp`: Execute `%prep` 141
12.1.2. `rpm -bc`: Execute `%prep`, `%build` 142
12.1.3. `rpm -bi`: Execute `%prep`, `%build`, `%install` 143
12.1.4. `rpm -bb`: Execute `%prep`, `%build`, `%install`, Package (bin) 144
12.1.5. `rpm -ba`: Execute `%prep`, `%build`, `%install`, Package (bin, src) 145
12.1.6. `rpm -bl`: Check `%files` List 146
12.1.7. `--short-circuit`: Force Build to Start at a Particular Stage .. 149
12.1.8. `--buildarch <arch>`: Perform a Build for the `<arch>` Architecture 151
12.1.9. `--buildos <os>`: Perform Build for the `<os>` Operating System 152
12.1.10. `--sign`: Add a Digital Signature to the Package 152
12.1.11. `--test`: Create, Save Build Scripts for Review 153
12.1.12. `--clean`: Clean Up After Build 154
12.1.13. `--buildroot <path>`: Execute `%install` Using `<path>` As the Root 155
12.1.14. `--timecheck <secs>`: Print a Warning if Files to Be Packaged Are More Than `<secs>` Old 158
12.1.15. `-vv`: Display Debugging Information 159
12.1.16. `--quiet`: Produce As Little Output As Possible 159
12.1.17. `--rcfile <rcfile>`: Set Alternate rpmrc File to `<rcfile>` 160
12.2. Other Build-Related Commands 160
12.2.1. `rpm --recompile`: What Does It Do? 160
12.2.2. `rpm --rebuild`: What Does It Do? 161
12.3. Summary 162

13   Inside the Spec File   **163**

13.1. Comments: Notes Ignored by RPM 164

13.2. Tags: Data Definitions 164

   13.2.1. Package Naming Tags 165

   13.2.2. Descriptive Tags 166

   13.2.3. Dependency Tags 169

   13.2.4. Architecture- and Operating System–Specific Tags 172

   13.2.5. Directory-Related Tags 174

   13.2.6. Source and Patch Tags 175

13.3. Scripts: RPM's Workhorse 178

   13.3.1. Build-Time Scripts 178

   13.3.2. Install/Erase-Time Scripts 181

   13.3.3. Verification-Time Script—The `%verifyscript` Script 183

13.4. Macros: Helpful Shorthand for Package Builders 183

   13.4.1. The `%setup` Macro 184

   13.4.2. The `%patch` Macro 191

13.5. The `%files` List 194

13.6. Directives for the `%files` List 194

   13.6.1. File-Related Directives 195

   13.6.2. Directory-Related Directives 197

13.7. The Lone Directive: `%package` 200

   13.7.1. `-n <string>`: Use `<string>` As the Entire
Subpackage Name 201

13.8. Conditionals 201

   13.8.1. The `%ifarch` Conditional 202

   13.8.2. The `%ifnarch` Conditional 202

   13.8.3. The `%ifos` Conditional 203

   13.8.4. The `%ifnos` Conditional 203

   13.8.5. The `%else` Conditional 203

   13.8.6. The `%endif` Conditional 203

13.9. Summary... 204

14   Adding Dependency Information to a Package   **205**

14.1. An Overview of Dependencies 206

14.2. Automatic Dependencies 206

   14.2.1. The Automatic Dependency Scripts 207

   14.2.2. Automatic Dependencies: An Example 208

   14.2.3. The `autoreqprov` Tag: Disable Automatic
Dependency Processing 209

14.3. Manual Dependencies 209

   14.3.1. The `requires` Tag 209

   14.3.2. The `conflicts` Tag 211

   14.3.3. The `provides` Tag 212

14.4. To Summarize 213

15   Making a Relocatable Package   215

15.1. Why Relocatable Packages? 216
15.2. The `prefix` tag: Relocation Central 216
15.3. Relocatable Wrinkles: Things to Consider 217
    15.3.1. `%files` List Restrictions 218
    15.3.2. Relocatable Packages Must Contain Relocatable Software ... 218
    15.3.3. The Relocatable Software Is Referenced by
    Other Software 219
15.4. Building a Relocatable Package 219
    15.4.1. Tying Up the Loose Ends 221
    15.4.2. Test-Driving a Relocatable Package 222

16   Making a Package That Can Build Anywhere   225

16.1. Using Build Roots in a Package 226
    16.1.1. Some Things to Consider 229
16.2. Having RPM Use a Different Build Area 230
    16.2.1. Setting Up a Build Area 230
    16.2.2. Directing RPM to Use the New Build Area 231
    16.2.3. Performing a Build in a New Build Area 231
16.3. Specifying File Attributes 233
    16.3.1. `%attr`: How Does It Work? 233
    16.3.2. Betcha Thought We Forgot 235

17   Adding PGP Signatures to a Package   237

17.1. Why Sign a Package? 238
17.2. Getting Ready to Sign 238
    17.2.1. Preparing PGP: Creating a Key Pair 238
    17.2.2. Preparing RPM 240
17.3. Signing Packages 241
    17.3.1. `--sign`: Sign a Package at Build Time 241
    17.3.2. `--resign`: Replace a Package's Signature(s) 243
    17.3.3. `--addsign`: Add a Signature to a Package 244

18   Creating Subpackages   247

18.1. What Are Subpackages? 248
18.2. Why Are Subpackages Needed? 248
18.3. Our Sample Spec File: Subpackages Galore! 248
18.4. Spec File Changes for Subpackages 249
    18.4.1. The Subpackage's Preamble 249
    18.4.2. The `%files` List 253
    18.4.3. Install and Erase Time Scripts 255
18.5. Build-Time Scripts: Unchanged for Subpackages 257
    18.5.1. Our Spec File: One Last Look 257
18.6. Building Subpackages 259
    18.6.1. Giving Subpackages the Once-Over 260

19   Building Packages for Multiple Architectures and Operating Systems   263

19.1. Architectures and Operating Systems: A Primer 264

    19.1.1. Let's Just Call Them Platforms 265

19.2. What Does RPM Do to Make Multiplatform Packaging Easier? 265

    19.2.1. Automatic Detection of the Build Platform 265

    19.2.2. Automatic Detection of the Install Platform 265

    19.2.3. Platform-Dependent Tags 265

    19.2.4. Platform-Dependent Conditionals 266

19.3. Build and Install Platform Detection 266

    19.3.1. Platform-Specific `rpmrc` Entries 266

    19.3.2. Overriding Platform Information at Build Time 268

    19.3.3. Overriding Platform Information at Install Time 268

19.4. `optflags`: The Other `rpmrc` File Entry 269

19.5. Platform-Dependent Tags 269

    19.5.1. The `excludexxx` Tags 270

    19.5.2. The `exclusivexxx` Tags 270

19.6. Platform-Dependent Conditionals 270

    19.6.1. Common Features of All Conditionals 271

    19.6.2. `%ifxxx` 272

    19.6.3. `%ifnxxx` 272

19.7. Hints and Kinks 273

20   Real-World Package Building   275

20.1. An Overview of Amanda 276

20.2. Initial Building Without RPM 276

    20.2.1. Setting Up a Test Build Area 277

    20.2.2. Getting Software to Build 278

    20.2.3. Installing and Testing 279

20.3. Initial Building with RPM 281

    20.3.1. Generating Patches 281

    20.3.2. Making a First-Cut Spec File 283

    20.3.3. Getting the Original Sources Unpacked 285

    20.3.4. Getting Patches Properly Applied 286

    20.3.5. Letting RPM Do the Building 287

    20.3.6. Letting RPM Do the Installing 288

    20.3.7. Testing RPM's Handiwork 289

20.4. Package Building 289

    20.4.1. Creating the `%files` List 291

    20.4.2. Testing those first packages 296

    20.4.3. Finishing Touches 297

21   A Guide to the RPM Library API   305

21.1. An Overview of rpmlib 306

21.2. rpmlib Functions 306

    21.2.1. Error Handling 306

    21.2.2. Getting Package Information 307

21.2.3. Variable Manipulation 308
21.2.4. rpmrc-Related Information 309
21.2.5. RPM Database Manipulation 311
21.2.6. RPM Database Traversal 312
21.2.7. RPM Database Search 313
21.2.8. Package Manipulation 315
21.2.9. Package and File Verification 318
21.2.10. Dependency-Related Operations 319
21.2.11. Diagnostic Output Control 322
21.2.12. Signature Verification 323
21.2.13. Header Manipulation 324
21.2.14. Header Entry Manipulation 326
21.2.15. Header Iterator Support 327
21.3. Sample Code 328
21.3.1. Example #1 328
21.3.2. Example #2 330
21.3.3. Example #3 333

Part III Appendixes

A   **The Format of the RPM File**   **337**

A.1. The RPM File-Naming Convention 338
A.2. The RPM File Format 339
A.2.1. Parts of an RPM File 339
A.3. Tools for Studying RPM Files 349
A.4. Identifying RPM Files with the file(1) Command 351

B   **The rpmrc File**   **353**

B.1. Using the --showrc Option 354
B.2. Different Places an rpmrc File Resides 355
B.2.1. /usr/lib/rpmrc 355
B.2.2. /etc/rpmrc 358
B.2.3. .rpmrc in the User's Login Directory 358
B.2.4. File Specified by the --rcfile Option 358
B.3. rpmrc File Syntax 358
B.4. rpmrc File Entries 359
B.4.1. arch_canon 359
B.4.2. os_canon 359
B.4.3. buildarchtranslate 359
B.4.4. buildostranslate 360
B.4.5. arch_compat 360
B.4.6. os_compat 360
B.4.7. builddir 361
B.4.8. buildroot 361
B.4.9. cpiobin 361
B.4.10. dbpath 361
B.4.11. defaultdocdir 361

B.4.12. `distribution` 362
B.4.13. `excludedocs` 362
B.4.14. `ftpport` 362
B.4.15. `ftpproxy` 362
B.4.16. `messagelevel` 362
B.4.17. `netsharedpath` 362
B.4.18. `optflags` 363
B.4.19. `packager` 363
B.4.20. `pgp_name` 363
B.4.21. `pgp_path` 364
B.4.22. `require_distribution` 364
B.4.23. `require_icon` 364
B.4.24. `require_vendor` 364
B.4.25. `rpmdir` 364
B.4.26. `signature` 365
B.4.27. `sourcedir` 365
B.4.28. `specdir` 365
B.4.29. `srcrpmdir` 365
B.4.30. `timecheck` 365
B.4.31. `tmppath` 365
B.4.32. `topdir` 366
B.4.33. `vendor` 366

C   Concise RPM Command Reference   367
C.1. Global Options 368
C.2. Informational Options 368
C.3. Query Mode 368
    C.3.1. Package Specification Options for Query Mode 368
    C.3.2. Information Selection Options for Query Mode 369
C.4. Verify Mode 369
    C.4.1. Options for Verify Mode 370
C.5. Install Mode 370
    C.5.1. Options for Install Mode 370
C.6. Upgrade Mode 371
    C.6.1. Options for Upgrade Mode 371
C.7. Erase Mode 371
    C.7.1. Options for Erase Mode 372
C.8. Build Mode 372
    C.8.1. Build Mode Stages 372
    C.8.2. Options for Build Mode 372
C.9. Rebuild Mode 373
    C.9.1. Options for Rebuild Mode 373
C.10. Recompile Mode 373
    C.10.1. Options for Recompile Mode 373
C.11. Resign Mode 373
    C.11.1. Options for Resign Mode 373

C.12. Add Signature Mode 373
    C.12.1. Options for Add Signature Mode 374
C.13. Check Signature Mode 374
    C.13.1. Options for Check Signature Mode 374
C.14. Initialize Database Mode 374
    C.14.1. Options for Initialize Database Mode 374
C.15. Rebuild Database Mode 374
    C.15.1. Options to Rebuild Database Mode 374

D   **Available Tags for `queryformat`**   **375**
D.1. List of `--queryformat` Tags 376

E   **Concise Spec File Reference**   **387**
E.1. Comments 388
E.2. The Preamble 388
    E.2.1. Package-Naming Tags 388
    E.2.2. Descriptive Tags 388
    E.2.3. Dependency Tags 390
    E.2.4. Architecture- and Operating System–Specific Tags 391
    E.2.5. Directory-Related Tags 392
    E.2.6. Source and Patch Tags 393
E.3. Scripts 394
    E.3.1. BuildTime Scripts 394
    E.3.2. Install and EraseTime Scripts 395
    E.3.3. Verification Scripts 396
E.4. Macros 396
    E.4.1. The `%setup` Macro 396
    E.4.2. The `%patch` Macro 397
E.5. The `%files` List 398
E.6. Directives for the `%files` List 399
    E.6.1. File-Related Directives 399
    E.6.2. Directory-Related Directives 400
E.7. The `%package` Directive 401
    F.7.1. The `%package -n` Option 401
E.8. Conditionals 401
    E.8.1. The `%ifarch` Conditional 401
    E.8.2. The `%ifnarch` Conditional 402
    E.8.3. The `%ifos` Conditional 402
    E.8.4. The `%ifnos` Conditional 402
    E.8.5. The `%else` Conditional 402
    E.8.6. The `%endif` Conditional 402

F   **RPM-Related Resources**   **403**
F.1. Where to Get RPM 404
    F.1.1. FTP Sites 404
    F.1.2. What Do I Need? 406

F.2. Where to Talk About RPM 407
   F.2.1. The `rpm-list` Mailing List 408
   F.2.2. The `redhat-list` Mailing List 408
   F.2.3. The `redhat-digest` Mailing List 408
F.3. RPM on the World Wide Web 409
F.4. RPM's License 409
   Preamble 410
   GNU General Public License 411
   How to Apply These Terms to Your New Programs 415

G   An Introduction to PGP   417

G.1. PGP: Privacy for Regular People 418
   G.1.1. Keys Your Locksmith Wouldn't Understand 418
   G.1.2. Are RPM Packages Encrypted? 419
   G.1.3. Do All RPM Packages Have Digital Signatures? 420
   G.1.4. So Much to Cover, So Little Time 420
G.2. Installing PGP for RPM's Use 420
   G.2.1. Obtaining PGP 420
   G.2.2. Building PGP 422
   G.2.3. Ready to Go! 423

Index   425

Acknowledgments

Writing a book is similar to entering a long-term relationship with an obsessive partner. Throughout the nine months it took to write this book, life went on: job changes, births, deaths, and even a hurricane. Throughout it all, the book demanded constant attention. Therefore, I'd like to thank the people who made it possible to focus on the book to the exclusion of nearly everything else. My wife, Deb, and son, Matt, supported and encouraged me throughout, even when I was little more than a reclusive houseguest hunched over the computer in the study. Additionally, Deb acted as my editor and indexer, eventually reading the book completely three times! Thank you both.

Thanks also to Marc Ewing and Erik Troan, RPM architects extraordinaire. Without their programming savvy, RPM wouldn't be the elegant tool it is. Without their boundless patience, my many questions would have gone unanswered, and this book would have been much less than it is now. I hope you find this book a worthy companion to your programming handiwork.

Rik Faith provided some much-needed information about PMS and PM, two of RPM's ancestors. Thank you! A tip of the RPM hat also goes to Kitty Jarrett and the rest of the crew at Sams. This book wouldn't have been what it is today without your involvement.

Finally, a great big thank you goes to Jessica and the gang at L'il Dino Subs, Jennifer and her crew at the Cary Barnes & Noble coffee shop, and Mom and her "kids" at Schlotzsky's Deli in Durham. If all of you hadn't let me sit around writing for hours, this book wouldn't be nearly as fat as it is. And neither would I!

About the Author

Edward C. Bailey is an operating systems specialist with more than 15 years of experience in OpenVMS, UNIX, Linux, and Windows NT. He currently provides high-level systems support at the National Institute of Environmental Health Sciences in Research Triangle Park, North Carolina. He lives in Cary, North Carolina, with his wife and son.

Tell Us What You Think!

As a reader, you are the most important critic and commentator of our books. We value your opinion and want to know what we're doing right, what we could do better, what areas you'd like to see us publish in, and any other words of wisdom you're willing to pass our way. You can help us make strong books that meet your needs and give you the computer guidance you require.

Do you have access to CompuServe or the World Wide Web? Then check out our CompuServe forum by typing GO SAMS at any prompt. If you prefer the World Wide Web, check out our site at http://www.mcp.com.

> **NOTE**
>
> If you have a technical question about this book, call the technical support line at 317-581-3833 or send e-mail to support@mcp.com.

As the team leader of the group that created this book, I welcome your comments. You can fax, e-mail, or write me directly to let me know what you did or didn't like about this book—as well as what we can do to make our books stronger. Here's the information:

Fax: 317-581-4669

E-mail: opsys_mgr@sams.mcp.com

Mail: Dean Miller
      Comments Department
      Sams Publishing
      201 W. 103rd Street
      Indianapolis, IN 46290

Introduction

Linux and RPM: A Brief History

Welcome! This is a book about the Red Hat Package Manager or, as it is known to its friends, RPM. The history of RPM is inextricably linked to the history of Linux, so a bit of Linux history may be in order. Linux is a full-featured implementation of a UNIX-like operating system, and has taken the computing world by storm.

And for good reason: With the addition of Linux, an Intel-based personal computer that had previously been prisoner of the dreaded Windows hourglass is transformed into a fully multitasking, network-capable personal workstation. All for the cost of the time required to download, install, and configure the software.

Of course, if you're not the type to tinker with downloaded software, you can get a CD-ROM containing Linux and associated software. The amount of tinkering required with these distributions varies widely. The phrase "You get what you pay for" is never more true than in the area of Linux distributions.

One distribution bears the curious name *Red Hat Linux*. Produced by a company of the same name, this Linux distribution is different. One of the key decisions a new Linux user needs to make is which of the many different parts of the distribution to install on his system. Most distributions use some sort of menu, making it easy to pick and choose. Red Hat Linux is no different.

But what is different about Red Hat Linux is that the creators of the distribution wanted their customers to have the ability to make the same choices long after the installation process was over. Some commercial UNIX systems have this capability (called *package management*), and a few Linux distributors were trying to come up with something similar, but none had the extensive scope present in RPM.

Over time, Red Hat Linux has become the most popular distribution available. For it to edge out the previous leader (known as Slackware) in just two years is amazing. There has to be a reason for this kind of success, and a good part of the reason is RPM. But until now, there has been precious little in terms of RPM documentation. You could say that RPM's ease of use has made detailed instructions practically unnecessary, and you'd be right.

However, there are always people who want to know more about their computers, and given the popularity of Red Hat Linux, this alone would have made a book on RPM worthwhile.

But there's more to the story than that.

There is a truism in the world of free software that goes something like this: If there's a better solution freely available, use it! RPM is no exception to the rule. Put under the terms of the GNU General Public License (meaning: RPM cannot be made proprietary by anyone, not even Bill Gates), RPM started to attract the attention of others in the Linux, UNIX, and free software communities.

At present, RPM is used by several commercial software companies producing Linux applications. They find that RPM makes it easier to get their products into the hands of their customers. They also find that it can even make the process of building their software easier. (Those of you who develop software for fun and profit, stick around. The second half of this book will show you everything you need to know to get your software "RPM-ized.")

People have also ported RPM to several commercial UNIX systems, including DEC's Digital UNIX, IBM's AIX, and Silicon Graphics's IRIX. Why? The simple answer is that it makes it easier to install, upgrade, and uninstall software. If all these people are using RPM, shouldn't you?

Parts of the Book and Who They're For

This book is divided into two major sections. The first section is for anyone who needs to know how to use RPM on his system. Given the state of the Linux arena today, this could include just about anyone, including people who are new to Linux or even UNIX. So those of you who think that

```
ls -FAl !*¦less
```

is serious magic (or maybe even a typing error), relax. We'll explain everything you'll need to know in the first section.

The book's second half covers all there is to know about building packages using RPM. Because software engineering on Linux and UNIX systems requires in-depth knowledge of the operating system, available tools, and basic programming concepts, we're going to assume that the reader has sufficient background in these areas. Feel free to browse through the second half, but don't hesitate to seek additional sources of information if you find the going a bit tough.

I

RPM and Computer Users: How to Use RPM to Effectively Manage Your Computer

1

An Introduction to Package Management

1.1. What Are Packages and Why Manage Them?

To determine what packages are and why it's important to manage them, let's go back to the basics for a moment. Computers process information. To process information you must have a few things:

- A computer (obviously)
- Some information to process (also obviously)
- A program to do the processing (still pretty obviously)

Unless these three things come together, very little information processing is going to happen. But each of these items has its own requirements that need to be satisfied before things can get exciting.

Take the computer, for example. While it needs things such as electricity and a cool, dry place to operate, it also needs access to the other two items—information and programs—in order to do its thing. The way to get information and programs into a computer is to place them in the computer's mass storage. These days, mass storage invariably means a disk drive. Putting information and programs on the disk drive means that they are stored as files.

Okay, let's look at the information. Does information have any particular needs? Well, it needs sufficient space on the disk drive, but more importantly, it needs to be in the proper format for the program that will be processing it. That's it for information.

Finally, we have the program. What does it need? Like the information, it needs sufficient disk space on the disk drive. But there are many other things it might need:

- It might need information to process, in the correct format, named properly, and in the appropriate area on a disk drive.
- It might need one or more configuration files. These are files that control the program's behavior and permit some level of customization. Like the information, these files must be in the proper format, named properly, and in the appropriate area on a disk. We'll be referring to them by their other name—config files—throughout the book.
- It might need to have work areas on a disk and need to be named properly and located in the appropriate area.
- It might even need other programs, each with their own requirements.
- Although not strictly required by the program itself, the program might come with one or more files containing documentation. These files can be very handy for the humans trying to get the program to do their bidding!

As you can imagine, this can get pretty complicated. It's not so bad once everything is set up properly, but how do things get set up properly in the first place? There are two possibilities:

■ After reading the documentation that comes with the program you'd like to use, copy the various programs, config files, and information onto your computer, making sure they are all named correctly and are located in the proper place, and that there is sufficient disk space to hold them all. Then make the appropriate changes to the configuration file(s). Finally, run any setup programs that are necessary, giving them whatever information they require to do their job.

■ Let the computer do it for you.

If it seems like the first choice isn't so bad, consider how many files you'll need to keep track of. On a typical Linux system, it's not unusual to have more than 20,000 different files. That's a lot of documentation reading, file copying, and configuring! And what happens when you want a newer version of a program? More of the same!

Some people think the second alternative is easier. RPM was made for them.

1.1.1. Enter the Package

When you consider that computers are very good at keeping track of large amounts of data, the idea of giving your computer the job of riding herd over 20,000 files seems like a good one. And that's exactly what package management software does. But what is a package?

A package in the computer sense is very similar to a package in the physical sense. Both are used to keep related objects together in the same place. Both need to be opened before the contents can be used. Both can have a packing slip taped to the side, identifying the contents.

Normally, package management systems take all the various files containing programs, data, documentation, and configuration information, and place them in one specially formatted file— a package file. In the case of RPM, the package file is sometimes called a *package*, an .rpm *file*, or even an *RPM*. All these terms refer to a package containing software meant to be installed using RPM.

What types of software are normally found in a package? There are no hard-and-fast rules, but normally a package's contents consist of one of the following types of software:

■ A collection of one or more programs that perform a single, well-defined task. This is normally what people think of as an application. Word processors and programming languages would fit into this category.

■ A specific part of an operating system. Examples include system initialization scripts, a particular command shell, or the software required to support a Web server.

1.1.1.1. Advantages of a Package

One of the most obvious benefits to having a package is that the package is one easily manageable chunk. If you move it from one place to another, there's no risk of any part getting left behind. Although this is the most obvious advantage, it's not the biggest one. The biggest advantage is that the package can contain the knowledge about what it takes to install itself on your computer. And if the package contains the steps required to install itself, the package can also contain the steps required to uninstall itself. What used to be a painful manual process is now a straightforward procedure. What used to be a mass of 20,000 files becomes a couple hundred packages.

1.1.2. Manage Your Packages or They Will Manage You

A couple hundred packages? Even though the use of packages has decreased the complexity of managing a system by an order of magnitude, it hasn't yet gotten to the level of being a no-brainer. It's still necessary to keep track of what packages are installed on your system. And if some packages require other packages in order to be installed or operate correctly, these should be tracked as well.

1.1.2.1. Packages Lead Active Lives

If you start looking at a computer system as a collection of packages, you'll find that a distinct set of operations will take place on those packages time and time again:

■ New packages are installed. Maybe it's a spreadsheet you'll use to keep track of expenses, or the latest shoot-'em-up game, but in either case it's new and you want it.

■ Old packages are replaced with newer versions. The company that wrote the word processor you use daily comes out with a new version. You'll probably want to install the new version and remove the old one.

■ Packages are removed entirely. Perhaps that overhyped strategy game just didn't cut it. You have better things to do with that disk space, so get rid of the game!

With this much activity going on, it's easy to lose track of things. What types of package information should be available to keep you informed?

1.1.2.2. Keeping Track of Packages

Just as certain operations are performed on packages, there are also certain types of information that will make it easier to make sense of the packages installed on your system:

■ Certainly you'd like to be able to see what packages are installed. It's easy to forget whether the fax program you tried a few months ago is still installed.

■ It would be nice to be able to get more detailed information on a specific package. This might consist of anything from the date the package was installed to a list of files it installed on your system.

■ Being able to access this information in a variety of ways can be helpful, too. Instead of simply finding out what files a package installed, it might be handy to be able to name a particular file and find out which package installed it.

■ If this amount of detail is possible, it should be possible to see if the way a package is presently installed varies from the way it was originally installed. It's not at all unusual to make a mistake and delete one file—or 100. Being able to tell if one or more packages are missing files could greatly simplify the process of getting an ailing system back on its feet again.

■ Files containing configuration information can be a real headache. If it were possible to pay extra attention to these files and make sure any changes made to them weren't lost, life would certainly be a lot easier.

1.2. Package Management: How to Do It

Well, all this sounds great: easy install, upgrade, and deletion of packages; getting package information presented several different ways; making sure packages are installed correctly; and even tracking changes to config files. But how do you do it?

As mentioned earlier, the obvious answer is to let the computer do it. Many groups have tried to create package management software. There are two basic approaches:

■ Some package management systems concentrate on the specific steps required to manipulate a package.

■ Other package management systems take a different approach, keeping track of the files on the system and manipulating packages by concentrating on the files involved.

Each approach has its good and bad points. In the first method, it's easy to install new packages, somewhat difficult to remove old ones, and almost impossible to obtain any meaningful information about installed packages.

The second method makes it easy to obtain information about installed packages and fairly easy to install and remove packages. The main problem with using this method is that there may not be a well-defined way to execute any commands required during the installation or removal process.

In practice, no package management system uses one approach or the other; all are a mixture of the two. The exact mix and design goals will dictate how well a particular package management system meets the needs of the people using it. At the time Red Hat Software started work on its Linux distribution, there were a number of package management systems in use, each with a different approach to making package management easier.

1.2.1. The Ancestors of RPM

Because this is a book about the Red Hat Package Manager, a good way to see what RPM is all about is to look at the package management software that preceded RPM.

1.2.1.1. RPP

RPP was used in the first Red Hat Linux distributions. Many of RPP's features would be recognizable to anyone who has worked with RPM. Some of these innovative features are

- Simple, one-command installation and uninstallation of packages.
- Scripts that can run before and after installation and uninstallation of packages.
- Package verification. The files of individual packages can be checked to see that they haven't been modified since they were installed.
- Powerful querying. The database of packages can be queried for information about installed packages, including file lists, descriptions, and more.

Although RPP possessed several of the features that were important enough to continue on as parts of RPM today, it had some weaknesses, too:

- It didn't use *pristine sources*. Every program is made up of programming language statements stored in files. This source code is later translated into a binary language that the computer can execute. RPP's packages were based on source code that had been modified specifically for RPP. Since the sources were no longer as the program's creator had written them, they were no longer *pristine*. This is a bad idea for a number of fairly technical reasons. Not using pristine sources made it difficult for package developers to keep things straight, particularly if they were building hundreds of different packages.
- It couldn't guarantee that executables were built from packaged sources. The process of building a package for RPP was such that there was no way to ensure that the executable programs were built from the source code contained in an RPP source package. Once again, this was a problem for package builders, especially those who had large numbers of packages to build.
- It had no support for multiple architectures. As people started using RPP, it became obvious that the package managers that were unable to simplify the process of building packages for more than one architecture, or type of computer, were going to be at a disadvantage. This was a problem, particularly for Red Hat Software, because it was starting to look at the possibility of creating Linux distributions for other architectures, such as the Digital Alpha.

Even with these problems, RPP was one of the things that made the first Red Hat Linux distributions unique. Its ability to simplify the process of installing software was a real boon to many of Red Hat's customers, particularly those with little experience in Linux.

1.2.1.2. PMS

While Red Hat Software was busy with RPP, another group of Linux devotees was hard at work with its package management system. Known as PMS, its development, lead by Rik Faith, attacked the problem of package management from a slightly different viewpoint.

Like RPP, PMS was used to package a Linux distribution. This distribution was known as the *BOGUS distribution*, and all the software in it was built from original unmodified sources. Any changes that were required were patched in during the process of building the software. This is the concept of *pristine sources* and is PMS's most important contribution to RPM. The importance of pristine sources cannot be overstated. It allows the packager to quickly release new versions of software and to immediately see what changes were made to the software.

The chief disadvantages of PMS were weak querying ability, no package verification, no multiple architecture support, and poor database design.

1.2.1.3. PM

Later, Rik Faith and Doug Hoffman, working under contract for Red Hat Software, produced PM. The design combined all the important features of RPP and PM, including one-command installation and uninstallation, scripts run before and after installation and uninstallation, package verification, advanced querying, and pristine sources. However, it retained RPP's and PMS's chief disadvantages: weak database design and no support for multiple architectures.

PM was very close to a viable package management system, but it wasn't quite ready for prime time. It was never used in a commercially available product.

1.2.1.4. RPM Version 1

With two major forays into package management behind them, Marc Ewing and Erik Troan went to work on a third attempt. This one would be called the Red Hat Package Manager, or RPM.

Although it built on the experiences of PM, PMS, and RPP, RPM was quite different under the hood. RPM was written in the Perl programming language for fast development. Version 1 of RPM focused on addressing the flaws of its ancestors. In some cases, the flaws were eliminated, while in others the problems remained.

Some of the successes of RPM version 1 were

■ Automatic handling of configuration files. The contents of config files are often changed from what they were in the original package, making it hard for a package manager to know how a particular config file should be handled during installations, upgrades, and erasures. PM made an attempt at config file handling, but in RPM it was further improved. In many respects, this feature is the key to RPM's power and flexibility.

■ Ease of rebuilding large numbers of packages. By making it easy for people who were trying to create a Linux distribution consisting of several hundred packages, RPM was a step in the right direction.

■ Ease of use. Many of the concepts used in RPP had withstood the test of time and were used in RPM. For instance, the ability to verify the installation of a package was one of the features that set RPP apart. It was adapted and expanded in RPM version 1.

But RPM version 1 wasn't perfect. There were a number of flaws, some of them major:

■ It was slow. While the use of Perl made RPM's development proceed more quickly, it also meant that RPM wouldn't run as quickly as it would have had it been written in C.

■ Its database design was fragile. Unfortunately, under RPM version 1 it was not unusual for there to be problems with the database. While dedicating a database to package management was a good idea, the implementation used in RPM version 1 left a lot to be desired.

■ It was big. This is another artifact of using Perl. Normally, RPM's size requirements were not an issue, except in one area. When performing an initial system installation, RPM was run from a small, floppy-based system environment. The need to have Perl available meant that space on the boot floppies was always a problem.

■ It didn't support multiple architectures (different types of computers) well. The need to have a package manager support more than one type of computer hadn't been acknowledged before. With RPM version 1, an initial stab was taken at the problem, but the implementation was incomplete. Nonetheless, RPM had been ported to a number of other computer systems. It was becoming obvious that the issue of multiarchitecture support was not going away and had to be addressed.

■ The package file format wasn't extensible. This made it very difficult to add functionality since any change to the file format would cause older versions of RPM to break.

Even though their Linux distribution was a success, and RPM was much of the reason for it, Ewing and Troan knew that some changes were going to be necessary to carry RPM to the next level.

1.2.1.5. The RPM of Today: Version 2

Looking back on their experiences with RPM version 1, Ewing and Troan made a major change to RPM's design: They rewrote it entirely in C. This did wonderful things to RPM's speed and size. Querying the database was quicker now, and there was no need to have Perl around just to do package management.

In addition, the database format was redesigned to improve both performance and reliability. Displaying package information can take as little as a tenth of the time spent in RPM version 1, for example.

Realizing RPM's potential in the non-Linux arena, Ewing and Troan also created `rpmlib`, a library of RPM routines that allow the use of RPM functionality in other programs. RPM's ability to function on more than one architecture was also enhanced. Finally, the package file format was made more extensible, clearing the way for future enhancements to RPM.

So is RPM perfect? No program can ever reach perfection, and RPM is no exception. But as a package manager that can run on several different types of systems, RPM has a lot to offer, and it will only get better. Let's take a look at the design criteria that drove the development of RPM.

1.3. RPM Design Goals

The design goals of RPM could best be summed up with the phrase "something for everyone." While the main reason for the existence of RPM was to make it easier for Red Hat Software to build the several hundred packages that comprised the Linux distribution, it was not the only reason RPM was created. The following sections take a look at the various requirements the Red Hat team used in its design of RPM.

1.3.1. Making It Easy to Get Packages on and off the System

As you've learned in this chapter, the act of installing a package can involve many complex steps. Entrusting these steps to a person who may not have the necessary experience is a strategy for failure. So the goal for RPM was to make it as easy as possible for anyone to install and uninstall packages. These are complex and error-prone operations, which RPM should handle for the user.

The other side of this issue is that RPM should give the package builder almost total control in terms of how the package is installed. The reason for this is simple: If the package builders do their homework, their packages should install and uninstall properly.

1.3.2. Making It Easy to Verify That a Package Was Installed Correctly

Because software problems are a fact of life, the ability to verify the proper installation of a package is vital. If done properly, it should be possible to catch a variety of problems, including things such as missing or modified files.

1.3.3. Making It Easy for the Package Builder

Although we're dedicating an entire book to package management, it really should be a small portion of the package builder's job. Why? He's got better things to do! If the package builders are the people who are actually creating the software to be packaged, that's where they should be spending the majority of their time.

Even if the package builder isn't actually writing software, he still has better things to do than worry about building packages. For instance, he might be responsible for building many packages. The less time spent on building an individual package, the more packages that can be built.

1.3.4. Making It Start with the Original Source Code

It was deemed important that RPM start with the original, unmodified source code. Why is this so important?

Using the original sources makes it possible to separate the changes required to build the package from any changes implemented to fix bugs, add new features, or anything else. This is a good thing for package builders because many of them are not the original authors of the programs they package.

This separation makes it easy, months down the road, to know exactly what changes were made in order to get the package to build. This is important when a new version of the packaged software becomes available. Many times it's only necessary to apply the original package building changes to the newer software. At worst, the changes provide a starting point to determine what sorts of things might need to be changed in the new version.

1.3.5. Making It Work on Different Computer Architectures

One of the tougher things for a package builder to do is to take a program, make it run on more than one type of computer, and distribute packages for each. Because RPM makes it easy to use a program's original source code, add the changes necessary to get it to build, and produce a package for each architecture in one step, it can be pretty handy.

1.4. What's in a Package?

With all the magical things we've claimed that package management software in general (and RPM in particular) can do, you'd think there was a tiny computer guru bundled in every package. However, the reality is not that magical. The following sections give a quick overview of the more important parts of an RPM package.

> **NOTE**
>
> See Appendix A, "The Format of the RPM File, " for complete details on the contents of an `.rpm` file.

1.4.1. RPM's Package Labels

Every package built for RPM has to have a specific set of information that uniquely identifies it. We call this information a *package label*. Here are two sample package labels:

■ `nls-1.0-1`
■ `perl-5.001m-4`

Although these labels look like they have very little in common, in fact they both follow RPM's package labeling convention. There are three different components in every package label. Let's look at each one in order.

1.4.1.1. Component 1: The Software's Name

Every package label begins with the name of the software. The name might be derived from the name of the application packaged, or it might be a name describing a group of related programs bundled together by the package builder. The software names in the examples shown previously are `nls` and `perl`. As you can see, the software name is separated from the rest of the package label by a dash.

1.4.1.2. Component 2: The Software's Version

Next in the package label is an identifier that describes the version of the software being packaged. If the package builder bundled a number of related programs together, the software version is probably a number of the package builder's choosing. However, if the package consists of one major application, the software version normally comes directly from the application's developer. The actual version specification is quite flexible, as can be seen in the examples. The versions shown are `1.0` and `5.001m`. A dash separates the software version from the remainder of the package label.

1.4.1.3. Component 3: The Package's Release

The package release is the most unambiguous part of a package label. It is a number chosen by the package builder. It reflects the number of times the package has been rebuilt using the same version of software. Normally, the rebuilds are due to bugs uncovered after the package has been in use for a while. By tradition, the package release starts at 1. The package releases in the example are `1` and `4`.

1.4.2. Labels and Names: Similar but Distinct

Package labels are used internally by RPM. For example, if you ask RPM to list every installed package, it will respond with a list of package labels. When a package file is created, part of the filename consists of the package label. There is no technical requirement for this, but it does make it easier to keep track of things.

However, a package file may be renamed, and the new filename won't confuse RPM in the least because the package label is contained within the file. For a fairly technical view of the inside of a package file, see Appendix A.

1.4.3. Packagewide Information

Some of the information contained in a package is general in nature. This information includes such items as

- The date and time the package was built
- A description of the package's contents
- The total size of all the files installed by the package
- Information that allows the package to be grouped with similar packages
- A digital *signature* that can be used to verify the authenticity and integrity of the package

> **NOTE**
>
> For more information on RPM's signature checking capability, refer to section 7.1 in Chapter 7, "Using RPM to Verify Package Files."

1.4.4. Per-File Information

Each package also contains information about every file contained in the package. The information includes

- The name of every file and where it is to be installed
- Each file's permissions
- Each file's owner and group specifications
- The MD5 checksum of each file

> **NOTE**
>
> We'll discuss MD5 checksums in greater detail in section 6.1 of Chapter 6, "Using RPM to Verify Installed Packages."

- The file's contents

1.5. Summary

So a package management system uses the computer to keep track of all the various bits and pieces that comprise an application or an entire operating system. Most package management systems use a specially formatted file to keep everything together in a single, easily manageable entity, or package. Additionally, package management systems tend to provide one or more of the following functions:

- Installing new packages
- Removing old packages
- Upgrading from an old package to a new one
- Obtaining information about installed packages

RPM has been designed with Red Hat Software's past package management experiences in mind. PM and RPP provided most of these functions with varying degrees of success. Ewing and Troan have worked hard to make RPM better than its predecessors in every way. Now it's time to see how they did it and learn how to use RPM!

2

Using RPM to Install Packages

Table 2.1. Install-mode command syntax and options.

`rpm -i` *(or* `--install`*) Options* `file1.rpm...fileN.rp`		
Parameters		
`file1.rpm...fileN.rpm`	One or more RPM package files (URLs are usable)	
Install-Specific Options		**Section**
`-h (or --hash)`	Print hash marks (#) during install	2.3.2
`--test`	Perform install tests only	2.4.2
`--percent`	Print percentages during install	2.4.11
`--excludedocs`	Do not install documentation	2.4.7
`--includedocs`	Install documentation	2.4.8
`--replacepkgs`	Replace a package with a new copy of itself	2.4.3
`--replacefiles`	Replace files owned by another package	2.4.4
`--force`	Ignore package and file conflicts	2.4.6
`--noscripts`	Do not execute pre- and postinstall scripts	2.4.10
`--prefix <path>`	Relocate package to `<path>` if possible	2.4.9
`--ignorearch`	Do not verify package architecture	2.4.17
`--ignoreos`	Do not verify package operating system	2.4.18
`--nodeps`	Do not check dependencies	2.4.5
`--ftpproxy <host>`	Use `<host>` as the FTP proxy	2.4.16
`--ftpport <port>`	Use `<port>` as the FTP port	2.4.15
General Options		**Section**
`-v`	Display additional information	2.3.1
`-vv`	Display debugging information	2.4.1
`--root <path>`	Set alternate root to `<path>`	2.4.13
`--rcfile <rcfile>`	Set alternate rpmrc file to `<rcfile>`	2.4.12
`--dbpath <path>`	Use `<path>` to find the RPM database	2.4.14

2.1. `rpm -i`—What Does It Do?

Of the many things RPM can do, probably the one that users think of first, is the installation of software. As mentioned earlier, installing new software is a complex, error-prone job. RPM turns that process into a single command.

rpm -i (--install is equivalent) installs software that's been packaged into an RPM package file. It does this through the following process:

■ Performs dependency checks. Some packages will not operate properly unless some other package is installed, too. RPM makes sure the package being installed will have its dependency requirements met. It also ensures that the package's installation will not cause dependency problems for other already-installed packages.

■ Checks for conflicts. RPM performs a number of checks during this phase. These checks look for things such as attempts to install an already-installed package, attempts to install an older package over a newer version, or the possibility that a file might be overwritten.

■ Performs any tasks required before the install. There are cases where one or more commands must be given prior to the actual installation of a package. RPM performs these commands exactly as directed by the package builder, thus eliminating a common source of problems during installations.

■ Decides what to do with config files. One of the features that really sets RPM apart from other package managers is the way it handles configuration files. Since these files are normally changed to customize the behavior of installed software, simply overwriting a config file would tend to make people angry—all their customizations would be gone! Instead, RPM analyzes the situation and attempts to do "the right thing" with config files, even if they weren't originally installed by RPM!

> **NOTE**
>
> To learn exactly what "the right thing" means, turn to section 4.1.1 in Chapter 4, "Using RPM to Upgrade Packages," for more details.

■ Unpacks files from the package and puts them in the proper place. This is the step most people think of when they think about installing software. Each package file contains a list of files that are to be installed, as well as their destination on your system. In addition, many other file attributes, such as permissions and ownerships, are set correctly by RPM.

■ Performs any tasks required after the install. Very often a new package requires that one or more commands be executed after the new files are in place. An example of this is running ldconfig to make new shared libraries accessible.

■ Keeps track of what has been done. Every time RPM installs a package on your system, it uses its database to keep track of the files it installed. The database contains a wealth of information necessary for RPM to do its job. For example, RPM uses the database when it checks for possible conflicts during an install.

2.2. Performing an Install

Let's have RPM install a package. The only thing necessary is to give the command `rpm -i`, followed by the name of the package file:

```
# rpm -i eject-1.2-2.i386.rpm
#
```

At this point, all the steps outlined previously have been performed. The package is now installed. Note that the filename need not adhere to RPM's file-naming convention:

```
# mv eject-1.2-2.i386.rpm baz.txt
# rpm -i baz.txt
#
```

In this case, we changed the name of the package file `eject-1.2-2.i386.rpm` to `baz.txt` and then proceeded to install the package. The result is identical to the previous install; that is, the `eject-1.2-2` package successfully installed. The name of the package file, although normally incorporating the package label, is not used by RPM during the installation process. RPM uses the contents of the package file, which means that even if the file were placed on a DOS floppy and the name truncated, the installation would still proceed normally.

2.2.1. URLs: Another Way to Specify Package Files

If you've surfed the World Wide Web, you've no doubt noticed the way Web pages are identified. Here's an example:

```
http://www.redhat.com/support/docs/rpm/RPM-HOWTO/RPM-HOWTO.html
```

This is called a *uniform resource locator*, or *URL*. RPM can also use URLs, although they look a little bit different. Here's one:

```
ftp://ftp.redhat.com/pub/redhat/code/rpm/rpm-2.3-1.i386.rpm
```

`ftp:` signifies that this URL is a File Transfer Protocol URL. As the name implies, this type of URL is used to move files around. The section containing `ftp.redhat.com` specifies the hostname, or the name of the system where the package file resides.

The remainder of the URL (`/pub/redhat/code/rpm/rpm-2.3-1.i386.rpm`) specifies the path to the package file, followed by the package file itself.

RPM's use of URLs gives you the ability to install a package located on the other side of the world, with a single command:

```
# rpm -i ftp://ftp.gnomovision.com/pub/rpms/foobar-1.0-1.i386.rpm
#
```

This command would use anonymous FTP to obtain the `foobar` version 1.0 package file and install it on your system. Of course, anonymous FTP (no username and password required) is not always available. Therefore, the URL may also contain a username and password preceding the hostname:

```
ftp://smith:mypass@ftp.gnomovision.com/pub/rpms/foobar-1.0-1.i386.rpm
```

However, entering a password where it can be seen by anyone looking at your screen is a bad idea. So try this format:

```
ftp://smith@ftp.gnomovision.com/pub/rpms/foobar-1.0-1.i386.rpm
```

RPM will prompt you for your password, and you'll be in business:

```
# rpm -i ftp://smith@ftp.gnomovision.com /pub/rpms/apmd-2.4-1.i386.rpm
Password for smith@ftp.gnomovision.com: mypass (not echoed)
#
```

After you enter a valid password, RPM installs the package.

On some systems, the FTP daemon doesn't run on the standard port 21. Normally this is done for the sake of enhanced security. Fortunately, there is a way to specify a nonstandard port in a URL:

```
ftp://ftp.gnomovision.com:1024/pub/rpms/foobar-1.0-1.i386.rpm
```

This URL will direct the FTP request to port 1024. The --ftpport option is another way to specify the port. This option is discussed later in the chapter, in section 2.4.15.

2.2.2. A Warning Message You Might Never See

Depending on circumstances, the following message might be rare or very common. While performing an ordinary install, RPM prints a warning message:

```
# rpm -i cdp-0.33-100.i386.rpm
warning: /etc/cdp-config saved as /etc/cdp-config.rpmorig
#
```

What does it mean? It has to do with RPM's handling of config files. In the previous example, RPM found a file (/etc/cdp-config) that didn't belong to any RPM-installed package. Because the cdp-0.33-100 package contains a file of the same name that is to be installed in the same directory, there is a problem.

RPM solves this the best way it can. It performs two steps:

1. It renames the original file to cdp-config.rpmorig.
2. It installs the new cdp-config file that came with the package.

Continuing our example, if we look in /etc, we see that this is exactly what has happened:

```
# ls -al /etc/cdp*
-rw-r--r--   1 root     root      119 Jun 23 16:00 /etc/cdp-config
-rw-rw-r--   1 root     root       56 Jun 14 21:44 /etc/cdp-config.rpmorig
#
```

This is the best possible solution to a tricky problem. The package is installed with a config file that is known to work. After all, the original file may be for an older, incompatible version of the software. However, the original file is saved so that it can be studied by the system administrator, who can decide whether the original file should be put back into service.

2.3. Two Handy Options

There are two options to `rpm -i` that work so well and are so useful that you might think they should be RPM's default behavior. They aren't, but using them requires only that you type an extra two characters, which are described in the following sections.

2.3.1. Getting a Bit More Feedback with `-v`

Even though `rpm -i` is doing many things, it's not very exciting, is it? When performing installs, RPM is pretty quiet unless something goes wrong. However, we can ask for a bit more output by adding `-v` to the command:

```
# rpm -iv eject-1.2-2.i386.rpm
Installing eject-1.2-2.i386.rpm
#
```

By adding `-v`, RPM displayed a simple status line. Using `-v` is a good idea, particularly if you're going to use a single command to install more than one package:

```
# rpm -iv *.rpm
Installing eject-1.2-2.i386.rpm
Installing iBCS-1.2-3.i386.rpm
Installing logrotate-1.0-1.i386.rpm
#
```

In this case, there were three `.rpm` files in the directory. By using a simple wildcard, it's as easy to install 1 package as it is to install 100!

2.3.2. `-h`: Perfect for the Impatient

Sometimes a package can be quite large. Other than watching the disk activity light flash, there's no assurance that RPM is working, and if it is, how far along it is. If you add `-h`, RPM will print 50 hash marks (#) as the install proceeds:

```
# rpm -ih eject-1.2-2.i386.rpm
##################################################
#
```

When all 50 hash marks are printed, the package is completely installed. Using `-v` with `-h` results in a very nice display, particularly when you're installing more than one package:

```
# rpm -ivh *.rpm
eject           ##################################################
iBCS            ##################################################
logrotate       ##################################################
#
```

2.4. Additional Options to `rpm -i`

Normally `rpm -i`, perhaps with `-v` and `-h`, is all you'll need. However, there may be times when a basic install is not going to get the job done. Fortunately, RPM has a wealth of install options to make the tough times a little easier. As with any other powerful tool, you should understand these options before putting them to use. Let's take a look at them.

2.4.1. Getting a Lot More Information with `-vv`

Sometimes it's necessary to have even more information than we can get with `-v`. By adding another v, we can start to see more of RPM's inner workings:

```
# rpm -ivv eject-1.2-2.i386.rpm
D: installing eject-1.2-2.i386.rpm
Installing eject-1.2-2.i386.rpm
D: package: eject-1.2-2 files test = 0
D: running preinstall script (if any)
D: setting file owners and groups by name (not id)
D: ///usr/bin/eject owned by root (0), group root (0) mode 755
D: ///usr/man/man1/eject.1 owned by root (0), group root (0) mode 644
D: running postinstall script (if any)
#
```

The lines starting with D: have been added by using `-vv`. The line ending with `files test = 0` means that RPM is going to install the package. If the number were nonzero, it would mean that the `--test` option is present, and RPM would not perform the install. For more information on using `--test` with `rpm -i`, see section 2.4.2.

Continuing with this example, we see that RPM next executes a preinstall script (if there is one), followed by the actual installation of the files in the package. There is one line for each file being installed, and that line shows the filename, ownership, group membership, and permissions (or mode) applied to the file. With larger packages, the output from `-vv` can become quite lengthy! Finally, RPM runs a postinstall script, if one exists for the package. We'll be discussing pre- and postinstall scripts in more detail in section 2.4.10.

In most cases, it will not be necessary to use `-vv`. It is normally used by software engineers working on RPM itself, and the output can change without notice. However, it's a handy way to gain insights into RPM's inner workings.

2.4.2. `--test`: Perform Installation Tests Only

There are times when it's more appropriate to take it slow and not try to install a package right away. RPM provides the `--test` option for that. As the names implies, it performs all the checks that RPM normally does during an install, but it stops short of actually performing the steps necessary to install the package:

```
# rpm -i --test eject-1.2-2.i386.rpm
#
```

Once again, there's not very much output. This is because the test succeeded; had there been a problem, the output would have been a bit more interesting. In this example, there are some problems:

```
# rpm -i --test rpm-2.0.11-1.i386.rpm
/bin/rpm conflicts with file from rpm-2.3-1
/usr/bin/gendiff conflicts with file from rpm-2.3-1
/usr/bin/rpm2cpio conflicts with file from rpm-2.3-1
/usr/bin/rpmconvert conflicts with file from rpm-2.3-1
/usr/man/man8/rpm.8 conflicts with file from rpm-2.3-1
error: rpm-2.0.11-1.i386.rpm cannot be installed
#
```

Note the version numbers. We're trying to install an older version of RPM (2.0.11) on top of a newer version (2.3). RPM faithfully reported the various file conflicts and summarized with a message saying that the install would not have proceeded, even if --test had not been on the command line.

The --test option will also catch dependency-related problems:

```
# rpm -i --test blather-7.9-1.i386.rpm
failed dependencies:
bother >= 3.1 is needed by blather-7.9-1
#
```

> **TIP**
>
> Here's a tip for all you script writers out there: RPM will return a nonzero status if the --test option detects problems.

2.4.3. --replacepkgs: Install the Package Even if It's Already Installed

The --replacepkgs option is used to force RPM to install a package that it believes to be installed already. This option is normally used if the installed package has been damaged somehow and needs to be fixed up.

To see how the --replacepkgs option works, let's first install some software:

```
# rpm -iv cdp-0.33-2.i386.rpm
Installing cdp-0.33-2.i386.rpm
#
```

Okay, now that we have cdp-0.33-2 installed, let's see what happens if we try to install the same version on top of itself:

```
# rpm -iv cdp-0.33-2.i386.rpm
Installing cdp-0.33-2.i386.rpm
package cdp-0.33-2 is already installed
error: cdp-0.33-2.i386.rpm cannot be installed
#
```

That didn't go very well. Let's see what adding `--replacepkgs` will do:

```
# rpm -iv --replacepkgs cdp-0.33-2.i386.rpm
Installing cdp-0.33-2.i386.rpm
#
```

Much better. The original package was replaced by a new copy of itself.

2.4.4. `--replacefiles`: Install the Package Even if It Replaces Another Package's Files

While the `--replacepkgs` option permits a package to be installed on top of itself, `--replacefiles` is used to allow a package to overwrite files belonging to a different package. Sounds strange? Let's go over it in a bit more detail.

One thing that sets RPM apart from many other package managers is that it keeps track of all the files it installs in a database. Each file's database entry contains a variety of information about the file, including a means of summarizing the file's contents. By using these summaries, known as MD5 checksums, RPM can determine whether a particular file is going to be replaced by a file with the same name but different contents. The following paragraphs give an example.

> **NOTE**
>
> We'll get more into this aspect of RPM in Chapter 6, "Using RPM to Verify Installed Packages," when we discuss `rpm -V`.

Package A installs a file (we'll call it `/bin/foo.bar`). When Package A is installed, `foo.bar` resides happily in the `/bin` directory. In the RPM database, there is an entry for `/bin/foo.bar`, including the file's MD5 checksum.

However, there is another package, B. Package B also has a file called `foo.bar` that it wants to install in `/bin`. There can't be two files in the same directory with the same name. The files are different; their MD5 checksums do not match. What happens if Package B is installed? Let's find out. Here, we've installed a package:

```
# rpm -iv cdp-0.33-2.i386.rpm
Installing cdp-0.33-2.i386.rpm
#
```

Okay, no problem there. But we have another package to install. In this case, it is a new release of the cdp package. Note that RPM's detection of file conflicts does not depend on the two packages being related. It is strictly based on the name of the file, the directory in which it resides, and the file's MD5 checksum. Here's what happens when we try to install the package:

```
# rpm -iv cdp-0.33-3.i386.rpm
Installing cdp-0.33-3.i386.rpm
```

```
/usr/bin/cdp conflicts with file from cdp-0.33-2
error: cdp-0.33-3.i386.rpm cannot be installed
#
```

What's happening? The package cdp-0.33-2 has a file, /usr/bin/cdp, that it installed. Sure enough, there it is. Let's note the size and creation date of the file for future reference:

```
# ls -al /usr/bin/cdp
-rwxr-xr-x 1 root root 34460 Feb 25 14:27 /usr/bin/cdp
#
```

The package we just tried to install, cdp-0.33-3 (note the different release), also installs a file cdp in /usr/bin. Since there is a conflict, the two packages' cdp files must be different—their checksums don't match. Because of this, RPM won't let the second package install. But with --replacefiles, we can force RPM to let /usr/bin/cdp from cdp-0.33-3 replace /usr/bin/cdp from cdp-0.33-2:

```
# rpm -iv --replacefiles cdp-0.33-3.i386.rpm
Installing cdp-0.33-3.i386.rpm
#
```

Taking a closer look at the copy of /usr/bin/cdp that was just installed, we find that they certainly are different, both in size and creation date:

```
# ls -al /usr/bin/cdp
-rwxr-xr-x 1 root root 34444 Apr 24 22:37 /usr/bin/cdp
#
```

File conflicts should be relatively rare occurrences. They happen only when two packages attempt to install files with the same name but different contents. There are two possible reasons for this to happen:

■ Installing a newer version of a package without erasing the older version. A newer version of a package is a wonderful source of file conflicts against older versions—the filenames remain the same, but the contents change. We used it in our example because it's an easy way to show what happens when there are file conflicts. However, it is usually a bad idea to do this as a way to upgrade packages. RPM has a special option for this (rpm -U) that is discussed in Chapter 4.

■ Installing two unrelated packages that each install a file with the same name. This may happen because of poor package design (hence the file's residing in more than one package) or a lack of coordination between the people building the packages.

2.4.4.1. --replacefiles **and Config Files**

What happens if a conflicting file is a config file that you've sweated over and worked on until it's just right? Will issuing a --replacefiles on a package with a conflicting config file blow all your changes away?

No! RPM won't cook your goose. (You'll have to do that yourself!) It will save any changes you've made, to a config file called `file.rpmsave`. Let's give it a try.

As system administrator, you want to make sure your new users have a rich environment the first time they log in. So you've come up with a really nifty `.bashrc` file that will be executed whenever they log in. Knowing that everyone will enjoy your wonderful `.bashrc` file, you place it in `/etc/skel`. That way, every time a new account is created, your `.bashrc` will be copied into the new user's login directory.

Not realizing that the `.bashrc` file you modified in `/etc/skel` is listed as a config file in a package called (strangely enough) `etcskel`, you decide to experiment with RPM using the `etcskel` package. First you try to install it:

```
# rpm -iv etcskel-1.0-100.i386.rpm
etcskel /etc/skel/.bashrc conflicts with file from etcskel-1.0-3
error: etcskel-1.0-100.i386.rpm cannot be installed
#
```

Hmmm. That didn't work. Wait a minute! You can add `--replacefiles` to the command and it should install just fine:

```
# rpm -iv --replacefiles etcskel-1.0-100.i386.rpm
Installing etcskel-1.0-100.i386.rpm
warning: /etc/skel/.bashrc saved as /etc/skel/.bashrc.rpmsave
#
```

Wait a minute. That's my customized `.bashrc`! Was it really saved? Let's see:

```
# ls -al /etc/skel/
total 8 -rwxr-xr-x 1 root root 186 Oct 12 1994 .Xclients
-rw-r--r-- 1 root root 1126 Aug 23 1995 .Xdefaults
-rw-r--r-- 1 root root 24 Jul 13 1994 .bash logout
-rw-r--r-- 1 root root 220 Aug 23 1995 .bash profile
-rw-r--r-- 1 root root 169 Jun 17 20:02 .bashrc
-rw-r--r-- 1 root root 159 Jun 17 20:46 .bashrc.rpmsave
drwxr-xr-x 2 root root 1024 May 13 13:18 .xfm
lrwxrwxrwx 1 root root 9 Jun 17 20:46 .xsession -> .Xclients
# cat /etc/skel/.bashrc.rpmsave
# .bashrc
# User specific aliases and functions
# Modified by the sysadmin
uptime
# Source global definitions
if [ -f /etc/bashrc ]; then
. /etc/bashrc
fi
#
```

Whew! You heave a sigh of relief and study the new `.bashrc` to see if the changes need to be integrated into your customized version.

2.4.4.2. `--replacefiles` Can Mean Trouble Down the Road

Although `--replacefiles` can make today's difficult install easier, it can mean big headaches in the future. When the time comes for erasing the packages involved in a file conflict, bad things can happen. What bad things? Well, files can be deleted. Here's how, in three easy steps:

1. Two packages are installed. When the second package is installed, there is a conflict with a file installed by the first package. Therefore, the `--replacefiles` option is used to force RPM to replace the conflicting file with the one from the second package.

2. At some point in the future, the second package is erased.

3. The conflicting file is gone!

Let's look at an example. First, we install a new package. Next, we take a look at a file it installed, noting the size and creation date:

```
# rpm -iv cdp-0.33-2.i386.rpm
Installing cdp-0.33-2.i386.rpm
# ls -al /usr/bin/cdp
-rwxr-xr-x 1 root root (34460 Feb 25 14:27) /usr/bin/cdp
#
```

Next, we try to install a newer release of the same package. It fails:

```
# rpm -iv cdp-0.33-3.i386.rpm
Installing cdp-0.33-3.i386.rpm
/usr/bin/cdp conflicts with file from cdp-0.33-2
error: cdp-0.33-3.i386.rpm cannot be installed
#
```

So we use `--replacefiles` to convince the newer package to install. We note that the newer package installed a file on top of the file originally installed:

```
# rpm -iv --replacefiles cdp-0.33-3.i386.rpm
Installing cdp-0.33-3.i386.rpm
# ls -al /usr/bin/cdp
-rwxr-xr-x 1 root root 34444 Apr 24 22:37 /usr/bin/cdp
#
```

The original cdp file, 34,460 bytes long and dated February 25, has been replaced with a file with the same name but 34,444 bytes long and from April 24. The original file is long gone.

Next, we erased the package we just installed. Finally, we tried to find the file:

```
# rpm -e cdp-0.33-3
# ls -al /usr/bin/cdp
ls: /usr/bin/cdp: No such file or directory
#
```

> **NOTE**
>
> For more information on erasing packages with rpm -e, see Chapter 3.

The file is gone because /usr/bin/cdp from the first package was replaced when the second package was installed using the --replacefiles option. Then, when the second package was erased, the /usr/bin/cdp file was removed since it belonged to the second package. If the first package had been erased first, there would have been no problem because RPM would have realized that the first package's file had already been deleted and would have left the file in place.

The only problem with this state of affairs is that the first package is still installed, except for /usr/bin/cdp. So now there's a partially installed package on the system. What to do? Perhaps it's time to exercise your newfound knowledge by issuing an rpm -i --replacepkgs command to fix up the first package.

2.4.5. --nodeps: Do Not Check Dependencies Before Installing Package

One day it'll happen. You'll be installing a new package, when suddenly, the install bombs:

```
# rpm -i blather-7.9-1.i386.rpm
failed dependencies:
bother >= 3.1 is needed by blather-7.9-1
#
```

What happened? The problem is that the package you're installing requires another package to be installed in order for it to work properly. In our example, the blather package won't work properly unless the bother package (and more specifically, bother version 3.1 or later) is installed. Since our system doesn't have an appropriate version of bother installed at all, RPM aborted the installation of blather.

Now, 99 times out of 100, this is exactly the right thing for RPM to do. After all, if the package doesn't have everything it needs to work properly, why try to install it? Well, as with everything else in life, there are exceptions to the rule. And that is why there is a --nodeps option.

Adding the --nodeps options to an install command directs RPM to ignore any dependency-related problems and to complete the package installation. Going back to our earlier example, let's add the --nodeps option to the command line and see what happens:

```
# rpm -i --nodeps blather-7.9-1.i386.rpm
#
```

The package was installed without a peep. Whether it will work properly is another matter, but it is installed. In general, it's not a good idea to use --nodeps to get around dependency problems. The package builders included the dependency requirements for a reason, and it's best not to second-guess them.

2.4.6. `--force`: The Big Hammer

Adding `--force` to an install command is a way of saying "Install it anyway!" In essence, it adds `--replacepkgs` and `--replacefiles` to the command. Like a big hammer, `--force` is an irresistible force (no pun intended) that makes things happen. In fact, the only thing that will prevent an install from proceeding when `--force` is used is a dependency conflict.

And as with a big hammer, it pays to fully understand why you need to use `--force` before actually using it.

2.4.7. `--excludedocs`: Do Not Install Documentation for This Package

RPM has a number of good features. One of them is that RPM classifies the files it installs into one of three categories:

- ■ Config files
- ■ Files containing documentation
- ■ All other files

RPM uses the `--excludedocs` option to prevent files classified as documentation from being installed. In the following example, we know that the package contains documentation, specifically, the man page: `/usr/man/man1/cdp.1`. Let's see how `--excludedocs` keeps it from being installed:

```
# rpm -iv --excludedocs cdp-0.33-3.i386.rpm
Installing cdp-0.33-3.i386.rpm
# ls -al /usr/man/man1/cdp.1
ls: /usr/man/man1/cdp.1: No such file or directory
#
```

The primary reason to use `--excludedocs` is to save disk space. The savings can be sizable. For example, on an RPM-installed Linux system, there can be more than 5,000 documentation files, using nearly 50MB.

If you like, you can make `--excludedocs` the default for all installs. To do this, simply add the following line to `/etc/rpmrc`, `.rpmrc` in your login directory, or the file specified with the `--rcfile` option:

```
excludedocs: 1
```

After that, every time an `rpm -i` command is run, it will not install any documentation files. For more information on rpmrc files, see Appendix B, "The `rpmrc` File."

2.4.8. --includedocs: Install Documentation for This Package

As the name implies, --includedocs directs RPM to install any files marked as being documentation. This option is normally not required, unless the rpmrc file entry excludedocs: 1 is included in the referenced rpmrc file. Here's an example. Note that in this example, /etc/rpmrc contains excludedocs: 1, which directs RPM not to install documentation files:

```
# ls /usr/man/man1/cdp.1
ls: /usr/man/man1/cdp.1: No such file or directory
# rpm -iv cdp-0.33-3.i386.rpm
Installing cdp-0.33-3.i386.rpm
# ls /usr/man/man1/cdp.1
ls: /usr/man/man1/cdp.1: No such file or directory
#
```

Here we've checked to make sure that the cdp man page did not previously exist on the system. Then after installing the cdp package, we find that the excludedocs: 1 in /etc/rpmrc did its job: The man page wasn't installed. Let's try it again, this time adding the --includedocs option:

```
# ls /usr/man/man1/cdp.1
ls: /usr/man/man1/cdp.1: No such file or directory
# rpm -iv --includedocs cdp-0.33-3.i386.rpm
Installing cdp-0.33-3.i386.rpm
# ls /usr/man/man1/cdp.1
-rw-r--r-- 1 root root 4550 Apr 24 22:37 /usr/man/man1/cdp.1
#
```

The --includedocs option overrode the rpmrc file's excludedocs: 1 entry, causing RPM to install the documentation file.

2.4.9. --prefix <path>: Relocate the Package to <path>, if Possible

Some packages give the person installing them flexibility in determining where on his system they should be installed. These are known as *relocatable packages*. A relocatable package differs from a package that cannot be relocated in only one way—the definition of a default prefix. Because of this, it takes a bit of additional effort to determine whether a package is relocatable. But here's an RPM command that can be used to find out:

```
rpm -qp --queryformat "%{defaultprefix\}\n" <packagefile>
```

> **NOTE**
>
> You can find more about RPM's query commands in Chapter 5, "Getting Information About Packages."

Just replace `<packagefile>` with the name of the package file you want to check out. If the package is not relocatable, you'll only see the word (`none`). If, on the other hand, the command displays a path, the package is relocatable. Unless specified otherwise, every file in the package will be installed somewhere below the path specified by the default prefix.

What if you want to specify otherwise? Easy. Just use the `--prefix` option. Let's give it a try:

```
# rpm -qp --queryformat "%fdefaultprefixg\n" cdplayer-1.0-1.i386.rpm
/usr/local
# rpm -i --prefix /tmp/test cdplayer-1.0-1.i386.rpm
#
```

Here we've used our magic query command to determine that the `cdplayer` package is relocatable. It normally installs below `/usr/local`, but we wanted to move it around. By adding the `--prefix` option, we were able to make the package install in `/tmp/test`. If we take a look there, we'll see that RPM created all the necessary directories to hold the package's files:

```
# ls -1R /tmp/test/
total 2
drwxr-xr-x 2 root root 1024 Dec 16 13:21 bin/
drwxr-xr-x 3 root root 1024 Dec 16 13:21 man/
/tmp/test/bin:
total 41
-rwxr-xr-x 1 root root 40739 Oct 14 20:25 cdp*
lrwxrwxrwx 1 root root 17 Dec 16 13:21 cdplay -> /tmp/test/bin/cdp*

/tmp/test/man:
total 1 drwxr-xr-x 2 root root 1024 Dec 16 13:21 man1/

/tmp/test/man/man1:
total 5
-rwxr-xr-x 1 root root 4550 Oct 14 20:25 cdp.1*
#
```

2.4.10. `--noscripts`: Do Not Execute Pre- and Postinstall Scripts

Before we talk about the `--noscripts` option, we need to cover a bit of background. In section 2.4.1, you saw some output from an install using the `-vv` option. As you can see, there are two lines that mention preinstall and postinstall scripts. When some packages are installed, they may require that certain programs be executed before, after, or before and after the package's files are copied to disk.

> **NOTE**
>
> It's possible to use RPM's query command to see if a package has pre- or postinstall scripts. See section 5.2.2 in Chapter 5 for more information.

The `--noscripts` option prevents these scripts from being executed during an install. This is a very dangerous thing to do! The `--noscripts` option is really meant for package builders to use during the development of their packages. By preventing the pre- and postinstall scripts from running, a package builder can keep a buggy package from bringing down his development system. Once the bugs are found and eliminated, the `--noscripts` option is no longer necessary.

2.4.11. `--percent`: Not Meant for Human Consumption

An option that will probably never be very popular is `--percent`. This option is meant to be used by programs that interact with the user, perhaps presenting a graphical user interface for RPM. When the `--percent` option is used, RPM displays a series of numbers. Each number is a percentage that indicates how far along the install is. When the number reaches 100%, the install is complete. Here's an example:

```
# rpm -i --percent iBCS-1.2-3.i386.rpm
%f iBCS:1.2:3
%% 0.002140
%% 1.492386
%% 5.296632
%% 9.310026
%% 15.271010
%% 26.217846
%% 31.216000
%% 100.000000
%% 100.000000
#
```

The list of percentages will vary depending on the number of files in the package, but every package ends at 100% when completely installed.

2.4.12. `--rcfile <rcfile>`: Use `<rcfile>` As an Alternate `rpmrc` File

The `--rcfile` option is used to specify a file containing default settings for RPM. Normally, this option is not needed. By default, RPM uses `/etc/rpmrc` and a file named `.rpmrc` located in your login directory.

This option would be used if there were a need to switch between several sets of RPM defaults. Software developers and package builders will normally be the only people using the `--rcfile` option. For more information on `rpmrc` files, see Appendix B.

2.4.13. `--root <path>`: Use `<path>` As an Alternate Root

Adding `--root <path>` to an install command forces RPM to assume that the directory specified by `<path>` is actually the root directory. The `--root` option affects every aspect of the install process, so pre- and postinstall scripts are run with `<path>` as their root directory (using `chroot(2)`. In addition, RPM expects its database to reside in the directory specified by the `dbpath` `rpmrc` file entry, relative to `<path>`. (For more information on `rpmrc` file entries, see Appendix B.)

Normally, this option is used only during an initial system install or when a system has been booted off a rescue disk and some packages need to be reinstalled.

2.4.14. --dbpath *<path>*: Use *<path>* to Find an RPM Database

In order for RPM to do its handiwork, it needs access to an RPM database. Normally, this database exists in the directory specified by the rpmrc file entry dbpath. By default, dbpath is set to /var/lib/rpm.

Although the dbpath entry can be modified in the appropriate rpmrc file, the --dbpath option is probably a better choice when the database path needs to be changed temporarily. An example of a time the --dbpath option would come in handy is when it's necessary to examine an RPM database copied from another system. Granted, it's not a common occurrence, but it's difficult to handle any other way.

2.4.15. --ftpport *<port>*: Use *<port>* in FTP-Based Installs

Back in section 2.2.1 you saw how RPM can access package files with the use of a URL. You also learned that some systems may not use the standard FTP port. In those cases, it's necessary to give RPM the proper port number to use. As mentioned earlier, one approach is to embed the port number in the URL itself.

Another approach is to use the --ftpport option. RPM will access the desired port when this option, along with the port number, is added to the command line. In cases where the desired port seldom changes, it may be entered in an rpmrc file by using the ftpport entry. For more information on the use of rpmrc files, see Appendix B.

2.4.16. --ftpproxy *<host>*: Use *<host>* As a Proxy in FTP-Based Installs

Many companies and Internet service providers (ISPs) employ various methods to protect their network connections against misuse. One of these methods is to use a system that will process all FTP requests on behalf of the other systems on the company or ISP network. Having a single computer act as a proxy for the other systems serves to protect the other systems against any FTP-related misuse.

When RPM is employed on a network with an FTP proxy system, it will be necessary for RPM to direct all its FTP requests to the FTP proxy. RPM will send its FTP requests to the specified proxy system when the --ftpproxy option, along with the proxy hostname, is added to the command line.

In cases where the proxy host seldom changes, you can enter it in an rpmrc file by using the ftpproxy entry.

2.4.17. `--ignorearch`: Do Not Verify Package Architecture

When a package file is created, RPM specifies the architecture, or type of computer hardware, for which the package was created. This is a good thing because the architecture is one of the main factors in determining whether a package written for one computer is going to be compatible with another computer.

When a package is installed, RPM uses the `arch_compat rpmrc` entries to determine what are normally considered compatible architectures. Unless you're porting RPM to a new architecture, you shouldn't make any changes to these entries. (You'll find more on `arch_compat` in section 19.3.1 in Chapter 19, "Building Packages for Multiple Architectures and Operating Systems.") Although RPM attempts to make the right decisions regarding package compatibility, there are times when it errs on the side of conservatism. In those cases, it's necessary to override RPM's decision. The `--ignorearch` option is used in those cases. When it's added to the command line, RPM will not perform any architecture-related checking.

> **CAUTION**
>
> Unless you really know what you're doing, you should never use --ignorearch!

2.4.18. `--ignoreos`: Do Not Verify the Package Operating System

When a package file is created, RPM specifies the operating system for which the package was created. This is good because the operating system is one of the main factors in determining whether a package written for one computer is going to be compatible with another computer.

When a package is installed, RPM uses the `os_compat rpmrc` entries to determine what are normally considered compatible operating systems. Unless you're porting RPM to a new operating system, you shouldn't make any changes to these entries. (You'll find more on `oscompat` in section 19.3.1 in Chapter 19.) Although RPM attempts to make the right decisions regarding package compatibility, there are times when it errs on the side of conservatism. In those cases, it's necessary to override RPM's decision. The `--ignoreos` option is used in those cases. When it's added to the command line, RPM will not perform any operating system–related checking.

> **CAUTION**
>
> Unless you really know what you're doing, you should never use --ignoreos!

3

Using RPM to Erase Packages

Table 3.1. Erase-mode command syntax and options.

rpm -e *(or* --erase*) Options* pkg1...pkg*N*		
Parameters		
pkg1...pkg*N*	One or more installed packages	
Erase-Specific Options		***Section***
--test	Perform erase tests only	3.3.1
--noscripts	Do not execute pre- and postuninstall scripts	3.3.3
--nodeps	Do not check dependencies	3.3.2
General Options		***Section***
-vv	Display debugging information	3.2.1
--root *<path>*	Set alternate root to *<path>*	3.3.5
--rcfile *<rcfile>*	Set alternate rpmrc file to *<rcfile>*	3.3.4
--dbpath *<path>*	Use *<path>* to find the RPM database	3.3.6

3.1. rpm -e: What Does It Do?

The rpm -e command (--erase is equivalent) removes, or erases, one or more packages from the system. RPM performs a series of steps whenever it erases a package:

1. It checks the RPM database to make sure that no other packages depend on the package being erased.
2. It executes a preuninstall script (if one exists).
3. It checks whether any of the package's config files have been modified. If so, it saves copies of them.
4. It reviews the RPM database to find every file listed as being part of the package, and if a file does not belong to another package, deletes the file.
5. It executes a postuninstall script (if one exists).
6. It removes all traces of the package (and the files belonging to it) from the RPM database.

That's quite a bit of activity for a single command. No wonder RPM can be such a time-saver!

3.2. Erasing a Package

The most basic erase command is

```
# rpm -e eject
#
```

In this case, the eject package was erased. There isn't much in the way of feedback, is there? Could we get more if we added -v?

```
# rpm -ev eject
#
```

Still nothing. However, another option can be counted on to give a wealth of information. You'll learn about it in the next section.

3.2.1. Getting More Information with -vv

By adding -vv to the command line, we can often get a better feel for what's going on inside RPM. The -vv option was really meant for the RPM developers, and its output may change, but it is a great way to gain insight into RPM's inner workings. Let's try it with rpm -e:

```
# rpm -evv eject
D: uninstalling record number 286040
D: running preuninstall script (if any)
D: removing files test = 0
D: /usr/man/man1/eject.1 - removing
D: /usr/bin/eject - removing
D: running postuninstall script (if any)
D: removing database entry
D: removing name index
D: removing group index
D: removing file index for /usr/bin/eject
D: removing file index for /usr/man/man1/eject.1
#
```

Although -v had no effect on RPM's output, -vv gave us a torrent of output. But what does it tell us?

First, RPM displays the package's record number. The number is normally of use only to people that work on RPM's database code.

Next, RPM executes a preuninstall script, if one exists. This script can execute any commands required to remove the package before any files are actually deleted.

The files test = 0 line indicates that RPM is to actually erase the package. If the number had been nonzero, RPM would only be performing a test of the package erasure. This happens when the --test option is used. Refer to section 3.3.1 for more information on the use of the --test option with rpm -e.

The next two lines log the actual removal of the files comprising the package. Packages with many files can result in a lot of output when using -vv!

Next, RPM executes a postuninstall script, if one exists. Like the preuninstall script, this script is used to perform any processing required to cleanly erase the package. Unlike the preuninstall script, however, the postuninstall script runs after all the package's files have been removed.

Finally, the last five lines show the process RPM uses to remove every trace of the package from its database. From the messages, we can see that the database contains some per-package data, followed by information on every file installed by the package.

3.3. Additional Options

If you're interested in a complex command with lots of options, rpm -e is not the place to look. There just aren't that many different ways to erase a package! But there are a few options you should know about.

3.3.1. --test: Go Through the Process of Erasing the Package, But Do Not Erase It

If you're a bit gun-shy about erasing a package, you can use the --test option first to see what rpm -e would do:

```
# rpm -e --test bother
removing these packages would break dependencies:
bother >= 3.1 is needed by blather-7.9-1
#
```

It's pretty easy to see that the blather package wouldn't work very well if bother were erased. To be fair, however, RPM wouldn't have erased the package in this example unless we used the --nodeps option, which we'll discuss shortly.

However, if there are no problems erasing the package, you won't see very much:

```
# rpm -e --test eject
#
```

We know, based on previous experience, that -v doesn't give us any additional output with rpm -e. However, we do know that -vv works wonders. Let's see what it has to say:

```
# rpm -evv --test eject
D: uninstalling record number 286040
D: running preuninstall script (if any)
D: would remove files test = 1
D: /usr/man/man1/eject.1 - would remove
D: /usr/bin/eject - would remove
D: running postuninstall script (if any)
D: would remove database entry
#
```

As you can see, the output is similar to that of a regular erase command using the -vv option, with the following exceptions:

■ The would remove files test = 1 line ends with a nonzero number. This is because --test has been added. If the command hadn't included --test, the number would have been 0, and the package would have been erased.

- There is a line for each file that RPM would have removed, each one ending with `would remove` instead of `removing`.
- There is only one line at the end, which states `would remove database entry`, versus the multiline output showing the cleanup of the RPM database during an actual erase.

By using `--test` in conjunction with `-vv`, it's easy to see exactly what RPM would do during an actual erase.

3.3.2. `--nodeps`: Do Not Check Dependencies Before Erasing Package

It's likely that one day while erasing a package, you'll see something like this:

```
# rpm -e bother
removing these packages would break dependencies:
bother >= 3.1 is needed by blather-7.9-1
#
```

What happened? The problem is that one or more of the packages installed on your system require the package you're trying to erase. Without it, they won't work properly. In our example, the `blather` package won't work properly unless the `bother` package (and more specifically, `bother` version 3.1 or later) is installed. Since we're trying to erase `bother`, RPM aborted the erasure.

Now, 99 times out of 100, this is exactly the right thing for RPM to do. After all, if the package is needed by other packages, why try to erase it? As with everything else in life, there are exceptions to the rule. And that is why there is a `--nodeps` option.

Adding the `--nodeps` options to an erase command directs RPM to ignore any dependency-related problems and to erase the package. Going back to our previous example, let's add the `--nodeps` option to the command line and see what happens:

```
# rpm -e --nodeps bother
#
```

The package was erased without a peep. Whether the blather package will work properly is another matter. In general, it's not a good idea to use `--nodeps` to get around dependency problems. The package builders included the dependency requirements for a reason, and it's best not to second-guess them.

3.3.3. `--noscripts`: Do Not Execute Pre- and Postuninstall Scripts

In section 3.2.1 we used the `-vv` option to see what RPM was actually doing when it erased a package. We noted that there were two scripts, a preuninstall and a postuninstall, that were used to execute commands required during the process of erasing a package.

The `--noscripts` option prevents these scripts from being executed during an erase. This is a very dangerous thing to do! The `--noscripts` option is really meant for package builders to use during the development of their packages. By preventing the pre- and postuninstall scripts from running, a package builder can keep a buggy package from bringing down his development system. After the bugs are found and eliminated, there's very little need to prevent these scripts from running; in fact, doing so can cause problems!

3.3.4. `--rcfile` *`<rcfile>`*: Read *`<rcfile>`* for RPM Defaults

The `--rcfile` option is used to specify a file containing default settings for RPM. Normally, this option is not needed. By default, RPM uses `/etc/rpmrc` and a file named `.rpmrc` located in your login directory.

This option would be used if there were a need to switch between several sets of RPM defaults. Software developers and package builders will normally be the only people using the `--rcfile` option. For more information on `rpmrc` files, see Appendix B, "The `rpmrc` File."

3.3.5. `--root` *`<path>`*: Use *`<path>`* As the Root

Adding `--root` *`<path>`* to an erase command forces RPM to assume that the directory specified by *`<path>`* is actually the root directory. The `--root` option affects every aspect of the erase process, so pre- and postuninstall scripts are run with *`<path>`* as their root directory (using `chroot(2)`, if you must know). In addition, RPM expects its database to reside in the directory specified by the `dbpath` `rpmrc` file entry, relative to *`<path>`*.

Normally this option is only used during an initial system install, or when a system has been booted off a rescue disk and some packages need to be re-installed.

3.3.6. `--dbpath` *`<path>`*: Use *`<path>`* to Find the RPM Database

In order for RPM to do its work, it needs access to an RPM database. Normally, this database exists in the directory specified by the `rpmrc` file entry, `dbpath`. By default, `dbpath` is set to `/var/lib/rpm`.

Although the `dbpath` entry can be modified in the appropriate `rpmrc` file, the `--dbpath` option is probably a better choice when the database path needs to be changed temporarily. An example of a time the `--dbpath` option would come in handy is when it's necessary to examine an RPM database copied from another system. Granted, it's not a common occurrence, but it's difficult to handle any other way.

3.4. `rpm -e` and Config Files

If you've made changes to a configuration file that was originally installed by RPM, your changes won't be lost if you erase the package. Say, for example, that we've made changes to /etc/skel/ .bashrc (a config file), which was installed as part of the etcskel package. Later, we remove etcskel:

```
# rpm -e etcskel
#
```

But if we take a look in /etc/skel, here's what we see:

```
# ls -al
total 5
drwxr-xr-x 3 root root 1024 Jun 17 22:01 .
drwxr-xr-x 8 root root 2048 Jun 17 19:01 ..
-rw-r--r-- 1 root root 152 Jun 17 21:54 .bashrc.rpmsave
drwxr-xr-x 2 root root 1024 May 13 13:18 .xfm
#
```

Sure enough, .bashrc.rpmsave is a copy of your modified .bashrc file! Remember, however, that this feature only works with config files. Not sure how to determine which files RPM thinks are config files? Chapter 5, "Getting Information About Packages," specifically section 5.2.2, shows you how.

3.5. Watch Out!

RPM takes most of the work out of removing software from your system, and that's great. But of course there's a downside. RPM also makes it easy to erase packages that are critical to your system's continued operation. Here are some examples of packages not to erase:

■ RPM: RPM will happily uninstall itself. No problem, though. You'll just re-install it with rpm -i….Oops!

■ Bash: The Bourne-again shell may not be the shell you use, but certain parts of many Linux systems (such as the scripts executed during system startup and shutdown) use /bin/sh, which is a symbolic link to /bin/bash. No /bin/bash, no /bin/sh. No /bin/sh, no system!

In many cases, RPM's dependency processing will prevent inadvertent erasures from causing massive problems. However, if you're not sure, use rpm -q to get more information about the package you'd like to erase. (See Chapter 5 for more information on rpm -q.)

4

Using RPM to Upgrade Packages

Table 4.1. Upgrade-mode command syntax and options.

`rpm -U` *(or* `--upgrade`*) Options* `file1.rpm...fileN.rpm`		
Parameters		
`file1.rpm...fileN.rpm`	One or more RPM package files (URLs are usable)	
Upgrade-Specific Options		**Section**
`-h (or --hash)`	Hash marks (#) during upgrade*	2.3.2
`--oldpackage`	Permit upgrading to an older package	4.3.1
`--test`	Perform upgrade tests only*	2.4.2
`--excludedocs`	Do not install documentation*	2.4.7
`--includedocs`	Install documentation*	2.4.8
`--replacepkgs`	Replace a package with a new copy of itself*	2.4.3
`--replacefiles`	Replace files owned by another package*	2.4.4
`--force`	Ignore package and file conflicts	4.3.2
`--percent`	Print percentages during upgrade*	2.4.11
`--noscripts`	Do not execute pre- and postinstall scripts	4.3.3
`--prefix <path>`	Relocate package to *<path>* if possible*	2.4.9
`--ignorearch`	Do not verify package architecture*	2.4.17
`--ignoreos`	Do not verify package operating system*	2.4.18
`--nodeps`	Do not check dependencies*	2.4.5
`--ftpproxy <host>`	Use *<host>* as the FTP proxy*	2.4.16
`--ftpport <port>`	Use *<port>* as the FTP port*	2.4.15
General Options		**Section**
`-v`	Display additional information*	2.3.1
`-vv`	Display debugging information*	2.4.1
`--root <path>`	Set alternate root to *<path>**	2.4.13
`--rcfile <rcfile>`	Set alternate rpmrc file to *<rcfile>**	2.4.12
`--dbpath <path>`	Use *<path>* to find the RPM database*	2.4.14

*This option behaves identically to the same option used with rpm -i. See Chapter 2, "Using RPM to Install Packages," for more information on this option.

4.1. `rpm -U`: What Does It Do?

If there were one RPM command that could win over friends, it would be RPM's upgrade command. After all, anyone who has ever tried to install a newer version of any software knows what a traumatic experience it can be. With RPM, though, this process is reduced to a single command: `rpm -U`. The `rpm -U` command (`--upgrade` is equivalent) performs two distinct operations:

- It installs the desired package.
- It erases all older versions of the package, if any exist.

If it sounds to you like `rpm -U` is nothing more than an `rpm -i` command (see Chapter 2) followed by the appropriate number of `rpm -e` commands (see Chapter 3, "Using RPM to Erase Packages"), you'd be exactly right. In fact, we'll be referring to Chapters 2 and 3 as we discuss `rpm -U`, so if you haven't at least skimmed those chapters yet, you might want to do that now.

Although some people might think it's a cheap shot to claim that RPM performs an upgrade when in fact it's just doing the equivalent of a couple other commands, in reality it's a very smart thing to do. Carefully crafting RPM's package installation and erasure commands to do the work required during an upgrade makes RPM more tolerant of misuse by preserving important files even if an upgrade isn't being done.

If RPM had been written with a very smart upgrade command, and the install and erase commands couldn't handle upgrade situations at all, installing a package could overwrite a modified configuration file. Likewise, erasing a package would also mean that config files could be erased. Not a good situation! However, RPM's approach to upgrades makes it possible to handle even the most tricky situation—having multiple versions of a package installed simultaneously.

4.1.1. Config File Magic

While the `rpm -i` and `rpm -e` commands each do their part to keep config files straight, it is with `rpm -U` that the full power of RPM's config file handling shows through. There are no fewer than six different scenarios that RPM takes into account when handling config files.

In order to make the appropriate decisions, RPM needs information. The information used to decide how to handle config files is a set of three large numbers known as MD5 checksums. An MD5 checksum is produced when a file is used as the input to a complex series of mathematical operations. The resulting checksum has a unique property in that any change to the file's contents will result in a change to the checksum of that file. (Actually, there's a 1 in 2^{128} chance a change will go undetected, but for all practical purposes, it's as close to perfect as we can get.) Therefore, MD5 checksums are a powerful tool for quickly determining whether two different files have the same contents.

The three checksums RPM uses to determine what should be done with a config file are

■ The MD5 checksum of the file when it was originally installed. We'll call this the checksum of the original file.

■ The MD5 checksum of the file as it exists at upgrade time. We'll call this the checksum of the current file.

■ The MD5 checksum of the corresponding file in the new package. We'll call this the checksum of the new file.

Let's take a look at the various combinations of checksums, see what RPM will do because of them, and discuss why. In the following examples, we'll use the letters X, Y, and Z in place of lengthy MD5 checksums.

4.1.1.1. Original File = X, Current File = X, New File = X

In this case, the file originally installed was never modified. Or, as some sticklers for detail may note, it may have been modified, and subsequently those modifications were undone. The file in the new version of the package is identical to the file on disk.

In this case, RPM installs the new file, overwriting the original. You might be wondering why anyone would go to the trouble of installing the new file if it's just the same as the existing one. The reason is that aspects of the file other than its name and contents might have changed. The file's ownership, for example, might be different in the new version.

4.1.1.2. Original File = X, Current File = X, New File = Y

The original file has not been modified, but the file in the new package is different. Perhaps the difference represents a bug fix or a new feature. It makes no difference to RPM.

In this case, RPM installs the new file, overwriting the original. This makes sense. If it didn't, RPM would never permit newer, modified versions of software to be installed! The original file is not saved because it had not been changed. A lack of changes here means that no site-specific modifications were made to the file.

4.1.1.3. Original File = X, Current File = Y, New File = X

Here we have a file that was changed at some point. However, the new file is identical to the existing file prior to the local modifications.

In this case, RPM takes the viewpoint that since the original file and the new file are identical, the modifications made to the original version must still be valid for the new version. It leaves the existing, modified file in place.

4.1.1.4. Original File = X, Current File = Y, New File = Y

At some point the original file was modified and those modifications happen to make the file identical to the new file. Perhaps the modification was made to fix a security problem, and the new version of the file has the same fix applied to it.

In this case, RPM installs the new version, overwriting the modified original. The same philosophy used in the first scenario applies here: Although the file has not changed, perhaps some other aspect of the file has, so the new version is installed.

4.1.1.5. Original File = X, Current File = Y, New File = Z

Here the original file was modified at some point. The new file is different from both the original and the modified versions of the original file.

RPM is not able to analyze the contents of the files and determine what is going on. In this instance, it takes the best possible approach. The new file is known to work properly with the rest of the software in the new package—at least the people building the new package should have ensured that it does. The modified original file is an unknown: It might work with the new package and it might not. So RPM installs the new file.

But the existing file was definitely modified. Someone made an effort to change the file for some reason. Perhaps the information contained in the file is still of use. Therefore, RPM saves the modified file, naming it `file.rpmsave`, and prints a warning so the user knows what happened:

```
warning: /etc/skel/.bashrc saved as /etc/skel/.bashrc.rpmsave
```

4.1.1.6. Original File = None , Current File = ??, New File = ??

While RPM doesn't use checksums in this particular case, we'll describe it in those terms for the sake of consistency. In this instance, RPM had not installed the file originally, so there is no original checksum.

Because the file had not originally been installed as part of a package, there is no way for RPM to determine whether the file currently in place had been modified. Therefore, the checksums for the current file and the new file are irrelevant; they cannot be used to clear up the mystery.

When this happens, RPM renames the file `file.rpmorig`, prints a warning, and installs the new file. This way, any modifications contained in the original file are saved. The system administrator can review the differences between the original and the newly installed files and determine what action should be taken.

As you can see, in the majority of cases RPM will automatically take the proper course of action when performing an upgrade. It is only when config files have been modified and are to be overwritten that RPM leaves any postupgrade work for the system administrator. Even in those cases, many times the modified files are not worth saving and can be deleted.

4.2. Upgrading a Package

The most basic version of the `rpm -U` command is simply `rpm -U`, followed by the name of an `.rpm` package file:

```
# rpm -U eject-1.2-2.i386.rpm
#
```

Here, RPM performed all the steps necessary to upgrade the `eject-1.2-2` package, faster than could have been done by hand. As in RPM's install command, uniform resource locators, or URLs, can also be used to specify the package file. (For more information on RPM's use of URLs, see section 2.2.1 in Chapter 2.)

4.2.1. `rpm -U`'s Dirty Little Secret

Well, in the preceding example, we didn't tell the whole story. There was no older version of the eject package installed. Yes, it's true. `rpm -U` works just fine as a replacement for the normal install command `rpm -i`.

This is another, more concrete, example of the strength of RPM's method of performing upgrades. Because RPM's install command is smart enough to handle upgrades, RPM's upgrade command is really just another way to specify an install. Some people never even bother to use RPM's install command; they always use `rpm -U`. Maybe the `-U` should stand for, "Uh, do the right thing...."

4.3. They're Nearly Identical

Given the fact that `rpm -U` can be used as a replacement to `rpm -i`, it follows that most of the options available for `rpm -U` are identical to those used with `rpm -i`. Therefore, to keep the duplication to a minimum, we'll discuss only those options that are unique to `rpm -U` or that behave differently from the same option when used with `rpm -i`. The table at the beginning of this chapter shows all valid options to RPM's upgrade command and indicates which are identical to those used with `rpm -i`.

4.3.1. `--oldpackage`: Upgrade to an Older Version

This option might be used a bit more by people who like to stay on the bleeding edge of new versions of software, but eventually everyone will probably need to use it. Usually, the situation plays out like this:

1. You hear about some new software that sounds pretty nifty, so you download the `.rpm` file and install it.

2. The software is great! It does everything you ask for and more. You end up using it every day for the next few months.

3. You hear that a new version of your favorite software is available. You waste no time in getting the package. You upgrade the software by using `rpm -U`. No problem!

4. Fingers arched in anticipation, you launch the new version. Your computer's screen goes blank!

Looks like a bug in the new version. Now what do you do? Hmmm. Maybe you can just "upgrade" to the older version. Let's try to go back to release 2 of `cdp-0.33` from release 3:

```
# rpm -Uv cdp-0.33-2.i386.rpm
Installing cdp-0.33-2.i386.rpm
package cdp-0.33-3 (which is newer) is already installed
error: cdp-0.33-2.i386.rpm cannot be installed
#
```

That didn't work very well. At least it told us just what the problem was: We were trying to upgrade to an older version of a package that is already installed. Fortunately, there's a special option for just this situation: `--oldpackage`. Let's give it a try:

```
# rpm -Uv --oldpackage cdp-0.33-2.i386.rpm
Installing cdp-0.33-2.i386.rpm
#
```

By using the `--oldpackage` option, release 3 of `cdp-0.33` is history and has been replaced by release 2.

4.3.2. `--force`: The Big Hammer

Adding `--force` to an upgrade command is a way of saying "Upgrade it anyway!" In essence, it adds `--replacepkgs`, `--replacefiles`, and `--oldpackage` to the command. Like a big hammer, `--force` is an irresistible force (pun intended) that makes things happen. In fact, the only thing that will prevent an upgrade with `--force` from proceeding is a dependency conflict.

It pays to fully understand why you need to use `--force` before actually using it.

4.3.3. `--noscripts`: Do Not Execute Install and Uninstall Scripts

The `--noscripts` option prevents a package's pre- and postinstall scripts from being executed. This is no different from the option's behavior when used with RPM's install command. However, there is an additional point to consider when the option is used during an upgrade. The following example uses specially built packages that display messages when their scripts are executed by RPM:

```
# rpm -i bother-2.7-1.i386.rpm
This is the bother 2.7 preinstall script
This is the bother 2.7 postinstall script
#
```

In this case, a package has been installed. As expected, its scripts are executed. Next, let's upgrade this package:

```
# rpm -U bother-3.5-1.i386.rpm
This is the bother 3.5 preinstall script
This is the bother 3.5 postinstall script
This is the bother 2.7 preuninstall script
This is the bother 2.7 postuninstall script
#
```

This is a textbook example of the sequence of events during an upgrade. The new version of the package is installed (as shown by the pre- and postinstall scripts being executed). Finally, the previous version of the package is removed (showing the pre- and postuninstall scripts being executed). There are really no surprises here. It worked just the way it was meant to.

This time, let's use the --noscripts option when the time comes to perform the upgrade:

```
# rpm -i bother-2.7-1.i386.rpm
This is the bother 2.7 preinstall script
This is the bother 2.7 postinstall script
#
```

Again, the first package is installed and its scripts are executed. Now let's try the upgrade using the --noscripts option:

```
# rpm -U --noscripts bother-3.5-1.i386.rpm
This is the bother 2.7 preuninstall script
This is the bother 2.7 postuninstall script
#
```

The difference here is that the --noscripts option prevented the new package's scripts from executing. The scripts from the package being erased were still executed.

5

Getting Information
About Packages

Table 5.1. Query-mode command syntax and options.

`rpm  -q` *(or* `--query`*) Options*		
Package Selection Options		*Section*
`pkg1...pkgN`	Query installed package(s)	5.2.1.1
`-p <file>` (or `-`)	Query package file `<file>` (URLs are usable)	5.2.1.4
`-f <file>`	Query package owning `<file>`	5.2.1.3
`-a`	Query all installed packages	5.2.1.2
`--whatprovides <x>`	Query packages providing capability `<x>`	5.2.1.6
`-g <group>`	Query packages belonging to group `<group>`	5.2.1.5
`--whatrequires <x>`	Query packages requiring capability `<x>`	5.2.1.7
Information Selection Options		*Section*
`<null>`	Display full package label	5.2.2
`-i`	Display summary package information	5.2.2.1
`-l`	Display list of files in package	5.2.2.2
`-c`	Display list of configuration files	5.2.2.4
`-d`	Display list of documentation files	5.2.2.5
`-s`	Display list of files in package, with state	5.2.2.6
`--scripts`	Display install, uninstall, verify scripts	5.2.2.10
`--queryformat` (or `--qf`)	Display queried data in custom format	5.2.2.11
`--dump`	Display all verifiable information for each file	5.2.2.9
`--provides`	Display capabilities package provides	5.2.2.7
`--requires` (or `-R`)	Display capabilities package requires	5.2.2.8
General Options		*Section*
`-v`	Display additional information	5.2.2.3
`-vv`	Display debugging information	5.2.3
`--root <path>`	Set alternate root to `<path>`	5.2.4
`--rcfile <rcfile>`	Set alternate rpmrc file to `<rcfile>`	5.2.5
`--dbpath <path>`	Use `<path>` to find the RPM database	5.2.6

5.1. `rpm -q`: What Does It Do?

One of the nice things about using RPM is that the packages you manage don't end up going into some kind of black hole. Nothing would be worse than to install, upgrade, and erase several different packages and not have a clue as to what's on your system. In fact, RPM's query function can help you get out of sticky situations such as the following:

■ You're poking around your system and you come across a file that you just can't identify. Where did it come from?

■ Your friend sends you a package file and you have no idea what the package does, what it installs, or where it originally came from.

■ You know that you installed XFree86 a couple months ago, but you don't know what version and you can't find any documentation on it.

The list could go on, but you get the idea. The `rpm -q` command is what you need. If you're the kind of person who doesn't like to have more options than you know what to do with, `rpm -q` might look imposing. But fear not. Once you have a handle on the basic structure of an RPM query, it'll be a piece of cake.

5.2. The Parts of an RPM Query

It becomes easy to construct a query command when you understand the individual parts. First is the `-q` (you can also use `--query`, if you like). After all, you need to tell RPM what function to perform, right? The rest of a query command consists of two distinct parts: package selection (or what packages you'd like to query) and information selection (or what information you'd like to see). Let's take a look at package selection first.

5.2.1. Query Commands, Part I: Package Selection

The first thing you'll need to decide when issuing an RPM query is what package (or packages) you'd like to query. RPM has several ways to specify packages, so you have quite an assortment to choose from.

5.2.1.1. The Package Label

Earlier chapters discuss RPM's package label, a string that uniquely identifies every installed package. Every label contains three pieces of information:

■ The name of the packaged software
■ The version of the packaged software
■ The package's release number

When issuing a query command using package labels, you must always include the package name. You can also include the version and even the release, if you like. The only restrictions are that each part of the package label specified must be complete and that if any parts of the package label are missing, all parts to the right must be omitted as well. This second restriction is just a long way of saying that if you specify the release, you must specify the version as well. Let's look at a few examples.

Say, for instance, you've recently installed a new version of the C libraries, but you can't remember the version number:

```
# rpm -q libc
libc-5.2.18-1
#
```

In this type of query, RPM returns the complete package label for all installed packages that match the given information. In this example, if version 5.2.17 of the C libraries were also installed, its package label would have been displayed, too.

In this example, we've included the version as well as the package name:

```
# rpm -q rpm-2.3
rpm-2.3-1
#
```

Note, however, that RPM is a bit picky about specifying package names. Here are some queries for the C library that won't work:

```
# rpm -q LibC
package LibC is not installed
#
```

```
# rpm -q lib
package lib is not installed
#
```

```
# rpm -q "lib*"
package lib* is not installed
#
```

```
# rpm -q libc-5
package libc-5 is not installed
#
```

```
# rpm -q libc-5.2.1
package libc-5.2.1 is not installed
#
```

As you can see, RPM is case sensitive about package names and cannot match partial names, version numbers, or release numbers. Nor can it use the wildcard characters we've come to know and love. As we've seen, however, RPM can perform the query when more than one field of the package label is present. In this case, rpm -q libc-5.2.18, or even rpm -q libc-5.2.18-1 would have found the package, libc-5.2.18-1.

Querying based on package labels may seem a bit restrictive. After all, you need to know the exact name of a package in order to perform a query on it. But there are other ways of specifying packages.

5.2.1.2. -a: Query All Installed Packages

Want lots of information fast? Using the -a option, you can query every package installed on your system. Here's an example:

```
# rpm -qa
ElectricFence-2.0.5-2
ImageMagick-3.7-2
...
tetex-xtexsh-0.3.3-8
lout-3.06-4
#
```

On a system installed using RPM, the number of packages can easily be 200 or more; we've deleted most of the output.

The -a option can produce mountains of output, which makes it a prime candidate for piping through the many Linux/UNIX commands available. One of the prime candidates would be a pager such as more, so that the list of installed packages could be viewed a screenful at a time.

Another handy command to pipe rpm -qa's output through is grep. In fact, using grep, it's possible to get around RPM's lack of built-in wildcard processing:

```
# rpm -qa | grep -i sysv
SysVinit-2.64-2
#
```

In this example, we were able to find the SysVinit package even though we didn't have the complete package name or capitalization.

5.2.1.3. -f <file>: Query the Package Owning <file>

How many times have you found a program sitting on your system and wondered what it does? Well, if the program was installed by RPM as part of a package, it's easy to find out. Simply use the -f option. For example, you find a strange program called ls in /bin (okay, it is a contrived example). Wonder what package installed it? It's as easy as this to find out:

```
# rpm -qf /bin/ls
fileutils-3.12-3
#
```

If you happen to point RPM to a file it didn't install, you'll get a message similar to the following:

```
# rpm -qf .cshrc
file /home/ed/.cshrc is not owned by any package
#
```

It's possible that you'll get the not owned by any package message in error. Here's an example of how it can happen:

```
# rpm -qf /usr/X11/bin/xterm
file /usr/X11/bin/xterm is not owned by any package
#
```

As you can see, we're trying to find out what package the xterm program is part of. The first example failed, which might lead you to believe that xterm really isn't owned by any package.

However, let's look at a directory listing:

```
# ls -lF /usr
...
lrwxrwxrwx 1 root root    5 May 13 12:46 X11 -> X11R6/
drwxrwxr-x 7 root root 1024 Mar 21 00:21 X11R6/
...
#
```

> **NOTE**
>
> I've truncated the list; normally /usr is quite a bit more crowded than this.

The key here is the line ending with X11 -> X11R6/. This is known as a *symbolic link,* or *symlink.* It's a way of referring to a file (here, a directory file) by another name. In this case, if we used the path /usr/X11 or /usr/X11R6, it shouldn't make a difference. It certainly doesn't make a difference to programs that simply want access to the file. But it does make a difference to RPM because RPM doesn't use the filename to access the file. RPM uses the filename as a key into its database. It would be very difficult, if not impossible, to keep track of all the symlinks on a system and try every possible path to a file during a query.

What to do? There are two options:

■ Make sure you always specify a path free of symlinks. This can be pretty tough, though. An alternative approach is to use namei to track down symlinks:

```
# namei /usr/X11/bin/xterm
f: /usr/X11/bin/xterm
d /
d usr
l X11 -> X11R6
d X11R6
d bin
- xterm
#
```

It's pretty easy to see the X11 to X11R6 symlink. Using this approach you can enter the nonsymlinked path and get the desired results:

```
# rpm -qf /usr/X11R6/bin/xterm
XFree86-3.1.2-5
#
```

■ Change your directory to the one holding the file you want to query. Even if you use a symlinked path to get there, querying the file should then work as you'd expect:

```
# cd /usr/X11/bin
# rpm -qf xterm
XFree86-3.1.2-5
#
```

So if you get a not owned by any package error and you think it might not be true, try one of these approaches.

5.2.1.4. -p *<file>*: Query a Specific RPM Package File

Until now, every means of specifying a package to an RPM query focused on packages that had already been installed. While it's certainly very useful to be able to dredge up information about packages that are already on your system, what about packages that haven't yet been installed? The -p option can do that for you.

One situation where this capability would help occurs when the name of a package file has been changed. Because the name of the file containing a package has nothing to do with the name of the package (although by tradition it's nice to name package files consistently), we can use this option to find out exactly what package a file contains:

```
# rpm -qp foo.bar
rpm-2.3-1
#
```

With one command, RPM gives you the answer. (On most Linux systems, the file command can be used to obtain similar information. See Appendix A, "The Format of the RPM File," for details on how to add this capability to your system's file command.)

The -p option can also use URLs to specify package files. See section 2.2.1 in Chapter 2, "Using RPM to Install Packages," for more information on using URLs.

There's one last trick up -p's sleeve—it can also perform a query by reading a package from standard input. Here's an example:

```
# cat bother-3.5-1.i386.rpm | rpm -qp
- bother-3.5-1
#
```

We piped the output of cat into RPM. The dash at the end of the command line directs RPM to read the package from standard input.

5.2.1.5. -g *<group>*: Query Packages Belonging to Group *<group>*

When a package is built, the package builder must classify the package, grouping it with other packages that perform similar functions. RPM gives you the ability to query installed packages based on their groups. For example, there is a group known as Base, which consists of packages that provide low-level structure for a Linux distribution. Let's see what installed packages make up the Base group:

```
# rpm -qg Base
setup-1.5-1
pamconfig-0.50-5
filesystem-1.2-1
crontabs-1.3-1
dev-2.3-1
etcskel-1.1-1
initscripts-2.73-1
mailcap-1.0-3
pam-0.50-17
passwd-0.50-2
redhat-release-4.0-1
rootfiles-1.3-1
termcap-9.12.6-5
#
```

One thing to keep in mind is that group specifications are case sensitive. Issuing the command rpm -qg base won't produce any output.

5.2.1.6. --whatprovides *<x>*: Query the Packages That Provide Capability *<x>*

RPM provides extensive support for dependencies between packages. Basically, a package might require what another package provides. The thing that is required and provided can be a shared library's soname (which is used to determine compatibility between different versions of the library). It can also be a character string chosen by the package builder. In any case, it's important to be able to display which packages provide a given capability.

This is just what the --whatprovides option does. When the option, followed by a capability, is added to a query command, RPM will select the packages that provide the capability. Here's an example:

```
# rpm -q --whatprovides module-info
kernel-2.0.18-5
#
```

In this case, the only package that provides the module-info capability is kernel-2.0.18-5.

5.2.1.7. --whatrequires *<x>*: Query the Packages That Require Capability *<x>*

The --whatrequires option is the logical complement to the --whatprovides option described earlier. It is used to display which packages require the specified capability. Expanding on the example we started with --whatprovides, let's see which packages require the module-info capability:

```
# rpm -q --whatrequires module-info
kernelcfg-0.3-2
#
```

There's only one package that requires module-info: kernelcfg-0.3-2.

5.2.2. Querying Commands, Part II: Information Selection

After specifying the package (or packages) you wish to query, you'll need to figure out just what information you'd like RPM to retrieve. As you've seen, by default RPM only returns the complete package label. But there's much more to a package than that. Here, we'll explore every information selection option available.

5.2.2.1. -i: Display Package Information

Adding -i to rpm -q tells RPM to give you some information on the package or packages you've selected. For the sake of clarity, let's take a look at what it gives you and explain what you're looking at:

```
# rpm -qi rpm
Name         : rpm                   Distribution: Red Hat Linux Vanderbilt
Version      : 2.3                         Vendor: Red Hat Software
Release      : 1                       Build Date: Tue Dec 24 09:07:59 1996
Install date: Thu Dec 26 23:01:51 1996  Build Host: porky.redhat.com
Group        : Utilities/System        Source RPM: rpm-2.3-1.src.rpm
Size         : 631157
Summary      : Red Hat Package Manager
Description :
RPM is a powerful package manager, which can be used to build, install, query,
verify, update, and uninstall individual software packages. A package
consists of an archive of files, and package information, including name,
version, and description.
#
```

There's quite a bit of information here, so let's go through it entry by entry:

- ■ Name—The name of the package you queried. Usually (but not always) it bears some resemblance to the name of the underlying software.

- ■ Version— The version number of the software, as specified by the software's original creator.

- ■ Release—The number of times a package consisting of this software has been packaged. If the version number should change, the release number should start over again at 1.

As you've probably noticed, these three pieces of information comprise the package label we've come to know and love. Continuing, we have these:

- ■ Install date—This is the time when the package was installed on your system.
- ■ Group—In our example, this looks suspiciously like a path. If you went searching madly for a directory tree by that name, you'd come up dry—it isn't a set of directories at all.

  When a package builder starts to create a new package, he enters a list of words that describe the software. The list, which goes from least specific to most specific, attempts to categorize the software in a concise manner. The primary use for the group is to enable graphically oriented package managers based on RPM to present packages grouped by function. Red Hat Linux's glint command does this.

■ `Size`—This is the size (in bytes) of every file in this package. It might make your decision to erase an unused package easier if you see six or more digits here.

■ `Summary`—This is a concise description of the packaged software.

■ `Description`—This is a verbose description of the packaged software. Some descriptions might be more, well, descriptive than others, but hopefully it will be enough to clue you in as to the software's role in the greater scheme of things.

■ `Distribution`—The word `Distribution` is really not the best name for this field. `Product` might be a better choice. In any case, this is the name of the product this package is a part of.

■ `Vendor`—The organization responsible for building this package.

■ `Build Date`—The time the package was created.

■ `Build Host`—The name of the computer system that built the package. Note to software packagers: Choose your build machine names wisely! A silly or offensive name might be embarrassing.

■ `Source RPM`—The process of building a package results in two files:

  ■ The package file used to install the packaged software. This is sometimes called the *binary package*.

  ■ The package file containing the source code and other files used to create the binary package file. This is known as the *source RPM package file*. This is the filename that is displayed in this field.

  Unless you want to make changes to the software, you probably won't need to worry about source packages. But if you do, stick around because the second part of this book is for you.

5.2.2.2. `-l`: Display the Package's File List

Adding `-l` to `rpm -q` tells RPM to display the list of files that are installed by the specified package or packages. If you've used `ls` before, you won't be surprised by RPM's file list.

Here's a look at one of the smaller packages on Red Hat Linux—`adduser`:

```
# rpm -ql adduser
/usr/sbin/adduser
#
```

The `adduser` package consists of only one file, so there's only one filename displayed.

5.2.2.3. `-v`: Display Additional Information

In some cases, the `-v` option can be added to a query command for additional information. The `-l` option we've been discussing is an example of just such a case. Note how the `-v` option adds verbosity:

```
# rpm -qlv adduser
-rwxr-xr-x- root root 3894 Feb 25 13:45 /usr/sbin/adduser
#
```

Looks a lot like the output from ls, doesn't it? Looks can be deceiving. Everything you see here is straight from RPM's database. However, the format is identical to that of ls, so it's more easily understood. If this is Greek to you, consult the ls man page.

5.2.2.4. -c: Display the Package's List of Configuration Files

When -c is added to an rpm -q command, RPM will display the configuration files that are part of the specified package or packages. As mentioned earlier in the book, config files are important because they control the behavior of the packaged software. Let's take a look at the list of config files for XFree86:

```
# rpm -qc XFree86
/etc/X11/fs/config
/etc/X11/twm/system.twmrc
/etc/X11/xdm/GiveConsole
/etc/X11/xdm/TakeConsole
/etc/X11/xdm/Xaccess
/etc/X11/xdm/Xresources
/etc/X11/xdm/Xservers
/etc/X11/xdm/Xsession
/etc/X11/xdm/Xsetup 0
/etc/X11/xdm/chooser
/etc/X11/xdm/xdm-config
/etc/X11/xinit/xinitrc
/etc/X11/xsm/system.xsm
/usr/X11R6/lib/X11/XF86Config
#
```

These are the files you'd want to look at first if you were looking to customize XFree86 for your particular needs. Just like -l, we can also add v for more information:

```
# rpm -qcv XFree86
-r--r--r--- root root 423 Mar 21 00:17 /etc/X11/fs/config
...
lrwxrwxrwx- root root 30 Mar 21 00:29 /usr/X11R6/lib/X11/XF86Config
-> ../../../../etc/X11/XF86Config
#
```

Note that last file: RPM will display symbolic links, as well.

5.2.2.5. -d: Display a List of the Package's Documentation

When -d is added to a query, we get a list of all files containing documentation for the named package or packages. This is a great way to get up to speed when you're having problems with unfamiliar software. As with -c and -l, you'll see either a simple list of filenames or (if you've added -v) a more comprehensive list. Here's an example that might look daunting at first, but really isn't:

```
# rpm -qdcf /sbin/dump
/etc/dumpdates
```

```
/usr/doc/dump-0.3-5
/usr/doc/dump-0.3-5/CHANGES
/usr/doc/dump-0.3-5/COPYRIGHT
/usr/doc/dump-0.3-5/INSTALL
/usr/doc/dump-0.3-5/KNOWNBUGS
/usr/doc/dump-0.3-5/THANKS
/usr/doc/dump-0.3-5/dump-0.3.announce
/usr/doc/dump-0.3-5/dump.lsm
/usr/doc/dump-0.3-5/linux-1.2.x.patch
/usr/man/man8/dump.8
/usr/man/man8/rdump.8
/usr/man/man8/restore.8
/usr/man/man8/rmt.8
/usr/man/man8/rrestore.8
#
```

Let's take that alphabet soup set of options one letter at a time:

- ■ q—Performs a query.
- ■ d—Lists all documentation files.
- ■ c—Lists all config files.
- ■ f—Queries the package that owns the specified file (/sbin/dump in this case).

The list of files represents all the documentation and config files that apply to the package owning /sbin/dump.

5.2.2.6. -s: Display the State of Each File in the Package

Unlike the past three sections, which deal with lists of files of one type or another, adding -s to a query will list the state of the files that comprise one or more packages. I can hear you out there; you're saying, "What is the state of a file?" For every file that RPM installs, there is an associated state. There are four possible states:

- ■ normal—A file in the normal state has not been modified by installing another package on the system.
- ■ replaced—Files in the replaced state have been modified by installing another package on the system.
- ■ not installed—A file is classified as not installed when it isn't installed. This state is normally seen only if the package was partially installed. An example of a partially installed package would be one that was installed with the --excludedocs option. Using this option, no documentation files would be installed. The RPM database would still contain entries for these missing files, but their state would be not installed.
- ■ net shared—The net shared state is used to alert RPM to the fact that a file is on a shared filesystem and should not be erased. This happens when several computers use NFS to mount the same filesystem. If one computer erased a package that contained files on a shared filesystem, the other computers sharing that filesystem would then have incompletely installed copies of the erased package. Files will be in the net shared state when two things happen:

- The `netsharedpath` rpmrc file entry has been changed from its default (null) value.
- The file is to be installed in a directory within a net shared path.

Here's an example showing how file states appear:

```
# rpm -qs adduser
normal /usr/sbin/adduser
#
```

The `normal` at the start of the line is the state, followed by the filename.

The file state is one of the tools RPM uses to determine the most appropriate action to take when packages are installed or erased.

Would the average person need to check the states of files? Not really. But if there should be problems, this kind of information can help get things back on track.

5.2.2.7. `--provides`: Display Capabilities Provided by the Package

By adding `--provides` to a query command, you can see the capabilities provided by one or more packages. If the package doesn't provide any capabilities, the `--provides` option produces no output:

```
# rpm -q --provides rpm
#
```

However, if a package does provide capabilities, they will be displayed:

```
# rpm -q --provides foonly
index
#
```

It's important to remember that capabilities are not filenames. In the preceding example, the `foonly` package contains no file called `index`; it's just a character string the package builder chose. This is no different from the following example:

```
# rpm -q --provides libc
libm.so.5
libc.so.5
#
```

While there might be symlinks by those names in `/lib`, capabilities are a property of the package, not a file contained in the package!

5.2.2.8. `--requires`: Display Capabilities Required by the Package

The `--requires` option (`-R` is equivalent) is the logical complement to the `--provides` option. It displays the capabilities required by the specified package(s). If a package has no requirements, there's no output (or, in later versions of RPM, the word `none`):

```
# rpm -q --requires adduser
#
```

In cases where there are requirements, they are displayed as follows:

```
# rpm -q --requires rpm
libz.so.1
libdb.so.2
libc.so.5
#
```

It's also possible that you'll come across something like this:

```
# rpm -q --requires blather
bother >= 3.1
#
```

Packages may also be built to require another package. This requirement can also include specific versions. In the preceding example, the bother package is required by blather (specifically, a version of bother greater than or equal to 3.1).

Here's something worth understanding. Let's say we decide to track down the bother that blather says it requires. If we use RPM's query capabilities, we could use the --whatprovides package selection option to try to find it:

```
# rpm -q --whatprovides bother
no package provides bother
#
```

No dice. This might lead you to believe that the blather package has a problem. The moral of this story is that, when trying to find out which package fulfills another package's requirements, it's a good idea to also try a simple query using the requirement as a package name. Continuing our earlier example, let's see if there's a package called bother:

```
# rpm -q bother
bother-3.5-1
#
```

Bingo! However, if we see what capabilities the bother package provides, we come up dry:

```
# rpm -q --provides bother
#
```

The reason for the lack of output is that all packages, by default, provide their package name (and version).

5.2.2.9. --dump: Display All Verifiable Information for Each File

The --dump option is used to display every piece of information RPM has on one or more files listed in its database. The information is listed in a very concise fashion. Because the --dump option displays file-related information, the list of files must be chosen by using the -l, -c, or -d options (or some combination thereof):

```
# rpm -ql --dump adduser
/usr/sbin/adduser 4442 841083888 ca5fa53dc74952aa5b5e3a5fa5d8904b 0100755
root root 0 0 0 X
#
```

What does all this stuff mean? Let's go through it, item by item:

- `/usr/sbin/adduser` is simple: It's the name of the file being dumped.
- `4442` is the size of the file, in bytes.
- How about `841083888`? It's the time the file was last modified, in seconds past the UNIX zero date of January 1, 1970.
- `ca5fa53dc74952aa5b5e3a5fa5d8904b` is the MD5 checksum of the file's contents, all 128 bits of it.
- If you guessed `0100755` was the file's mode, you were right.
- The first `root` represents the file's owner.
- The second `root` is the file's group.
- We'll take the next part (`0 0`) in one chunk. The first `0` shows whether the file is a config file. If `0`, as in this case, the file is not a config file. The next `0` shows whether the file is documentation. Again, since there is a `0` here, this file isn't documentation either.
- The final `0` represents the file's major and minor numbers. These are set only for device special files. Otherwise, it will be `0`.
- If the file were a symlink, the spot taken by `X` would contain a path pointing to the linked file.

Normally, the `--dump` option is used by people who want to extract the file-related information from RPM and process it somehow.

5.2.2.10. `--scripts`: Show Scripts Associated with a Package

If you add `--scripts` (that's two dashes) to a query, you get to see a little bit more of RPM's underlying magic:

```
# rpm -q --scripts XFree86
preinstall script:
(none)

postinstall script:
/sbin/ldconfig
/sbin/pamconfig --add --service=xdm --password=none --sesslist=none


preuninstall script:
(none)

postuninstall script:
/sbin/ldconfig
if [ "$1" = 0 ] ; then
/sbin/pamconfig --remove --service=xdm --password=none --sesslist=none
fi
```

```
verify script:
(none)

#
```

In this particular case, the `XFree86` package has two scripts: One labeled `postinstall` and one labeled `postuninstall`. As you might imagine, the postinstall script is executed just after the package's files have been installed; the `postuninstall` script is executed just after the package's files have been erased.

Based on the labels in this example, you'd probably imagine that a package can have as many as five different scripts. You'd be right:

■ The `preinstall` script, which is executed just before the package's files are installed.

■ The `postinstall` script, which is executed just after the package's files are installed.

■ The `preuninstall` script, which is executed just before the package's files are removed.

■ The `postuninstall` script, which is executed just after the package's files are removed.

■ And finally, the `verify` script. While it's easy to figure out the other scripts' functions based on their name, what does a script called `verify` do? Well, we haven't gotten to it yet, but packages can also be verified for proper installation. This script is used during verification. (For more information on package verification, see section 6.1 in Chapter 6, "Using RPM to Verify Installed Packages.")

Is this something you'll need very often? As in the case of displaying file states, not really. But when you need it, you really need it!

5.2.2.11. `--queryformat`: Construct a Custom Query Response

Okay, say you're still not satisfied. You'd like some additional information, or you think a different format would be easier on the eyes. Maybe you want to take some information on the packages you've installed and run it through a script for some specialized processing. You can do it, using the `--queryformat` option. In fact, if you look back at the output of the `-i` option, you'll notice that RPM was using `--queryformat` internally. Here's how it works: On the RPM command line, include `--queryformat`. Right after that, enter a format string, enclosed in single quotes (`'`).

The format string can consist of a number of different components:

■ Literal text, including escape sequences

■ Tags, with optional field width, formatting, and iteration information

■ Array iterators

Let's look at each of these components.

5.2.2.11.1. Literal Text

Any part of a format string that is not associated with tags or array iterators will be treated as literal text. Literal text is just that: It's text that is printed just as it appears in the format string. In fact, a format string can consist of nothing but literal text, although the output wouldn't tell us much about the packages being queried. Let's give the --queryformat option a try, using a format string with nothing but literal text:

```
# rpm -q --queryformat 'This is a test!' rpm
This is a test!#
```

The RPM command might look a little unusual, but if you take out the --queryformat option, along with its format string, you'll see that this is just an ordinary query of the rpm package. When the --queryformat option is present, RPM will use the text immediately following the option as a format string. In this case, the format string is 'This is a test!'. The single quotes are required. Otherwise, it's likely that your shell will complain about some of the characters contained in the average format string.

The output of this command appears on the second line. As you can see, the literal text from the format string was printed exactly as it was entered.

5.2.2.11.2. Carriage Control Escape Sequences

Wait a minute. What is that # doing at the end of the output? Well, that's our shell prompt. You see, we didn't direct RPM to move to a new line after producing the output, so the shell prompt ended up being tacked to the end of the output.

Is there a way to fix that? Yes, there is. We need to use an escape sequence. An escape sequence is a sequence of characters that starts with a backslash (\). Escape sequences add carriage control information to a format string. The following escape sequences can be used:

- ■ \a—Produces a bell sound or similar alert.
- ■ \b—Backspaces one character.
- ■ \f—Outputs a form-feed character.
- ■ \n—Outputs a newline character sequence.
- ■ \r—Outputs a carriage return character.
- ■ \t—Causes a horizontal tab.
- ■ \v—Causes a vertical tab.
- ■ \\—Displays a backslash character.

Based on this list, it seems that an \n escape sequence at the end of the format string will put our shell prompt on the next line:

```
# rpm -q -queryformat 'This is a test!\n' rpm
This is a test!
#
```

Much better.

5.2.2.11.3. Tags

The most important parts of a format string are the tags. Each tag specifies what information is to be displayed and can optionally include field width, as well as justification and data formatting instructions. (RPM uses printf to do --queryformat formatting. Therefore, you can use any of the printf format modifiers discussed in the printf(3) man page.)

But for now, let's look at the basic tag. In fact, let's look at three: the tags that print the package name, version, and release. Strangely enough, these tags are called NAME, VERSION, and RELEASE. In order to be used in a format string, the tag names must be enclosed in curly braces and preceded by a percent sign. Let's give it a try:

```
# rpm -q --queryformat '%{NAME}%{VERSION}%{RELEASE}\n' rpm
rpm2.31
#
```

Let's add a dash between the tags and see if that makes the output a little easier to read:

```
# rpm -q --queryformat '%{NAME}-%{VERSION}-%{RELEASE}\n' rpm
rpm-2.3-1
#
```

Now our format string outputs standard package labels.

5.2.2.11.4. Field Width and Justification

Sometimes it's desirable to allocate fields of a particular size for a tag. This is done by putting the desired field width between the tag's leading percent sign and the opening curly brace. Using our package-label–producing format string, let's allocate a 20-character field for the version:

```
# rpm -q --queryformat '%{NAME}-%20{VERSION}-%{RELEASE}\n' rpm
rpm-                 2.3-1
#
```

The result is a field of 20 characters: 17 spaces followed by the 3 characters that make up the version.

In this case the version field is right-justified; that is, the data is printed at the far right of the output field. We can left-justify the field by preceding the field width specification with a dash:

```
# rpm -q --queryformat '%{NAME}-%-20{VERSION}-%{RELEASE}\n' rpm
rpm-2.3              -1
#
```

Now the version is printed at the far left of the output field. You might be wondering what would happen if the field width specification didn't leave enough room for the data being printed. The field width specification can be considered the minimum width the field will take. If the data being printed is wider, the field will expand to accommodate the data.

5.2.2.11.5. Modifiers—Making Data More Readable

While RPM does its best to appropriately display the data from a --queryformat, there are times when you'll need to lend a helping hand. Here's an example. Say we want to display the name of each installed package, followed by the time the package was installed. Looking through the available tags, we see INSTALLTIME. Great! Looks like this will be simple:

```
# rpm -qa --queryformat '%{NAME} was installed on %{INSTALLTIME}\n'
setup was installed on 845414601
pamconfig was installed on 845414602
filesystem was installed on 845414607
...
rpm was installed on 851659311
pgp was installed on 846027549
#
```

Well, that's a lot of output, but it's not very useful. What are those numbers? RPM didn't lie—they're the times the packages were installed. The problem is that the times are being displayed in their numeric form used internally by the operating system, and humans like to see the day, month, year, and so on.

Fortunately, there's a modifier for just this situation. The name of the modifier is :date, and it follows the tag name. Let's try our example again, this time using :date:

```
# rpm -qa --queryformat '%{NAME} was installed on %{INSTALLTIME:date}\n'
setup was installed on Tue Oct 15 17:23:21 1996
pamconfig was installed on Tue Oct 15 17:23:22 1996
filesystem was installed on Tue Oct 15 17:23:27 1996
...
rpm was installed on Thu Dec 26 23:01:51 1996
pgp was installed on Tue Oct 22 19:39:09 1996
#
```

That sure is a lot easier to understand, isn't it?

Here's a list of the available modifiers:

- The :date modifier displays dates in human-readable form. It transforms 846027549 into Tue Oct 22 19:39:09 1996.

- The :perms modifier displays file permissions in an easy-to-read format. It changes -32275 to -rwxr-xr-x-.

- The :depflags modifier displays the version comparison ags used in dependency processing in human-readable form. It turns 12 into >=.

- The :fflags modifier displays a c if the file has been marked as being a configuration file, a d if the file has been marked as being a documentation file, and blank otherwise. Thus, 2 becomes d.

5.2.2.11.6. Array Iterators

Until now, we've been using tags that represent single data items. There is, for example, only one package name or installation date for each package. However, other tags can represent many different pieces of data. One such tag is FILENAMES, which can be used to display the names of every file contained in a package.

Let's put together a format string that will display the package name, followed by the name of every file that package contains. We'll try it on the adduser package first since it contains only one file:

```
# rpm -q --queryformat '%{NAME}: %{FILENAMES}\n' adduser
adduser: /usr/sbin/adduser
#
```

Hey, not bad: Got it on the first try. Now let's try it on a package with more than one file:

```
# rpm -q --queryformat '%{NAME}: %{FILENAMES}\n' etcskel
etcskel: (array)
#
```

Hmmm. What went wrong? It worked before. Well, it worked before because the adduser package contained only one file. The FILENAMES tag points to an array of names, so when there is more than one file in a package, there's a problem.

But there is a solution. It's called an *iterator*. An iterator can step through each entry in an array, producing output as it goes. Iterators are created when square braces enclose one or more tags and literal text. Since we want to iterate through the FILENAMES array, let's enclose that tag in the iterator:

```
# rpm -q --queryformat '%{NAME}: [%{FILENAMES}]\n' etcskel
etcskel: /etc/skel/etc/skel/.Xclients/etc/skel/.Xdefaults/etc/skel/.ba
#
```

There was more output: It went right off the screen in one long line. The problem? We didn't include a newline escape sequence inside the iterator. Let's try it again:

```
# rpm -q --queryformat '%{NAME}: [%{FILENAMES}\n]' etcskel
etcskel: /etc/skel
/etc/skel/.Xclients
/etc/skel/.Xdefaults
/etc/skel/.bash logout
/etc/skel/.bash profile
/etc/skel/.bashrc
/etc/skel/.xsession
#
```

That's more like it. If we wanted, we could put another file-related tag inside the iterator. If we included the FILESIZES tag, we'd be able to see the name of each file, as well as how big it was:

```
# rpm -q --queryformat '%{NAME}: [%{FILENAMES} (%{FILESIZES} bytes) \n]'\
> etcskel
etcskel: /etc/skel (1024 bytes)
/etc/skel/.Xclients (551 bytes)
/etc/skel/.Xdefaults (3785 bytes)
/etc/skel/.bash logout (24 bytes)
/etc/skel/.bash profile (220 bytes)
/etc/skel/.bashrc (124 bytes)
/etc/skel/.xsession (9 bytes)
#
```

That's pretty nice. But it would be even nicer if the package name appeared on each line, along with the filename and size. Maybe if we put the NAME tag inside the iterator:

```
# rpm -q --queryformat '[%{NAME}: %{FILENAMES} (%{FILESIZES} bytes) \n]'\
> etcskel
etcskel: /etc/skel(parallel array size mismatch)#
```

The error message says it all. The FILENAMES and FILESIZES arrays are the same size. The NAME tag isn't even an array. Of course the sizes don't match!

5.2.2.11.7. Iterating Single-Entry Tags

If a tag has only one piece of data, it's possible to put it in an iterator and have its one piece of data displayed with every iteration. This is done by preceding the tag name with an equal sign. Let's try it on our current example:

```
# rpm -q --queryformat '[%{=NAME}: %{FILENAMES} (%{FILESIZES} bytes) \n]'\
> etcskel
etcskel: /etc/skel (1024 bytes)
etcskel: /etc/skel/.Xclients (551 bytes)
etcskel: /etc/skel/.Xdefaults (3785 bytes)
etcskel: /etc/skel/.bash logout (24 bytes)
etcskel: /etc/skel/.bash profile (220 bytes)
etcskel: /etc/skel/.bashrc (124 bytes)
etcskel: /etc/skel/.xsession (9 bytes)
#
```

That's about all there is to format strings. Now, if RPM's standard output doesn't give you what you want, you have no reason to complain. Just --queryformat it!

5.2.2.11.8. In Case You Were Wondering…

What's that? You say you don't know what tags are available? You can use RPM's --querytags option. When used as the only option (that is, rpm --querytags), it produces a list of available tags. It should be noted that RPM displays the complete tag name. For instance, RPMTAG_ARCH is the complete name, yet you'll only need to use ARCH in your format string. Here's a partial example of the --querytags option in action:

```
# rpm --querytags
RPMTAG_NAME
RPMTAG_VERSION
RPMTAG_RELEASE
...
 RPMTAG_VERIFYSCRIPT
#
```

Be forewarned: The full list is quite lengthy. At the time this book was written, there were more than 60 tags! You'll notice that each tag is printed in uppercase and is preceded with RPMTAG_. If we were to use that last tag, RPMTAG_VERIFYSCRIPT, in a format string, it could be specified in any of the following ways:

```
%{RPMTAG_VERIFYSCRIPT}
```

```
%{RPMTAG_VerifyScript}
```

```
%{RPMTAG_VeRiFyScRiPt}
```

```
%{VERIFYSCRIPT}
```

```
%{VerifyScript}
```

```
%{VeRiFyScRiPt}
```

The only hard-and-fast rule regarding tags is that if you include the RPMTAG_ prefix, it must be all uppercase. The fourth example here shows the traditional way of specifying a tag: prefix omitted, all uppercase. The choice, however, is yours.

One other thing to keep in mind is that not every package will have every type of tagged information available. In cases where the requested information is not available, RPM will display (none) or (unknown). There are also a few tags that, for one reason or another, will not produce useful output when they are used in a format string. For a comprehensive list of queryformat tags, see Appendix D, "Available Tags for --queryformat."

5.2.3. Getting a Lot More Information with -vv

Sometimes it's necessary to have even more information than we can get with -v. By adding another v, we can start to see more of RPM's inner workings:

```
# rpm -qvv rpm
D: opening database in //var/lib/rpm/
D: querying record number 2341208
rpm-2.3-1
#
```

The lines starting with D: have been added by using -vv. We can see where the RPM database is located and what record number contains information on the rpm-2.3-1 package. Following that is the usual output.

In the vast majority of cases, it will not be necessary to use -vv. It is normally used by software engineers working on RPM itself, and the output can change without notice. However, it's a handy way to gain insight into RPM's inner workings.

5.2.4. --root *<path>*: Use *<path>* As an Alternate Root

Adding --root *<path>* to a query command forces RPM to assume that the directory specified by *<path>* is actually the root directory. In addition, RPM expects its database to reside in the directory specified by the dbpath rpmrc file entry, relative to *<path>*.

Normally, this option is only used during an initial system install or when a system has been booted off a rescue disk and some packages need to be re-installed in order to restore normal operation.

5.2.5. `--rcfile` *<rcfile>*: Use *<rcfile>* As an Alternate `rpmrc` File

The `--rcfile` option is used to specify a file containing default settings for RPM. Normally, this option is not needed. By default, RPM uses `/etc/rpmrc` and a file named `.rpmrc`, located in your login directory.

This option would be used if there were a need to switch between several sets of RPM options. Software developers and package builders will be the people using `--rcfile`. For more information on `rpmrc` files, see Appendix B, "The `rpmrc` Files"

5.2.6. `--dbpath` *<path>*: Use *<path>* to Find an RPM Database

In order for RPM to do its work, it needs access to an RPM database. Normally, this database exists in the directory specified by the `rpmrc` file entry `dbpath`. By default, `dbpath` is set to `/var/lib/rpm`.

Although the `dbpath` entry can be modified in the appropriate `rpmrc` file, the `--dbpath` option is probably a better choice when the database path needs to be changed temporarily. An example of a time when the `--dbpath` option would come in handy is when it's necessary to examine an RPM database copied from another system. Granted, it's not a common occurrence, but it's difficult to handle any other way.

5.3. A Few Handy Queries

The following sections describe some examples of situations you might find yourself in, and ways you can use RPM to get the information you need. Keep in mind that these are just examples. Don't be afraid to experiment!

5.3.1. Finding Config Files Based on a Program Name

You're setting up a new system, and you'd like to implement some systemwide aliases for people using the Bourne again shell, `bash`. The problem is you just can't remember the name of the systemwide initialization file used by `bash`, or where it resides:

```
# rpm -qcf /bin/bash
/etc/bashrc
#
```

Rather than spend your time trying to hunt down the file, RPM finds it for you in seconds.

5.3.2. Learning More About an Uninstalled Package

Practically any option can be combined with -qp to extract information from an .rpm file. Let's say you have an unknown .rpm file, and you'd like to know a bit more before installing it:

```
# rpm -qpil foo.bar
Name        : rpm              Distribution: Red Hat Linux Vanderbilt
Version     : 2.3                   Vendor: Red Hat Software
Release     : 1                 Build Date: Tue Dec 24 09:07:59 1996
Install date:    (none)         Build Host: porky.redhat.com
Group       : Utilities/System  Source RPM: rpm-2.3-1.src.rpm
Size        : 631157
Summary     : Red Hat Package Manager
Description :
RPM is a powerful package manager, which can be used to build, install,
query, verify, update, and uninstall individual software packages. A package
consists of an archive of files, and package information, including name,
version, and description.
/bin/rpm
/usr/bin/find-provides
/usr/bin/find-requires
/usr/bin/gendiff
/usr/bin/rpm2cpio
/usr/doc/rpm-2.3-1
...
 /usr/src/redhat/SOURCES
/usr/src/redhat/SPECS
/usr/src/redhat/SRPMS
#
```

By displaying the package information, we know that we have a package file containing RPM version 2.3. We can then peruse the file list and see exactly what it would install before installing it.

5.3.3. Finding Documentation for a Specific Package

Picking on bash some more, you realize that your knowledge of the software is lacking. You'd like to see when it was installed on your system and what documentation is available for it:

```
# rpm -qid bash
Name        :bash               Distribution: Red Hat Linux (Picasso)
Version     :1.14.6                  Vendor: Red Hat Software
Release     :2                   Build Date: Sun Feb 25 13:59:26 1996
Install date:    Mon May 13 12:47:22 1996 Build Host: porky.redhat.com
Group       :Shells               Source RPM: bash-1.14.6-2.src.rpm
Size        :486557
Description :GNU Bourne Again Shell (bash)
/usr/doc/bash-1.14.6-2
/usr/doc/bash-1.14.6-2/NEWS
/usr/doc/bash-1.14.6-2/README
/usr/doc/bash-1.14.6-2/RELEASE
/usr/info/bash.info.gz
/usr/man/man1/bash.1
#
```

You never realized that there could be so much documentation for a shell!

5.3.4. Finding Similar Packages

Looking at bash's information, we see that it belongs to the group Shells. You're not sure what other shell packages are installed on your system. If you can find other packages in the Shells group, you'll have found the other installed shells:

```
# rpm -qa --queryformat '%10{NAME} %20{GROUP}\n' ¦ grep -i shells
      ash      Shells
     bash      Shells
      csh      Shells
       mc      Shells
     tcsh      Shells
#
```

Now you can query each of these packages and learn more about them, too.

> **NOTE**
>
> Did you see this example and say to yourself, "Hey, they could've used the -g option to query for that group directly"? If you did, you've been paying attention. This is a more general way of searching the RPM database for information. We just happened to search by group in this example.

5.3.5. Finding Recently Installed Packages, Part I

Let's say you installed a new package a few days ago. All you know for certain is that the package installed a new command in the /bin directory. Let's try to find the package:

```
# find /bin -type f -mtime -14 ¦ rpm -qF
rpm-2.3-1
#
```

Looks like RPM version 2.3 was installed sometime in the last two weeks.

5.3.6. Finding Recently Installed Packages, Part II

Another way to see which packages were recently installed is to use the --queryformat option:

```
# rpm -qa --queryformat\
> '%{installtime} %{name}-%{version}-%{release} %{installtime:date}\n'\
> ¦ sort -nr +1 ¦ sed -e 's/^[^ ]* //'
rpm-devel-2.3-1 Thu Dec 26 23:02:05 1996
rpm-2.3-1 Thu Dec 26 23:01:51 1996
pgp-2.6.3usa-2 Tue Oct 22 19:39:09 1996
...
 pamconfig-0.50-5 Tue Oct 15 17:23:22 1996
setup-1.5-1 Tue Oct 15 17:23:21 1996
#
```

By having RPM include the installation time in numeric form, it was simple to sort the packages and then use sed to remove the user-unfriendly numeric time.

5.3.7. Finding the Largest Installed Packages

Let's say that you're running low on disk space and you'd like to see what packages you have installed, along with the amount of space each package takes up. You'd also like to see the largest packages first so you can get back as much disk space as possible:

```
# rpm -qa --queryformat\
> '%{name}-%{version}-%{release} %{size}\n'\
> | sort -nr +1
kernel-source-2.0.18-5 20608472
tetex-0.3.4-3 19757371
emacs-el-19.34-1 12259914
...
rootfiles-1.3-1 3494
mkinitrd-1.0-1 1898
redhat-release-4.0-1 22
#
```

If you don't build custom kernels or use T_EX, it's easy to see how much space could be reclaimed by removing those packages.

6

Using RPM to Verify Installed Packages

Table 6.1. Verify-mode command syntax and options.

`rpm -V` *(or* `--verify`*, or* `-y`*) Options*

	Package Selection Options	Section
`pkg1...pkgN`	Verify named package(s)	6.3.1
`-p <file>`	Verify against package file `<file>`	6.3.4
`-f <file>`	Verify package owning `<file>`	6.3.3
`-a`	Verify all installed packages	6.3.2
`-g <group>`	Verify packages belonging to group `<group>`	6.3.5
	Verify-Specific Options	**Section**
`--noscripts`	Do not execute verification script	6.3.7
`--nodeps`	Do not verify dependencies	6.3.6
`--nofiles`	Do not verify file attributes	6.3.8
	General Options	**Section**
`-v`	Display additional information	6.3.9
`-vv`	Display debugging information	6.3.10
`--root <path>`	Set alternate root to `<path>`	6.3.12
`--rcfile <rcfile>`	Set alternate rpmrc file to `<rcfile>`	6.3.13
`--dbpath <path>`	Use `<path>` to find the RPM database	6.3.11

6.1. `rpm -V`: What Does It Do?

From time to time, it's necessary to make sure that everything on your system is okay. Are you sure the packages you've installed are still configured properly? Have there been any changes made that you don't know about? Did you mistakenly start a recursive delete in /usr and now you have to assess the damage?

RPM can help. It can alert you to changes made to any of the files installed by RPM. Also, if a package requires capabilities provided by another package, it can make sure the other package is installed, too.

The command `rpm -V` (or `-y`, or `--verify`, which are equivalent) verifies an installed package. Before we see how this is done, let's take a step back and look at the big picture.

Every time a package is installed, upgraded, or erased, the changes are logged in RPM's database. It's necessary for RPM to keep track of this information; otherwise, it wouldn't be able to perform these operations correctly. You can think of the RPM database (and the disk space it consumes) as being the price of admission for the easy package management that RPM provides. (Actually, the price is fairly low. For a completely RPM-based Linux distribution, it would be unusual to have a database over 5MB.)

The RPM database reflects the configuration of the system on which it resides. When RPM accesses the database to see how files should be manipulated during an install, upgrade, or erase, it is using the database as a mirror of the system's configuration.

However, we can also use the system configuration as a mirror of the RPM database. What does this backward view give us? What purpose would be served?

The purpose would be to see if the system configuration accurately reflects the contents of the RPM database. If the system configuration doesn't match the database, we can reach one of two conclusions:

The RPM database has become corrupt. The system configuration is unchanged.

The RPM database is intact. The system configuration has changed.

While RPM databases occasionally are corrupted, it is a sufficiently rare occurrence that the second conclusion is much more likely. So RPM gives us a powerful verification tool, essentially for free.

6.1.1. What Does It Verify?

It would be handy if RPM did nothing more than verify that every file installed by a package actually exists on your system. In reality, RPM does much more. It makes sure that if a package depends on other packages to provide certain capabilities, the necessary packages are, in fact, installed. If the package builder created one, RPM will also run a special verification script that can verify aspects of the package's installation that RPM cannot.

Finally, every file installed by RPM is examined. No fewer than the following nine attributes of each file can be checked:

■ Owner
Group
Mode
MD5 checksum
Size
Major number
Minor number
Symbolic link string
Modification time

Let's take a look at each of these attributes and why they are good things to check.

6.1.1.1. File Ownership

Most operating systems today keep track of each file's creator. This is done primarily for resource accounting. Linux and UNIX also use file ownership to help determine access rights to the file. In addition, some files, when executed by a user, can temporarily change the user's ID, normally to a more privileged ID. Therefore, any change of file ownership may have far-reaching effects on data security and system availability.

6.1.1.2. File Group

In a similar manner to file ownership, a group specification is attached to each file. Primarily used for determining access rights, a file's group specification can also become a user's group ID, should that user execute the file's contents. Therefore, any changes in a file's group specification are important and should be monitored.

6.1.1.3. File Mode

Encompassing the file's permissions, the mode is a set of bits that specifies permitted access for the file's owner, group members, and everyone else. Even more important are two additional bits that determine whether a user's group or user ID should be changed if he executes the program contained in the file. Since these little bombshells can let any user become root for the duration of the program, it pays to be extra careful with a file's permissions.

6.1.1.4. MD5 Checksum

The MD5 checksum of a file is simply a 128-bit number that is mathematically derived from the contents of the file. The MD5 algorithm was designed by Ron Rivest, the *R* in the popular RSA public-key encryption algorithm. The *MD* in MD5 stands for *message digest*, which is a pretty accurate description of what it does.

Unlike literary digests, an MD5 checksum conveys no information about the contents of the original file. However, it possesses one unique trait: Any change to the file, no matter how small, results in a change to the MD5 checksum. (From a strictly theoretical standpoint, this is not entirely true. Using the lingo of cryptologists, it is believed to be "computationally infeasible" to find two messages that produce the same MD5 checksum.)

RPM creates MD5 checksums of all files it manipulates, and stores them in its database. For all intents and purposes, if one of these files is changed, the MD5 checksum will change, and RPM will detect it.

6.1.1.5. File Size

As if the use of MD5 isn't enough, RPM also keeps track of file sizes. A difference of even 1 byte more or less will not go unnoticed.

6.1.1.6. Major Number

Device character and block files possess a major number. The major number is used to communicate information to the device driver associated with the special file. For instance, under Linux the special files for SCSI disk drives should have a major number of 8, while the major number for an IDE disk drive's special file would be 3. As you can imagine, any change to a file's major number can have disastrous effects and is tracked by RPM.

6.1.1.7. Minor Number

A file's minor number is similar in concept to the major number, but conveys different information to the device driver. In the case of disk drives, this information can consist of a unit identifier. If the minor number changes, RPM will detect it.

6.1.1.8. Symbolic Link

If the file in question is really a symbolic link, the text string containing the name of the linked-to file is checked.

6.1.1.9. Modification Time

Most operating systems keep track of the date and time that a file was last modified. RPM uses this to its advantage by keeping modification times in its database.

6.2. When Verification Fails: rpm -V Output

When verifying a package, RPM produces output only if there is a verification failure. When a file fails verification, the format of the output is a bit cryptic, but it packs all the information you need into one line per file. Here is the format:

```
SM5DLUGT c file
```

In this syntax the following things are true:

- ■ S is the file size.
- ■ M is the file's mode.
- ■ 5 is the MD5 checksum of the file.
- ■ D is the file's major and minor numbers.
- ■ L is the file's symbolic link contents.
- ■ U is owner of the file.
- ■ G is the file's group.

- ■ T is the modification time of the file.
- ■ c appears only if the file is a configuration file. This is handy for quickly identifying config files, as they are very likely to change, and therefore, very unlikely to verify successfully.
- ■ *file* is the file that failed verification. The complete path is listed to make it easy to find.

It's unlikely that every file attribute will fail to verify, so each of the eight attribute flags will only appear if there is a problem. Otherwise, a . will be printed in that flag's place. Let's look at an example or two. In this case, the mode, MD5 checksum, and modification time for the specified file have failed to verify:

```
# rpm -V Xfree86
.M5....T /usr/X11R6/lib/X11/fonts/misc/fonts.dir
#
```

The file is not a config file (note the absence of a c between the attribute list and the filename).

In the following, the size, checksum, and modification time of the system password file have all changed:

```
# rpm -V setup
S.5....T c /etc/passwd
#
```

The c indicates that this is a config file.

This last example illustrates what RPM does when a file that should be there is missing entirely:

```
# rpm -V at
missing    /var/spool/at/spool
#
```

6.2.1. Other Verification Failure Messages

When rpm -V finds other problems, the output is a bit easier to understand:

```
# rpm -V blather
Unsatisfied dependencies for blather-7.9-1:    bother >= 3.1
#
```

It's pretty easy to see that the blather package requires at least version 3.1 of the bother package.

The output from a package's verification script is a bit harder to categorize because the script's contents, as well as its messages, are entirely up to the package builder.

6.3. Selecting What to Verify and How

There are several ways to verify packages installed on your system. If you've taken a look at RPM's query command, you'll find that many of them are similar. Let's start with the simplest method of specifying packages: the package label.

6.3.1. The Package Label: Verify an Installed Package Against the RPM Database

You can simply follow the rpm -V command with all or part of a package label. As with every other RPM command that accepts package labels, you'll need to carefully specify each part of the label you include. Keep in mind that package names are case sensitive, so rpm -V *PackageName* and rpm -V *packagename* are not the same. Let's verify the initscripts package:

```
# rpm -V initscripts
#
```

Although it looks like RPM didn't do anything, the following steps were performed:

1. For every file in the package, RPM checked the nine file attributes discussed earlier.
2. If the package was built with dependencies, the RPM database was searched to ensure that the packages that satisfy those dependencies were installed.
3. If the package was built with a verification script, that script was executed.

In our example, each of these steps was performed without error—the package verified successfully. Remember, with rpm -V you'll only see output if a package fails to verify.

6.3.2. -a: Verify All Installed Packages Against the RPM Database

If you add -a to rpm -V, you can easily verify every installed package on your system. It might take a while, but when it's done, you'll know exactly what's been changed on your system:

```
# rpm -Va
.M5....T    /usr/X11R6/lib/X11/fonts/misc/fonts.dir
missing     /var/spool/at/.lockfile
missing     /var/spool/at/spool
S.5....T    /usr/lib/rhs/glint/icon.pyc
..5....T  c /etc/inittab
..5.....    /usr/bin/loadkeys
#
```

Don't be too surprised if rpm -Va turns up a surprising number of files that failed verification. RPM's verification process is very strict! In many cases, the changes flagged don't indicate problems—they are only an indication of your system's configuration being different from what the builders of the installed packages had on their systems. Also, some attributes change during normal system operation. It would be wise to check into each verification failure, just to make sure.

6.3.3. -f *<file>*: Verify the Package Owning *<file>* Against the RPM Database

Imagine this: You're hard at work when a program you've used a million times before suddenly stops working. What do you do? Well, before using RPM, you probably tried to find other files associated with that program and see if they had changed recently.

Now you can let RPM do at least part of that sleuthing for you. Simply direct RPM to verify the package owning the ailing program:

```
% rpm -Vf /sbin/cardmgr
S.5....T c /etc/sysconfig/pcmcia
%
```

Hmmmm. Looks like a config file was recently changed.

This isn't to say that using RPM to verify a package will always get you out of trouble, but it's such a quick step that it should be one of the first things you try. Here's an example of rpm -Vf not working out as well:

```
% rpm -Vf /etc/blunder
file /etc/blunder is not owned by any package
%
```

Note that the issue surrounding RPM and symbolic links mentioned in Chapter 5, "Getting Information About Packages," also applies to rpm -Vf. Watch those symlinks!

6.3.4. -p *<file>*: Verify Against a Specific Package File

Unlike the previous options to rpm -V, each of which verifies one or more packages against RPM's database, the -p option performs the same verification, but against a package file. Why on earth would you want to do this when the RPM database is sitting there, just waiting to be used?

Well, what if you didn't have an RPM database? While it isn't a common occurrence, power failures, hardware problems, and inadvertent deletions (along with nonexistent backups) can leave your system sans database. Then your system hiccups; what do you do now?

This is where a CD full of package files can be worth its weight in gold. Simply mount the CD and verify to your heart's content:

```
# rpm -Vp /mnt/cdrom/RedHat/RPMS/i386/adduser-1.1-1.i386.rpm
#
```

Whatever else might be wrong with this system, at least we can add new users. But what if you have many packages to verify? It would be a very slow process doing it one package at a time. That's where the next option comes in handy.

6.3.5. -g *<group>*: Verify Packages Belonging to *<group>*

When a package is built, the package builder must classify the package, grouping it with other packages that perform similar functions. RPM gives you the ability to verify installed packages based on their groups. For example, there is a group known as Shells. This group consists of packages that contain, strangely enough, shells. Let's verify the proper installation of every shell-related package on the system:

```
# rpm -Vg Shells
missing /etc/bashrc
#
```

One thing to keep in mind is that group specifications are case sensitive. Issuing the command rpm -Vg shells wouldn't verify many packages:

```
# rpm -Vg shells
group shells does not contain any packages
#
```

6.3.6. --nodeps: Do Not Check Dependencies Before Erasing Package

When the --nodeps option is added to a verify command, RPM will bypass its dependency verification processing. In this example, we've added the -vv option to the command line so we can watch RPM at work:

```
# rpm -Vvv rpm
D: opening database in //var/lib/rpm/
D: verifying record number 2341208
D: dependencies: looking for libz.so.1
D: dependencies: looking for libdb.so.2
D: dependencies: looking for libc.so.5
#
```

As you can see, the rpm package provides three different capabilities:

- libz.so.1
- libdb.so.2
- libc.so.5

If we add the --nodeps option, the dependency verification of the three capabilities is no longer performed:

```
# rpm -Vvv --nodeps rpm
D: opening database in //var/lib/rpm/
D: verifying record number 2341208
#
```

The line D: verifying record number 2341208 indicates that RPM's normal file-based verification proceeded normally.

6.3.7. --noscripts: Do Not Execute Verification Script

Adding the --noscripts option to a verify command prevents execution of the verification scripts of each package being verified. In the following example, the package verification script is executed:

```
# rpm -Vvv bother
D: opening database in //var/lib/rpm/
D: verifying record number 616728
D: verify script found - running from file /var/tmp/rpm-321.vscript
+ PATH=/sbin:/bin:/usr/sbin:/usr/bin:/usr/X11R6/bin
+ export PATH
+ echo This is the bother 3.5 verification script
This is the bother 3.5 verification script
#
```

While the actual script is not very interesting, it did execute when the package was being verified. In the next example, we'll use the --noscripts option to prevent its execution:

```
# rpm -Vvv --noscripts bother
D: opening database in //var/lib/rpm/
D: verifying record number 616728
#
```

As expected, the output is identical to the prior example, minus the lines dealing with the verification script, of course.

6.3.8. --nofiles: Do Not Verify File Attributes

The --nofiles option disables RPM's file-related verification processing. When this option is used, only the verification script and dependency verification processing are performed. In this example, the package has a file-related verification problem:

```
# rpm -Vvv bash
D: opening database in //var/lib/rpm/
D: verifying record number 279448
D: dependencies: looking for libc.so.5
D: dependencies: looking for libtermcap.so.2
missing /etc/bashrc
#
```

When the --nofiles option is added, the missing file doesn't cause a message anymore:

```
# rpm -Vvv --nofiles bash
D: opening database in //var/lib/rpm/
D: verifying record number 279448
D: dependencies: looking for libc.so.5
D: dependencies: looking for libtermcap.so.2
#
```

This is not to say that the missing file problem is solved, just that no file verification was performed.

6.3.9. -v: Display Additional Information

Although RPM won't report an error with the command syntax if you include the -v option, you won't see much in the way of additional output:

```
# rpm -Vv bash
#
```

Even if there are verification errors, adding -v won't change the output:

```
# rpm -Vv apmd
S.5....T /etc/rc.d/init.d/apm
S.5....T /usr/X11R6/bin/xapm
#
```

The only time that the -v option will produce output is when the package being verified has a verification script. Any normal output from the script won't be displayed by RPM when run without -v (note that failure messages will always be displayed):

```
# rpm -V bother
#
```

But when -v is added, the script's non-error-related output is displayed:

```
# rpm -Vv bother
This is the bother 0.5 verification script
#
```

6.3.10. -vv: Display Debugging Information

Sometimes it's necessary to have even more information than we can get with -v. By adding another v, that's just what we'll get:

```
# rpm -Vvv rpm
D: opening database in //var/lib/rpm/
D: verifying record number 2341208
D: dependencies: looking for libz.so.1
D: dependencies: looking for libdb.so.2
D: dependencies: looking for libc.so.5
#
```

The lines starting with D: have been added by using -vv. We can see where the RPM database is located and what record number contains information on the rpm-2.3-1 package. Following that is the list of dependencies that the rpm package requires.

In the vast majority of cases, it will not be necessary to use -vv. It is normally used by software engineers working on RPM itself, and the output can change without notice. However, it's a handy way to gain insights into RPM.

6.3.11. --dbpath *<path>*: Use *<path>* to Find an RPM Database

In order for RPM to do its handiwork, it needs access to an RPM database. Normally, this database exists in the directory specified by the rpmrc file entry, dbpath. By default, dbpath is set to /var/lib/rpm. Although the dbpath entry can be modified in the appropriate rpmrc file, the --dbpath option is probably a better choice when the database path needs to be changed temporarily. An example of a time the --dbpath option would come in handy is when it's necessary to examine an RPM database copied from another system. Granted, it's not a common occurrence, but it's difficult to handle any other way.

6.3.12. --root *<path>*: Set Alternate Root to *<path>*

Adding --root *<path>* to a verify command forces RPM to assume that the directory specified by *<path>* is actually the root directory. In addition, RPM expects its database to reside in the directory specified by the dbpath rpmrc file entry, relative to *<path>*. (For more information on rpmrc file entries, see Appendix B, "The rpmrc File.")

Normally this option is only used during an initial system install or when a system has been booted off a rescue disk.

6.3.13. --rcfile *<rcfile>*: Set Alternate rpmrc File to *<rcfile>*

The --rcfile option is used to specify a file containing default settings for RPM. Normally, this option is not needed. By default, RPM uses /etc/rpmrc and a file named .rpmrc, located in your login directory.

This option would be used if there were a need to switch between several sets of RPM options. Software developer and package builders will be the people using --rcfile. For more information on rpmrc files, see Appendix B.

6.4. We've Lied to You

Not really; we just omitted a few details until you've had a chance to see rpm -V in action. These details are described in the following sections.

6.4.1. RPM Controls What Gets Verified

Depending on the type of file being verified, RPM will not verify every possible attribute. Table 6.2 shows the attributes checked for each of the different file types.

Table 6.2. File attributes verified for each file type.

File Type	*File Size*	*Mode*	*MD5 Check-sum*	*Major Number*	*Minor Number*	*Symlink String*	*Owner*	*Group*	*Modification Time*
Directory									
File		X					X	X	
Symbolic Links		X				X	X	X	
FIFO		X					X	X	
Devices		X		X	X		X	X	
Regular Files	X	X	X				X	X	X

6.4.2. The Package Builder Can Also Control What Gets Verified

When a package builder creates a new package, he can control what attributes are to be verified on a file-by-file basis. The reasons for excluding specific attributes from verification can be quite involved, but here's an example just to give you the flavor: When a person logs into a system, there are device files associated with that user's terminal session. In order for the terminal device (called tty) to function properly, the owner and group of the device must change to that of the person logging in. Therefore, if RPM were to verify the package that created the tty device files, any ttys that were in use at the time would fail to verify. However, by using the %verify directive (see Chapter 13, "Inside the Spec File," for details on %verify), a package builder can save you from trivial verification failures.

7

Using RPM to Verify
Package Files

Table 7.1. Package verification syntax and options.

`rpm -K` *(or* `--checksig`*) Options* `file1.rpm...fileN.rpm`		
	Parameters	
`file1.rpm...fileN.rpm`	One or more RPM package files (URLs are usable)	
	Checksig-Specific Options	***Section***
`--nopgp`	Do not verify PGP signatures	7.3.5
	General Options	***Section***
`-v`	Display additional information	7.3.1
`-vv`	Display debugging information	7.3.6
`--rcfile <rcfile>`	Set alternate `rpmrc` file to `<rcfile>`	7.3.7

7.1. `rpm -K`: What Does It Do?

One aspect of RPM is that you can get a package from the Internet and easily install it. But what do you know about that package file? Is the organization listed as being the vendor of the package really the organization that built it? Did someone make unauthorized changes to it? Can you trust that, if installed, it won't mail a copy of your password file to a system cracker?

Features built into RPM allow you to make sure that the package file you've just gotten won't cause you problems after it's installed, whether the package was corrupted by line noise when you downloaded it or something more sinister happened to it.

The command `rpm -K` (the option `--checksig` is equivalent) verifies a package file. Using this command, it is easy to make sure the file has not been changed in any way. `rpm -K` can also be used to make sure that the package was actually built by the organization listed as being the package's vendor. That's all very impressive, but how does it do that? Well, it just needs help from some "pretty good" software.

7.1.1. Pretty Good Privacy: RPM's Assistant

The "pretty good" software we're referring to is known as *pretty good privacy*, or *PGP*. While all the information on PGP could fill a book (or several), we've provided a quick introduction to help you get started.

If PGP is new to you, a quick glance through Appendix G, "An Introduction to PGP," should get you well on your way to understanding, building, and installing PGP. If, on the other hand, you've got PGP already installed and have sent an encrypted message or two, you're probably more than ready to continue with this chapter.

7.2. Configuring PGP for rpm -K

After PGP is properly built and installed, the actual configuration for RPM is trivial. Here's what needs to be done:

1. PGP must be in your path. If PGP's usage message doesn't come up when you enter pgp at your shell prompt, you'll need to add PGP's directory to your path.

2. PGP must be able to find the public keyring file that you want to use when checking package file signatures. You can use two methods to direct PGP to the public keyring:

   ■ Set the PGPPATH environment variable to point to the directory containing the public keyring file.

   ■ Set the pgp_path rpmrc file entry to point to the directory containing the public keyring file. For more information on rpmrc files, rpmrc file entries, and how to use them, please see Appendix B, "The rpmrc File."

Now we're ready.

7.3. Using rpm -K

After all the preliminaries with PGP, it's time to get down to business. First, we need to get the package builder's public key and add it to the public keyring file used by RPM. You'll need to do this once for each package builder whose packages you'll want to check. This is what you'll need to do:

```
# pgp -ka RPM-PGP-KEY ./pubring.pgp
Pretty Good Privacy(tm) 2.6.3a   Public key encryption for the masses.
(c) 1990-96 Philip Zimmermann, Phil's Pretty Good Software. 1996-03-04
Uses the RSAREF(tm) Toolkit, which is copyright RSA Data Security, Inc.
Distributed by the Massachusetts Institute of Technology.
Export of this software may be restricted by the U.S. government.
Current time: 1996/06/01 22:50 GMT

Looking for new keys...
pub 1024/CBA29BF9 1996/02/20 Red Hat Software, Inc. <redhat@redhat.com>

Checking signatures...


Keyfile contains:
1 new key(s)

One or more of the new keys are not fully certified.
Do you want to certify any of these keys yourself (y/N)? n
#
```

Here we've added Red Hat Software's public key, since we're going to check some package files produced by them. The file RPM-PGP-KEY contains the key. At the end, PGP asks whether we want to certify the new key. We've answered no because it isn't necessary to certify keys to verify package files.

Next, we'll verify a package file:

```
# rpm -K rpm-2.3-1.i386.rpm
rpm-2.3-1.i386.rpm: size pgp md5 OK
#
```

While the output might seem somewhat anticlimactic, we can now be nearly 100% certain that this package was produced by Red Hat Software, Inc., and is unchanged from Red Hat's original copy.

The output from this command shows that there are actually three distinct features of the package file that are checked by the -K option:

- The size message indicates that the size of the packaged files has not changed.
- The pgp message indicates that the digital signature contained in the package file is a valid signature of the package file contents, and was produced by the organization that originally signed the package.
- The md5 message indicates that a checksum contained in the package file and calculated when the package was built matches a checksum calculated by RPM during verification. Because the two checksums match, it is unlikely that the package has been modified.

The OK means that each of these tests was successful. If any had failed, the name would have been printed in parentheses. A bit later in the chapter, we'll see what happens when there are verification problems.

7.3.1. -v: Display Additional Information

Adding v to a verification command will produce more interesting output:

```
# rpm -Kv rpm-2.3-1.i386.rpm
rpm-2.3-1.i386.rpm:
Header+Archive size OK: 278686 bytes
Good signature from user "Red Hat Software, Inc. <redhat@redhat.com>".
Signature made 1996/12/24 18:37 GMT using 1024-bit key, key ID CBA29BF9

WARNING: Because this public key is not certified with a trusted signature,
it is not known with high confidence that this public key actually belongs
to: "Red Hat Software, Inc. <redhat@redhat.com>".
MD5 sum OK: 8873682c5e036a307dee87d990e75349
#
```

With a bit of digging, we can see that each of the three tests was performed, and each passed. The reason for that dire-sounding warning is that PGP is meant to operate without a central authority managing key distribution. PGP certifies keys based on webs of trust. For example, if an acquaintance of yours creates a public key, you can certify it by attaching your digital signature to it. Then anyone who knows and trusts you can also trust your acquaintance's public key.

In this case, the key came directly from a mass-produced Red Hat Linux CD-ROM. If someone were trying to masquerade as Red Hat Software, Inc., then he'd have certainly gone through a lot of trouble to do so. In this case, the lack of a certified public key is not a major problem, given the fact that the CD-ROM came directly from the Red Hat Software offices.

> **NOTE**
>
> Red Hat Software's public key is also available from its Web site at `http://www.redhat.com/redhat/contact.html`. The RPM sources also contain the key and are available from their FTP site at `ftp://ftp.redhat.com/pub/redhat/code/rpm`.

7.3.2. When the Package Is Not Signed

As mentioned earlier, not every package you'll run across is going to be signed. If this is the case, here's what you'll see from RPM:

```
# rpm -K bother-3.5-1.i386.rpm
bother-3.5-1.i386.rpm: size md5 OK
#
```

Note the lack of a pgp message. The size and md5 messages indicate that the package still has size and checksum information that verified properly. In fact, all recently produced package files will have these verification measures built in automatically.

If you happen to run across an older unsigned package, you'll know it right away:

```
# rpm -K apmd-2.4-1.i386.rpm
apmd-2.4-1.i386.rpm: No signature available
#
```

Older package files had only a PGP-based signature; if that were missing, there would be nothing left to verify.

7.3.3. When You Are Missing the Correct Public Key

If you happen to forget to add the correct public key to RPM's keyring, you'll see the following response:

```
# rpm -K rpm-2.3-1.i386.rpm
rpm-2.3-1.i386.rpm: size (PGP) md5 OK (MISSING KEYS)
#
```

Here the PGP in parentheses indicates that there's a problem with the signature, and the message at the end of the line (MISSING KEYS) shows what the problem is. Basically, RPM asked PGP to verify the package against a key that PGP didn't have, and PGP complained.

7.3.4. When a Package Just Doesn't Verify

Eventually it's going to happen: You go to verify a package, and it fails. We'll look at an example of a package that fails verification a bit later. Before we do that, let's make a package that won't verify in order to demonstrate how sensitive RPM's verification is.

First, we made a copy of a signed package, rpm-2.3-1.i386.rpm. We called the copy rpm-2.3-1.i386-bogus.rpm. Next, using Emacs (in hexl-mode, for all you Emacs buffs), we changed the first letter of the name of the system that built the original package. The file rpm-2.3-1.i386-bogus.rpm is now truly bogus: It has been changed from the original file.

Although the change was a small one, it still showed up when the package file was queried. Here's a listing from the original package:

```
# rpm -qip rpm-2.3-1.i386.rpm
Name       : rpm              Distribution: Red Hat Linux Vanderbilt
Version    : 2.3                    Vendor: Red Hat Software
Release    : 1                  Build Date: Tue Dec 24 09:07:59 1996
Install date: (none)           Build Host: porky.redhat.com
Group      : Utilities/System  Source RPM: rpm-2.3-1.src.rpm
Size       : 631157
Summary    : Red Hat Package Manager
Description :
RPM is a powerful package manager, which can be used to build, install,
query, verify, update, and uninstall individual software packages. A
package consists of an archive of files, and package information, including
name, version, and description.
#
```

And here's the same listing from the bogus package file:

```
# rpm -qip rpm-2.3-1.i386-bogus.rpm
Name       : rpm              Distribution: Red Hat Linux Vanderbilt
Version    : 2.3                    Vendor: Red Hat Software
Release    : 1                  Build Date: Tue Dec 24 09:07:59 1996
Install date: (none)           Build Host: qorky.redhat.com
Group      : Utilities/System  Source RPM: rpm-2.3-1.src.rpm
Size       : 631157
Summary    : Red Hat Package Manager
Description :
RPM is a powerful package manager, which can be used to build, install,
query, verify, update, and uninstall individual software packages. A
package consists of an archive of files, and package information, including
name, version, and description.
#
```

Notice that the build hostname changed from `porky.redhat.com` to `qorky.redhat.com`. Using the `cmp` utility to compare the two files, we find that the difference occurs at byte 1201, which changed from p (octal 160), to q (octal 161):

```
# cmp -cl rpm-2.3-1.i386.rpm rpm-2.3-1.i386-bogus.rpm
  1201 160 p    161 q
#
```

People versed in octal numbers will note that only one bit has been changed in the entire file. That's the smallest possible change you can make! Let's see how our bogus friend fares:

```
# rpm -K rpm-2.3-1.i386-bogus.rpm
rpm-2.3-1.i386-bogus.rpm: size PGP MD5 NOT OK
#
```

Given that the command's output ends with NOT OK in big capital letters, it's obvious there's a problem. Since the word size was printed in lowercase, the bogus package's size was okay, which makes sense: We only changed the value of one bit, without adding or subtracting anything else.

However, the PGP signature, printed in uppercase, didn't verify. This makes sense, too. The package that was signed by Red Hat Software has been changed. The fact that the package's MD5 checksum also failed to verify provides further evidence that the bogus package is just that: bogus.

7.3.5. --nopgp: Do Not Verify Any PGP Signatures

Perhaps you want to be able to verify packages but, for one reason or another, you cannot use PGP. Maybe you don't have a trustworthy source of the necessary public keys, or maybe it's illegal to possess encryption (like PGP) software in your country. Is it still possible to verify packages?

Certainly. In fact, we've already done it, in section 7.3.3. You lose the ability to verify the package's origins, as well as some level of confidence in the package's integrity, but the size and MD5 checksums still give some measure of assurance as to the package's state.

Of course, when PGP can't be used, the output from a verification always looks like something's wrong:

```
# rpm -K rpm-2.3-1.i386.rpm
rpm-2.3-1.i386.rpm: size (PGP) md5 OK (MISSING KEYS)
#
```

The --nopgp option directs RPM to ignore PGP entirely. If we use the --nopgp option on the preceding example, we find that things look a whole lot better:

```
# rpm -K --nopgp rpm-2.3-1.i386.rpm
rpm-2.3-1.i386.rpm: size md5 OK
#
```

7.3.6. -vv: Display Debugging Information

You'll probably never have to use it, but the -vv option will give you insights into how RPM verifies packages. Here's an example:

```
# rpm -Kvv rpm-2.3-1.i386.rpm
D: New Header signature
D: magic: 8e ad e8 01
D: got : 8e ad e8 01
D: Signature size: 236
D: Signature pad : 4
D: sigsize : 240
D: Header + Archive: 278686
D: expected size : 278686
rpm-2.3-1.i386.rpm:
Header+Archive size OK: 278686 bytes
Good signature from user "Red Hat Software, Inc. <redhat@redhat.com>".
Signature made 1996/12/24 18:37 GMT using 1024-bit key, key ID CBA29BF9

WARNING: Because this public key is not certified with a trusted signature,
it is not known with high confidence that this public key actually belongs
to: "Red Hat Software, Inc. <redhat@redhat.com>".
MD5 sum OK: 8873682c5e036a307dee87d990e75349
#
```

The lines starting with D: represent extra output produced by the -vv option. This output is normally used by software developers in the course of adding new features to RPM and is subject to change, but there's no law against looking at it.

Briefly, the output shows that RPM has detected a new-style signature block, containing size, MD5 checksum, and PGP signature information. The size of the signature, the size of the package file's header and archive sections, and the expected size of those sections are all displayed.

7.3.7. --rcfile <rcfile>: Use <rcfile> As an Alternate rpmrc File

The --rcfile option is used to specify a file containing default settings for RPM. Normally, this option is not needed. By default, RPM uses /etc/rpmrc and a file named .rpmrc located in your login directory.

This option would be used if there were a need to switch between several sets of RPM defaults. Software developers and package builders will normally be the only people using the --rcfile option. For more information on rpmrc files, see Appendix B.

8

Miscellanea

As with any other large, complex subject, there are always some leftovers—things that just don't seem to fit in any one category. RPM is no exception. This chapter covers those aspects of RPM that can only be called "miscellanea."

8.1. Other RPM Options

The options described in the following sections normally are not used on a day-to-day basis. However, some of them can be quite important when the need arises. One such option is `--rebuilddb`.

8.1.1. `--rebuilddb`: Rebuild RPM Database

We all hope the day never comes, and for many of us, it never does. But still, there is a chance that one day, while you're busy using RPM to install or upgrade a package, you'll see this message:

```
free list corrupt (42)- contact rpm-list@redhat.com
```

When this happens, you'll find there's very little that you can do, RPM-wise. However, before you fire off an e-mail to the RPM mailing list, you might try the `--rebuilddb` option. The format of the command is simple:

```
rpm --rebuilddb
```

The command produces no output. After a few minutes, it completes with nary a peep. Here's an example of `--rebuilddb` being used on an RPM database that wasn't corrupt. First, let's look at the files that comprise the database:

```
# cd /var/lib/rpm
# ls
total 3534
-rw-r--r--    1 root     root         1351680 Oct 17 10:35 fileindex.rpm
-rw-r--r--    1 root     root           16384 Oct 17 10:35 groupindex.rpm
-rw-r--r--    1 root     root           16384 Oct 17 10:35 nameindex.rpm
-rw-r--r--    1 root     root         2342536 Oct 17 10:35 packages.rpm
-rw-r--r--    1 root     root           16384 Oct 17 10:35 providesindex.rpm
-rw-r--r--    1 root     root           16384 Oct 17 10:35 requiredby.rpm
#
```

Then, issue the command:

```
# rpm --rebuilddb
#
```

After a few minutes, the command completes, and we take a look at the files again:

```
# ls
total 3531
-rw-r--r--    1 root     root         1351680 Oct 17 20:50 fileindex.rpm
-rw-r--r--    1 root     root           16384 Oct 17 20:50 groupindex.rpm
-rw-r--r--    1 root     root           16384 Oct 17 20:50 nameindex.rpm
-rw-r--r--    1 root     root         2339080 Oct 17 20:50 packages.rpm
```

```
-rw-r--r--   1 root     root          16384 Oct 17 20:50 providesindex.rpm
-rw-r--r--   1 root     root          16384 Oct 17 20:50 requiredby.rpm
#
```

You'll note that packages.rpm decreased in size. This is due to a side-effect of the --rebuilddb option. While it is going through the database, it is getting rid of unused portions of the database. Our example was performed on a newly installed system where only one or two packages had been upgraded, so the reduction in size was small. For a system that has been through a complete upgrade, the difference would be more dramatic.

Does this mean that you should rebuild the database every once in a while? Not necessarily. Since RPM eventually will make use of the holes, there's no major advantage to regular rebuilds. However, when an RPM-based system has undergone a major upgrade, it certainly wouldn't hurt to spend a few minutes using --rebuilddb to clean things up.

8.1.2. --initdb: Create a New RPM Database

If you are already using RPM, the --initdb option is one you'll probably never have to use. The --initdb option is used to create a new RPM database. That's why you'll probably not need it if you're already using RPM: You already have an RPM database.

It might seem that the --initdb option would be dangerous. After all, won't it trash your current database if you mistakenly use it? Fortunately, the answer is no. If there is an RPM database in place already, it's still perfectly safe to use the option, even though it won't accomplish much. As an example, here's a listing of the files that make up the RPM database on a Red Hat Linux system:

```
# ls /var/lib/rpm
total 3559
-rw-r--r--   1 root     root          16384 Jan 8 22:10 conflictsindex.rpm
-rw-r--r--   1 root     root        1351680 Jan 8 22:10 fileindex.rpm
-rw-r--r--   1 root     root          16384 Jan 8 22:10 groupindex.rpm
-rw-r--r--   1 root     root          16384 Jan 8 22:10 nameindex.rpm
-rw-r--r--   1 root     root        2349640 Jan 8 22:10 packages.rpm
-rw-r--r--   1 root     root          16384 Jan 8 22:10 providesindex.rpm
-rw-r--r--   1 root     root          16384 Jan 8 22:10 requiredby.rpm
#
```

Next, let's use the --initdb option, just to see what it does to this database:

```
# rpm --initdb
# ls /var/lib/rpm
total 3559
-rw-r--r--   1 root     root          16384 Jan 8 22:10 conflictsindex.rpm
-rw-r--r--   1 root     root        1351680 Jan 8 22:10 fileindex.rpm
-rw-r--r--   1 root     root          16384 Jan 8 22:10 groupindex.rpm
-rw-r--r--   1 root     root          16384 Jan 8 22:10 nameindex.rpm
-rw-r--r--   1 root     root        2349640 Jan 8 22:10 packages.rpm
-rw-r--r--   1 root     root          16384 Jan 8 22:10 providesindex.rpm
-rw-r--r--   1 root     root          16384 Jan 8 22:10 requiredby.rpm
#
```

Since an RPM database existed already, the `--initdb` option did no harm to it—there was no change to the database files.

The only other option that can be used with `--initdb` is `--dbpath`. This permits the easy creation of a new RPM database in the directory specified with the `--dbpath` option.

8.1.3. `--quiet`: Produce As Little Output As Possible

Adding the `--quiet` option to any RPM command directs RPM to produce as little output as possible. For example, RPM's build command (the subject of Part II, "RPM and Developers: How to Distribute Your Software More Easily with RPM") normally produces reams of output; by adding the `--quiet` option, this is all you'll see:

```
# rpm -ba --quiet bother-3.5.spec
Package: bother
1 block
3 blocks
#
```

The `--quiet` option can silence even the mighty `-vv` option:

```
# rpm -Uvv --quiet eject-1.2-2.i386.rpm
#
```

8.1.4. `--help`: Display a Help Message

RPM includes a concise built-in help message for those times when you need a reminder about a particular command. Normally, you'll want to use the `--help` option by itself, although you might want to pipe the output through a pager such as `less`, since the output is more than one screen long:

```
# rpm --help¦less

RPM version 2.3
Copyright (C) 1995 - Red Hat Software
This may be freely redistributed under the terms of the GNU Public License
usage:
--help                 - print this message
--version      - print the version of rpm being used
all modes support the following arguments:
--rcfile <file>        - use <file> instead of /etc/rpmrc and $HOME/.rpmrc
-v                           - be a little more verbose
-vv                          - be incredibly verbose (for debugging)
-q                     - query mode
--root <dir>           - use <dir> as the top level directory
--dbpath <dir>         - use <dir> as the directory for the database
--queryformat <s>      - use s as the header format (implies -i)
install, upgrade and query (with -p) allow ftp URL's to be used in place of
file names as well as the following options:

--ftpproxy <host>      - hostname or IP of ftp proxy

--ftpport <port>       - port number of ftp server (or proxy)
```

This is just the first screen of RPM's help command. To see the rest, give the command a try. Practically everything there is to know about RPM is present in the `--help` output. It's a bit too concise to learn RPM from, but it's enough to refresh your memory when the syntax of a particular option escapes you.

8.1.5. `--version`: Display the Current RPM Version

If you're not sure what version of RPM is presently installed on your system, the easiest way to find out is to ask RPM itself using the `--version` option:

```
# rpm --version
RPM version 2.3
#
```

8.2. Using `rpm2cpio`

From time to time, you might find it necessary to extract one or more files from a package file. One way to do this would be the following:

1. Install the package.
2. Make a copy of the file(s) you need.
3. Erase the package.

An easier way would be to use `rpm2cpio`.

8.2.1. `rpm2cpio`: What Does It Do?

As the name implies, `rpm2cpio` takes an RPM package file and converts it to a `cpio` archive. Because it's written to be used primarily as a filter, there's not much to be specified. `rpm2cpio` takes only one argument, and even that's optional!

The optional argument is the name of the package file to be converted. If there is no filename specified on the command line, `rpm2cpio` will simply read from standard input and convert that to a `cpio` archive. Let's give it a try:

```
# rpm2cpio logrotate-1.0-1.i386.rpm
0707020001a86a000081a40000000000000000000000001313118bb000002c200000008000
00003000000000000000000000000190000e73eusr/man/man8/logrotate.8." logrotate
- log file rotator
.TH rpm 8 "28 November 1995" "Red Hat Software" "Red Hat Linux"
.SH NAME
```

Note that this is only the first few lines of output.

What on earth is all that stuff? Remember that `rpm2cpio` is written as a filter. It writes the `cpio` archive contained in the package file to standard output, which, if you've not redirected it somehow, is your screen. Here's a more reasonable example:

```
# rpm2cpio logrotate-1.0-1.i386.rpm > blah.cpio
# file blah.cpio
blah.cpio: ASCII cpio archive (SVR4 with CRC)
#
```

Here we've directed `rpm2cpio` to convert the `logrotate` package file. We've also redirected `rpm2cpio`'s output to a file called `blah.cpio`. Next, using the `file` command, we find that the resulting file is indeed a bona fide `cpio` archive file. The following command is entirely equivalent to the previous one and shows `rpm2cpio`'s capability to read the package file from its standard input:

```
# cat logrotate-1.0-1.i386.rpm ¦ rpm2cpio > blah.cpio
#
```

8.2.2. A More Real-World Example: Listing the Files in a Package File

While there's nothing wrong with using `rpm2cpio` to create a `cpio` archive file, it takes a few more steps and uses a bit more disk space than is strictly necessary. A somewhat cleaner approach would be to pipe `rpm2cpio`'s output directly into `cpio`:

```
# rpm2cpio logrotate-1.0-1.i386.rpm ¦ cpio -t
usr/man/man8/logrotate.8
usr/sbin/logrotate
14 blocks
#
```

In this example, we used the `-t` option to direct `cpio` to produce a table of contents of the archive created by `rpm2cpio`. This can make it much easier to get the right filename and path when you want to extract a file.

8.2.3. Extracting One or More Files from a Package File

Continuing the previous example, let's extract the man page from the `logrotate` package. In the table of contents, we see that the full path is `usr/man/man8/logrotate.8`. All we need to do is to use the filename and path as shown here:

```
# rpm2cpio logrotate-1.0-1.i386.rpm ¦cpio -ivd usr/man/man8/logrotate.8
usr/man/man8/logrotate.8
14 blocks
#
```

In this case, the `cpio` options `-i`, `-v`, and `-d` direct `cpio` to do the following:

1. Extract one or more files from an archive.
2. Display the names of any files processed, along with the size of the archive file, in 512-byte blocks. (Note that the size displayed by `cpio` is the size of the `cpio` archive and not the package file.)
3. Create any directories that precede the filename specified in the `cpio` command.

So where did the file end up? The last option (-d) to cpio provides a hint. Let's take a look:

```
# ls -al
total 5
-rw-rw-r-- 1 root root 3918 May 30 11:02 logrotate-1.0-1.i386.rpm
drwx------ 3 root root 1024 Jul 14 12:42 usr
# cd usr
# ls -al
total 1
drwx------ 3 root root 1024 Jul 14 12:42 man
# cd man
# ls -al
total 1
drwx------ 2 root root 1024 Jul 14 12:42 man8
# cd man8
# ls -al
total 1
-rw-r--r-- 1 root root 706 Jul 14 12:42 logrotate.8
# cat logrotate.8
.\" logrotate - log file rotator
.TH rpm 8 "28 November 1995" "Red Hat Software" "Red Hat Linux"
.SH NAME
logrotate \- log file rotator
.SH SYNOPSIS
\fBlogrotate\fP [configfiles]
.SH DESCRIPTION
\fBlogrotate\fP is a tool to prevent log files from growing without
. . .
```

Since the current directory didn't have a usr/man/man8/ path in it, the -d option caused cpio to create all the directories leading up to the logrotate.8 file in the current directory. Based on this, it's probably safest to use cpio outside the normal system directories unless you're comfortable with cpio and you know what you're doing!

8.3. Source Package Files and How to Use Them

One day, you may run across a package file with a name similar to the following:

etcskel-1.0-3.src.rpm

Notice the src. Is that a new kind of computer? If you use RPM on an Intel-based computer, you'd normally expect to find i386 there. Maybe someone messed up the name of the file. Well, we know that the file command can display information about a package file, even if the filename has been changed. We've used it before to figure out what package a file contains:

```
# file foo.bar
foo.bar: RPM v2 bin i386 eject-1.2-2
#
```

In this example, foo.bar is an RPM version 2 file. bin indicates that the file contains an executable package, and i386 means that the package was built for Intel processors. The package is called eject version 1.2, release 2.

Let's try the `file` command on this mystery file to see what we can find out about it:

```
# file etcskel-1.0-3.src.rpm
etcskel-1.0-3.src.rpm: RPM v2 src i386 etcskel-1.0-3
#
```

Well, it's a package file all, right—for version 1.0, release 3 of the `etcskel` package. It's in RPM version 2 format and built for Intel-based systems. But what does the `src` mean?

8.3.1. A Gentle Introduction to Source Code

This package file contains not the executable, or *binary*, files that a normal package contains, but rather the source files required to create those binaries. When a programmer creates a new program, he writes the instructions, often called *code*, in one or more files. The source code is then compiled into a binary that can be executed by the computer.

As part of the process of building package files (a process covered in great detail in Part II), two types of package files are created:

- The binary, or executable, package file
- The source package file

The source package contains everything needed to re-create not only the programs and associated files that are contained in the binary package file, but the binary and source package files themselves.

8.3.2. Do You Really Need More Information Than This?

The following discussion is going to get rather technical. Unless you're the type of person who likes to modify other people's code, chances are you won't need much more information than this. But if you're still interested, let's explore further.

8.3.3. So What Can I Do with It?

One thing you can do with source package files is install them. Let's try an install of a source package:

```
# rpm -i cdp-0.33-3.src.rpm
#
```

Well, that doesn't tell us very much and (take our word for it) adding -v doesn't improve the situation appreciably. Let's haul out the big guns and try -vv:

```
# rpm -ivv cdp-0.33-3.src.rpm
D: installing cdp-0.33-3.src.rpm
Installing cdp-0.33-3.src.rpm
D: package is a source package major = 2
D: installing a source package
D: sources in: ///usr/src/redhat/SOURCES
```

```
D: spec file in: ///usr/src/redhat/SPECS
D: file "cdp-0.33-cdplay.patch" complete
D: file "cdp-0.33-fsstnd.patch" complete
D: file "cdp-0.33.spec" complete
D: file "cdp-0.33.tgz" complete
D: renaming ///usr/src/redhat/SOURCES/cdp-0.33.spec
to
///usr/src/redhat/SPECS/cdp-0.33.spec
#
```

What does this output say? Well, RPM recognizes that the file is a source package. It mentions that sources (we know what they are) are in /usr/src/redhat/SOURCES. Let's take a look:

```
# ls -al /usr/src/redhat/SOURCES/
-rw-rw-r-- 1 root root 364 Apr 24 22:35 cdp-0.33-cdplay.patch
-rw-r--r-- 1 root root 916 Jan 8 12:07 cdp-0.33-fsstnd.patch
-rw-r--r-- 1 root root 148916 Nov 10 1995 cdp-0.33.tgz
#
```

Some files there seem to be related to cdp. The two files ending with .patch are patches to the source. RPM permits patches to be processed when building binary packages. The patches are bundled along with the original, unmodified sources in the source package.

The last file is a gzipped tar file. If you've gotten software off the Internet, you're probably familiar with tar files, gzipped or not. If we look inside the file, we should see all the usual kinds of things: readme files, a makefile or two, and some source code:

```
# tar ztf cdp-0.33.tgz
cdp-0.33/COPYING
cdp-0.33/ChangeLog
cdp-0.33/INSTALL
cdp-0.33/Makefile
cdp-0.33/README
cdp-0.33/cdp
cdp-0.33/cdp-0.33.lsm
cdp-0.33/cdp.1
cdp-0.33/cdp.1.Z
cdp-0.33/cdp.c
cdp-0.33/cdp.h
. . .
#
```

There's more, but you get the idea. Okay, so there are the sources. But what is that spec file mentioned in the output? It mentions something about /usr/src/redhat/SPECS, so let's see what we have in that directory:

```
# ls -al /usr/src/redhat/SPECS
-rw-r--r-- 1 root root 397 Apr 24 22:36 cdp-0.33.spec
```

Without making a long story too short, a spec file contains information used by RPM to create the binary and source packages. Using the spec file, RPM does the following:

1. Unpacks the sources.
2. Applies patches (if any exist).

3. Builds the software.

4. Creates the binary package file.

5. Creates the source package file.

6. Cleans up after itself.

The neatest part of this is that RPM does all this automatically, under the control of the spec file. That's about all we're going to say about how RPM builds packages. For more information, please see Part II.

8.3.4. Stick with Us!

As noted several times, we'll be covering the subject of building packages with RPM in Part II. Be forewarned, however: Package building, while straightforward, is not a task for people new to programming. But if you've written a program or two, you'll probably find RPM's package building a piece of cake.

II

RPM and Developers:
How to Distribute
Your Software More
Easily with RPM

9

The Philosophy
Behind RPM

As you saw in Part I, "RPM and Computer Users: How to Use RPM to Effectively Manage Your Computer," RPM can make life much easier for the user. With automated installs, up-grades, and erasures, RPM can take a lot of the guesswork out of keeping a computer system up-to-date.

But what about people who sling code for a living? Does RPM have anything to offer them? Yes! One of the best things about RPM is that although it was designed to make life easier for users, it was written by people who would be using it to build many packages. So the design philosophy of RPM has a definite bias toward making life easier for developers. The following sections list some of the reasons you should consider building packages with RPM.

9.1. Pristine Sources

Although many developers might use RPM to package their own software, just as many, if not more, are going to be packaging software that they have not written. Therefore, there are some aspects to RPM's design that are geared toward third-party package builders. One such aspect is RPM's use of pristine sources.

When a third-party package builder decides to package someone else's software, he often gets the software from the Net, normally as a `tar` file compressed with something like GNU zip. That's probably about the only generalization we can make when talking about software that is eligible for packaging. Once we look inside the `tar` file, there is a world of possible differences:

■ The application could be available in pure source form, in pure binary form, or some combination of both.

■ The application might have been written to be built using `make`, `imake`, or a script included with the sources. Or, it might have to be built entirely by hand.

■ The application might need to be configured prior to use. Maybe it uses GNU `configure`, a custom configuration script, or one or more files that need to be edited to reflect the target environment.

■ The application might have been written to reside in specific directories, and those directories do not exist, or are not appropriate on the target system.

■ The application might not even support the target environment, requiring all manner of changes to port it to the target environment.

We could go on, but you probably get the idea. It's a rare application that comes off the Net ready to package, and the changes required vary widely. What to do?

This is where the concept of pristine sources comes in. RPM is designed to use the sources as they come from the application's developer, no matter how it has been packaged and config-ured. The main benefit is that the changes you as a package builder need to make remain sepa-rate from the original sources, in a distinct collection of patches.

This may not sound like much of an advantage, but consider how this would work if a new version of the application came out. If the new version had a few localized bug fixes, it's entirely possible that the original patches could be applied and a new package built, with a single RPM command. Even if the patches didn't apply cleanly, it would at least give an indication as to what might need to be done to get the new version built and packaged.

If your users sometimes customize packages, having pristine sources makes it easier for them, too. They can see what patches you've created and can easily add their own.

Another benefit to using pristine sources is that it makes keeping track of multiple versions of a package simple. Instead of keeping patched sources around, or battling a revision control system, it's only necessary to keep the following:

- The original sources in their `tar` file
- A copy of the patches you applied to get the application to build
- A file used by RPM to control the package-building process

With these three items, it's possible to easily build the package at any time. Keeping track of multiple versions only entails keeping track of each version of these three components, rather than hundreds or thousands of patched source files.

In fact, it gets better than that. RPM can also build a source package containing these three components. The source package, named using RPM's standard naming convention, keeps everything you need to re-create a specific version of a package in one uniquely named file. Keeping track of multiple versions of multiple packages is simply a matter of keeping the appropriate source packages around. Everything else can be built from them.

9.2. Easy Builds

RPM makes it easy to build packages. Just as with the use of pristine sources, the fact that the build process is simple is an even greater advantage to the third-party package builders responsible for many packages than it is to a one-package software development house. But in either case, RPM's ease of building is a welcome relief. The following sections document some of the ways that RPM makes building packages a straightforward process.

9.2.1. Reproducible Builds

One of the biggest problems facing developers is reproducing a particular build. This problem is the main reason so much effort is put into creating and deploying version control systems to manage sources.

Although RPM cannot compete with a full-blown revision control system, it does an excellent job of keeping in one place everything required to build a particular version of a package. Remember the source package mentioned earlier? With one command, RPM can open the package, extract the sources, patch them, perform a build, and create a new binary package, ready for your users. The best part is that the binary package will be the same every time you build it because everything needed to create it is kept in one source package.

9.2.2. Unattended Builds

As mentioned earlier, completely building a package takes only one RPM command. This makes it easy to set up automated build procedures that can build 100 packages as easily as 1. Anything from a single package consisting of 1 application to the several hundred packages that comprise an entire operating system can be built automatically using RPM.

9.3. Multiarchitecture/Operating System Support

It has always been a fact for software developers that their applications may need to be ported to multiple operating systems. It is also becoming more common that a particular operating system might run on several different platforms, or architectures.

RPM's capability to support multiple architectures and operating systems makes it easy to build the same package for many OS/platform combinations. A package might be configured to build on only one architecture/OS combination, or on several. The only limitation is the application's portability.

9.4. Easier for Your Users

While we are primarily concerned with RPM's advantages from the developer's point of view, it's worth looking at RPM from the user's standpoint for a moment. After all, if RPM makes life easier for your users, that can translate into lower support costs.

9.4.1. Easy Upgrades

Probably the biggest headache for user and developer alike is the upgrade of an application, or worse yet, an entire operating system! RPM can make upgrading a one-step process. With one command, a new package can be installed, and the remnants of the old package removed.

9.4.2. Intelligent Configuration File Handling

Configuration files—nearly every application has them. They might go by different names, but they all control the behavior of their application. Users normally customize config files to their liking and would be upset if their customizations were lost during the installation, upgrade, or removal of a package.

RPM takes special care with a user's config files. By using MD5 checksums, RPM can determine what action is most appropriate with a config file. If a config file has been modified by the user and has to be replaced, it is saved. That way a user's modifications are never lost.

9.4.3. Powerful Query Capabilities

RPM uses a database to keep track of all files it installs. RPM's database provides other benefits, such as the wide variety of information that can be easily retrieved from it. RPM's query command makes it easy for users to quickly answer a number of questions, such as the following:

- Where did this file come from? Is it part of a package?
- What does this package do?
- What packages are installed on my system?

These are just a few examples of the many ways RPM can provide information about one or more packages on a user's system.

9.4.4. Easy Package Verification

Another way that RPM leverages the information stored in its database is by providing an easy way to verify that a package is properly installed. With this capability, RPM makes it easy to determine, for example, what packages were damaged by a wildcard delete in /usr/bin. In addition, RPM's verification command can detect changes to file attributes, such as a file's permissions, ownership, and size.

9.5. To Summarize

RPM was written by developers for developers. It makes building packages as easy as possible, even if the software being packaged hasn't been developed in-house. In addition, RPM presents some significant advantages to users, thereby reducing support needs.

Chapter 10, "The Basics of Developing with RPM," introduces the basic concepts of package building with RPM.

10

The Basics of Developing with RPM

Now that we've seen the design philosophy of RPM, let's look at the nuts and bolts of RPM's build process. Building a package is similar to compiling code—there are inputs, an engine that does the dirty work, and outputs.

10.1. The Inputs

There are three different kinds of inputs that are used to drive RPM's build process. Two of the three inputs are required, and the third, strictly speaking, is optional. But unless you're packaging your own code, chances are you'll need it.

10.1.1. The Sources

First and foremost are the sources. After all, without them, there wouldn't be much to build! In the case of packaging someone else's software, the sources should be kept as the author distributed them, which usually means a compressed `tar` file. RPM can handle other archive formats, but a bit more up-front effort is required.

In any case, you should not modify the sources used in the package building process. If you're a third-party package builder, the sources should be just the way you got them from the author's FTP site. If it's your own software, the choice is up to you, but you should consider starting with your mainstream sources.

10.1.2. The Patches

Why all the emphasis on unmodified sources? Because RPM gives you the ability to automatically apply patches to them. Usually, the nature of these patches falls into one of the following categories:

- The patch addresses an issue specific to the target system. This could include changing makefiles to install the application into the appropriate directories, or resolving cross-platform conflicts, such as replacing BSD system calls with their SYSV counterparts.

- The patch creates files that are normally created during a configuration step in the installation process. Many times, it's necessary to edit either configuration files or scripts in order to set things up for compilation. In other cases, a configuration utility needs to be run before the sources are compiled. In either instance, the patches create the environment required for proper compilation.

10.1.2.1. Creating the Patches

While it might sound a bit daunting to take into account the types of patches outlined here, it's really quite simple. Here's how it's done:

1. Unpack the sources.
2. Rename the top-level directory. Make it end with `.orig`, for example.
3. Unpack the sources again, leaving the top-level directory name unchanged.

The source tree that you created the second time will be the one you'll use to get the software to build.

If the software builds with no changes required, that's great—you won't need a patch. But if you had to make any changes, you'll have to create a set of patches. To do so, simply clean the source directory of any binaries. Then issue a recursive `diff` command to compare the source tree you used for the build against the original, unmodified source tree. It's as easy as that!

10.1.3. The Spec File

The spec file is at the heart of RPM's packaging building process. Similar in concept to a makefile, it contains information required by RPM to build the package, as well as instructions telling RPM how to build it. The spec file also dictates exactly what files are a part of the package and where they should be installed.

As you might imagine, with this many responsibilities, the spec file format can be a bit complex. However, it's broken into several sections, making it easier to handle. All told, there are eight sections:

■ The preamble—The preamble contains information that will be displayed when users request information about the package. This includes a description of the package's function, the version number of the software, and so on. Also contained in the preamble are lines identifying sources, patches, and even an icon to be used if the package is manipulated by graphical interface.

■ The prep section—The prep section is where the actual work of building a package starts. As the name implies, this section is where the necessary preparations are made prior to the actual building of the software. In general, if anything needs to be done to the sources prior to building the software, it needs to happen in the prep section. Usually, this boils down to unpacking the sources.

The contents of this section are an ordinary shell script. However, RPM does provide two macros to make life easier. One macro can unpack a compressed `tar` file and `cd` into the source directory. The other macro easily applies patches to the unpacked sources.

■ The build section—Like the prep section, the build section consists of a shell script. As you might guess, this section is used to perform whatever commands are required to actually compile the sources. This section could consist of a single make command, or be more complex if the build process required it. Since most software today is built using make, there are no macros available in this section.

■ The install section—Also containing a shell script, the install section is used to perform the commands required to actually install the software. If the software's author added an install target in the makefile, this section might only consist of a make install command. Otherwise, you'd need to add the usual assortment of cp, mv, or install commands to get the job done.

■ Install and uninstall scripts—Whereas the previous sections contain either information required by RPM to build the package or the actual commands to do the deed, this section is different. It consists of scripts that will be run on the user's system when the package is actually installed or removed. RPM can execute a script in the following instances:

   ■ Prior to the package being installed

   ■ After the package has been installed

   ■ Prior to the package being erased

   ■ After the package has been erased

One example of when this capability would be required is when a package contains shared libraries. In this case, ldconfig would need to be run after the package is installed or erased. As another example, if a package contains a shell, the file /etc/shells would need to be updated appropriately when the package was installed or erased.

■ The verify script—This is another script that is executed on the user's system. It is executed when RPM verifies the package's proper installation. Although RPM does most of the work verifying packages, this script can be used to verify aspects of the package that are beyond RPM's capabilities.

■ The clean section—Another script that can be present is a script that can clean things up after the build. This script is rarely used because RPM normally does a good job of clean-up in most build environments.

■ The file list—The last section consists of a list of files that will comprise the package. Additionally, a number of macros can be used to control file attributes when installed, as well as to denote which files are documentation and which contain configuration information. The file list is very important; if it is missing, no package will be built.

10.2. The Engine: RPM

At the center of the action is RPM. It performs a number of steps during the build process:

1. It executes the commands and macros in the prep section of the spec file.
2. It checks the contents of the file list.
3. It executes the commands and macros in the build section of the spec file.
4. It executes the commands and macros in the install section of the spec file. Any macros in the file list are executed at this time, too.
5. It creates the binary package file.
6. It creates the source package file.

By using different options on the RPM command line, the build process can be stopped at any of these steps. This makes the initial building of a package that much easier because it is then possible to see whether each step completed successfully before continuing to the next step.

10.3. The Outputs

The end product of this entire process is a source package file and a binary package file.

10.3.1. The Source Package File

The source package file is a specially formatted archive that contains the following files:

■ The original compressed tar file(s)
■ The spec file
■ The patches

Because the source package contains everything needed to create the binary package, create the source package, and provide the original sources, it's a great way to distribute source code. As mentioned earlier, it's also a great way to archive all the information needed to rebuild a particular version of the package.

10.3.2. The Binary RPM

The binary package file is the one part of the entire RPM building process that is most visible to the user. It contains the files that comprise the application, along with any additional information needed to install and erase it. The binary package file is where the rubber hits the road.

10.4. And Now...

Now that we've seen, in broad-brush terms, the way RPM builds packages, let's take a look at an actual build. Chapter 11, "Building Packages: A Simple Example," does just that, showing how simple it can be to build a package.

11

Building Packages:
A Simple Example

In Chapter 10, "The Basics of Developing with RPM," we looked at RPM's build process from a conceptual level. In this chapter, we will be performing an actual build using RPM. In order to keep things understandable for this first pass, the build will be very simple. Once we've covered the basics, we'll present more real-world examples in later chapters.

11.1. Creating the Build Directory Structure

RPM requires a set of directories in which to perform the build. Although the directories' locations and names can be changed, it's best to use the default layout. Note that if you've installed RPM, the build directories are most likely in place already.

The normal directory layout consists of a single top-level directory (the default name is /usr/src/redhat) with five subdirectories. The five subdirectories and their functions are

- ■ /usr/src/redhat/SOURCES—Contains the original sources, patches, and icon files.
- ■ /usr/src/redhat/SPECS—Contains the spec files used to control the build process.
- ■ /usr/src/redhat/BUILD—The directory in which the sources are unpacked and the software is built.
- ■ /usr/src/redhat/RPMS—Contains the binary package files created by the build process.
- ■ /usr/src/redhat/SRPMS—Contains the source package files created by the build process.

In general, there are no special requirements that need to be met when creating these directories. In fact, the only important requirement is that the BUILD directory be part of a filesystem with sufficient free space to build the largest package expected. Here is a directory listing showing a typical build directory tree:

```
# ls -lF /usr/src/redhat
total 5
drwxr-xr-x 3 root root 1024 Aug 5 13:12 BUILD/
drwxr-xr-x 3 root root 1024 Jul 17 17:51 RPMS/
drwxr-xr-x 4 root root 1024 Aug 4 22:31 SOURCES/
drwxr-xr-x 2 root root 1024 Aug 5 13:12 SPECS/
drwxr-xr-x 2 root root 1024 Aug 4 22:28 SRPMS/
#
```

Now that we have the directories ready to go, it's time to prepare for the build. For the remainder of this chapter, we'll be building a fictional piece of software known as cdplayer.

> **NOTE**
>
> The cdplayer software is a mercilessly hacked version of cdp, which was written by Sariel Har-Peled. The software was hacked to provide a simple sample package and in no way represents the fine work done by Sariel on cdp.

11.2. Getting the Sources

The first thing we need to do in order to build a package for cdplayer is to obtain the sources. Being avid cdplayer fans from way back, we know that the latest source can be found at GnomoVision's FTP site, so we go get a copy.

We now have a gzipped tar file of cdplayer version 1.0 on our system. After putting a copy in the SOURCES directory, we're ready to tell RPM what to do with it.

11.3. Creating the Spec File

The way we direct RPM in the build process is to create a spec file. As we saw in Chapter 10, the spec file contains eight different sections, most of which are required. Let's go through each section and create cdplayer's spec file as we go.

11.3.1. The Preamble

The preamble contains a wealth of information about the package being built and the people who built it. Here's cdplayer's preamble:

```
#
# Sample spec file for cdplayer app...
#
Summary: A CD player app that rocks!
Name: cdplayer
Version: 1.0
Release: 1
Copyright: GPL
Group: Applications/Sound
Source: ftp://ftp.gnomovision.com/pub/cdplayer/cdplayer-1.0.tgz
URL: http://www.gnomovision.com/cdplayer/cdplayer.html
Distribution: WSS Linux
Vendor: White Socks Software, Inc.
Packager: Santa Claus <sclaus@northpole.com>

%description
It slices! It dices! It's a CD player app that can't be beat. By using
the resonant frequency of the CD itself, it is able to simulate 20X
oversampling. This leads to sound quality that cannot be equaled with
more mundane software...
```

In general, the preamble consists of entries, one per line, that start with a tag followed by a colon, and then some information. For example, the line starting with Summary: gives a short description of the packaged software that can be displayed by RPM. The order of the lines is not important, as long as they appear in the preamble.

Let's take a look at each line and see what function it performs:

- Name—The `name` line defines what the package will actually be called. In general, it's a good idea to use the name of the software. The name will also be included in the package label and the package filename.

- Version—The `version` line should be set to the version of the software being packaged. The version will also be included in the package label and the package filename.

- Release—The `release` is a number used to represent the number of times the software, at the present version, has been packaged. You can think of it as the package's version number. The release is also part of the package label and package filename.

- Copyright—The `copyright` line is used to hold the packaged software's copyright information. This makes it easy to determine which packages can be freely redistributed and which cannot. In our case, `cdplayer` is made available under the terms of the GNU General Public License, so we've put `GPL` on the line.

- Group—The `group` line is used to hold a string that defines how the packaged software should be grouped with other packages. The string consists of a series of words separated by slashes. From left to right, the words describe the packaged software more explicitly. We grouped `cdplayer` under `Applications` because it is an application, and then under `Sound` because it is an application that is sound related.

- Source—The `source` line serves two purposes:
  - To document where the packaged software's sources can be found
  - To give the name of the source file as it exists in the `SOURCES` subdirectory

  In our example, the `cdplayer` sources are contained in the file `cdplayer-1.0.tgz`, which is available from `ftp.gnomovision.com`, in the directory `/pub/cdplayer`. RPM actually ignores everything prior to the last filename in the source line, so the first part of the source string could be anything you'd like. Traditionally, the source line contains a uniform resource locator, or URL.

- URL—The `URL` line is used to contain a URL, like the source line. How are they different? While the source line is used to provide the source filename to RPM, the URL line points to documentation for the software being packaged.

- Distribution—The `distribution` line contains the name of the product that the packaged software is a part of. In the Linux world, the operating system is often packaged together into a distribution, hence the name. Because we're using a fictional application in this example, we've filled in the `distribution` line with the name of a fictional distribution. There's no requirement that the spec file contain a distribution line, so individuals will probably omit this.

- Vendor—The vendor line identifies the organization that distributes the software. Maintaining our fictional motif, we've invented a fictional company, White Socks Software, to add to our spec file. Individuals will probably omit this as well.

- Packager—The packager line is used to identify the organization that actually packaged the software, as opposed to the author of the software. In our example, we've chosen the greatest packager of them all, Santa Claus, to work at White Socks Software. Note that we've included contact information, in the form of an e-mail address.

- Description—The description line is a bit different, in that it starts with a percent sign. It is also different because the information can take up more than one line. It is used to provide a more detailed description of the packaged software than the summary line.

- A comment on comments—At the top of the spec file are three lines, each starting with a pound sign. These are comments and can be sprinkled throughout the spec file to make it more easily understood.

11.3.2. The %prep Section

With the preamble, we provided a wealth of information. The majority of this information is meant for human consumption. Only the name, version, release, and source lines have a direct bearing on the package building process. However, in the %prep section, the focus is entirely on directing RPM through the process of preparing the software for building.

It is in the %prep section that the build environment for the software is created, starting with removing the remnants of any previous builds. Following this, the source archive is expanded. Here is what the %prep section looks like in our sample spec file:

```
%prep
rm -rf $RPM_BUILD_DIR/cdplayer-1.0
zcat $RPM_SOURCE_DIR/cdplayer-1.0.tgz ¦ tar -xvf -
```

If the %prep section looks like a script, that's because it is. Any sh constructs can be used here, including expansion of environment variables (such as the $RPM BUILD DIR variable defined by RPM), and piping the output of zcat through tar. (For more information on the environment variables used in the build-time scripts, see section 13.3.1 in Chapter 13, "Inside the Spec File.")

In this case, we perform a recursive delete in the build directory to remove any old builds. We then uncompress the gzipped tar file and extract its contents into the build directory.

Quite often, the sources may require patching in order to build properly. The %prep section is the appropriate place to patch the sources, but in this example, no patching is required. Fear not, however, because we'll explore patching in all its glory in Chapter 20, "Real-World Package Building," when we build a more complex package.

11.3.2.1. Making Life Easier with Macros

While the `%prep` section as we've described it isn't that difficult to understand, RPM provides macros to make life even easier. In this simple example, there's precious little that can be made easier, but macros will prevent many headaches when it's time to build more complex packages. The macro we'll introduce here is the `%setup` macro.

The average gzipped `tar` file is `%setup`'s stock in trade. Like the hand-crafted `%prep` section described earlier, it cleans up old build trees and then uncompresses and extracts the files from the original source. While `%setup` has a number of options that we'll cover in later chapters, for now all we need for a `%prep` section is this:

```
%prep
%setup
```

That is simpler than our `%prep` section, so let's use the `%setup` macro instead. The `%setup` macro has a number of options to handle many different situations. For more information on this and other macros, see section 13.4 in Chapter 13.

In this example, the `%prep` section is complete. Next comes the actual build.

11.3.3. The `%build` Section

Not surprisingly, the part of the spec file that is responsible for performing the build is the `%build` section. Like the `%prep` section, the `%build` section is an ordinary `sh` script. Unlike the `%prep` section, there are no macros. The reason for this is that the process of building software is going to be either very easy or highly complicated. In either case, macros won't help much. In our example, the build process is simple:

```
%build
make
```

Thanks to the `make` utility, only one command is necessary to build the `cdplayer` application. In the case of an application with more esoteric build requirements, the `%build` section could get a bit more interesting.

11.3.4. The `%install` Section

The `%install` section is executed as a `sh` script, just like `%prep` and `%build`. If the application is built with `make` and the makefile has an install target, the `%install` section will also be straightforward. The `cdplayer` application is a good example of this:

```
%install
make install
```

If the application doesn't have a means of automatically installing itself, you must create a script to do so and place it in the `%install` section.

11.3.5. The %files Section

The %files section is different from the others in that it contains a list of the files that are part of the package. Always remember that if it isn't in the %files list, it won't be put in the package! Here's the %files section for cdplayer:

```
%files
%doc README
/usr/local/bin/cdp
/usr/local/bin/cdplay
/usr/local/man/man1/cdp.1
```

The line starting with %doc is an example of RPM's handling of different file types. As you might guess, %doc stands for *documentation*. The %doc directive is used to mark files as being documentation. In this example, the README file will be placed in a package-specific directory, located in /usr/doc, and called cdplayer-1.0-1. It's also possible to mark files as documentation and have them installed in other directories. This is covered in more detail in section 13.6.1 in Chapter 13.

The rest of the files in the example are shown with complete paths. This is necessary because the files will actually be installed in those directories by the application's makefile. Since RPM needs to be able to find the files prior to packaging them, complete paths are required.

11.3.5.1. How Do You Create the File List?

Since RPM automates so many aspects of software installation, it's easy to fall into the trap of assuming that RPM does everything for you. Not so! One task that is still a manual process is creating the file list. While it may seem at first glance that it could be automated somehow, it's actually a more difficult problem than it seems.

Since the majority of an application's files are installed by its makefile, RPM has no control over that part of the build process and therefore cannot automatically determine which files should be part of the package. Some people have attempted to use a modified version of install that logs the name of every file it installs. But not every makefile uses install, or if it does, uses it sporadically.

Another attempted approach was to obtain a list of every file on the build system, immediately before and after a build, and use the differences as the file list. While this approach will certainly find every file that the application installed, it can also pick up extraneous files, such as system logs, files in /tmp, and the like. The only way to begin to make this approach workable would be to do nothing else on the build system, which is highly inconvenient. This approach also precludes building more than one package on the system at any given time.

At present, the best way to create the file list is to read the makefile to see what files it installs, verify this list against the files installed on the build system, and create the list.

11.3.6. The Missing Spec File Sections

Our sample spec file is somewhat simplistic and it's missing two sections that might be used in more complex situations. We'll go over each one briefly here. More complete information on these sections will be given at various points in the book.

11.3.6.1. The Install/Uninstall Scripts

One missing section to our spec file is the section that would define one or more of four possible scripts. The scripts are executed at various times when a package is installed or erased.

The scripts can be executed at the following points:

- Before a package is installed
- After a package is installed
- Before a package is erased
- After a package is erased

We'll see how these scripts are used in Chapter 20.

11.3.6.2. The %clean Section

The other missing section has the rather descriptive title %clean. This section can be used to clean up any files that are not part of the application's normal build area. For example, if the application creates a directory structure in /tmp as part of its build, it will not be removed. By adding a sh script to the %clean section, such situations can be handled gracefully, right after the binary package is created.

11.4. Starting the Build

Now it's time to begin the build. First, we change directory into the directory holding cdplayer's spec file:

```
# cd /usr/src/redhat/SPECS
#
```

Next, we start the build with an rpm -b command:

```
# rpm -ba cdplayer-1.0.spec
```

The a following the -b option directs RPM to perform all phases of the build process. Sometimes it is necessary to stop at various phases during the initial build to resolve problems that crop up while writing the spec file. In these cases, other letters can be used after the -b in order to stop the build at the desired phase. For this example, however, we will continue through the entire build process.

In this example, the only other argument to the build command is the name of the package's spec file. This can be wildcarded to build more than one package, but in our example, we'll stick with one.

Let's look at RPM's output during the build:

```
* Package: cdplayer
+ umask 022
+ echo Excuting: %prep
Excuting: %prep
+ cd /usr/src/redhat/BUILD
+ cd /usr/src/redhat/BUILD
+ rm -rf cdplayer-1.0
+ gzip -dc /usr/src/redhat/SOURCES/cdplayer-1.0.tgz
+ tar -xvvf -
drwxrwxr-x root/users          0 Aug  4 22:30 1996 cdplayer-1.0/
-rw-r--r-- root/users      17982 Nov 10 01:10 1995 cdplayer-1.0/COPYING
-rw-r--r-- root/users        627 Nov 10 01:10 1995 cdplayer-1.0/ChangeLog
-rw-r--r-- root/users        482 Nov 10 01:11 1995 cdplayer-1.0/INSTALL
.
.
.
-rw-r--r-- root/users       2720 Nov 10 01:10 1995 cdplayer-1.0/struct.h
-rw-r--r-- root/users        730 Nov 10 01:10 1995 cdplayer-1.0/vol.c
-rw-r--r-- root/users       2806 Nov 10 01:10 1995 cdplayer-1.0/volume.c
-rw-r--r-- root/users       1515 Nov 10 01:10 1995 cdplayer-1.0/volume.h
+ [ 0 -ne 0 ]
+ cd cdplayer-1.0
+ cd /usr/src/redhat/BUILD/cdplayer-1.0 + chown -R root.root .
+ chmod -R a+rX,g-w,o-w .
+ exit 0
```

The output continues, but let's stop here for a moment and discuss what has happened so far.

At the start of the output, RPM displays the package name (cdplayer), sets the umask, and starts executing the %prep section. Thanks to the %setup macro, RPM then changes directory into the build area, removes any existing old sources, and extracts the sources from the original compressed tar file. Although each file is listed as it is extracted, we've omitted most of the files listed to save space.

The %setup macro continues by changing directory into cdplayer's top-level source directory and setting the file ownership and permissions properly. As you can see, it does quite a bit of work for you.

Let's take a look at the output from the %build section next:

```
+ umask 022
+ echo Excuting: %build
Excuting: %build
+ cd /usr/src/redhat/BUILD
+ cd cdplayer-1.0
+ make
gcc -Wall -O2 -c -I/usr/include/ncurses cdp.c
gcc -Wall -O2 -c -I/usr/include/ncurses color.c
gcc -Wall -O2 -c -I/usr/include/ncurses display.c
```

```
gcc -Wall -O2 -c -I/usr/include/ncurses misc.c
gcc -Wall -O2 -c -I/usr/include/ncurses volume.c
volume.c: In function 'mix_set_volume':
volume.c:67: warning: implicit declaration of function 'ioctl'
gcc -Wall -O2 -c -I/usr/include/ncurses hardware.c
gcc -Wall -O2 -c -I/usr/include/ncurses database.c
gcc -Wall -O2 -c -I/usr/include/ncurses getline.c
gcc -o cdp cdp.o color.o display.o misc.o volume.o hardware.o database.o
getline.o -I/usr/include/ncurses -L/usr/lib -lncurses
groff -Tascii -man cdp.1 ¦ compress >cdp.1.Z
+ exit 0
```

There are no surprises here. After setting the umask and changing directory into cdplayer's top-level directory, RPM issues the make command we put into the spec file. The rest of the output comes from make as it actually builds the software. Next comes the %install section:

```
+ umask 022
+ echo Excuting: %install
Excuting: %install
+ cd /usr/src/redhat/BUILD
+ cd cdplayer-1.0
+ make install
chmod 755 cdp
chmod 644 cdp.1.Z
cp cdp /usr/local/bin
ln -s /usr/local/bin/cdp /usr/local/bin/cdplay
cp cdp.1 /usr/local/man/man1
+ exit 0
```

Just as in the previous sections, RPM again sets the umask and changes directory into the proper directory. It then executes cdplayer's install target, installing the newly built software on the build system. Those of you who carefully studied the spec file might have noticed that the README file is not part of the install section. It's not a problem, as we see here:

```
+ umask 022
+ echo Excuting: special doc
Excuting: special doc
+ cd /usr/src/redhat/BUILD
+ cd cdplayer-1.0
+ DOCDIR=//usr/doc/cdplayer-1.0-1
+ rm -rf //usr/doc/cdplayer-1.0-1
+ mkdir -p //usr/doc/cdplayer-1.0-1
+ cp -ar README //usr/doc/cdplayer-1.0-1
+ exit 0
```

After the customary umask and cd commands, RPM constructs the path that will be used for cdplayer's documentation directory. It then cleans out any preexisting directory and copies the README file into it. The cdplayer app is now installed on the build system. The only thing left to do is to create the actual package files and perform some housekeeping. The binary package file is created first:

```
Binary Packaging: cdplayer-1.0-1
Finding dependencies...
Requires (2): libc.so.5 libncurses.so.2.0
```

```
usr/doc/cdplayer-1.0-1
usr/doc/cdplayer-1.0-1/README
usr/local/bin/cdp
usr/local/bin/cdplay
usr/local/man/man1/cdp.1
93 blocks
Generating signature: 0
Wrote: /usr/src/redhat/RPMS/i386/cdplayer-1.0-1.i386.rpm
```

The first line says it all: RPM is creating the binary package for cdplayer version 1.0, release 1. Next, RPM determines what packages are required by cdplayer-1.0-1. Part of this process entails running ldd on each executable program in the package. In this example, the package requires the libraries libc.so.5 and libncurses.so.2.0. Other dependency information can be included in the spec file, but for our example we'll keep it simple.

Following the dependency information, is a list of every directory and file included in the package. The list displayed is actually the output of cpio, which is the archiving software used by RPM to bundle the package's files. 93 blocks is also printed by cpio.

The line Generating signature: 0 means that RPM has not been directed to add a PGP signature to the package file. During this time, however, RPM still adds two signatures that can be used to verify the size and the MD5 checksum of the package file. Finally, we see confirmation that RPM has created the binary package file.

At this point, the application has been built and the application's files have been packaged. There is no longer any need for any files created during the build, so they may be removed. In the case of the sources extracted into RPM's build directory, we can see that, at worst, they will be removed the next time the package is built. But what if there were files we needed to remove? Well, they could be deleted here, in the %clean section:

```
+ umask 022
+ echo Excuting: %clean
Excuting: %clean
+ cd /usr/src/redhat/BUILD
+ cd cdplayer-1.0
+ exit 0
```

In this example, there are no other files outside the build directory that are created during cdplayer's build, so we don't need to expend any additional effort to clean things up.

The very last step performed by RPM is to create the source package file:

```
Source Packaging: cdplayer-1.0-1
cdplayer-1.0.spec
cdplayer-1.0.tgz
80 blocks
Generating signature: 0
Wrote: /usr/src/redhat/SRPMS/cdplayer-1.0-1.src.rpm
#
```

This file includes everything needed to re-create a binary package file as well as a copy of itself. In this example, the only files needed to do that are the original sources and the spec file. In cases where the original sources need to be modified, the source package includes one or more patch files. As when the binary package was created, we see cpio's output listing each file archived, along with the archive's block size.

Just like a binary package, a source package file can have a PGP signature attached to it. In our case, we see that a PGP signature was not attached. The last message from RPM is to confirm the creation of the source package. Let's take a look at the end products. First, look at the binary package:

```
# ls -1F /usr/src/redhat/RPMS/i386/cdplayer-1.0-1.i386.rpm
-rw-r--r-- 1 root root 24698 Aug 6 22:22 RPMS/i386/cdplayer-1.0-1.i386.rpm
#
```

Note that we built cdplayer on an Intel-based system, so RPM placed the binary package files in the i386 subdirectory.

Next, look at the source package file:

```
# ls -1F /usr/src/redhat/SRPMS/cdplayer-1.0-1.src.rpm
-rw-r--r-- 1 root root 41380 Aug 6 22:22 SRPMS/cdplayer-1.0-1.src.rpm
#
```

Everything went perfectly—we now have binary and source package files ready to use. But sometimes things don't go so well.

11.5. When Things Go Wrong

This example is a bit of a fairy tale in that it went perfectly the first time. In real life, it often takes several tries to get it right.

11.5.1. Problems During the Build

As alluded to earlier in the chapter, RPM can stop at various points in the build process. This allows package builders to look through the build directory and make sure everything is proceeding properly. If there are problems, stopping during the build process permits them to see exactly what is going wrong and where. Here is a list of points at which RPM can be stopped during the build:

- After the %prep section
- After doing some cursory checks on the %files list
- After the %build section
- After the %install section
- After the binary package has been created

In addition, there is a method that permits the package builder to short-circuit the build process and direct RPM to skip over the initial steps. This is handy when the application is not yet ready for packaging and needs some fine-tuning. This way, once the package builds, installs, and operates properly, the required patches to the original sources can be created and plugged into the package's spec file.

11.5.2. Testing Newly Built Packages

Of course, the fact that an application has been packaged successfully doesn't necessarily mean that it will operate correctly when the package is actually installed. Testing is required. In the case of our example, it's perfect and doesn't need such testing. (As we said, it's a fairy tale!) But the following paragraphs explain how testing would proceed.

The first step is to find a test system. If you thought of simply using the build system, try again! Think about it—in the course of building the package, the build system actually had the application installed on it. That is how RPM gets the files that are to be packaged: by building the software, installing it, and grabbing copies of the installed files, which are found using the `%files` list.

Some of you dissenters who have read the first half of the book might be wondering why not just install the package on the build system using the `--replacefiles` option. That way, it'll just blow away the files installed by the build process and replace them with the packaged files. Well, you folks get a bzzzzt, too!

Say, for example, that the software you're packaging installs a bunch of files—maybe 100. What does this mean? Well, for one thing, it means that the package's `%files` list is going to be quite large. For another thing, the sheer number of files makes it likely that you'll miss 1 or 2. What would happen then?

When RPM builds the software, there's no problem: The software builds and the application's makefile merrily installs all the files. The next step in RPM's build process is to collect the files by reading the `%files` list and to add each file listed to a `cpio` archive. What happens to the files you've missed? Nothing. They aren't added to the package file, but they are on your build system, installed just where they should be.

Next, when the package is installed using `--replacefiles`, RPM dutifully installs each of the packaged files, replacing the ones originally installed on the build system. The missed files? They aren't overwritten by RPM since they weren't in the package. But they're still on disk, right where the application expects them to be! If you go to test the application then, it will find every file it needs. But not every file came from the package. Bad news! Using a different system on which the application had never been built is one sure way to test for missing files.

11.6. Summary

That wraps up our fictional build. Now that we have some experience with RPM's build process, we can take a more in-depth look at RPM's build command.

12

rpm -b
Command Reference

Table 12.1. Build-mode command syntax and options.

`rpm -b <stage>` *Options* `file1.spec...fileN.spec`

	<stage>	*Section*
p	Execute `%prep`	12.1.1
c	Execute `%prep`, `%build`	12.1.2
i	Execute `%prep`, `%build`, `%install`	12.1.3
b	Execute `%prep`, `%build`, `%install`; Package (bin)	12.1.4
a	Execute `%prep`, `%build`, `%install`; Package (bin, src)	12.1.5
l	Check `%files` list	12.1.6
	Parameters	
spec1...spec*N*	One or more spec files	
	Build-Specific Options	*Section*
--short-circuit	Force build to start at particular stage (`-bc`, `-bi` only)	12.1.7
--test	Create, save build scripts for review	12.1.11
--clean	Clean up after build	12.1.12
--sign	Add a digital signature to the package	12.1.10
--buildroot *<root>*	Execute `%install` using *<root>* as the root	12.1.13
--buildarch *<arch>*	Perform build for the *<arch>* architecture	12.1.8
--buildos *<os>*	Perform build for the *<os>* operating system	12.1.9
--timecheck *<secs>*	Print a warning if files are over *<secs>* old	12.1.14
	General Options	*Section*
-vv	Display debugging information	12.1.15
--quiet	Produce as little output as possible	12.1.16
--rcfile *<rcfile>*	Set alternate `rpmrc` file to *<rcfile>*	12.1.17

12.1. `rpm -b`: What Does It Do?

When RPM is invoked with the `-b` option, the process of building a package is started. The rest of the command will determine exactly what is to be built and how far the build should proceed. This chapter explores every aspect of `rpm -b`.

An RPM build command must have two additional pieces of information, over and above `rpm -b`:

■ The names of one or more spec files representing software to be packaged

■ The desired stage at which the build is to stop

As discussed in Chapter 10, "The Basics of Developing with RPM," the spec file is one of the inputs to RPM's build process. It contains the information necessary for RPM to perform the build and package the software.

RPM goes through a number of stages during a build. By specifying that the build process is to stop at a certain stage, the package builder can monitor the build's progress, make any changes necessary, and restart the build. Let's start by looking at the various stages that can be specified in a build command.

12.1.1. rpm -bp: Execute %prep

The command rpm -bp directs RPM to execute the very first step in the build process.

In the spec file, this step is labeled %prep. Every command in the %prep section will be executed when the -bp option is used.

Here's a simple %prep section from the spec file we used in Chapter 11, "Building Packages: A Simple Example":

```
%prep
%setup
```

This %prep section consists of a single %setup macro. When using rpm -bp against this spec file, we can see exactly what %setup does:

```
# rpm -bp cdplayer-1.0.spec
* Package: cdplayer
+ umask 022
+ echo Executing: %prep
Executing: %prep
+ cd /usr/src/redhat/BUILD
+ cd /usr/src/redhat/BUILD
+ rm -rf cdplayer-1.0
+ gzip -dc /usr/src/redhat/SOURCES/cdplayer-1.0.tgz
+ tar -xvvf -
drwxrwxr-x root/users          0 Aug  4 22:30 1996 cdplayer-1.0/
-rw-r--r-- root/users      17982 Nov 10 01:10 1995 cdplayer-1.0/COPYING
-rw-r--r-- root/users        627 Nov 10 01:10 1995 cdplayer-1.0/ChangeLog
...
-rw-r--r-- root/users       2806 Nov 10 01:10 1995 cdplayer-1.0/volume.c
-rw-r--r-- root/users       1515 Nov 10 01:10 1995 cdplayer-1.0/volume.h
+ [ 0 -ne 0 ]
+ cd cdplayer-1.0
+ cd /usr/src/redhat/BUILD/cdplayer-1.0
+ chown -R root.root .
+ chmod -R a+rX,g-w,o-w .
+ exit 0
#
```

First, RPM confirms that the cdplayer package is the subject of this build. Then it sets the umask and starts executing the %prep section. At this point, the %setup macro is doing its thing. It changes directory into the build area and removes any old copies of cdplayer's build tree.

Next, %setup unzips the sources and uses tar to create the build tree. We've removed the complete listing of files, but be prepared to see lots of output if the software being packaged is large.

Finally, %setup changes directory into cdplayer's build tree and changes ownership and file permissions appropriately. exit 0 signifies the end of the %prep section and, therefore, the end of the %setup macro. Because we used the -bp option, RPM stopped at this point. Let's see what RPM left in the build area:

```
# cd /usr/src/redhat/BUILD
# ls -l
total 1
drwxr-xr-x 2 root root 1024 Aug 4 22:30 cdplayer-1.0
#
```

There's the top-level directory. Changing directory into cdplayer-1.0, we find that the sources are ready to be built:

```
# cd cdplayer-1.0
# ls -1F
total 216
-rw-r--r--    1 root     root     17982 Nov 10  1995 COPYING
-rw-r--r--    1 root     root       627 Nov 10  1995 ChangeLog
...
-rw-r--r--    1 root     root      2806 Nov 10  1995 volume.c
-rw-r--r--    1 root     root      1515 Nov 10  1995 volume.h
#
```

We can see that %setup's chown and chmod commands did what they were supposed to—the files are owned by root, with permissions set appropriately.

If not stopped by the -bp option, the next step in RPM's build process would be to build the software. RPM can also be stopped at the end of the %build section in the spec file. This is done by using the -bc option.

12.1.2. rpm -bc: Execute %prep, %build

When the -bc option is used during a build, RPM stops once the software has been built. In terms of the spec file, every command in the %build section will be executed. In the following example, we've removed the output from the %prep section to cut down on the redundant output, but keep in mind that it is executed nonetheless:

```
# rpm -bc cdplayer-1.0.spec
* Package: cdplayer
Executing: %prep
...
+ exit 0
Executing: %build
+ cd /usr/src/redhat/BUILD
+ cd cdplayer-1.0
+ make
gcc -Wall -O2 -c -I/usr/include/ncurses cdp.c
gcc -Wall -O2 -c -I/usr/include/ncurses color.c
gcc -Wall -O2 -c -I/usr/include/ncurses display.c
```

```
gcc -Wall -O2 -c -I/usr/include/ncurses misc.c
gcc -Wall -O2 -c -I/usr/include/ncurses volume.c
volume.c: In function 'mix_set_volume':
volume.c:67: warning: implicit declaration of function 'ioctl'
gcc -Wall -O2 -c -I/usr/include/ncurses hardware.c
gcc -Wall -O2 -c -I/usr/include/ncurses database.c
gcc -Wall -O2 -c -I/usr/include/ncurses getline.c
gcc -o cdp cdp.o color.o display.o misc.o volume.o hardware.o database.o
getline.o -I/usr/include/ncurses -L/usr/lib -lncurses
groff -Tascii -man cdp.1 ¦ compress >cdp.1.Z
+ exit 0
#
```

After the command, we see RPM executing the %prep section (which we've removed almost entirely). Next, RPM starts executing the contents of the %build section. In our sample spec file, the %build section looks like this:

```
%build
make
```

We see that prior to the make command, RPM changes directory into cdplayer's top-level directory. RPM then starts the make, which ends with the groff command. At this point, the execution of the %build section has been completed. Because the -bc option was used, RPM stops at this point.

The next step in the build process would be to install the newly built software. This is done in the %install section of the spec file. RPM can be stopped after the install has taken place by using the -bi option.

12.1.3. rpm -bi: Execute %prep, %build, %install

By using the -bi option, RPM is directed to stop once the software is completely built and installed on the build system. Here's what the output of a build using the -bi option looks like:

```
# rpm -bi cdplayer-1.0.spec
* Package: cdplayer
Executing: %prep
...
+ exit 0
Executing: %build
...
+ exit 0
Executing: %install
+ cd /usr/src/redhat/BUILD
+ cd cdplayer-1.0
+ make install
chmod 755 cdp
chmod 644 cdp.1.Z
cp cdp /usr/local/bin
ln -s /usr/local/bin/cdp /usr/local/bin/cdplay
cp cdp.1 /usr/local/man/man1
+ exit 0
+ umask 022
+ echo Executing: special doc
```

```
Executing: special doc
+ cd /usr/src/redhat/BUILD
+ cd cdplayer-1.0
+ DOCDIR=//usr/doc/cdplayer-1.0-1
+ rm -rf //usr/doc/cdplayer-1.0-1
+ mkdir -p //usr/doc/cdplayer-1.0-1
+ cp -ar README //usr/doc/cdplayer-1.0-1
+ exit 0
#
```

As before, we've cut out most of the previously described sections. In this example, the %install section looks like this:

```
%install
make install
```

After the %prep and %build sections, the %install section is executed. Looking at the output, we see that RPM changes directory into cdplayer's top-level directory and issues the make install command, the sole command in the %install section. The output from that point until the first exit 0 is from makefile's install target.

The remaining commands are due to the contents of the spec file's %files list. Here's what it looks like:

```
%files
%doc README
/usr/local/bin/cdp
/usr/local/bin/cdplay
/usr/local/man/man1/cdp.1
```

The line responsible is %doc README. The %doc tag identifies the file as being documentation. RPM handles documentation files by creating a directory in /usr/doc and placing all documentation in it. The exit 0 at the end signifies the end of the %install section. RPM stops due to the -bi option.

The next step at which RPM's build process can be stopped is after the software's binary package file has been created. This is done using the -bb option.

12.1.4. rpm -bb: Execute %prep, %build, %install, Package (bin)

As stated at the end of the previous section, RPM's -bb option performs every step of the build process up to the point of creating the source package file. At that point it stops, as shown here:

```
# rpm -bb cdplayer-1.0.spec
* Package: cdplayer
Executing: %prep
...
+ exit 0
Executing: %build
...
+ exit 0
Executing: %install
...
```

```
+ exit 0
Executing: special doc
...
+ exit 0
Binary Packaging: cdplayer-1.0-1
Finding dependencies...
Requires (2): libc.so.5 libncurses.so.2.0
usr/doc/cdplayer-1.0-1
usr/doc/cdplayer-1.0-1/README
usr/local/bin/cdp
usr/local/bin/cdplay
usr/local/man/man1/cdp.1
93 blocks
Generating signature: 0
Wrote: /usr/src/redhat/RPMS/i386/cdplayer-1.0-1.i386.rpm
+ umask 022
+ echo Executing: %clean
Executing: %clean
+ cd /usr/src/redhat/BUILD
+ cd cdplayer-1.0
+ exit 0
#
```

After executing the %prep, %build, and %install sections and handling any special documentation files, RPM creates a binary package file. In the sample output, we see that first RPM performs automatic dependency checking. It does this by determining which shared libraries are required by the executable programs contained in the package. Next, RPM actually archives the files to be packaged, optionally signs the package file, and outputs the finished product.

The last part of RPM's output looks suspiciously like a section in the spec file being executed. In our example, there is no %clean section. If there were, however, RPM would have executed any commands in the section. In the absence of a %clean section, RPM simply issues the usual cd commands and exits normally.

12.1.5. rpm -ba: Execute %prep, %build, %install, Package (bin, src)

The -ba option directs RPM to perform all the stages in building a package. With this one command, RPM does the following:

1. Unpacks the original sources.
2. Applies patches (if desired).
3. Builds the software.
4. Installs the software.
5. Creates the binary package file.
6. Creates the source package file.

That's quite a bit of work for one command! Here it is, in action:

```
# rpm -ba cdplayer-1.0.spec
* Package: cdplayer
Executing: %prep
...
+ exit 0
Executing: %build
...
+ exit 0
Executing: %install
...
+ exit 0
Executing: special doc
...
+ exit 0
Binary Packaging: cdplayer-1.0-1
...
Executing: %clean
...
+ exit 0
Source Packaging: cdplayer-1.0-1
cdplayer-1.0.spec
cdplayer-1.0.tgz
80 blocks
Generating signature: 0
Wrote: /usr/src/redhat/SRPMS/cdplayer-1.0-1.src.rpm
#
```

As in previous examples, RPM executes the %prep, %build, and %install sections, handles any special documentation files, creates a binary package file, and cleans up after itself.

The final step in the build process is to create a source package file. As the output shows, it consists of the spec file and the original sources. A source package may optionally include one or more patch files, although in our example, cdplayer requires none.

At the end of a build using the -ba option, the software has been successfully built and packaged in both binary and source form. But there are a few more build-time options we can use. One of them is the -bl option.

12.1.6. rpm -bl: Check %files List

There's one last option that may be specified with rpm -b, but unlike the others, which indicate the stage at which the build process is to stop, this option performs a variety of checks on the %files list in the named spec file. When l is added to rpm -b, the command does the following:

- Expands the spec file's %files list and checks that each file listed actually exists.
- Determines what shared libraries the software requires by examining every executable file listed.
- Determines what shared libraries are provided by the package.

Why is it necessary to do all this checking? When would it be useful? Keep in mind that the %files list must be generated manually. By using the -bl option, the following steps are all that's necessary to create a %files list:

■ Writing the %files list

■ Using the -bl option to check the %files list

■ Making any necessary changes to the %files list

It may take more than one iteration through these steps, but eventually the list check will pass. Using the -bl option to check the %files list is certainly better than starting a two-hour package build, only to find out at the very end that the list contains a misspelled filename.

Here's an example of the -bl option in action:

```
# rpm -bl cdplayer-1.0.spec
Package: cdplayer
File List Check: cdplayer-1.0-1
Finding dependencies...
Requires (2): libc.so.5 libncurses.so.2.0
#
```

It's hard to see exactly what RPM is doing from the output, but if we add -vv, we can get a bit more information:

```
# rpm -bl -vv cdplayer-1.0.spec
D: Switched to BASE package
D: Source(0) = sunsite.unc.edu:/pub/Linux/apps/sound/cds/cdplayer-1.0.tgz
D: Switching to part: 12
D: fileFile =
D: Switched to package: (null)
D: Switching to part: 2
D: fileFile =
D: Switching to part: 3
D: fileFile =
D: Switching to part: 4
D: fileFile =
D: Switching to part: 10
D: fileFile =
D: Switched to package: (null)
* Package: cdplayer
File List Check: cdplayer-1.0-1
D: ADDING: /usr/doc/cdplayer-1.0-1
D: ADDING: /usr/doc/cdplayer-1.0-1/README
D: ADDING: /usr/local/bin/cdp
D: ADDING: /usr/local/bin/cdplay
D: ADDING: /usr/local/man/man1/cdp.1
D: md5(/usr/doc/cdplayer-1.0-1/README) = 2c149b2fb1a4d65418131a19b242601c
D: md5(/usr/local/bin/cdp) = 0f2a7a2f81812c75fd01c52f456798d6
D: md5(/usr/local/bin/cdplay) = d41d8cd98f00b204e9800998ecf8427e
D: md5(/usr/local/man/man1/cdp.1) = b32cc867ae50e2bdfa4d6780b084adfa
Finding dependencies...
D: Adding require: libncurses.so.2.0
D: Adding require: libc.so.5
Requires (2): libc.so.5 libncurses.so.2.0
#
```

Looking at this more verbose output, it's easy to see that there's a great deal going on. Some of it is not directly pertinent to checking the %files list, however. For example, the output extending from the first line to the line reading * Package: cdplayer reflects processing that takes place during actual package building and can be ignored.

Following that section is the actual %files list check. In this section, every file named in the %files list is checked to make sure it exists. The phrase ADDING: again reflects RPM's package building roots. When using the -bl option, however, RPM is simply making sure the files exist on the build system. If the --timecheck option (described a bit later, in section 12.1.14) is present, the checks required by that option are performed here, as well.

After the list check, the MD5 checksums of each file are calculated and displayed. While this information is vital during actual package building, it is not used when using the -bl option.

Finally, RPM determines which shared libraries the listed files require. In this case, there are only two: libc.so.5 and libncurses.so.2.0. While not strictly a part of the list-checking process, displaying shared library dependencies can be quite helpful at this point. It can point out possible problems, such as assuming that the target systems have a certain library installed when, in fact, they do not.

So far, we've only seen what happens when the %files list is correct. Let's see what happens where the list has problems. In this example, we've added a bogus file to the package's %files list:

```
# rpm -bl cdplayer-1.0.spec
Package: cdplayer
File List Check: cdplayer-1.0-1
File not found: /usr/local/bin/bogus
Build failed.
#
```

Reflecting more of its package building roots, rpm -bl says that the build failed. But the bottom line is that there is no such file as /usr/bin/bogus. In this example, we made the name obviously wrong, but in a more real-world setting, the name will more likely be a misspelling in the %files list. Okay, let's correct the %files list and try again:

```
# rpm -bl cdplayer-1.0.spec
Package: cdplayer
File List Check: cdplayer-1.0-1
File not found: /usr/local/bin/cdplay
Build failed.
#
```

Another error! In this case the file is spelled correctly, but it is not on the build system, even though it should be. Perhaps it was deleted accidentally. In any case, let's rebuild the software and try again:

```
# rpm -bi cdplayer-1.0.spec
* Package: cdplayer
Executing: %prep
...
```

```
+ exit 0
Executing: %build
...
+ exit 0
Executing: %install
...
ln -s /usr/local/bin/cdp /usr/local/bin/cdplay
...
+ exit 0
Executing: special doc
...
+ exit 0
#


# rpm -bl cdplayer-1.0.spec
Package: cdplayer
File List Check: cdplayer-1.0-1
Finding dependencies...
Requires (2): libc.so.5 libncurses.so.2.0
#
```

Done! The moral to this story is that using rpm -bl and fixing the error it flagged doesn't necessarily mean your %files list is ready for prime time: Always run it again to make sure!

12.1.7. --short-circuit: Force Build to Start at a Particular Stage

Although it sounds dangerous, the --short-circuit option can be your friend. This option is used during the initial development of a package. Earlier in the chapter, we explored stopping RPM's build process at different stages. Using --short-circuit, we can start the build process at different stages.

One time that --short-circuit comes in handy is when you're trying to get software to build properly. Just think what it would be like—you're hacking away at the sources, trying a build, getting an error, and hacking some more to fix that error. Without --short-circuit, you'd have to do the following:

1. Make your change to the sources.
2. Use tar to create a new source archive.
3. Start a build with something like rpm -bc.
4. See another bug.
5. Go back to step 1.

Pretty cumbersome! Since RPM's build process is designed to start with the sources in their original tar file, unless your modifications end up in that tar file, they won't be used in the next build. (As mentioned in Chapter 10, if the original sources need to be modified, the modifications should be kept as a separate set of patches. However, during development, it makes more sense to not generate patches every time a change to the original source is made.)

But there's another way. Just follow these steps:

1. Place the original source tar file in RPM's SOURCES directory.
2. Create a partial spec file in RPM's SPECS directory (be sure to include a valid Source line).
3. Issue an rpm -bp to properly create the build environment.

Now use --short-circuit to attempt a compile. Here's an example:

```
# rpm -bc --short-circuit cdplayer-1.0.spec
* Package: cdplayer
+ umask 022
+ echo Executing: %build
Executing: %build
+ cd /usr/src/redhat/BUILD
+ cd cdplayer-1.0
+ make
gcc -Wall -O2 -c -I/usr/include/ncurses cdp.c
gcc -Wall -O2 -c -I/usr/include/ncurses color.c
gcc -Wall -O2 -c -I/usr/include/ncurses display.c
gcc -Wall -O2 -c -I/usr/include/ncurses misc.c
gcc -Wall -O2 -c -I/usr/include/ncurses volume.c
volume.c: In function 'mix_set_volume':
volume.c:67: warning: implicit declaration of function 'ioctl'
gcc -Wall -O2 -c -I/usr/include/ncurses hardware.c
gcc -Wall -O2 -c -I/usr/include/ncurses database.c
gcc -Wall -O2 -c -I/usr/include/ncurses getline.c
gcc -o cdp cdp.o color.o display.o misc.o volume.o
    hardware.o database.o getline.o -I/usr/include/ncurses
    -L/usr/lib -lncurses
groff -Tascii -man cdp.1 ¦ compress >cdp.1.Z
+ exit 0
#
```

Normally, the -bc option instructs RPM to stop the build after the %build section of the spec file has been executed. By adding --short-circuit, however, RPM starts the build by executing the %build section and stops when everything in %build has been executed.

There is only one other build stage that can be --short-circuited: the install stage. The reason for this restriction is to make it difficult to bypass RPM's use of pristine sources. If it were possible to --short-circuit to -bb or -ba, a package builder might take the easy way out and simply hack at the build tree until the software built successfully, then package the hacked sources. So, RPM will only --short-circuit to -bc or -bi. Nothing else will do.

What exactly does an rpm -bi --short-circuit do, anyway? Like an rpm -bc --short-circuit, it starts executing at the named stage, which in this case is %install. Note that the build environment must be ready to perform an install before attempting to --short-circuit to the %install stage. If the software installs via make install, make will automatically compile the software anyway.

And what happens if the build environment isn't ready and a --short-circuit is attempted? Let's see:

```
# rpm -bi --short-circuit cdplayer-1.0.spec
* Package: cdplayer
+ umask 022
+ echo Executing: %install
Executing: %install
+ cd /usr/src/redhat/BUILD
+ cd cdplayer-1.0
/var/tmp/rpmbu01157aaa: cdplayer-1.0: No such file or directory
Bad exit status
#
```

RPM blindly started executing the %install stage, but came to an abrupt halt when it attempted to change directory into cdplayer-1.0, which didn't exist. After giving a descriptive error message, RPM exited with a failure status. Except for some minor differences, rpm -bc would have failed in the same way.

12.1.8. --buildarch *<arch>*: Perform a Build for the *<arch>* Architecture

The --buildarch option is used to override RPM's architecture detection logic. The option is followed by the desired architecture name. Here's an example:

```
# rpm -ba --buildarch i486 cdplayer-1.0.spec
Package. cdplayer
...
Binary Packaging: cdplayer-1.0-1
...
Wrote: /usr/src/redhat/RPMS/i486/cdplayer-1.0-1.i486.rpm
...
Wrote: /usr/src/redhat/SRPMS/cdplayer-1.0-1.src.rpm
#
```

We've removed most of RPM's output from this example, but the main thing we can see from this example is that the package was built for the i486 architecture, due to the inclusion of the --buildarch option on the command line. We can also see that RPM wrote the binary package in the architecture-specific directory, /usr/src/redhat/RPMS/i486. Using RPM's --queryformat option confirms the package's architecture:

```
# rpm -qp --queryformat '%{arch}\n'\
> /usr/src/redhat/RPMS/i486/cdplayer-1.0-1.i486.rpm
i486
#
```

For more information on build packages for multiple architectures, see Chapter 19, "Building Packages for Multiple Architectures and Operating Systems."

12.1.9. `--buildos` `<os>`: Perform Build for the `<os>` Operating System

The `--buildos` option is used to override RPM's operating system detection logic. The option is followed by the desired operating system name. Here's an example:

```
# rpm -ba --buildos osf1 cdplayer-1.0.spec
...
Binary Packaging: cdplayer-1.0-1
...
Wrote: /usr/src/redhat/RPMS/i386/cdplayer-1.0-1.i386.rpm
Source Packaging: cdplayer-1.0-1
...
Wrote: /usr/src/redhat/SRPMS/cdplayer-1.0-1.src.rpm
#
```

There's nothing in the build output that explicitly states that the build operating system has been set to osf1. Let's see if `--queryformat` will tell us:

```
# rpm -qp --queryformat '%{os}\n'\
> /usr/src/redhat/RPMS/i386/cdplayer-1.0-1.i386.rpm
osf1
#
```

The package was indeed built for the specified operating system. For more information on building packages for multiple operating systems, see Chapter 19.

12.1.10. `--sign`: Add a Digital Signature to the Package

The `--sign` option directs RPM to add a digital signature to the package being built. Currently, this is done using PGP. Here's an example of `--sign` in action:

```
# rpm -ba --sign cdplayer-1.0.spec
Enter pass phrase: <passphrase> (not echoed)
Pass phrase is good.
Package: cdplayer
...
Binary Packaging: cdplayer-1.0-1
...
Generating signature: 1002
Wrote: /usr/src/redhat/RPMS/i386/cdplayer-1.0-1.i386.rpm
...
Source Packaging: cdplayer-1.0-1
...
Generating signature: 1002
Wrote: /usr/src/redhat/SRPMS/cdplayer-1.0-1.src.rpm
#
```

The most obvious effect of adding the `--sign` option to a build command is that RPM then asks for your private key's passphrase. After entering the passphrase (which isn't echoed), the build proceeds as usual. The only other difference between this and a nonsigned build is that the Generating signature: lines have a nonzero value.

Let's check the source and binary packages we've just created to see if they are, in fact, signed:

```
# rpm --checksig /usr/src/redhat/SRPMS/cdplayer-1.0-1.src.rpm
/usr/src/redhat/SRPMS/cdplayer-1.0-1.src.rpm: size pgp md5 OK
# rpm --checksig /usr/src/redhat/RPMS/i386/cdplayer-1.0-1.i386.rpm
/usr/src/redhat/RPMS/i386/cdplayer-1.0-1.i386.rpm: size pgp md5 OK
#
```

The fact that there is a pgp in --checksig's output indicates that the packages have been signed.

For more information on signing packages, see Chapter 17, "Adding PGP Signatures to a Package." Appendix G, "An Introduction to PGP," contains information on obtaining and installing PGP.

12.1.11. --test: Create, Save Build Scripts for Review

There are times when it might be necessary to get a more in-depth view of a particular build. By using the --test option, it's easy. When --test is added to a build command, the scripts RPM would normally use to actually perform the build are created and saved for you to review. Let's see how it works:

```
# rpm -ba --test cdplayer-1.0.spec
Package: cdplayer
#
```

Unlike in a normal build, there's not much output. But the --test option has caused a set of scripts to be written and saved for you. Where are they?

If you are using a customized rpmrc file, the scripts will be written to the directory specified by the rpmrc entry tmppath. If you haven't changed this setting, RPM, by default, writes the scripts in /var/tmp. Here they are:

```
# ls -l /var/tmp
total 4
-rw-rw-r--   1 root     root          670 Sep 17 20:35 rpmbu00236aaa
-rw-rw-r--   1 root     root          449 Sep 17 20:35 rpmbu00236baa
-rw-rw-r--   1 root     root          482 Sep 17 20:35 rpmbu00236caa
-rw-rw-r--   1 root     root          552 Sep 17 20:35 rpmbu00236daa
#
```

Each file contains a script that performs a given part of the build. Here's the first file:

```
#!/bin/sh -e
# Script generated by rpm

RPM_SOURCE_DIR="/usr/src/redhat/SOURCES"
RPM_BUILD_DIR="/usr/src/redhat/BUILD"
RPM_DOC_DIR="/usr/doc"
RPM_OPT_FLAGS="-O2 -m486 -fno-strength-reduce"
RPM_ARCH="i386"
RPM_OS="Linux"
RPM_ROOT_DIR="/tmp/cdplayer"
RPM_BUILD_ROOT="/tmp/cdplayer"
RPM_PACKAGE_NAME="cdplayer"
```

```
RPM_PACKAGE_VERSION="1.0"
RPM_PACKAGE_RELEASE="1"
set -x

umask 022
echo Executing: %prep
cd /usr/src/redhat/BUILD

cd /usr/src/redhat/BUILD
rm -rf cdplayer-1.0
gzip -dc /usr/src/redhat/SOURCES/cdplayer-1.0.tgz ¦ tar -xvvf -
if [ $? -ne 0 ]; then
  exit $?
fi
cd cdplayer-1.0
cd /usr/src/redhat/BUILD/cdplayer-1.0
chown -R root.root .
chmod -R a+rX,g-w,o-w .
```

As you can see, this script contains the `%prep` section from the spec file. The script starts by defining a number of environment variables and then leads into the `%prep` section. In the spec file used in this build, the `%prep` section consists of a single `%setup` macro. In this file, we can see exactly how RPM expands that macro. The remaining files follow the same basic layout— a section-defining environment variables, followed by the commands to be executed.

Note that the `--test` option will only create script files for each build stage, as specified in the command line. For example, if the previous command were changed to

 # rpm -bp --test cdplayer-1.0.spec
#

only one script file, containing the `%prep` commands, would be written. In any case, no matter what RPM build command is used, the `--test` option can let you see exactly what is going to happen during a build.

12.1.12. `--clean`: Clean Up After Build

The `--clean` option can be used to ensure that the package's build directory tree is removed at the end of a build. Although it can be used with any build stage, it doesn't always make much sense to do so:

```
# rpm -bp --clean cdplayer-1.0.spec
* Package: cdplayer
Executing: %prep
...
+ exit 0
+ echo Executing: sweep
Executing: sweep
+ cd /usr/src/redhat/BUILD
+ rm -rf cdplayer-1.0
+ exit 0
#
```

In this example, we see a typical `%prep` section being executed. The line `+ echo Executing:` `sweep` indicates the start of `--clean`'s activity. After changing directory into the build directory, RPM issues a recursive delete on the package's top-level directory.

As noted previously, this particular example doesn't make much sense. We're only executing the `%prep` section, which creates the package's build tree, and using `--clean`, which removes it! Using `--clean` with the `-bc` option isn't very productive either, as the newly built software remains in the build tree. Once again, there would be no remnants left after `--clean` has done its thing.

Normally, the `--clean` option is used once the software builds and can be packaged successfully. It is particularly useful when more than one package is to be built, since `--clean` ensures that the filesystem holding the build area will not fill up with build trees from each package.

Note also that the `--clean` option only removes the files that reside in the software's build tree. If there are any files that the build creates outside this hierarchy, it will be necessary to write a script for the spec file's `%clean` section.

12.1.13. `--buildroot` *<path>*: Execute `%install` Using *<path>* As the Root

The `--buildroot` option can make two difficult situations much easier:

- Performing a build without affecting the build system
- Allowing non-root users to build packages

Let's study the first situation in a bit more detail. Say, for example, that `sendmail` is to be packaged. In the course of creating a `sendmail` package, the software must be installed. This would mean that critical `sendmail` files, such as `sendmail.cf` and aliases, would be overwritten. Mail handling on the build system would almost certainly be disrupted.

In the second case, it's certainly possible to set permissions such that non-root users can install software, but highly unlikely that any system administrator worth his salt would do so. What can be done to make these situations more tenable?

The `--buildroot` option is used to instruct RPM to use a directory other than `/` as a build root. The term *build root* is a bit misleading, in that the build root is not the root directory under which the software is built. Rather, it is the root directory for the install phase of the build. When a build root is not specified, the software being packaged is installed relative to the build system's root directory `/`.

However, it's not enough to just specify a build root on the command line. The spec file for the package must be set up to support a build root. If you don't make the necessary changes, this is what you'll see:

```
# rpm -ba --buildroot /tmp/foo cdplayer-1.0.spec
Package can not do build prefixes
Build failed.
#
```

Chapter 16, "Making a Package That Can Build Anywhere," has complete instructions on the modifications necessary to configure a package to use an alternate build root, as well as methods to permit users to build packages without root access. Assuming that the necessary modifications have been made, here is what the build would look like:

```
# rpm -ba --buildroot /tmp/foonly cdplayer-1.0.spec
* Package: cdplayer
Executing: %prep
+ cd /usr/src/redhat/BUILD
...
+ exit 0
Executing: %build
+ cd /usr/src/redhat/BUILD
+ cd cdplayer-1.0
...
+ exit 0
+ umask 022
Executing: %install
+ cd /usr/src/redhat/BUILD
+ cd cdplayer-1.0
+ make ROOT=/tmp/foonly install
install -m 755 -o 0 -g 0 -d /tmp/foonly/usr/local/bin/
install -m 755 -o 0 -g 0 cdp /tmp/foonly/usr/local/bin/cdp
rm -f /tmp/foonly/usr/local/bin/cdplay
ln -s /tmp/foonly/usr/local/bin/cdp /tmp/foonly/usr/local/bin/cdplay
install -m 755 -o 0 -g 0 -d /tmp/foonly/usr/local/man/man1/
install -m 755 -o 0 -g 0 cdp.1 /tmp/foonly/usr/local/man/man1/cdp.1
+ exit 0
Executing: special doc
+ cd /usr/src/redhat/BUILD
+ cd cdplayer-1.0
+ DOCDIR=/tmp/foonly//usr/doc/cdplayer-1.0-1
+ rm -rf /tmp/foonly//usr/doc/cdplayer-1.0-1
+ mkdir -p /tmp/foonly//usr/doc/cdplayer-1.0-1
+ cp -ar README /tmp/foonly//usr/doc/cdplayer-1.0-1
+ exit 0
Binary Packaging: cdplayer-1.0-1
Finding dependencies...
Requires (2): libc.so.5 libncurses.so.2.0
usr/doc/cdplayer-1.0-1
usr/doc/cdplayer-1.0-1/README
usr/local/bin/cdp
usr/local/bin/cdplay
usr/local/man/man1/cdp.1
93 blocks
Generating signature: 0
Wrote: /usr/src/redhat/RPMS/i386/cdplayer-1.0-1.i386.rpm
+ umask 022
+ echo Executing: %clean
Executing: %clean
+ cd /usr/src/redhat/BUILD
```

```
+ cd cdplayer-1.0
+ exit 0
Source Packaging: cdplayer-1.0-1
cdplayer-1.0.spec
cdplayer-1.0.tgz
82 blocks
Generating signature: 0
Wrote: /usr/src/redhat/SRPMS/cdplayer-1.0-1.src.rpm
#
```

As the somewhat edited output shows, the %prep, %build, and %install sections are executed in RPM's normal build directory. However, the --buildroot option comes into play when the make install is done. As we can see, the ROOT variable is set to /tmp/foonly, which was the value following --buildroot on the command line. From that point on, we can see that make substituted the new build root value during the install phase.

The build root is also used when documentation files are installed. The documentation directory cdplayer-1.0-1 is created in /tmp/foonly/usr/doc, and the README file is placed in it.

The only remaining difference that results from using --buildroot is that the files to be included in the binary package are not located relative to the build system's root directory. Instead, they are located relative to the build root /tmp/foonly. The resulting binary and source package files are functionally equivalent to packages built without the use of --buildroot.

12.1.13.1. Using --buildroot Can Bite You!

Although the --buildroot option can solve some problems, using a build root can actually be dangerous. How? Consider the following situation:

- A spec file is configured to have a build root of /tmp/blather, for instance.
- In the %prep section (or the %clean section; it doesn't matter—the end result is the same), there is an rm -rf $RPM BUILD ROOT command to clean out any old installed software.
- You decide to build the software so that it installs relative to your system's root directory, so you enter the following command: rpm -ba --buildroot / foo.spec.

The end result? Since specifying / as the build root sets $RPM BUILD ROOT to /, that innocuous little rm -rf $RPM BUILD ROOT turns into rm -rf /! A recursive delete, starting at your system's root directory, might not be a total disaster if you catch it quickly, but in either case, you'll be testing your ability to restore from backup (er, you do have backups, don't you?).

The moral of this story is to be very careful when using --buildroot. A good rule of thumb is to always specify a unique build root. For example, instead of specifying /tmp as a build root (and possibly losing your system's directory for holding temporary files), use the path /tmp/mypackage, where the directory mypackage is used only by the package you're building.

12.1.14. --timecheck <secs>: Print a Warning if Files to Be Packaged Are More Than <secs> Old

While it's possible to detect many errors in the %files list using rpm -bl, there is another type of problem that can't be detected. Consider the following scenario:

- A package you're building creates the file /usr/bin/foo.
- Because of a problem with the package's makefile, foo is never copied into /usr/bin.
- An older, incompatible version of foo, created several months ago, already exists in /usr/bin.
- RPM creates the binary package file.

Is the incompatible /usr/bin/foo included in the package? You bet it is! If only there were some way for RPM to catch this type of problem.

Well, there is! If you add --timecheck, followed by a number, RPM will check each file being packaged to see if the file is more than the specified number of seconds old. If it is, a warning message is displayed. The --timecheck option works with either the -ba or -bl options. Here's an example using -bl:

```
# rpm -bl --timecheck 3600 cdplayer-1.0.spec
* Package: cdplayer
File List Check: cdplayer-1.0-1
warning: TIMECHECK failure: /usr/doc/cdplayer-1.0-1/README
Finding dependencies...
Requires (2): libc.so.5 libncurses.so.2.0
#
```

In this example, the file /usr/doc/cdplayer-1.0-1/README is more than 3,600 seconds, or 1 hour, old. If we take a look at the file, we find that it is as follows (note that the package was built substantially later than November 1995!):

```
# ls -al /usr/doc/cdplayer-1.0-1/README
-rw-r--r-- 1 root root 1085 Nov 10 1995 README
#
```

In this case, the warning from --timecheck is no cause for alarm. Since the README file was simply copied from the original source, which was created November 10, 1995, its date is unchanged. If the file had been an executable or a library that was supposedly built recently, --timecheck's warning should be taken more seriously.

If you'd like to set a default time check value of one hour, you can include the following line in your rpmrc file:

```
timecheck: 3600
```

This value can still be overridden by a value on the command line, if desired. For more information on the use of rpmrc files, see Appendix B, "The rpmrc File."

12.1.15. -vv: Display Debugging Information

Unlike most other RPM commands, there is no -v option for rpm -b. That's because the command's default is to be verbose. However, even more information can be obtained by adding -vv. Here's an example:

```
# rpm -bp -vv cdplayer-1.0.spec
D: Switched to BASE package
D: Source(0) = sunsite.unc.edu:/pub/Linux/apps/sound/cds/cdplayer-1.0.tgz
D: Switching to part: 12
D: fileFile =
D: Switched to package: (null)
D: Switching to part: 2
D: fileFile =
D: Switching to part: 3
D: fileFile =
D: Switching to part: 4
D: fileFile =
D: Switching to part: 10
D: fileFile =
D: Switched to package: (null)
* Package: cdplayer
D: RUNNING: %prep
+ umask 022
+ echo Executing: %prep
Executing: %prep
+ cd /usr/src/redhat/BUILD
+ cd /usr/src/redhat/BUILD
+ rm -rf cdplayer-1.0
+ gzip -dc /usr/src/redhat/SOURCES/cdplayer-1.0.tgz
+ tar -xvvf -
drwxrwxr-x root/users        0 Aug  4 22:30 1996 cdplayer-1.0/
-rw-r--r-- root/users    17982 Nov 10 01:10 1995 cdplayer-1.0/COPYING
...
-rw-r--r-- root/users     1515 Nov 10 01:10 1995 cdplayer-1.0/volume.h
+ [ 0 -ne 0 ]
+ cd cdplayer-1.0
+ cd /usr/src/redhat/BUILD/cdplayer-1.0
+ chown -R root.root .
+ chmod -R a+rX,g-w,o-w .
+ exit 0
#
```

Most of the output generated by the -vv option is preceded by a D:. In this example, the additional output represents RPM's internal processing during the start of the build process. Using the -vv option with other build commands will produce different output.

12.1.16. --quiet: Produce As Little Output As Possible

As mentioned earlier, the build command is normally verbose. The --quiet option can be used to cut down on the command's output:

```
# rpm -ba --quiet cdplayer-1.0.spec
Package: cdplayer
```

```
volume.c: In function 'mix_set_volume':
volume.c:67: warning: implicit declaration of function 'ioctl'
90 blocks
82 blocks
#
```

This is the entire output from a package build of `cdplayer`. Note that warning messages (actually, anything sent to `stdout`) are still printed.

12.1.17. `--rcfile` *<rcfile>*: Set Alternate `rpmrc` File to *<rcfile>*

The `--rcfile` option is used to specify a file containing default settings for RPM. Normally, this option is not needed. By default, RPM uses `/etc/rpmrc` and a file named `.rpmrc` located in your login directory.

This option would be used if there were a need to switch between several sets of RPM defaults. Software developers and package builders will normally be the only people using the `--rcfile` option. For more information on `rpmrc` files, see Appendix B.

12.2. Other Build-Related Commands

Two other commands also perform build-related functions. However, they do not use the `rpm -b` command syntax we've been studying so far. Instead of specifying the name of the spec file, as with `rpm -b`, it's necessary to specify the name of the source package file.

Why the difference in syntax? The reason has to do with the differing functions of these commands. Unlike `rpm -b`, where the name of the game is to get software packaged into binary and source package files, these commands use an already-existing source package file as input. Let's take a look at them in the following sections.

12.2.1. `rpm --recompile`: What Does It Do?

The `--recompile` option directs RPM to perform the following steps:

1. Install the specified source package file.
2. Unpack the original sources.
3. Build the software.
4. Install the software.
5. Remove the software's build directory structure.

While you might think this sounds a great deal like an install of the source package file, followed by an `rpm -bi`, this is not entirely the case. Using `--recompile`, the only file required is the source package file. After the software is built and installed, the only thing left, other than the newly installed software, is the original source package file.

The --recompile option is normally used when a previously installed package needs to be recompiled. --recompile comes in handy when software needs to be compiled against a new version of the kernel.

Here's what RPM displays during a --recompile:

```
# rpm --recompile cdplayer-1.0-1.src.rpm
Installing cdplayer-1.0-1.src.rpm
* Package: cdplayer
Executing: %prep
...
+ exit 0
Executing: %build
...
+ exit 0
Executing: %install
...
+ exit 0
Executing: special doc
...
+ exit 0
Executing: sweep
...
+ exit 0
#
```

The very first line shows RPM installing the source package. After that are ordinary executions of the %prep, %build, and %install sections of the spec file. Finally, the cleanup of the software's build directory takes place, just as if the --clean option had been specified.

Since rpm -i and rpm -U are not being used to install the software, the RPM database is not updated during a --recompile. This means that doing a --recompile on an already-installed package may result in problems down the road, when RPM is used to upgrade or verify the package.

12.2.2. rpm --rebuild: What Does It Do?

Package builders, particularly those who create packages for multiple architectures, often need to build their packages starting from the original sources. The --rebuild option does this, starting from a source package file. Here is the list of steps it performs:

1. Install the specified source package file.
2. Unpack the original sources.
3. Build the software.
4. Install the software.
5. Create a binary package file.
6. Remove the software's build directory tree.

Like the `--recompile` option, `--rebuild` cleans up after itself. The only difference between the two commands is that `--rebuild` also creates a binary package file. The only remnants of a `--rebuild` are the original source package, the newly installed software, and a new binary package file.

Package builders find this command especially handy because it allows them to create new binary packages using one command, with no additional cleanups required. There are two times when `--rebuild` is normally used:

- When the build environment (for example, compilers, libraries) has changed.
- When binary packages for a different architecture are to be built.

Here's an example of the `--rebuild` option in action:

```
# rpm --rebuild cdplayer-1.0-1.src.rpm
Installing cdplayer-1.0-1.src.rpm
* Package: cdplayer
Executing: %prep
...
+ exit 0
Executing: %build
...
+ exit 0
Executing: %install
...
+ exit 0
Executing: special doc
...
+ exit 0
Binary Packaging: cdplayer-1.0-1
...
Executing: %clean
...
+ exit 0
Executing: sweep
...
+ exit 0
#
```

The very first line shows RPM installing the source package. The lines after that are ordinary executions of the `%prep`, `%build`, and `%install` sections of the spec file. Next, a binary package file is created. Finally, the spec file's `%clean` section (if one exists) is executed. The cleanup of the software's build directory takes place, just as if the `--clean` option had been specified.

12.3. Summary

That completes our overview of the commands used to build packages with RPM. In Chapter 13, "Inside the Spec File," we'll look at the various macros that are available and how they can make life easier for the package builder.

13

Inside the Spec File

In this chapter, we're going to cover the spec file in detail. There are a number of different types of entries that comprise a spec file, and every one will be documented here. The different types of entries are

- Comments—Human-readable notes ignored by RPM.
- Tags—Data definitions.
- Scripts—A set of commands to be executed at specific times.
- Macros—A method of executing multiple commands easily.
- The `%files` list—A list of files to be included in the package.
- Directives—Used in the `%files` list to direct RPM to handle certain files in a specific way.
- Conditionals—Permit operating system– or architecture-specific preprocessing of the spec file.

Let's start by looking at comments.

13.1. Comments: Notes Ignored by RPM

Comments are a way to make RPM ignore a line in the spec file. The contents of a comment line are entirely up to the person writing the spec file.

To create a comment, enter an pound sign (#) at the start of the line. Any text following the comment character will be ignored by RPM. Here's an example of a comment:

```
# This is the spec file for playmidi 2.3...
```

Comments can be placed in any section of the spec file.

13.2. Tags: Data Definitions

Looking at a spec file, the first thing you'll see are a number of lines, all following the same basic format:

```
<something>:<something-else>
```

`<something>` is known as a *tag* because it is used by RPM to name or tag some data. The tag is separated from its associated data by a colon. The data is represented by `<something-else>`. Tags are grouped together at the top of the spec file, in a section known as the *preamble*. Here's an example of a tag and its data:

```
Vendor: White Socks Software, Inc.
```

In this example, the tag is `Vendor`. Tags are not case sensitive—they may be all uppercase, all lowercase, or anything in between. The `Vendor` tag is used to define the name of the organization producing the package. The data in this example is White Socks Software, Inc.. Therefore, RPM will store White Socks Software, Inc. as the vendor of the package.

Note also that spacing between the tag, the colon, and the data is unimportant. Given this, and the case insensitivity of the tag, each of the following lines is equivalent to the previous example:

```
VeNdOr : White Socks Software, Inc.

vendor:White Socks Software, Inc.

VENDOR : White Socks Software, Inc.
```

The bottom line is that you can make tag lines as neat or as ugly as you like—RPM won't mind either way. Note, however, that the tag's data might need to be formatted in a particular fashion. If there are any such restrictions, we'll mention them. The following sections group together tags of similar functions for easier reference, starting with the tags used to create the package name.

13.2.1. Package Naming Tags

The following tags are used by RPM to produce the package's final name. Since the name is always in this format:

```
<name>-<version>-<release>
```

it's only natural that the three tags are known as name, version, and release.

13.2.1.1. The name Tag

The name tag is used to define the name of the software being packaged. In most (if not all) cases, the name used for a package should be identical in spelling and case to the software being packaged. The name cannot contain any whitespace: If it does, RPM will only use the first part of the name (up to the first space). Therefore, if the name of the software being packaged is cdplayer, the name tag should be something like this:

```
Name: cdplayer
```

13.2.1.2. The version Tag

The version tag defines the version of the software being packaged. The version specified should be as close as possible to the format of the original software's version. In most cases, there should be no problem specifying the version just as the software's original developer did. However, there is a restriction: There can be no dashes in the version. If you forget, RPM will remind you:

```
# rpm -ba cdplayer-1.0.spec
Package: cdplayer
Illegal '-' char in version: 1.0-a
#
```

Spaces in the version will also cause problems, in that anything after the first space will be ignored by RPM. The bottom line is that you should stick with alphanumeric characters and periods, and you'll never have to worry about it. Here's a sample `version` tag:

```
Version: 1.2
```

13.2.1.3. The `release` Tag

The `release` tag can be thought of as the package's version. The release is traditionally an integer—for example, when a specific piece of software at a particular version is first packaged, the release should be 1. If it is necessary to repackage that software at the same version, the release should be incremented. When a new version of the software becomes available, the release should drop back to 1 when it is first packaged.

Note that we used the word *traditionally*. The only hard-and-fast restriction to the release format is that there can be no dashes in it. Be aware that if you buck tradition, your users may not understand what your release means.

It is up to the package builder to determine which build represents a new release and to update the release manually. Here is what a typical `release` tag might look like:

```
Release: 5
```

13.2.2. Descriptive Tags

Descriptive tags provide information primarily for people who want to know a bit more about the package and who produced it. They are part of the package file, and most of them can be seen by issuing an `rpm -qi` command.

13.2.2.1. The `%description` Tag

The `%description` tag is used to provide an in-depth description of the packaged software. The description should be several sentences describing, to an uninformed user, what the software does.

The `%description` tag is a bit different from the other tags in the preamble. For one, it starts with a percent sign. The other difference is that the data specified by the `%description` tag can span more than one line. In addition, a primitive formatting capability exists. If a line starts with a space, that line will be displayed verbatim by RPM. Lines that do not start with a space are assumed to be part of a paragraph and will be formatted by RPM. It's even possible to mix and match formatted and unformatted lines. Here are some examples:

```
%description
It slices! It dices! It's a CD player app that can't be beat. By using the
resonant frequency of the CD itself, it is able to simulate 20X
oversampling. This leads to sound quality that cannot be equaled with more
mundane software...
```

This example contains no explicit formatting. RPM will format the text as a single paragraph, breaking lines as needed. In the next example, we use a leading space to control the description's formatting:

```
%description
 It slices!
 It dices!
 It's a CD player app that can't be beat.
By using the resonant frequency of the CD itself, it is able to simulate
20X oversampling. This leads to sound quality that cannot be equaled with
more mundane software...
```

In this example, the first three lines will be displayed verbatim by RPM. The remainder of the text will be formatted by RPM. The text will be formatted as one paragraph. In the next example, we've added an additional wrinkle to %description formatting:

```
%description
It slices!
It dices!
It's a CD player app that can't be beat.

By using the resonant frequency of the CD itself, it is able to simulate
20X oversampling. This leads to sound quality that cannot be equaled with
more mundane software...
```

Here, we have a situation similar to the previous example, in that part of the text is formatted and part is not. However, the blank line separates the text into two paragraphs.

13.2.2.2. The summary Tag

The summary tag is used to define a one-line description of the packaged software. Unlike %description, summary is restricted to one line. RPM uses it when a succinct description of the package is needed. Here is an example of a summary line:

```
Summary: A CD player app that rocks!
```

13.2.2.3. The copyright Tag

The copyright tag is used to define the copyright terms applicable to the software being packaged. In many cases, this might be nothing more than GPL, for software distributed under the terms of the GNU General Public License, or something similar. Here's an example:

```
Copyright: GPL
```

13.2.2.4. The distribution Tag

The distribution tag is used to define a group of packages, of which this package is a part. Since Red Hat Software is in the business of producing a group of packages known as a Linux distribution, the name stuck. For example, if a suite of applications known as Doors '95 were produced, each package that is part of the suite would define its distribution line like this:

```
Distribution: Doors '95
```

13.2.2.5. The icon Tag

The icon tag is used to name a file containing an icon representing the packaged software. The file may be in either GIF or XPM format, although XPM is preferred. In either case, the background of the icon should be transparent. The file should be placed in RPM's SOURCES directory prior to performing a build, so no path is needed.

The icon is normally used by graphically oriented front ends to RPM. RPM itself doesn't use the icon, but it's stored in the package file and retained in RPM's database after the package is installed. A sample icon tag might look like this:

```
Icon: foo.xpm
```

13.2.2.6. The vendor Tag

The vendor tag is used to define the name of the entity that is responsible for packaging the software. Normally, this would be the name of an organization. Here's an example:

```
Vendor: White Socks Software, Inc.
```

13.2.2.7. The url Tag

The url tag is used to define a uniform resource locator (URL) that can be used to obtain additional information about the packaged software. At present, RPM doesn't actively make use of this tag. The data is stored in the package, however, and will be written into RPM's database when the package is installed. It's only a matter of time before some Web-based RPM adjunct makes use of this information, so make sure you include URLs! Something like this is all you'll need:

```
URL: http://www.gnomovision.com/cdplayer.html
```

13.2.2.8. The group Tag

The group tag is used to group packages together by the types of functionality they provide. The group specification looks like a path and is similar in function, in that it specifies more general groupings before more detailed ones. For example, a package containing a text editor might have the following group:

```
Group: Applications/Editors
```

In this example, the package is part of the Editors group, which is a part of the Applications group. Likewise, a spreadsheet package might have this group:

```
Group: Applications/Spreadsheets
```

This group tag indicates that under the Applications group are Editors and Spreadsheets, and probably some other subgroups as well.

How is this information used? It's primarily meant to permit graphical front ends to RPM to display packages in a hierarchical fashion. Of course, in order for groups to be as effective as possible, it's necessary for all package builders to be consistent in their groupings. In the case of packages for Linux, Red Hat Software has the definitive list. Therefore, Linux package builders should give serious consideration to using Red Hat Software's groups. The current group hierarchy is installed with every copy of RPM and is available in the RPM sources as well. Check out the file groups in RPM's documentation directory (normally /usr/doc/rpm-<version>), or in the top-level source directory.

13.2.2.9. The packager Tag

The packager tag is used to hold the name and contact information for the person or persons who built the package. Normally, this would be the person who actually built the package, or in a larger organization, a public relations contact. In either case, contact information such as an e-mail address or a phone number should be included so customers can send either money or hate mail, depending on their satisfaction with the packaged software. Here's an example of a packager tag:

```
Packager: Fred Foonly <fred@gnomovision.com>
```

13.2.3. Dependency Tags

One RPM feature that's been recently implemented is a means of ensuring that if a package is installed, the system environment has everything the package requires in order to operate properly. Likewise, when an installed package is erased, RPM can make sure no other package relies on the package being erased. This dependency capability can be very helpful when end users install and erase packages on their own. It makes it more difficult for them to paint themselves into a corner, package-wise.

However, in order for RPM to be able to take more than basic dependency information into account, the package builder must add the appropriate dependency information to the package. This is done by using the tags described in the following sections. Note, however, that adding dependency information to a package requires some forethought. For additional information on RPM's dependency processing, review Chapter 14, "Adding Dependency Information to a Package."

13.2.3.1. The provides Tag

The provides tag is used to specify a virtual package that the packaged software makes available when it is installed. Normally, this tag would be used when different packages provide equivalent services. For example, any package that allows a user to read mail might provide the mail-reader virtual package. Another package that depends on a mail reader of some sort could require the mail-reader virtual package. It would then install without dependency problems, if any one of several mail programs were installed. Here's what a `provides` tag might look like:

```
Provides: mail-reader
```

13.2.3.2. The `requires` Tag

The `requires` tag is used to warn RPM that the package needs to have certain capabilities available in order to operate properly. These capabilities refer to the name of another package or to a virtual package provided by one or more packages that use the `provides` tag. When the `requires` tag references a package name, you can include version comparisons by following the package name with a version specification and <, >, =, >= or <=. To get even more specific, you can include a package's release as well. Here's a `requires` tag in action, with a specific version requirement:

```
Requires: playmidi = 2.3
```

If the `requires` tag needs to perform a comparison against a serial number defined with the `serial` tag, the following would be the proper format:

```
Requires: playmidi =S 4
```

13.2.3.3. The `conflicts` Tag

The `conflicts` tag is the logical complement to the `requires` tag. The `requires` tag is used to specify what packages must be present in order for the current package to operate properly. The `conflicts` tag is used to specify what packages cannot be installed if the current package is to operate properly.

The `conflicts` tag has the same format as the `requires` tag—namely, the tag is followed by a real or virtual package name. Like `requires`, the `conflicts` tag also accepts version and release specifications:

```
Conflicts: playmidi = 2.3-1
```

If the `conflicts` tag needs to perform a comparison against a serial number defined with the `serial` tag, this would be the proper format:

```
Conflicts: playmidi =S 4
```

13.2.3.4. The `serial` Tag

The `serial` tag is another part of RPM's dependency and upgrade processing. The need for it is somewhat obscure, but goes something like this:

■ The package being built (call it package A) uses a version numbering scheme sufficiently obscure so that RPM cannot determine if one version is older or newer than another version.

■ Another package (package B) requires that package A be installed. More specifically, it requires RPM to compare package A's version against a specified minimum (or maximum) version.

Because RPM is unable to compare package A's version against the version specified by package B, there is no way to determine if package B's dependency requirements can be met. What to do?

The `serial` tag provides a way to get around this tricky problem. By specifying a simple integer serial number for each version, you are, in essence, directing how RPM interprets the relative age of the package. The key point to keep in mind is that in order for this to work, a unique serial number must be defined for each version of the software being packaged. In addition, the serial number must increment along with the version. Finally, the package that requires the serialized software needs to specify its version requirements in terms of the serial number.

Does it sound like a lot of trouble? You're right! If you find yourself in the position of needing to use this tag, take a deep breath and seriously consider changing the way you assign version numbers. If you're packaging someone else's software, perhaps you can convince him to make the change. Chances are, if RPM can't figure out the version number, most people can't, either! An example of a serial tag would look something like this:

```
Serial: 4
```

Note that RPM considers a package with a serial number as newer than a package without a serial number.

13.2.3.5. The `autoreqprov` Tag

The `autoreqprov` tag is used to control the automatic dependency processing performed when the package is being built. Normally, as each package is built, the following steps are performed:

■ All executable programs being packaged are analyzed to determine their shared library requirements. These requirements are automatically added to the package's requirements.

■ The soname (the name used to determine compatibility between different versions of a library) of each shared library being packaged is automatically added to the package's list of provides information.

By doing this, RPM reduces the need for package builders to manually add dependency information to their packages. However, there are times when RPM's automatic dependency processing may not be desirable. In those cases the `autoreqprov` tag can be used to disable automatic dependency processing.

To disable automatic dependency processing, add the following line:

```
AutoReqProv: no
```

(Note that 0 may be used instead of no.) Although RPM defaults to performing automatic dependency processing, the effect of the autoreqprov tag can be reversed by changing no to yes. (1 may be used instead of yes.)

13.2.4. Architecture- and Operating System–Specific Tags

As RPM gains popularity, more people are putting it to work on different types of computer systems. While this would not normally be a problem, things start to get a little tricky when either of the following situations becomes commonplace:

- A particular operating system is ported to several different hardware platforms, or architectures.
- A particular architecture runs several different operating systems.

The real bind occurs when RPM is used to package software for several of these different system environments. Without methods of controlling the build process based on architecture and operating system, package builders that develop software for more than one architecture or operating system will have a hard time indeed. The only alternative would be to maintain parallel RPM build environments and accept all the coordination headaches they would entail.

Fortunately, RPM makes it all easier than that. With the tags described in the following sections, it's possible to support package building under multiple environments, all from a single set of sources, patches, and a single spec file. For a more complete discussion of multiarchitecture package building, see Chapter 19, "Building Packages for Multiple Architectures and Operating Systems."

13.2.4.1. The excludearch Tag

The excludearch tag directs RPM to ensure that the package does not attempt to build on the excluded architecture(s). The reasons for preventing a package from building on a certain architecture might include the following:

- The software has not yet been ported to the excluded architecture.
- The software would serve no purpose on the excluded architecture.

An example of the first case might be that the software was designed based on the assumption that an integer is a 32-bit quantity. Obviously, this assumption is not valid on a 64-bit processor.

In the second case, software that depended on or manipulated low-level features of a given architecture should be excluded from building on a different architecture. Assembly language programs would fall into this category.

One or more architectures may be specified after the excludearch tag, separated by either spaces or commas. Here is an example:

```
ExcludeArch: sparc alpha
```

In this example, RPM would not attempt to build the package on either the Sun SPARC or Digital Alpha/AXP architectures. The package could build on any other architectures, however. If a build is attempted on an excluded architecture, the following message will be displayed, and the build will fail:

```
# rpm -ba cdplayer-1.0.spec
Arch mismatch!
cdplayer-1.0.spec doesn't build on this architecture
#
```

Note that if your goal is to ensure that a package will only build on one architecture, you should use the `exclusivearch` tag.

13.2.4.2. The exclusivearch Tag

The `exclusivearch` tag is used to direct RPM to ensure that the package is only built on the specified architecture(s). The reasons for this are similar to the those mentioned in section 13.2.5.1. However, the `exclusivearch` tag is useful when the package builder needs to ensure that only the specified architectures will build the package. This tag ensures that no future architectures will mistakenly attempt to build the package. This would not be the case if the `excludearch` tag were used to specify every architecture known at the time the package is built.

The syntax of the `exclusivearch` tag is identical to that of `excludearch`:

```
ExclusiveArch: sparc alpha
```

In this example, the package will only build on a Sun SPARC or Digital Alpha/AXP system.

Note that if your goal is to ensure that a package will not build on specific architectures, you should use the `excludearch` tag.

13.2.4.3. The excludeos Tag

The `excludeos` tag is used to direct RPM to ensure that the package does not attempt to build on the excluded operating system(s). This is usually necessary when a package is to be built on more than one operating system, but it is necessary to keep a particular operating system from attempting a build.

Note that if your goal is to ensure that a package will only build on one operating system, you should use the `exclusiveos` tag. Here's a sample `excludeos` tag:

```
ExcludeOS: linux irix
```

13.2.4.4. The exclusiveos Tag

The `exclusiveos` tag has the same syntax as `excludeos`, but it has the opposite logic. The `exclusiveos` tag is used to denote which operating system(s) should be exclusively permitted to build the package. Here's `exclusiveos` in action:

```
ExclusiveOS: linux
```

Note that if your goal is to ensure that a package will not build on a specific operating system, you should use the `excludeos` tag.

13.2.5. Directory-Related Tags

A number of tags are used to specify directories and paths that are used in various phases of RPM's build and install processes. There's not much more to say collectively about these tags, so let's dive right in and look them over.

13.2.5.1. The `prefix` Tag

The `prefix` tag is used when a relocatable package is to be built. A relocatable package can be installed normally or can be installed in a user-specified directory, by using RPM's `--prefix` install-time option. The data specified after the prefix tag should be the part of the package's path that may be changed during installation. For example, if the following prefix line were included in a spec file:

```
Prefix: /opt
```

and the following file were specified in the spec file's `%files` list:

```
/opt/blather/foonly
```

then the file `foonly` would be installed in `/opt/blather` if the package was installed normally. It would be installed in `/usr/local/blather` if the package was installed with the `--prefix /usr/local` option.

For more information about creating relocatable packages, see Chapter 15, "Making a Relocatable Package."

13.2.5.2. The `buildroot` Tag

The `buildroot` tag is used to define an alternate build root. The name is a bit misleading because the build root is actually used when the software is installed during the build process. In order for a build root to be defined and actually used, a number of issues must be taken into account. These issues are covered in Chapter 16, "Making a Package That Can Build Anywhere." This is what a `buildroot` tag would look like:

```
BuildRoot: /tmp/cdplayer
```

The `buildroot` tag can be overridden at build time by using the `--buildroot` command-line option.

13.2.6. Source and Patch Tags

In order to build and package software, RPM needs to know where to find the original sources. But it's not quite that simple. There might be more than one set of sources that need to be part of a particular build. In some cases, it might be necessary to prevent some sources from being packaged.

And then there is the matter of patches. It's likely that changes will need to be made to the sources, so it's necessary to specify a patch file. But the same issues that apply to source specifications are also applicable to patches. There might be more than one set of patches required.

The tags that are described in the following sections are crucial to RPM, so it pays to have a firm grasp of how they are used.

13.2.6.1. The source Tag

The source tag is central to nearly every spec file. Although it has only one piece of data associated with it, it performs two functions:

- It shows where the software's developer has made the original sources available.
- It gives RPM the name of the original source file.

While there is no hard-and-fast rule for the first function, it's generally considered best to put this information in the form of a URL. The URL should point directly to the source file itself. This is because of the source tag's second function.

As mentioned previously, the source tag also needs to direct RPM to the source file on the build system. How does it do this? There's only one requirement, and it is ironclad: The source filename must be at the end of the line as the final element in a path. Here's an example:

```
Source: ftp://ftp.gnomovision.com/pub/cdplayer-1.0.tgz
```

Given this source line, RPM will search its SOURCES directory for cdplayer-1.0.tgz. Everything prior to the filename is ignored by RPM. It's there strictly for any interested humans.

A spec file may contain more than one source tag. This is necessary for those cases where the software being packaged is contained in more than one source file. However, the source tags must be uniquely identified. This is done by appending a number to the end of the tag itself. In fact, RPM does this internally for the first source tag in a spec file, in essence turning it into source0. Therefore, if a package contains two source files, they may either be specified this way:

```
Source: blather-4.5.tar.gz
Source1: bother-1.2.tar.gz
```

or this way:

```
Source0: blather-4.5.tar.gz
Source1: bother-1.2.tar.gz
```

13.2.6.2. The nosource Tag

The nosource tag is used to direct RPM to omit one or more source files from the source package. Why would someone want to go to the trouble of specifying a source file, only to exclude it? The reasons for this can be varied, but let's look at one example: The software known as pretty good privacy, or PGP.

PGP contains encryption routines of such high quality that the U.S. government restricts their export. (There is also an international version that may be used in non-U.S. countries. See Appendix G, "An Introduction to PGP.") While it would be nice to create a PGP package file, the resulting package could not legally be transferred between the U.S. and other countries.

However, what if all files other than the original source were packaged using RPM? Well, a binary package made without PGP would be of little use, but what about the source package? It would contain the spec file, maybe some patches, and perhaps even an icon file. Since the controversial PGP software was not a part of the source package, this sanitized source package could be downloaded legally in any country. The person who downloaded a copy could then go about legally obtaining the PGP sources himself, place them in RPM's SOURCES directory, and create a binary package. He wouldn't even need to change the nosource tag. One rpm -ba command later, and the user would have a perfectly usable PGP binary package file.

Since there may be more than one source tag in a spec file, the format of the nosource tag is as follows:

```
nosource: <src-num>, <src-num>...<src-num>
```

<src-num> represents the number following the source tag. If there is more than one number in the list, the numbers may be separated by either commas or spaces. For example, consider a package containing the following source tags:

```
source: blather-4.5.tar.gz
Source1: bother-1.2.tar.gz
source2: blather-lib-4.5.tar.gz
source3: bother-lib-1.2.tar.gz
```

If the source files for blather and blather-lib were not to be included in the package, the following nosource line could be added:

```
NoSource: 0, 3
```

What about that 0? Keep in mind that the first unnumbered source tag in a spec file is automatically numbered 0 by RPM.

13.2.6.3. The patch Tag

The patch tag is used to identify which patches are associated with the software being packaged. The patch files are kept in RPM's SOURCES directory, so only the name of the patch file should be specified. Here is an example:

```
Patch: cdp-0.33-fsstnd.patch
```

There are no hard-and-fast requirements for naming the patch files, but traditionally the filename starts with the software name and version, separated by dashes. The next part of the patch file name usually includes one or more words indicating the reason for the patch. In the preceding example, the patch file contains changes necessary to bring the software into compliance with the Linux File System Standard, hence the `fsstnd` magic incantation.

RPM processes `patch` tags the same way it does `source` tags. Therefore, it's acceptable to use a URL on a `patch` line, too.

A spec file may contain more than one `patch` tag. This is necessary for those cases where the software being packaged requires more than one patch. However, the `patch` tags must be uniquely identified. This is done by appending a number to the end of the tag itself. In fact, RPM does this internally for the first `patch` tag in a spec file, in essence turning it into `patch0`. Therefore, if a package contains three patches, this method of specifying them:

```
Patch: blather-4.5-bugfix.patch
Patch1: blather-4.5-config.patch
Patch2: blather-4.5-somethingelse.patch
```

is equivalent to this one:

```
Patch0: blather-4.5-bugfix.patch
Patch1: blather-4.5-config.patch
Patch2: blather-4.5-somethingelse.patch
```

Either approach may be used, but the second method looks nicer.

13.2.6.4. The `nopatch` Tag

The `nopatch` tag is similar to the `nosource` tag discussed earlier. Just like the `nosource` tag, the `nopatch` tag is used to direct RPM to omit something from the source package. In the case of `nosource`, that something was one or more sources. For the `nopatch` tag, the something is one or more patches.

Since each `patch` tag in a spec file must be numbered, the `nopatch` tag uses those numbers to specify which patches are not to be included in the package. The `nopatch` tag is used in this manner:

```
NoPatch: 2 3
```

In this example, the source files specified on the `source2` and `source3` lines are not to be included in the build.

This concludes our study of RPM's tags. In the next section, we'll look at the various scripts that RPM uses to build, as well as to install and erase, packages.

13.3. Scripts: RPM's Workhorse

The scripts that RPM uses to control the build process are among the most varied and interesting parts of the spec file. Many spec files also contain scripts that perform a variety of tasks whenever the package is installed or erased.

The start of each script is denoted by a keyword. For example, the `%build` keyword marks the start of the script RPM will execute when building the software to be packaged. Note that, in the strictest sense of the word, these parts of the spec file are not scripts. For example, they do not start with the traditional invocation of a shell. However, the contents of each script section are copied into a file and executed by RPM as a full-fledged script. This is part of the power of RPM: Anything that can be done in a script can be done by RPM.

Let's start by looking at the scripts used during the build process.

13.3.1. Build-Time Scripts

The scripts that RPM uses during the building of a package follow the steps known to every software developer:

1. Unpack the sources.
2. Build the software.
3. Install the software.
4. Clean up.

Although each of the scripts performs a specific function in the build process, they share a common environment. Using RPM's `--test` option (described in section 12.1.11 in Chapter 12), we can see the common portion of each script. In the following example, we've taken the `cdplayer` package, issued an `rpm -ba --test cdplayer-1.0-1.spec`, and viewed the script files left in RPM's temporary directory. This section (with the appropriate package-specific values) is present in every script RPM executes during a build:

```
#!/bin/sh -e
# Script generated by rpm

RPM_SOURCE_DIR="/usr/src/redhat/SOURCES"
RPM_BUILD_DIR="/usr/src/redhat/BUILD"
RPM_DOC_DIR="/usr/doc"
RPM_OPT_FLAGS="-O2 -m486 -fno-strength-reduce"
RPM_ARCH="i386"
RPM_OS="Linux"
RPM_ROOT_DIR="/tmp/cdplayer"
RPM_BUILD_ROOT="/tmp/cdplayer"
RPM_PACKAGE_NAME="cdplayer"
RPM_PACKAGE_VERSION="1.0"
RPM_PACKAGE_RELEASE="1"
set -x

umask 022
```

As you can see, the script starts with the usual invocation of a shell (in this case, the Bourne shell). There are no arguments passed to the script. Next, a number of environment variables are set. Here's a brief description of each one:

- RPM_SOURCE_DIR—This environment variable gets its value from the rpmrc file entry sourcedir, which in turn can get part of its value from the topdir entry. It is the path RPM will prepend to the file, specified in the source tag line.

- RPM_BUILD_DIR—This variable is based on the builddir rpmrc file entry, which in turn can get part of its value from the topdir entry. This environment variable translates to the path of RPM's build directory, where most software will be unpacked and built.

- RPM_DOC_DIR—The value of this environment variable is based on the defaultdocdir rpmrc file entry. Files marked with the %doc directive can be installed in a subdirectory of defaultdocdir. For more information on the %doc directive, refer to section 13.6.1.

- RPM_OPT_FLAGS—This environment variable gets its value from the optflags rpmrc file entry. It contains options that can be passed on to the build procedures of the software being packaged. Normally this means either a configuration script or the make command itself.

- RPM_ARCH—As you might infer from the preceding example, this environment variable contains a string describing the build system's architecture.

- RPM_OS—This one contains the name of the build system's operating system.

- RPM_BUILD_ROOT—This environment variable is used to hold the build root, into which the newly built software will be installed. If no explicit build root has been specified (either by command-line option, spec file tag line, or rpmrc file entry), this variable will be null.

- RPM_PACKAGE_NAME—This environment variable gets its value from the name tag line in the package's spec file. It contains the name of the software being packaged.

- RPM_PACKAGE_VERSION—The version tag line is the source of this variable's translation. Predictably, this environment variable contains the software's version number.

- RPM_PACKAGE_RELEASE—This environment variable contains the package's release number. Its value is obtained from the release tag line in the spec file.

All these environment variables are set for your use to make it easier to write scripts that will do the right thing even if the build environment changes.

The script also sets an option that causes the shell to print out each command, complete with expanded arguments. Finally, the default permissions are set. Past this point, the scripts differ. Let's look at the scripts in the order in which they are executed.

13.3.1.1. The %prep Script

The %prep script is the first one RPM executes during a build. Prior to the %prep script, RPM has performed preliminary consistency checks, such as whether the spec file's source tag points to files that actually exist. Just prior to passing control over to the `%prep` script's contents, RPM changes directory into RPM's build area, which, by default, is `/usr/src/redhat/BUILD`.

At that point, it is the responsibility of the `%prep` script to do the following:

- Create the top-level build directory.
- Unpack the original sources into the build directory.
- Apply patches to the sources, if necessary.
- Perform any other actions required to get the sources into a ready-to-build state.

The first three items on this list are common to the vast majority of all software being packaged. Therefore, RPM has two macros that greatly simplify these routine functions.

You can find more information on RPM's `%setup` and `%patch` macros in section 13.4.

The last item on the list can include creating directories or anything else required to get the sources into a ready-to-build state. As a result, a `%prep` script can range from one line invoking a single `%setup` macro to many lines of tricky shell programming.

13.3.1.2. The `%build` Script

The `%build` script picks up where the `%prep` script left off. Once the `%prep` script has gotten everything ready for the build, the `%build` script is usually somewhat anticlimactic—normally invoking `make`, maybe a configuration script, and little else.

Like `%prep` before it, the `%build` script has the same assortment of environment variables to draw on. Also, like `%prep`, `%build` changes directory into the software's top-level build directory (located in `RPM_BUILD_DIR`, or usually called `<name>-<version>`).

Unlike `%prep`, there are no macros available for use in the `%build` script. The reason is simple: Either the commands required to build the software are simple (such as a single `make` command) or they are so unique that a macro wouldn't make it easier to write the script.

13.3.1.3. The `%install` Script

The environment in which the `%install` script executes is identical to those of the other scripts. Like the other scripts, the `%install` script's working directory is set to the software's top-level directory.

As the name implies, it is this script's responsibility to do whatever is necessary to actually install the newly built software. In most cases, this means a single `make install` command or a few commands to copy files and create directories.

13.3.1.4. The `%clean` Script

The `%clean` script, as the name implies, is used to clean up the software's build directory tree. RPM normally does this for you, but in certain cases (most notably in those packages that use a build root) you'll need to include a `%clean` script.

As usual, the %clean script has the same set of environment variables as the other scripts we've covered here. Since a %clean script is normally used when the package is built in a build root, the RPM_BUILD_ROOT environment variable is particularly useful. In many cases, a simple

```
rm -rf $RPM_BUILD_ROOT
```

will suffice. Keep in mind that this command in a %clean script can wreak havoc if used, say, with a build root of /. Section 12.1.13 in Chapter 12, "rpm -b Command Reference," discusses this in more detail.

13.3.2. Install/Erase-Time Scripts

The other type of scripts that are present in the spec file are those that are only used when the package is either installed or erased. There are four scripts, each one meant to be executed at different times during the life of a package:

- ◼ Before installation
- ◼ After installation
- ◼ Before erasure
- ◼ After erasure

Unlike the build-time scripts, there is little in the way of environment variables for these scripts. The only environment variable available is RPM_INSTALL_PREFIX, and that is only set if the package uses an installation prefix.

Unlike with the build-time scripts, there is an argument defined. The sole argument to these scripts is a number representing the number of instances of the package currently installed on the system, after the current package has been installed or erased. Sound tricky? It really isn't. Here's an example: Assume that a package, called blather-1.0, is being installed. No previous versions of blather have been installed. Because the software is being installed, only the %pre and %post scripts are executed. The argument passed to these scripts will be 1 since the number of blather packages installed is 1. (Or it will be 1 once the package is completely installed. Remember that the number is based on the number of packages installed after the current package's install or erase has completed.)

Continuing our example, a new version of the blather package, version 1.3, is now available. Clearly it's time to upgrade. What will the scripts' values be during the upgrade? As blather-1.3 is installing, its %pre and %post scripts will have an argument equal to 2 (1 for version 1.0 already installed, plus 1 for version 1.3 being installed). As the final part of the upgrade, it's then time to erase blather version 1.0. As the package is being removed, its %preun and %postun scripts are executed. Since there will be only one blather package (version 1.3) installed after version 1.0 is erased, the argument passed to version 1.0's scripts is 1.

To bring an end to this example, we've decided to erase blather 1.3. We just don't need it anymore. As the package is being erased, its %preun and %postun scripts will be executed.

Because there will be no `blather` packages installed once the erase completes, the argument passed to the scripts is `0`.

With all that said, of what possible use would this argument be? Well, it has two very interesting properties:

- When the first version of a package is installed, its `%pre` and `%post` scripts will be passed an argument equal to `1`.
- When the last version of a package is erased, its `%preun` and `%postun` scripts will be passed an argument equal to `0`.

Given these properties, it's trivial to write an install-time script that can take certain actions in specific circumstances. Usually, the argument is used in the `%preun` or `%postun` scripts to perform a special task when the last instance of a package is being erased.

What is normally done during these scripts? The exact tasks may vary, but in general, the tasks are any that need to be performed at these points in the package's existence. One very common task is to run `ldconfig` when shared libraries are installed or removed. But that's not the only use for these scripts. It's even possible to use the scripts to perform tests to ensure the package install/erasure should proceed.

Since each of these scripts will be executing on whatever system installs the package, it's necessary to choose the script's choice of tools carefully. Unless you're sure a given program is going to be available on all the systems that could possibly install your package, you should not use it in these scripts.

13.3.2.1. The `%pre` Script

The `%pre` script executes just before the package is to be installed. It is the rare package that requires anything to be done prior to installation; none of the 350 packages that comprise Red Hat Linux 4.0 make use of it.

13.3.2.2. The `%post` Script

The `%post` script executes after the package has been installed. One of the most popular reasons a `%post` script is needed is to run `ldconfig` to update the list of available shared libraries after a new one has been installed. Of course, other functions can be performed in a `%post` script. For example, packages that install shells use the `%post` script to add the shell name to `/etc/shells`.

If a package uses a `%post` script to perform some function, quite often it will include a `%postun` script that performs the inverse of the `%post` script, after the package has been removed.

13.3.2.3. The %preun Script

If there's a time when your package needs to have one last look around before the user erases it, the place to do it is in the %preun script. Anything that a package needs to do immediately prior to RPM taking any action to erase the package can be done here.

13.3.2.4. The %postun Script

The %postun script executes after the package has been removed. It is the last chance for a package to clean up after itself. Quite often, %postun scripts are used to run ldconfig to remove newly erased shared libraries from ld.so.cache.

13.3.3. Verification-Time Script—The %verifyscript Script

The %verifyscript script executes whenever the installed package is verified by RPM's verification command. The contents of this script are entirely up to the package builder, but in general the script should do whatever is necessary to verify the package's proper installation. Since RPM automatically verifies the existence of a package's files, along with other file attributes, the %verifyscript script should concentrate on different aspects of the package's installation. For example, the script might ensure that certain configuration files contain the proper information for the package being verified:

```
for n in ash bsh; do
    echo -n "Looking for $n in /etc/shells... "
    if ! grep "^/bin/${n}\$" /etc/shells > /dev/null; then
        echo "missing"
        echo "${n} missing from /etc/shells" >&2
    else
        echo "found"
    fi
done
```

In this script, the config file /etc/shells is checked to ensure that it has entries for the shells provided by this package.

It is worth noting that the script sends informational and error messages to stdout and error messages only to stderr. Normally RPM will only display error output from a verification script; the output sent to stdout is only displayed when the verification is run in verbose mode.

13.4. Macros: Helpful Shorthand for Package Builders

RPM does not support macros in the sense of ad hoc sequences of commands being defined as a macro and executed by simply referring to the macro name.

However, two parts of RPM's build process are fairly constant from one package to another: the unpacking and patching of sources. RPM makes two macros available to simplify these tasks:

- The %setup macro, which is used to unpack the original sources.
- The %patch macro, which is used to apply patches to the original sources.

These macros are used exclusively in the %prep script; it wouldn't make sense to use them anywhere else. The use of these macros is not mandatory—it is certainly possible to write a %prep script without them. But in the vast majority of cases they make life easier for the package builder.

13.4.1. The %setup Macro

As mentioned earlier, the %setup macro is used to unpack the original sources, in preparation for the build. In its simplest form, the macro is used with no options and gets the name of the source archive from the source tag specified earlier in the spec file. Let's look at an example. The cdplayer package has the following source tag:

```
Source: ftp://ftp.gnomovision.com/pub/cdplayer/cdplayer-1.0.tgz
```

and the following %prep script:

```
%prep
%setup
```

In this simple case, the %setup macro expands into the following commands:

```
cd /usr/src/redhat/BUILD
rm -rf cdplayer-1.0
gzip -dc /usr/src/redhat/SOURCES/cdplayer-1.0.tgz ¦ tar -xvvf -
if [ $? -ne 0 ]; then
  exit $?
fi
cd cdplayer-1.0
cd /usr/src/redhat/BUILD/cdplayer-1.0 chown -R root.root .
chmod -R a+rX,g-w,o-w .
```

As you can see, the %setup macro starts by changing directory into RPM's build area and removing any cdplayer build trees from previous builds. It then uses gzip to uncompress the original source (whose name was taken from the source tag), and pipes the result to tar for unpacking. The return status of the unpacking is tested. If successful, the macro continues.

At this point, the original sources have been unpacked. The %setup macro continues by changing directory into cdplayer's top-level directory. The two cd commands are an artifact of %setup's macro expansion. Finally, %setup makes sure every file in the build tree is owned by root and has appropriate permissions set.

But that's just the simplest way that %setup can be used. A number of other options can be added to accommodate different situations. Let's look at them.

13.4.1.1. -n *<name>*: Set Name of Build Directory

In the preceding example, the `%setup` macro simply uncompressed and unpacked the sources.

In this case, the `tar` file containing the original sources was created so that the top-level directory was included in the `tar` file. The name of the top-level directory was also identical to that of the `tar` file, which was in *<name>*-*<version>* format.

However, this is not always the case. Quite often, the original sources unpack into a directory whose name is different from the original `tar` file. Since RPM assumes that the directory will be called *<name>*-*<version>*, when the directory is called something else, it's necessary to use `%setup`'s -n option. Here's an example: Assume for a moment that the `cdplayer` sources, when unpacked, create a top-level directory named `cd-player`. In this case, our `%setup` line would look like this:

```
%setup -n cd-player
```

and the resulting commands would look like this:

```
cd /usr/src/redhat/BUILD
rm -rf cd-player
gzip -dc /usr/src/redhat/SOURCES/cdplayer-1.0.tgz ¦ tar -xvvf -
if [ $? -ne 0 ]; then
  exit $?
fi
cd cd-player
cd /usr/src/redhat/BUILD/cd-player
chown -R root.root .
chmod -R a+rX,g-w,o-w .
```

The results are identical to using `%setup` with no options, except for the fact that `%setup` now does a recursive delete on the directory `cd-player` (instead of `cdplayer-1.0`) and changes directory into `cd-player` (instead of `cdplayer-1.0`).

Note that all subsequent build-time scripts will change directory into the directory specified by the -n option. This makes -n unsuitable as a means of unpacking sources in directories other than the top-level build directory. In the following sections, we'll show a way around this restriction.

A quick word of warning: If the name specified with the -n option doesn't match the name of the directory created when the sources are unpacked, the build will stop pretty quickly, so it pays to be careful when using this option.

13.4.1.2. -c: Create Directory (and Change to It) Before Unpacking

How many times have you grabbed a `tar` file and unpacked it, only to find that it splattered files all over your current directory? Sometimes source archives are created without a top-level directory.

As you can see from the examples so far, `%setup` expects the archive to create its own top-level directory. If this isn't the case, you'll need to use the -c option.

This option simply creates the directory and changes directory into it before unpacking the sources. Here's what it looks like:

```
cd /usr/src/redhat/BUILD
rm -rf cdplayer-1.0
mkdir -p cdplayer-1.0
cd cdplayer-1.0
gzip -dc /usr/src/redhat/SOURCES/cdplayer-1.0.tgz ¦ tar -xvvf -
if [ $? -ne 0 ]; then
  exit $?
fi
cd /usr/src/redhat/BUILD/cdplayer-1.0
chown -R root.root .
chmod -R a+rX,g-w,o-w .
```

The only changes from using %setup with no options are the mkdir and cd commands, prior to the commands that unpack the sources. Note that you can use the -n option along with -c, so something like %setup -c -n blather works as expected.

13.4.1.3. -D: Do Not Delete Directory Before Unpacking Sources

The -D option keeps the %setup macro from deleting the software's top-level directory. This option is handy when the sources being unpacked are to be added to an already-existing directory tree. This would be the case when more than one %setup macro is used. Here's what %setup does when the -D option is employed:

```
cd /usr/src/redhat/BUILD
gzip -dc /usr/src/redhat/SOURCES/cdplayer-1.0.tgz ¦ tar -xvvf -
if [ $? -ne 0 ]; then
  exit $?
fi
cd cdplayer-1.0
cd /usr/src/redhat/BUILD/cdplayer-1.0
chown -R root.root .
chmod -R a+rX,g-w,o-w .
```

As advertised, the rm prior to the tar command is gone.

13.4.1.4. -T: Do Not Perform Default Archive Unpacking

The -T option disables %setup's normal unpacking of the archive file specified on the source0 line. Here's what the resulting commands look like:

```
cd /usr/src/redhat/BUILD
rm -rf cdplayer-1.0
cd cdplayer-1.0
cd /usr/src/redhat/BUILD/cdplayer-1.0
chown -R root.root .
chmod -R a+rX,g-w,o-w .
```

Doesn't make much sense, does it? There's a method to this madness. We'll see the -T in action in the next section.

13.4.1.5. -b *<n>*: Unpack the *n*th Sources Before Changing Directory

The -b option is used in conjunction with the source tag. Specifically, it is used to identify which of the numbered source tags in the spec file are to be unpacked.

The -b option requires a numeric argument matching an existing source tag. If a numeric argument is not provided, the build will fail:

```
# rpm -ba cdplayer-1.0.spec
Package: cdplayer
Need arg to %setup -b
Build failed.
#
```

Remembering that the first source tag is implicitly numbered 0, let's see what happens when the %setup line is changed to %setup -b 0:

```
cd /usr/src/redhat/BUILD
rm -rf cdplayer-1.0
gzip -dc /usr/src/redhat/SOURCES/cdplayer-1.0.tgz ¦ tar -xvvf -
if [ $? -ne 0 ]; then
  exit $?
fi
gzip -dc /usr/src/redhat/SOURCES/cdplayer-1.0.tgz ¦ tar -xvvf -
if [ $? -ne 0 ]; then
exit $?
fi
cd cdplayer-1.0
cd /usr/src/redhat/BUILD/cdplayer-1.0
chown -R root.root .
chmod -R a+rX,g-w,o-w .
```

That's strange. The sources were unpacked twice. It doesn't make sense until you realize that this is why there is a -T option. Since -T disables the default source file unpacking, and -b selects a particular source file to be unpacked, the two are meant to go together, like this:

```
%setup -T -b 0
```

Looking at the resulting commands, we find this:

```
cd /usr/src/redhat/BUILD
rm -rf cdplayer-1.0
gzip -dc /usr/src/redhat/SOURCES/cdplayer-1.0.tgz ¦ tar -xvvf -
if [ $? -ne 0 ]; then
  exit $?
fi
cd cdplayer-1.0
cd /usr/src/redhat/BUILD/cdplayer-1.0
chown -R root.root .
chmod -R a+rX,g-w,o-w .
```

That's more like it! Let's go on to the next option.

13.4.1.6. -a *<n>*: Unpack the *n*th Sources After Changing Directory

The -a option works similarly to the -b option, except that the sources are unpacked after changing directory into the top-level build directory. Like the -b option, -a requires -T in order to prevent two sets of unpacking commands. Here are the commands that a %setup -T -a 0 line would produce:

```
cd /usr/src/redhat/BUILD
rm -rf cdplayer-1.0
cd cdplayer-1.0
gzip -dc /usr/src/redhat/SOURCES/cdplayer-1.0.tgz ¦ tar -xvvf -
  if [ $? -ne 0 ]; then
exit $?
fi
cd /usr/src/redhat/BUILD/cdplayer-1.0
chown -R root.root .
chmod -R a+rX,g-w,o-w .
```

Note that there is no mkdir command to create the top-level directory prior to issuing a cd into it. In our example, adding the -c option will make things right:

```
cd /usr/src/redhat/BUILD
rm -rf cdplayer-1.0
mkdir -p cdplayer-1.0
cd cdplayer-1.0
gzip -dc /usr/src/redhat/SOURCES/cdplayer-1.0.tgz ¦ tar -xvvf -
if [ $? -ne 0 ]; then
  exit $?
fi
cd /usr/src/redhat/BUILD/cdplayer-1.0
chown -R root.root .
chmod -R a+rX,g-w,o-w .
```

The result is the proper sequence of commands for unpacking a tar file with no top-level directory.

13.4.1.7. Using %setup in a Multisource Spec File

If all these interrelated options seem like overkill for unpacking a single source file, you're right. The real reason for the various options is to make it easier to combine several separate source archives into a single, buildable entity. Let's see how they work in that type of environment.

For the purposes of this example, our spec file will have the following three source tags (yes, the source tags should include a URL pointing to the sources):

```
source: source-zero.tar.gz
source1: source-one.tar.gz
source2: source-two.tar.gz
```

To unpack the first source is not hard; all that's required is to use %setup with no options:

```
%setup
```

This produces the following set of commands:

```
cd /usr/src/redhat/BUILD
rm -rf cdplayer-1.0
gzip -dc /usr/src/redhat/SOURCES/source-zero.tar.gz | tar -xvvf -
if [ $? -ne 0 ]; then
  exit $?
fi
cd cdplayer-1.0
cd /usr/src/redhat/BUILD/cdplayer-1.0
chown -R root.root .
chmod -R a+rX,g-w,o-w .
```

If `source-zero.tar.gz` didn't include a top-level directory, we could have made one by adding the -c option:

```
%setup -c
```

which would result in the following:

```
cd /usr/src/redhat/BUILD
rm -rf cdplayer-1.0
mkdir -p cdplayer-1.0
cd cdplayer-1.0
gzip -dc /usr/src/redhat/SOURCES/source-zero.tar.gz | tar -xvvf -
if [ $? -ne 0 ]; then
  exit $?
fi
cd /usr/src/redhat/BUILD/cdplayer-1.0
chown -R root.root .
chmod -R a+rX,g-w,o-w .
```

Of course, if the top-level directory did not match the package name, the -n option could have been added:

```
%setup -n blather
```

which results in the following:

```
cd /usr/src/redhat/BUILD
rm -rf blather
gzip -dc /usr/src/redhat/SOURCES/source-zero.tar.gz | tar -xvvf -
if [ $? -ne 0 ]; then
  exit $?
fi
cd blather
cd /usr/src/redhat/BUILD/blather
chown -R root.root .
chmod -R a+rX,g-w,o-w .
```

Or this:

```
%setup -c -n blather
```

results in the following:

```
cd /usr/src/redhat/BUILD
rm -rf blather
```

```
mkdir -p blather
cd blather
gzip -dc /usr/src/redhat/SOURCES/source-zero.tar.gz ¦ tar -xvvf -
if [ $? -ne 0 ]; then
  exit $?
fi
cd /usr/src/redhat/BUILD/blather
chown -R root.root .
chmod -R a+rX,g-w,o-w .
```

Now let's add the second source file. Things get a bit more interesting here. First, we need to identify which source tag (and, therefore, which source file) we're talking about. So we need to use either the -a or -b option, depending on the characteristics of the source archive. For this example, let's say that -a is the option we want. Adding that option, plus a 1 to point to the source file specified in the source1 tag, we have this:

```
%setup -a 1
```

Since we've already seen that using the -a or -b option results in duplicate unpacking, we need to disable the default unpacking by adding the -T option:

```
%setup -T -a 1
```

Next, we need to make sure that the top-level directory isn't deleted. Otherwise, the first source file we just unpacked would be gone. That means we need to include the -D option to prevent that from happening. Adding this final option, and including the now complete macro in our %prep script, we now have this:

```
%setup
%setup -T -D -a 1
```

This will result in the following commands:

```
cd /usr/src/redhat/BUILD
rm -rf cdplayer-1.0
gzip -dc /usr/src/redhat/SOURCES/source-zero.tar.gz ¦ tar -xvvf -
if [ $? -ne 0 ]; then
  exit $?
fi
cd cdplayer-1.0
cd /usr/src/redhat/BUILD/cdplayer-1.0
chown -R root.root .
chmod -R a+rX,g-w,o-w .
cd /usr/src/redhat/BUILD
cd cdplayer-1.0
gzip -dc /usr/src/redhat/SOURCES/source-one.tar.gz ¦ tar -xvvf -
if [ $? -ne 0 ]; then
  exit $?
fi
cd /usr/src/redhat/BUILD/cdplayer-1.0
chown -R root.root .
chmod -R a+rX,g-w,o-w .
```

So far, so good. Let's include the last source file, but with this one, we'll say that it needs to be unpacked in a subdirectory of cdplayer-1.0 called database. Can we use %setup in this case?

We could, if `source-two.tgz` creates the database subdirectory. If not, then it'll be necessary to do it by hand. For the purposes of our example, let's say that `source-two.tgz` wasn't created to include the database subdirectory, so we'll have to do it ourselves. Here's our `%prep` script now:

```
%setup
%setup -T -D -a 1
mkdir database
cd database
gzip -dc /usr/src/redhat/SOURCES/source-two.tar.gz ¦ tar -xvvf -
```

Here's the resulting script:

```
cd /usr/src/redhat/BUILD
rm -rf cdplayer-1.0
gzip -dc /usr/src/redhat/SOURCES/source-zero.tar.gz ¦ tar -xvvf -
if [ $? -ne 0 ]; then
  exit $?
fi
cd cdplayer-1.0
cd /usr/src/redhat/BUILD/cdplayer-1.0
chown -R root.root .
chmod -R a+rX,g-w,o-w .
cd /usr/src/redhat/BUILD
cd cdplayer-1.0
gzip -dc /usr/src/redhat/SOURCES/source-one.tar.gz ¦ tar -xvvf -
if [ $? -ne 0 ]; then
  exit $?
fi
mkdir database
cd database
gzip -dc /usr/src/redhat/SOURCES/source-two.tar.gz ¦ tar -xvvf -
```

The three commands we added to unpack the last set of sources were added to the end of the `%prep` script.

The bottom line to using the `%setup` macro is that you can probably get it to do what you want, but don't be afraid to tinker. And even if `%setup` can't be used, it's easy enough to add the necessary commands to do the work manually. Above all, make sure you use the `--test` option when testing your `%setup` macros, so you can see what commands they're translating to.

13.4.2. The `%patch` Macro

The `%patch` macro, as its name implies, is used to apply patches to the unpacked sources.

In the following examples, our spec file has the following `patch` tag lines:

```
patch0: patch-zero
patch1: patch-one
patch2: patch-two
```

At its simplest, the `%patch` macro can be invoked without any options:

```
%patch
```

Here are the resulting commands:

```
echo "Patch #0:"
patch -p0 -s < /usr/src/redhat/SOURCES/patch-zero
```

The %patch macro nicely displays a message showing that a patch is being applied, and then invokes the patch command to actually do the dirty work. There are two options to the patch command:

- The -p option, which directs patch to remove the specified number of slashes (and any intervening directories) from the front of any filenames specified in the patch file. In this case, nothing will be removed.

- The -s option, which directs patch to apply the patch without displaying any informational messages. Only errors from patch will be displayed.

How did the %patch macro know which patch to apply? Keep in mind that, like the source tag lines, every patch tag is numbered, starting at 0. The %patch macro, by default, applies the patch file named on the patch (or patch0) tag line.

13.4.2.1. Specifying Which patch Tag to Use

The %patch macro actually has two different ways to specify the patch tag line it is to use. The first method is to simply append the number of the desired patch tag to the end of the %patch macro itself. For example, in order to apply the patch specified on the patch2 tag line, the following %patch macro could be used:

```
%patch2
```

The other approach is to use the -P option. This option is followed by the number of the patch tag line desired. Therefore, this line is identical in function to the previous one:

```
%patch -P 2
```

Note that the -P option will not apply the file specified on the patch0 line, by default. Therefore, if you choose to use the -P option to specify patch numbers, you'll need to use the following format when applying patch 0:

```
%patch -P 0
```

13.4.2.2. -p <#>: Strip <#> Leading Slashes and Directories from patch Filenames

The -p (note the lowercase *p*!) option is sent directly to the patch command. It is followed by a number, which specifies the number of leading slashes (and the directories in between) to strip from any filenames present in the patch file. For more information on this option, consult the patch man page.

13.4.2.3. -b *<name>*: Set the Backup File Extension to *<name>*

When the patch command is used to apply a patch, unmodified copies of the files patched are renamed to end with the extension .orig. The -b option is used to change the extension used by patch. This is normally done when multiple patches are to be applied to a given file. By doing this, copies of the file as it existed prior to each patch are readily available.

13.4.2.4. -E: Remove Empty Output Files

The -E option is passed directly to the patch program. When patch is run with the -E option, any output files that are empty after the patches have been applied are removed.

Now let's take %patch on a test drive.

13.4.2.5. An Example of the %patch Macro in Action

Using the sample patch tag lines we've used throughout this section, let's put together an example and look at the resulting commands. In our example, the first patch to be applied needs to have the root directory stripped. Its %patch macro will look like this:

```
%patch -p1
```

The next patch is to be applied to files in the software's lib subdirectory, so we'll need to add a cd command to get us there. We'll also need to strip an additional directory:

```
cd lib
%patch -P 1 -p2
```

Finally, the last patch is to be applied from the software's top-level directory, so we need to cd back up a level. In addition, this patch modifies some files that were also patched the first time, so we'll need to change the backup file extension:

```
cd ..
%patch -P 2 -p1 -b .last-patch
```

Here's what the %prep script (minus any %setup macros) looks like:

```
%patch -p1
cd lib
%patch -P 1 -p2
cd ..
%patch -P 2 -p1 -b .last-patch
```

And here's what the macros expand to:

```
echo "Patch #0:"
patch -p1 -s < /usr/src/redhat/SOURCES/patch-zero
cd lib
echo "Patch #1:"
patch -p2 -s < /usr/src/redhat/SOURCES/patch-one
cd ..
echo "Patch #2:"
patch -p1 -b .last-patch -s < /usr/src/redhat/SOURCES/patch-two
```

No surprises here. Note that the `%setup` macro leaves the current working directory set to the software's top-level directory, so our `cd` commands with their relative paths will do the right thing. Of course, we have environment variables available that could be used here, too.

13.4.2.6. Compressed Patch Files

If a patch file is compressed with `gzip`, RPM will automatically decompress it before applying the patch. Here's a compressed `patch` file as specified in the spec file:

```
Patch: bother-3.5-hack.patch.gz
```

This is part of the script RPM will execute when the `%prep` section is executed:

```
echo Executing: %prep
...
echo "Patch #0:"
gzip -dc /usr/src/redhat/SOURCES/bother-3.5-hack.patch.gz ¦ patch -p1 -s
...
```

First, the `patch` file is decompressed using `gzip`. The output from `gzip` is then piped into `patch`.

That's about it for RPM's macros. Next, let's take a look at the `%files` list.

13.5. The `%files` List

The `%files` list indicates to RPM which files on the build system are to be packaged. The list consists of one file per line. The file may have one or more directives preceding it. These directives give RPM additional information about the file.

Normally, each file includes its full path. The path performs two functions. First, it specifies the file's location on the build system. Second, it denotes where the file should be placed when the package is to be installed. (This is not entirely the case when a relocatable package is being built. For more information on relocatable packages, see Chapter 15.)

For packages that create directories containing hundreds of files, it can be quite cumbersome creating a list that contains every file. To make this situation a bit easier, if the `%files` list contains a path to a directory, RPM will automatically package every file in that directory, as well as every file in each subdirectory. Shell-style globbing, or wildcard expansion, can also be used in the `%files` list.

13.6. Directives for the `%files` List

The `%files` list may contain a number of different directives. They are used to do the following:

- Identify documentation and configuration files
- Ensure that a file has the correct permissions and ownership set

■ Control which aspects of a file are to be checked during package verification

■ Eliminate some of the tedium in creating the %files list

In the %files list, one or more directives may be placed on a line, separated by spaces, before one or more filenames. Therefore, if %foo and %bar are two %files list directives, they may be applied to a file baz in the following manner:

```
%foo %bar baz
```

Now it's time to take a look at the directives that inhabit the %files list.

13.6.1. File-Related Directives

RPM processes files differently according to their types. However, RPM does not have a method of automatically determining file types. Therefore, it is up to the package builder to appropriately mark files in the %files list. This is done using one of the following directives.

Keep in mind that not every file will need to be marked. As you read the following sections, you'll see that directives are used only in special circumstances. In most packages, the majority of files in the %files list will not need to be marked.

13.6.1.1. The %doc Directive

The %doc directive flags the filename(s) that follow as being documentation. RPM keeps track of documentation files in its database so that a user can easily find information about an installed package. In addition, RPM can create a package-specific documentation directory during installation and copy documentation into it. Whether or not this additional step is taken depends on how a file is specified. Here is an example:

```
%doc README
%doc /usr/local/foonly/README
```

The file README exists in the software's top-level directory during the build and is included in the package file. When the package is installed, RPM creates a directory in the documentation directory named the same as the package (that is, *<software>-<version>-<release>*) and copies the README file there. The newly created directory and the README file are marked in the RPM database as being documentation. The default documentation directory is /usr/doc and can be changed by setting the defaultdocdir rpmrc file entry. For more information on rpmrc files, see Appendix B.

The file /usr/local/foonly/README was installed into that directory during the build and is included in the package file. When the package is installed, the README file is copied into /usr/local/foonly and marked in the RPM database as being documentation.

13.6.1.2. The `%config` Directive

The `%config` directive is used to flag the specified file as being a configuration file. RPM performs additional processing for config files when packages are erased, and during installations and upgrades. This is due to the nature of config files: They are often changed by the system administrator, and those changes should not be lost.

There is a restriction to the `%config` directive: No more than one filename may follow the `%config`. This means that the following example is the only allowable way to specify config files:

```
%config /etc/foonly
```

Note that the full path to the file, as it is installed at build time, is required.

13.6.1.3. The `%attr` Directive

The `%attr` directive permits finer control over three key file attributes:

- The file's permissions, or mode
- The file's user ID
- The file's group ID

The `%attr` directive has the following format:

```
%attr(<mode>, <user>, <group>) file
```

The mode is specified in the traditional numeric format, while the user and group are specified as a string, such as `root`. Here's a sample `%attr` directive:

```
%attr(755, root, root) foo.bar
```

This would set `foo.bar`'s permissions to `755`. The file would be owned by user root, group root. If a particular attribute does not need to be specified (usually because the file is installed with that attribute set properly), that attribute may be replaced with a dash:

```
%attr(755, -, root) foo.bar
```

The main reason to use the `%attr` directive is to permit users without root access to build packages. The techniques for doing this (and a more in-depth discussion of the `%attr` directive) can be found in Chapter 16.

13.6.1.4. The `%verify` Directive

RPM's ability to verify the integrity of the software it has installed is impressive. But sometimes it's a bit too impressive. After all, RPM can verify as many as nine different aspects of every file. The `%verify` directive can control which of these file attributes are to be checked when an RPM verification is done. Here are the attributes, along with the names used by the `%verify` directive:

- Owner (`owner`)
- Group (`group`)
- Mode (`mode`)
- MD5 Checksum (`md5`)
- Size (`size`)
- Major Number (`maj`)
- Minor Number (`min`)
- Symbolic Link String (`symlink`)
- Modification Time (`mtime`)

How is `%verify` used? Say, for instance, that a package installs device files. Since the owner of a device will change, it doesn't make sense to have RPM verify the device file's owner/group and give out a false alarm. Instead, the following `%verify` directive could be used:

```
%verify(mode md5 size maj min symlink mtime) /dev/ttyS0
```

We've left out owner and group since we'd rather RPM not verify those. (RPM will automatically exclude file attributes from verification if it doesn't make sense for the type of file. In our example, getting the MD5 checksum of a device file is an example of such a situation.) However, if all you want to do is prevent RPM from verifying one or two attributes, you can use `%verify`'s alternate syntax:

```
%verify(not owner group) /dev/ttyS0
```

This use of `%verify` produces results identical to those in the previous example.

13.6.2. Directory-Related Directives

While the two directives in this section perform different functions, each is related to directories in some way. Let's see what they do.

13.6.2.1. The `%docdir` Directive

The `%docdir` directive is used to add a directory to the list of directories that will contain documentation. RPM includes the directories `/usr/doc`, `/usr/info`, and `/usr/man` in the `%docdir` list by default.

For example, if the following line is part of the `%files` list:

```
%docdir /usr/blather
```

any files in the %files list that RPM packages from /usr/blather will be included in the package as usual, but will also be automatically flagged as documentation. This directive is handy when a package creates its own documentation directory and contains a large number of files. Let's give it a try by adding the following line to our spec file:

```
%docdir /usr/blather
```

Our %files list contains no references to the several files the package installs in the /usr/blather directory. After building the package, looking at the package's file list shows this:

```
# rpm -qlp ../RPMS/i386/blather-1.0-1.i386.rpm
...
#
```

Wait a minute: There's nothing there, not even /usr/blather! What happened?

The problem is that %docdir only directs RPM to mark the specified directory as holding documentation. It doesn't direct RPM to package any files in the directory. To do that, we need to clue RPM in to the fact that there are files in the directory that must be packaged.

One way to do this is to simply add the files to the %files list:

```
%docdir /usr/blather
/usr/blather/INSTALL
```

Looking at the package, we see that INSTALL was packaged:

```
# rpm -qlp ../RPMS/i386/blather-1.0-1.i386.rpm
...
/usr/blather/INSTALL
#
```

Directing RPM to only show the documentation files, we see that INSTALL has indeed been marked as documentation, even though the %doc directive had not been used:

```
# rpm -qdp ../RPMS/i386/blather-1.0-1.i386.rpm
...
/usr/blather/INSTALL
#
```

Of course, if you go to the trouble of adding each file to the %files list, it wouldn't be that much more work to add %doc to each one. So the way to get the most benefit from %docdir is to add another line to the %files list:

```
%docdir /usr/blather
/usr/blather
```

Since the first line directs RPM to flag any file in /usr/blather as being documentation, and the second line tells RPM to automatically package any files found in /usr/blather, every single file in there will be packaged and marked as documentation:

```
# rpm -qdp ../RPMS/i386/blather-1.0-1.i386.rpm
/usr/blather
/usr/blather/COPYING
```

```
/usr/blather/INSTALL
/usr/blather/README
...
#
```

The %docdir directive can save quite a bit of effort in creating the %files list. The only caveat is that you must be sure the directory will only contain files you want marked as documentation. Keep in mind, also, that all subdirectories of the %docdired directory will be marked as documentation directories, too.

13.6.2.2. The %dir Directive

As mentioned in section 13.5, if a directory is specified in the %files list, the contents of that directory, and the contents of every directory under it, will automatically be included in the package. While this feature can be handy (assuming that you are sure that every file under the directory should be packaged), there are times when this could be a problem.

The way to get around this is to use the %dir directive. By adding this directive to the line containing the directory, RPM will package only the directory itself, regardless of what files are in the directory at the time the package is created. Here's an example of %dir in action.

The blather-1.0 package creates the directory /usr/blather as part of its build. It also puts several files in that directory. In the spec file, the /usr/blather directory is included in the %files list:

```
%files
...
/usr/blather
...
```

There are no other entries in the %files list that have /usr/blather as part of their path. After building the package, we use RPM to look at the files in the package:

```
# rpm -qlp ../RPMS/i386/blather-1.0-1.i386.rpm
...
/usr/blather
/usr/blather/COPYING
/usr/blather/INSTALL
/usr/blather/README
...
#
```

The files present in /usr/blather at the time the package was built were included in the package automatically, without entering their names in the %files list.

However, after changing the /usr/blather line in the %files list to this:

```
%dir /usr/blather
```

and rebuilding the package, a listing of the package's files now includes only the `/usr/blather` directory:

```
# rpm -qlp ../RPMS/i386/blather-1.0-1.i386.rpm
...
/usr/blather
...
#
```

13.6.2.3. `-f <file>`: Read the `%files` List from `<file>`

The `-f` option is used to direct RPM to read the `%files` list from the named file. Like the `%files` list in a spec file, the file named using the `-f` option should contain one filename per line and also include any of the directives named in this section.

Why is it necessary to read filenames from a file rather than have the filenames in the spec file? Here's a possible reason: The filenames' paths may contain a directory name that can be determined only at build time, such as an architecture specification. The list of files, minus the variable part of the path, can be created, and `sed` can be used at build time to update the path appropriately.

It's not necessary that every filename to be packaged reside in the file. If there are any filenames present in the spec file, they will be packaged as well:

```
%files latex -f tetex-latex-skel
/usr/bin/latex
/usr/bin/pslatex
...
```

Here, the filenames present in the file `tetex-latex-skel` would be packaged, followed by every filename following the `%files` line.

13.7. The Lone Directive: `%package`

While every directive we've seen so far is used in the `%files` list, the `%package` directive is different. It is used to permit the creation of more than one package per spec file and can appear at any point in the spec file. These additional packages are known as subpackages. Subpackages are named according to the contents of the line containing the `%package` directive. The format of the package directive is this:

```
%package: <string>
```

`<string>` should be a name that describes the subpackage. This string is appended to the base package name to produce the subpackage's name. For example, if a spec file contains a name tag value of `foonly` and a `%package doc` line, the subpackage name will be `foonly-doc`.

13.7.1. -n *<string>*: Use *<string>* As the Entire Subpackage Name

As mentioned earlier, the name of a subpackage normally includes the main package name. When the -n option is added to the %package directive, it directs RPM to use the name specified on the %package line as the entire package name. In the preceding example, the following %package line would create a subpackage named foonly-doc:

```
%package doc
```

The following %package line would create a subpackage named doc:

```
%package -n doc
```

The %package directive plays another role in subpackage building: to act as a place to collect tags that are specific to a given subpackage. Any tag placed after a %package directive will apply only to that subpackage.

Finally, the name string specified by the %package directive is also used to denote which parts of the spec file are a part of that subpackage. This is done by including the string (along with the -n option, if present on the %package line) on the starting line of the section that is to be subpackage specific. Here's an example:

```
...
%package -n bar
...
%post -n bar
...
```

In this heavily edited spec file segment, a subpackage called bar has been defined. Later in the file is a postinstall script. Because it has subpackage bar's name on the %post line, the postinstall script will be part of the bar subpackage only.

For more information on building subpackages, see Chapter 18, "Creating Subpackages."

13.8. Conditionals

While the exclude and exclusive tags (excludearch, exclusivearch, excludeos, and exclusiveos) provide some control over whether a package will be built on a given architecture and/or operating system, that control is still rather coarse.

For example, what should be done if a package will build under multiple architectures, but requires slightly different %build scripts? Or what if a package requires a certain set of files under one operating system, and an entirely different set under another operating system? The architecture and operating system–specific tags discussed earlier in the chapter do nothing to help in such situations. What can be done?

One approach would be to simply create different spec files for each architecture or operating system. While it would certainly work, this approach has two problems:

- More work. The existence of multiple spec files for a given package means that the effort required to make any changes to the package is multiplied by however many different spec files there are.

- More chance for mistakes. If any work needs to be done to the spec files, the fact they are separate means it is that much easier to forget to make the necessary changes to each one. There is also the chance of introducing mistakes each time changes are made.

The other approach is to somehow permit the conditional inclusion of architecture- or operating system–specific sections of the spec file. Fortunately, the RPM designers chose this approach, and it makes multiplatform package building easier and less prone to mistakes.

We discuss multiplatform package building in depth in Chapter 19. For now, let's take a quick look at RPM's conditionals.

13.8.1. The `%ifarch` Conditional

The `%ifarch` conditional is used to begin a section of the spec file that is architecture specific. It is followed by one or more architecture specifiers, each separated by commas or whitespace. Here is an example:

```
%ifarch i386 sparc
```

The contents of the spec file following this line would be processed only by Intel x86 or Sun SPARC–based systems. However, if only this line were placed in a spec file, this is what would happen if a build were attempted:

```
# rpm -ba cdplayer-1.0.spec
Unclosed %if
Build failed.
#
```

The problem that surfaced here is that any conditional must be closed by using either `%else` or `%endif`. We'll be covering them a bit later in the chapter.

13.8.2. The `%ifnarch` Conditional

The `%ifnarch` conditional is used in a similar fashion to `%ifarch`, except that the logic is reversed. If a spec file contains a conditional block starting with `%ifarch alpha`, that block would be processed only if the build were being done on a Digital Alpha/AXP-based system. However, if the conditional block started with `%ifnarch alpha`, that block would be processed only if the build were not being done on an Alpha.

Like %ifarch, %ifnarch can be followed by one or more architectures and must be closed by %else or %endif.

13.8.3. The %ifos Conditional

The %ifos conditional is used to control RPM's spec file processing based on the build system's operating system. It is followed by one or more operating system names. A conditional block started with %ifos must be closed by %else or %endif. Here's an example:

```
%ifos linux
```

The contents of the spec file following this line would be processed only if the build were done on a Linux system.

13.8.4. The %ifnos Conditional

The %ifnos conditional is the logical complement to %ifos—that is, if a conditional starting with the line %ifnos irix is present in a spec file, the file contents after the %ifnos will not be processed if the build system is running Irix. As always, a conditional block starting with %ifnos must be closed by %else or %endif.

13.8.5. The %else Conditional

The %else conditional is placed between an %if conditional of some persuasion, and an %endif. It is used to create two blocks of spec file statements, only one of which will be used in any given case. Here's an example:

```
%ifarch alpha
make RPM_OPT_FLAGS="$RPM_OPT_FLAGS -I ."
%else
make RPM_OPT_FLAGS="$RPM_OPT_FLAGS"
%endif
```

When a build is performed on a Digital Alpha/AXP, some additional flags are added to the make command. On all other systems, these flags are not added.

13.8.6. The %endif Conditional

A %endif is used to end a conditional block of spec file statements. It can follow one of the %if conditionals, or the %else. The %endif is always needed after a conditional; otherwise the build will fail. Here's a short conditional block, ending with an %endif:

```
%ifarch i386
make INTELFLAG=-DINTEL
%endif
```

In this example, we see that the conditional block started with an %ifarch and ended with an %endif.

13.9. Summary

Now that you have some more in-depth knowledge of the spec file, let's take a look at some of RPM's additional features. In the next chapter, we'll explore how to add dependency information to a package.

14

Adding Dependency Information to a Package

Since the very first version of RPM hit the streets, one of the side effects of RPM's ease of use was that it made it easier for people to break things. Because RPM made it so simple to erase packages, it became common for people to joyfully erase packages until something broke.

Usually this only bit people once, but even once was too much of a hassle if it could be prevented. With this in mind, the RPM developers gave RPM the capability to

■ Build packages that contain information on the capabilities they require.

■ Build packages that contain information on the capabilities they provide.

■ Store this `provides` and `requires` information in the RPM database.

In addition, they made sure RPM was able to display dependency information, as well as warn users if they were attempting to do something that would break a package's dependency requirements.

With these features in place, it became more difficult for someone to unknowingly erase a package and wreak havoc on a system.

14.1. An Overview of Dependencies

We've already alluded to the underlying concept of RPM's dependency processing. It is based on two key factors:

■ Packages advertise what capabilities they provide.

■ Packages advertise what capabilities they require.

By simply checking these two types of information, you can avoid many problems. For example, if a package requires a capability that is not provided by any already-installed package, that package cannot be installed and expected to work properly.

On the other hand, if a package is to be erased, but its capabilities are required by other installed packages, then it cannot be erased without causing other packages to fail.

As you might imagine, it's not quite that simple. But adding dependency information can be easy. In fact, in most cases, it's automatic!

14.2. Automatic Dependencies

When a package is built by RPM, if any file in the package's `%files` list is a shared library, the library's soname is automatically added to the list of capabilities the package provides. The soname is the name used to determine compatibility between different versions of a library.

Note that the soname is not a filename. In fact, no aspect of RPM's dependency processing is based on filenames. Many people new to RPM assume that a failed dependency represents a missing file. This is not the case.

Remember that RPM's dependency processing is based on knowing what capabilities are provided by a package and what capabilities a package requires. We've seen how RPM automatically determines what shared library resources a package provides. But does it automatically determine what shared libraries a package requires?

Yes! RPM does this by running `ldd` on every executable program in a package's `%files` list. Since `ldd` provides a list of the shared libraries each program requires, both halves of the equation are complete—that is, the packages that make shared libraries available, and the packages that require those shared libraries, are tracked by RPM. RPM can then take that information into account when packages are installed, upgraded, or erased.

14.2.1. The Automatic Dependency Scripts

RPM uses two scripts to handle automatic dependency processing. They reside in /usr/bin and are called `find-requires` and `find-provides`. We'll take a look at them in a minute, but first let's look at why there are scripts to do this sort of thing. Wouldn't it be better to have this built into RPM itself?

Actually, creating scripts for this sort of thing is a better idea. The reason? RPM has already been ported to a variety of different operating systems. Determining what shared libraries an executable requires, and the soname of shared libraries, is simple, but the exact steps required vary widely from one operating system to another. Putting this part of RPM into a script makes it easier to port RPM.

Let's take a look at the scripts that are used by RPM under the Linux operating system.

14.2.1.1. `find-requires`: Automatically Determine Shared Library Requirements

The `find-requires` script for Linux is quite simple:

```
#!/bin/sh

# note this works for both a.out and ELF executables

ulimit -c 0

filelist='xargs -r file ¦ fgrep executable ¦ cut -d: -f1 '

for f in $filelist; do
    ldd $f ¦ awk '/=>/ { print $1 }'
done ¦ sort -u ¦ xargs -r -n 1 basename ¦ sort -u
```

This script first creates a list of executable files. Then, for each file in the list, `ldd` determines the file's shared library requirements, producing a list of sonames. Finally, the list of sonames is sanitized by removing duplicates and any paths.

14.2.1.2. `find-provides`: Automatically Determine Shared Library Sonames

The `find-provides` script for Linux is a bit more complex, but still pretty straightforward:

```
#!/bin/bash

# This script reads filenames from STDIN and outputs any relevant
# provides information that needs to be included in the package.

filelist=$(grep "\\.so" | grep -v "^/lib/ld.so" |
xargs file -L 2>/dev/null | grep "ELF.*shared object" | cut -d: -f1)

for f in $filelist; do
    soname=$(objdump -p $f | awk '/SONAME/ {print $2}')

    if [ "$soname" != "" ]; then
        if [ ! -L $f ]; then
            echo $soname
        fi
    else
echo ${f##*/}
    fi
done | sort -u
```

First, a list of shared libraries is created. Then, for each file on the list, the soname is extracted and cleaned up, and duplicates are removed.

14.2.2. Automatic Dependencies: An Example

Let's take a widely used program, `ls`, the directory lister, as an example. On a Red Hat Linux system, `ls` is part of the `fileutils` package and is installed in `/bin`. Let's play the part of RPM during `fileutils`'s package build and run `find-requires` on `/bin/ls`. Here's what we'll see:

```
# find-requires
/bin/ls
<ctrl-d>
libc.so.5
#
```

The `find-requires` script returned `libc.so.5`. Therefore, RPM should add a requirement for `libc.so.5` when the `fileutils` package is built. We can verify that RPM did add `ls`'s requirement for `libc.so.5` by using RPM's `--requires` option to display `fileutils`'s requirements:

```
# rpm -q --requires fileutils
libc.so.5
#
```

Okay, that's the first half of the equation: RPM automatically detecting a package's shared library requirements. Now let's look at the second half of the equation: RPM detecting packages that provide shared libraries. Since the `libc` package includes, among others, the shared library `/lib/libc.so.5.3.12`, RPM would obtain its soname. We can simulate this by using `find-provides` to print out the library's soname:

```
# find-provides
/lib/libc.so.5.3.12
```

```
<ctrl-d>
libc.so.5
#
```

Okay, so /lib/libc.so.5.3.12's soname is libc.so.5. Let's see if the libc package really does provide the libc.so.5 soname:

```
# rpm -q --provides libc
libm.so.5
libc.so.5
#
```

Yes, there it is, along with the soname of another library contained in the package. In this way, RPM can ensure that any package requiring libc.so.5 will have a compatible library available as long as the libc package, which provides libc.so.5, is installed.

In most cases, automatic dependencies are enough to fill the bill. However, there are circumstances when the package builder has to manually add dependency information to a package. Fortunately, RPM's approach to manual dependencies is both simple and flexible.

14.2.3. The autoreqprov Tag: Disable Automatic Dependency Processing

There may be times when RPM's automatic dependency processing is not desired. In these cases, the autoreqprov tag may be used to disable it. This tag takes a yes/no or 0/1 value. For example, to disable automatic dependency processing, the following line may be used:

```
AutoReqProv: no
```

14.3. Manual Dependencies

You might have noticed that we've been using the words *requires* and *provides* to describe the dependency relationships between packages. As it turns out, these are the exact words used in spec files to manually add dependency information. Let's look at the first tag: requires.

14.3.1. The requires Tag

We've been deliberately vague when discussing exactly what it is that a package requires. Although we've used the word *capabilities*, in fact, manual dependency requirements are always represented in terms of packages. For example, if package foo requires that package bar is installed, it's only necessary to add the following line to foo's spec file:

```
requires: bar
```

Later, when the foo package is being installed, RPM will consider foo's dependency requirements met if any version of package bar is already installed. As long as the requiring and the providing packages are installed using the same invocation of RPM, the dependency checking will succeed. For example, the command `rpm -ivh *.rpm` will properly check for dependencies, even if the requiring package ends up being installed before the providing package.

If more than one package is required, they can be added to the `requires` tag, one after another, separated by commas and/or spaces. So if package `foo` requires packages `bar` and `baz`, the following line will do the trick:

```
requires: bar, baz
```

As long as any version of `bar` and `baz` is installed, `foo`'s dependencies will be met.

14.3.1.1. Adding Version Requirements

When a package has slightly more stringent needs, it's possible to require certain versions of a package. All that's necessary is to add the desired version number, preceded by one of the following comparison operators:

- `<`   Requires a package with a version less than the specified version.
- `<=`   Requires a package with a version less than or equal to the specified version.
- `=`   Requires a package with a version equal to the specified version.
- `>=`   Requires a package with a version greater than or equal to the specified version.
- `>`   Requires a package with a version greater than the specified version.

Continuing with our example, let's suppose that the required version of package `bar` actually needs to be at least 2.7, and that the `baz` package must be version 2.1—no other version will do. Here's what the `requires` tag line would look like:

```
requires: bar >= 2.7, baz = 2.1
```

We can get even more specific and require a particular release of a package:

```
requires: bar >= 2.7-4, baz = 2.1-1
```

14.3.1.2. When Version Numbers Aren't Enough

You might think that with all these features, RPM's dependency processing can handle every conceivable situation. You'd be right, except for the problem of version numbers. RPM needs to be able to determine which version numbers are more recent than others in order to perform its version comparisons.

It's pretty simple to determine that version 1.5 is older than version 1.6. But what about 2.01 and 2.1? Or 7.6a and 7.6? There's no way for RPM to keep up with all the different version-numbering schemes in use. But there is a solution; there are two, in fact.

14.3.1.2.1. Solution Number 1: Serial Numbers

When RPM can't decipher a package's version number, it's time to pull out the `serial` tag. This tag is used to help RPM determine version number ordering. Here's a sample `serial` tag line:

```
Serial: 42
```

This line indicates that the package has the serial number 42. What does the 42 mean? Only that this version of the package is older than the same package with the serial number 41, but younger than the same package with the serial number 43. If you think of serial numbers as being nothing more than very simple version numbers, you'll be on the mark.

In order to direct RPM to look at the serial number instead of the version number when doing dependency checking, it's necessary to append an `s` to the end of the conditional operator in the `requires` tag line. So if a package requires package `foo` to have a serial number equal to 42, the following tag line would be used:

```
Requires: foo =S 42
```

If the `foo` package needs to have a serial number greater than or equal to 42, this line would work:

```
Requires: foo >=S 42
```

It might seem that using serial numbers is a lot of extra trouble, and you're right. But there is an alternative.

14.3.1.2.2. Solution Number 2: Just Say No!

If you have the option between changing the software's version-numbering scheme or using serial numbers in RPM, consider changing the version-numbering scheme. Chances are, if RPM can't figure it out, most of the people using your software can't, either. But in case you aren't the author of the software you're packaging, and its version numbering scheme is giving RPM fits, the serial tag can help you out.

14.3.2. The `conflicts` Tag

The `conflicts` tag is the logical complement to the `requires` tag. It is used to specify which packages conflict with the current package. RPM will not permit conflicting packages to be installed unless overridden with the `--nodeps` option.

The `conflicts` tag has the same format as `requires`. It accepts a real or virtual package name and can optionally include version and release specifications or a serial number.

14.3.3. The `provides` Tag

Now that you've seen how it's possible to require a package using the `requires` tag, you're probably expecting that you'll need to use the `provides` tag in every single package. After all, RPM has to get those package names from somewhere, right?

While it is true that RPM needs to have the package names available, the `provides` tag is normally not required. It would actually be redundant because the RPM database already contains the name of every package installed. There's no need to duplicate that information.

But wait! We said earlier that manual dependency requirements are always represented in terms of packages. If RPM doesn't require the package builder to use the `provides` tag to provide the package name, then what is the `provides` tag used for?

14.3.3.1. Virtual Packages

Enter the virtual package. A virtual package is nothing more than a name specified with the `provides` tag. Virtual packages are handy when a package requires a certain capability, and that capability can be provided by any one of several packages. Here's an example: In order to work properly, `sendmail` needs a local delivery agent to handle mail delivery. There are a number of different local delivery agents available: `sendmail` will work just fine with any of them.

In this case, it doesn't make sense to force the use of a particular local delivery agent; as long as one's installed, `sendmail`'s requirements will have been satisfied. So `sendmail`'s package builder adds the following line to `sendmail`'s spec file:

```
requires: lda
```

There is no package with that name available, so `sendmail`'s requirements must be met with a virtual package. The creators of the various local delivery agents indicate that their packages satisfy the requirements of the `lda` virtual package by adding the following line to their packages' spec files:

```
provides: lda
```

> **NOTE**
>
> Note that virtual packages may not have version numbers.

Now, when `sendmail` is installed, as long as there is a package installed that provides the `lda` virtual package, there will be no problem.

14.4. To Summarize

RPM's dependency processing is based on tracking the capabilities a package provides and the capabilities a package requires. A package's requirements can come from two places:

- Shared library requirements, automatically determined by RPM
- The `requires` tag line, manually added to the package's spec file

These requirements can be viewed by using RPM's `--requires` query option. A specific requirement can be viewed by using the `--whatrequires` query option. Both options are fully described in Chapter 5, "Getting Information About Packages."

The capabilities a package provides can come from three places:

- Shared library sonames, automatically determined by RPM
- The `provides` tag line, manually added to the package's spec file
- The package's name (and optionally, the version/serial number)

The first two types of information can be viewed by using RPM's `--provides` query option. A specific capability can be viewed by using the `--whatprovides` query option. Both options are fully described in Chapter 5.

The package name and version are not considered capabilities that are explicitly provided. Therefore, if a search using `--provides` or `--whatprovides` comes up dry, try simply looking for a package by that name.

As you've probably gathered by now, using manual dependencies requires some level of synchronization between packages. This can be tricky, particularly if you're not responsible for both packages. But RPM's dependency processing can make life easier for your users.

15

Making a Relocatable Package

RPM has the capability to give users some latitude in deciding where packages are to be installed on their systems. However, package builders must first design their packages to give users this freedom.

That's all well and good, but why would the ability to relocate a package be all that important?

15.1. Why Relocatable Packages?

One of the many problems that plague a system administrator's life is disk space. Usually, there's not enough of it, and if there is enough, chances are it's in the wrong place. Here's a hypothetical example:

- Some new software comes out and is desired greatly by the user community.

- The system administrator carefully reviews the software's installation documentation prior to doing the installation. (Hey, we said it was hypothetical!) She notes that the software, all 150MB of it, installs into /opt.

- Frowning, the sysadmin fires off a quick df command:

```
# df
Filesystem     1024-blocks     Used   Available   Capacity   Mounted on
/dev/sda0          100118      28434       66514      30%      /
/dev/sda6          991995     365527      575218      39%      /usr
#
```

  Bottom line: There's no way 150MB of new software is going to fit on the root filesystem.

- Sighing heavily, the sysadmin ponders what to do next. If only there were some way to install the software somewhere on the /usr filesystem.

It doesn't have to be this way. RPM has the ability to make packages that can be installed with a user-specified prefix that dictates where the software will actually be placed. By making packages relocatable, the package builder can make life easier for sysadmins everywhere. But what exactly is a relocatable package?

A *relocatable package* is a package that is standard in every way, save one. When a prefix tag is added to a spec file, RPM will attempt to build a relocatable package.

Note the word *attempt*. A few conditions must be met before a relocatable package can be built successfully, and this chapter covers them all. But first, let's look at exactly how RPM can relocate a package.

15.2. The prefix tag: Relocation Central

The best way to explain how the prefix tag is used is to step through an example. Here's a sample prefix tag:

```
Prefix: /opt
```

In this example, the `prefix` path is defined as `/opt`. This means that, by default, the package will install its files under `/opt`. Let's assume that the spec file contains the following line in its `%files` list:

```
/opt/bin/baz
```

If the package is installed without any relocation, this file will be installed in `/opt/bin`. This is identical to how a nonrelocatable package is installed.

However, if the package is to be relocated on installation, the path of every file in the `%files` list is modified according to the following steps:

1. The part of the file's path that corresponds to the path specified on the `prefix` tag line is removed.
2. The user-specified relocation prefix is prepended to the file's path.

Using our `/opt/bin/baz` file as an example, let's assume that the user installing the package wishes to override the default prefix (`/opt`) with a new prefix, say `/usr/local/opt`. Following the previous steps, we first remove the original prefix from the file's path:

```
/opt/bin/baz becomes /bin/baz
```

Next, we add the user-specified prefix to the front of the remaining part of the filename:

```
/usr/local/opt + /bin/baz = /usr/local/opt/bin/baz
```

Now that the file's new path has been created, RPM installs the file normally. This part of it seems simple enough, and it is. But as mentioned earlier, there are a few things the package builder needs to consider before getting on the relocatable package bandwagon.

15.3. Relocatable Wrinkles: Things to Consider

While it's certainly no problem to add a `prefix` tag line to a spec file, it's necessary to consider a few other issues:

■ Every file in the `%files` list must start with the path specified on the `prefix` tag line.

■ The software must be written such that it can operate properly if relocated. Absolute symlinks are a prime example of this.

■ Other software must not rely on the relocatable package being installed in any particular location.

Let's cover each of these issues, starting with the `%files` list.

15.3.1. `%files` List Restrictions

As mentioned earlier, each file in the `%files` list must start with the relocation prefix. If this isn't done, the build will fail:

```
# rpm -ba cdplayer-1.0.spec
* Package: cdplayer
+ umask 022
+ echo Executing: %prep
...
Binary Packaging: cdplayer-1.0-1
Package Prefix = usr/local
File doesn't match prefix (usr/local): /usr/doc/cdplayer-1.0-1
File not found: /usr/doc/cdplayer-1.0-1
Build failed.
#
```

In our example, the build proceeded normally until the time came to create the binary package file. At that point RPM detected the problem. The error message says it all: The prefix line in the spec file (`/usr/local`) was not present in the first part of the file's path (`/usr/doc/cdplayer-1.0-1`). This stopped the build in its tracks.

The fact that every file in a relocatable package must be installed under the directory specified in the prefix line raises some issues. For example, what about a program that reads a configuration file normally kept in `/etc`? This question leads right into our next section.

15.3.2. Relocatable Packages Must Contain Relocatable Software

While this section's title seems pretty obvious, it's not always easy to tell if a particular piece of software can be relocated. Let's take a look at the question raised at the end of the previous section. If a program has been written to read its configuration file from `/etc`, there are three possible approaches to making that program relocatable:

- Set the prefix to `/etc` and package everything under `/etc`.
- Package everything somewhere other than `/etc` and leave out the config file entirely.
- Modify the program.

The first approach would certainly work from a purely technical standpoint, but not many people would be happy with a program that installed itself in `/etc`. So this approach isn't viable.

The second approach might be more appropriate, but it forces users to complete the install by having them create the config file themselves. If RPM's goal is to make software easier to install and remove, this is not a viable approach either!

The final approach might be the best. Once the program is installed, when the rewritten software is first run, it can see that no configuration file exists in `/etc` and create one. However, even though this would work, when the time came to erase the package, the config file would be left behind. RPM had never installed it, so RPM couldn't get rid of it. There's also the fact that this approach is probably more labor intensive than most package builders would like.

None of these approaches are very appealing, are they? Some software just doesn't relocate very well. In general, the following things are warning signs that relocation is going to be a problem:

■ The software contains one or more files that must be installed in specific directories.

■ The software refers to system files using relative paths (which is really just another way of saying that the software must be installed in a particular directory).

If these kinds of issues crop up, making the software relocatable is going to be tough.

15.3.3. The Relocatable Software Is Referenced by Other Software

Even assuming that the software is written so that it can be put in a relocatable package, there still might be a problem, which relates not to the relocatable software itself, but to other programs that reference the relocatable software.

For example, there are times when a package needs to execute other programs. This might include backup software that needs to send mail, or a communications program that needs to compress files. If these underlying programs were relocatable, and not installed where other packages expect them, they would be of little use.

Granted, this isn't a common problem, but it can happen. And for the package builder interested in building relocatable packages, it's an issue that needs to be explored. Unfortunately, this type of problem can be the hardest to find.

If, however, a software product has been found to be relocatable, the mechanics of actually building a relocatable package are pretty straightforward. Let's give it a try.

15.4. Building a Relocatable Package

For this example, we'll use our tried-and-true `cdplayer` application. Let's start by reviewing the spec file for possible problems:

```
#
# Sample spec file for cdplayer app...
#
Summary:A CD player app that rocks!
Name: cdplayer
...
%files
%doc README
/usr/local/bin/cdp
/usr/local/bin/cdplay
%doc /usr/local/man/man1/cdp.1
%config /etc/cdp-config
```

Everything looks all right, except for the `%files` list. There are files in `/usr/local/bin`, a man page in `/usr/local/man/man1`, and a config file in `/etc`. The prefix `/usr/local` would work pretty well, except for that `cdp-config` file.

For the sake of this first build, we'll declare the config file unnecessary and remove it from the %files list. We'll then add a prefix tag line, setting the prefix to /usr/local. After these changes are made, let's try a build:

```
# rpm -ba cdplayer-1.0.spec
* Package: cdplayer
+ umask 022
+ echo Executing: %prep
Executing: %prep
+ cd /usr/src/redhat/BUILD
+ cd /usr/src/redhat/BUILD
+ rm -rf cdplayer-1.0
+ gzip -dc /usr/src/redhat/SOURCES/cdplayer-1.0.tgz
...
Binary Packaging: cdplayer-1.0-1
Package Prefix = usr/local
File doesn't match prefix (usr/local): /usr/doc/cdplayer-1.0-1
File not found: /usr/doc/cdplayer-1.0-1
Build failed.
#
```

The build proceeded normally up to the point of actually creating the binary package. The Package Prefix = usr/local line confirms that RPM picked up our prefix tag line. But the build stopped—and on a file called /usr/doc/cdplayer-1.0-1. But that file isn't even in the %files list. What's going on?

Take a closer look at the %files list. See the line that reads %doc README? In section 13.6.1 in Chapter 13, "Inside the Spec File," we discussed how the %doc directive creates a directory under /usr/doc. That's the file that killed the build—the directory created by the %doc directive.

Let's temporarily remove that line from the %files list and try again:

```
# rpm -ba cdplayer-1.0.spec
* Package: cdplayer
+ umask 022
+ echo Executing: %prep
Executing: %prep
+ cd /usr/src/redhat/BUILD
+ cd /usr/src/redhat/BUILD
+ rm -rf cdplayer-1.0
+ gzip -dc /usr/src/redhat/SOURCES/cdplayer-1.0.tgz
...
Binary Packaging: cdplayer-1.0-1
Package Prefix = usr/local
Finding dependencies...
Requires (2): libc.so.5 libncurses.so.2.0
bin/cdp
bin/cdplay
man/man1/cdp.1
90 blocks
Generating signature: 0
Wrote: /usr/src/redhat/RPMS/i386/cdplayer-1.0-1.i386.rpm
+ umask 022
+ echo Executing: %clean
```

```
Executing: %clean
+ cd /usr/src/redhat/BUILD
+ cd cdplayer-1.0
+ exit 0
Source Packaging: cdplayer-1.0-1
cdplayer-1.0.spec
cdplayer-1.0.tgz
82 blocks
Generating signature: 0
Wrote: /usr/src/redhat/SRPMS/cdplayer-1.0-1.src.rpm
#
```

The build completed normally. Note how the files to be placed in the binary package file are listed, minus the prefix /usr/local. Some of you might be wondering why the cdp.1 file didn't cause problems. After all, it had a %doc directive, too. The answer lies in the way the file was specified. Since the file was specified using an absolute path, and that path started with the prefix /usr/local, there was no problem. A more complete discussion of the %doc directive can be found in section 13.6.1 in Chapter 13.

15.4.1. Tying Up the Loose Ends

In the course of building this package, we ran into two hitches:

- ■ The config file cdp-config couldn't be installed in /etc.
- ■ The README file could not be packaged using the %doc directive.

Both of these issues are due to the fact that the files' paths do not start with the default prefix path /usr/local. Does this mean that this package cannot be relocated? Possibly, but there are two options to consider. The first option is to review the prefix. For our example, if we chose the prefix /usr instead of /usr/local, the README file could be packaged using the %doc directive since the default documentation directory is /usr/doc. Another approach would be to use the %docdir directive to define another documentation-holding directory somewhere along the prefix path. (For more information on the %docdir directive, see section 13.6.2 in Chapter 13.)

This approach wouldn't work for /etc/cdp-config, though. To package that file, we'd need to resort to more extreme measures. Basically, this approach would entail packaging the file in an acceptable directory (something under /usr/local) and using the %post postinstall script to move the file to /etc. Pointing a symlink at the config file is another possibility.

Of course, this approach has some problems. First, you'll need to write a %postun script to undo what the %post script does. (Install and erase-time scripts have an environment variable, RPM_INSTALL_PREFIX, that can be used to write scripts that are able to act appropriately if the package is relocated. See section 13.3.2 in Chapter 13 for more information.) A %verifyscript that made sure the files were in place would be nice, too. Second, because the file or symlink wasn't installed by RPM, there's no entry for it in the RPM database. This reduces the utility of RPM's -c and -d options when issuing queries. Finally, if you actually move files around using the %post script, the files you move will not verify properly, and when the package is erased, your users will get some disconcerting messages when RPM can't find the moved files to erase them. If you have to resort to these kinds of tricks, it's probably best to forget trying to make the package relocatable.

15.4.2. Test-Driving a Relocatable Package

Looks like cdplayer is a poor candidate for being made relocatable. However, since we did get a hamstrung version to build successfully, we can use it to show how to test a relocatable package. First, let's see if the binary package file's prefix has been recorded properly. We can do this by using the --queryformat option to RPM's query mode:

```
# rpm -qp --queryformat '%{DEFAULTPREFIX}\n' cdplayer-1.0-1.i386.rpm
/usr/local
#
```

The DEFAULTPREFIX tag directs RPM to display the prefix used during the build. As we can see, it's /usr/local, just as we intended. The --queryformat option is discussed in section 5.2.2 of Chapter 5, "Getting Information About Packages."

So it looks like we have a relocatable package. Let's try a couple installs and see if we really can install it in different locations. First, let's try a regular install with no prefix specified:

```
# rpm -Uvh cdplayer-1.0-1.i386.rpm
cdplayer ##############################################
#
```

That seemed to work well enough. Let's see if the files went where we intended:

```
# ls -al /usr/local/bin
total 558
-rwxr-xr-x 1 root root 40739 Oct 7 13:23 cdp*
lrwxrwxrwx 1 root root 18 Oct 7 13:40 cdplay -> /usr/local/bin/cdp*
...
# ls -al /usr/local/man/man1
total 9
-rwxr-xr-x 1 root root 4550 Oct 7 13:23 cdp.1*
...
#
```

Looks good. Let's erase the package and reinstall it with a different prefix:

```
# rpm -e cdplayer
# rpm -Uvh --prefix /usr/foonly/blather cdplayer-1.0-1.i386.rpm
cdplayer ##############################################
#
```

Note that directories foonly and blather didn't exist prior to installing cdplayer.

RPM has another tag that can be used with the --queryformat option. It's called INSTALLPREFIX, and using it displays the prefix under which a package was installed. Let's give it a try:

```
# rpm -q --queryformat '%{INSTALLPREFIX}\n' cdplayer
/usr/foonly/blather
#
```

As you can see, it displays the prefix you entered on the command line. Let's see if the files were installed as directed:

```
# cd /usr/foonly/blather/
# ls -al
total 2
drwxr-xr-x 2 root root 1024 Oct  7 13:45 bin/
drwxr-xr-x 3 root root 1024 Oct  7 13:45 man/
#
```

So far, so good—the proper directories are there. Let's look at the man page first:

```
# cd /usr/foonly/blather/man/man1/
# ls -al
total 5
-rwxr-xr-x 1 root root 4550 Oct  7 13:23 cdp.1*
#
```

That looks okay. Now on to the files in bin:

```
# cd /usr/foonly/blather/bin
# ls -al
total 41
-rwxr-xr-x 1 root root 40739 Oct  7 13:23 cdp*
lrwxrwxrwx 1 root root    18 Oct  7 13:45 cdplay -> /usr/local/bin/cdp
#
```

Uh-oh. That cdplay symlink isn't right. What happened? If we look at cdplayer's makefile, we see the answer:

```
install: cdp cdp.1.Z
...
ln -s /usr/local/bin/cdp /usr/local/bin/cdplay
```

Ah, when the software is installed during RPM's build process, the makefile sets up the symbolic link. Looking back at the %files list, we see cdplay listed. RPM blindly packaged the symlink, complete with its nonrelocatable string. This is why we mentioned absolute symlinks as a prime example of nonrelocatable software.

Fortunately, this problem isn't that difficult to fix. All we need to do is change the line in the makefile that creates the symlink from this:

```
ln -s /usr/local/bin/cdp /usr/local/bin/cdplay
```

to this:

```
ln -s ./cdp /usr/local/bin/cdplay
```

Now cdplay will always point to cdp, no matter where it's installed. When building relocatable packages, relative symlinks are your friend!

After rebuilding the package, let's see if our modifications have the desired effect. First, a normal install with the default prefix:

```
# rpm -Uvh --nodeps cdplayer-1.0-1.i386.rpm
cdplayer #################################################
# cd /usr/local/bin/
# ls -al cdplay
lrwxrwxrwx 1 root root 18 Oct 8 22:32 cdplay -> ./cdp*
```

Next, we'll try a second install using the --prefix option (after we first delete the original package):

```
# rpm -e cdplayer
# rpm -Uvh --nodeps --prefix /a/dumb/prefix cdplayer-1.0-1.i386.rpm
cdplayer #################################################
# cd /a/dumb/prefix/bin/
# ls -al cdplay
lrwxrwxrwx 1 root root 30 Oct 8 22:34 cdplay -> ./cdp*
#
```

As you can see, the trickiest part about building relocatable packages is making sure the software you're packaging is up to the task. Once that part of the job is done, the actual modifications are straightforward.

16

Making a Package That Can Build Anywhere

Although RPM makes building packages as easy as possible, some of the default design decisions might not work well in a particular situation. Here are two situations where RPM's method of package building may cause problems:

■ You are unable to dedicate a system to RPM package building, or the software you're packaging would disrupt the build system's operation if it were installed.

■ You would like to package software, but you don't have root access to an appropriate build system.

Either of these situations can be resolved by directing RPM to build, install, and package the software in a different area on your build system. It requires a bit of additional effort to accomplish this, but taken a step at a time, it is not dificult. Basically, the process can be summed up by addressing the following steps:

■ Writing the package's spec file to support a build root

■ Directing RPM to build software in a user-specified build area

■ Specifying file attributes that RPM needs to set on installation

The methods discussed here are not required in every situation. For example, a system administrator developing a package on a production system may only need to add support for a build root. On the other hand, a student wishing to build a package on a university system will need to get around the lack of root access by implementing every method described here.

16.1. Using Build Roots in a Package

Part of the process of packaging software with RPM is to actually build the software and install it on the build system. The installation of software can be accomplished only by someone with root access, so a nonprivileged user will certainly need to handle RPM's installation phase differently. There are times, however, when even a person with root access will not want RPM to copy new files into the system's directories. As mentioned earlier, the reason might be due to the fact that the software being packaged is already in use on the build system. Another reason might be as mundane as not having enough free space available to perform the install into the default directories.

Whatever the reason, RPM provides the capability to direct a given package to install into an alternate root. This alternate root is known as a *build root*. Several requirements must be met in order for a build root to be utilized:

■ A default build root must be defined in the package's spec file.

■ The installation method used by the software being packaged must be able to support installation in an alternate root.

The first part is easy. It entails adding the following line to the spec file:

```
BuildRoot: <root>
```

Of course, you would replace *<root>* with the name of the directory in which you'd like the software to install. (Keep in mind that the build root can be overridden at build time using the `--buildroot` option or the `buildroot` `rpmrc` file entry. See Chapter 12, "rpm -b Command Reference," for more details.) If, for example, you specify a build root of `/tmp/foo`, and the software you're packaging installs a file `bar` in `/usr/bin`, you'll find `bar` residing in `/tmp/foo/usr/bin` after the build.

A note for you nonroot package builders: Make sure you can actually write to the build root you specify! Those of you with root access should also make sure you choose your build root carefully. For a variety of reasons, it's not a good idea to declare a build root of `/`. We'll get into the reasons shortly.

The final requirement for adding build root support is to make sure the software's installation method can support installing into an alternate root. The difficulty in meeting this requirement can range from dead simple to nearly impossible. There are probably as many different ways of approaching this as there are packages to build. But in general, some variant of the following approach is used:

■ The environment variable `RPM_BUILD_ROOT` is set by RPM and contains the value of the build root to be used when the software is built and installed.

■ The `%install` section of the spec file is modified to use `RPM_BUILD_ROOT` as part of the installation process.

■ If the software is installed using `make`, the makefile is modified to use `RPM_BUILD_ROOT` and to create any directories that may not exist at installation time.

Here's an example of how these components work together to utilize a build root. First, there's the definition of the build root in the spec file:

```
BuildRoot: /tmp/cdplayer
```

This line defines the build root as being `/tmp/cdplayer`. All the files installed by this software will be placed under the `cdplayer` directory. Next is the spec file's `%install` section:

```
%install
make ROOT="$RPM_BUILD_ROOT" install
```

Since the software we're packaging uses `make` to perform the actual install, we simply define the environment variable `ROOT` to be the path defined by `RPM_BUILD_ROOT`. So far, so good. Things really start to get interesting in the software's makefile, though:

```
install: cdp cdp.1.Z
# chmod 755 cdp
# cp cdp /usr/local/bin
install -m 755 -o 0 -g 0 -d $(ROOT)/usr/local/bin/
install -m 755 -o 0 -g 0 cdp $(ROOT)/usr/local/bin/cdp
# ln -s /usr/local/bin/cdp /usr/local/bin/cdplay
ln -s ./cdp $(ROOT)/usr/local/bin/cdplay
# cp cdp.1 /usr/local/man/man1
install -m 755 -o 0 -g 0 -d $(ROOT)/usr/local/man/man1/
install -m 755 -o 0 -g 0 cdp.1 $(ROOT)/usr/local/man/man1/cdp.1
```

In this example, the commented lines were the original ones. The uncommented lines perform the same function, but also support installation in the root specified by the environment variable ROOT.

One point worth noting is that the makefile now takes extra pains to make sure the proper directory structure exists before installing any files. This is often necessary because build roots are deleted, in most cases, after the software has been packaged. This is why install is used with the -d option: to make sure the necessary directories have been created.

Let's see how it works:

```
# rpm -ba cdplayer-1.0.spec
* Package: cdplayer
Executing: %prep
+ cd /usr/src/redhat/BUILD
...
+ exit 0
Executing: %build
+ cd /usr/src/redhat/BUILD
+ cd cdplayer-1.0
...
+ exit 0
+ umask 022
Executing: %install
+ cd /usr/src/redhat/BUILD
+ cd cdplayer-1.0
+ make ROOT=/tmp/cdplayer install
install -m 755 -o 0 -g 0 -d /tmp/cdplayer/usr/local/bin/
install -m 755 -o 0 -g 0 cdp /tmp/cdplayer/usr/local/bin/cdp
ln -s ./cdp /tmp/cdplayer/usr/local/bin/cdplay
install -m 755 -o 0 -g 0 -d /tmp/cdplayer/usr/local/man/man1/
install -m 755 -o 0 -g 0 cdp.1 /tmp/cdplayer/usr/local/man/man1/cdp.1
+ exit 0
Executing: special doc
+ cd /usr/src/redhat/BUILD
+ cd cdplayer-1.0
+ DOCDIR=/tmp/cdplayer//usr/doc/cdplayer-1.0-1
+ rm -rf /tmp/cdplayer//usr/doc/cdplayer-1.0-1
+ mkdir -p /tmp/cdplayer//usr/doc/cdplayer-1.0-1
+ cp -ar README /tmp/cdplayer//usr/doc/cdplayer-1.0-1
+ exit 0
Binary Packaging: cdplayer-1.0-1
Finding dependencies...
Requires (2): libc.so.5 libncurses.so.2.0
usr/doc/cdplayer-1.0-1
usr/doc/cdplayer-1.0-1/README
usr/local/bin/cdp
usr/local/bin/cdplay
usr/local/man/man1/cdp.1
93 blocks
Generating signature: 0
Wrote: /usr/src/redhat/RPMS/i386/cdplayer-1.0-1.i386.rpm
+ umask 022
+ echo Executing: %clean
Executing: %clean
+ cd /usr/src/redhat/BUILD
```

```
+ cd cdplayer-1.0
+ exit 0
Source Packaging: cdplayer-1.0-1
cdplayer-1.0.spec
cdplayer-1.0.tgz
82 blocks
Generating signature: 0
Wrote: /usr/src/redhat/SRPMS/cdplayer-1.0-1.src.rpm
#
```

Looking over the output from the %install section, we first see that the RPM_BUILD_ROOT environment variable in the make install command has been replaced with the path specified earlier in the spec file on the BuildRoot: line. The ROOT environment variable used in the makefile now has the appropriate value, as can be seen in the various install commands that follow.

Note also that we use install's -d option to ensure that every directory in the path exists before we actually install the software. Unfortunately, we can't do this and install the file in one command.

Looking at the section labeled Executing: special doc, we find that RPM is doing something similar for us. It starts by making sure there is no preexisting documentation directory. Next, RPM creates the documentation directory and copies files into it.

The remainder of this example is identical to that of a package being built without a build root being specified. However, although the output is identical, there is one crucial difference. When the binary package is created, instead of simply using each line in the %files list verbatim, RPM prepends the build root path first. If this weren't done, RPM would attempt to find the files, relative to the system's root directory, and would, of course, fail. Because of the automatic prepending of the build root, it's important to not include the build root path in any %files list entry. Otherwise, the files would not be found by RPM, and the build would fail.

Although RPM has to go through a bit of extra effort to locate the files to be packaged, the resulting binary package is indistinguishable from the same package created without using a build root.

16.1.1. Some Things to Consider

Once the necessary modifications have been made to support a build root, it's necessary for the package builder to keep some issues in mind. The first is that the build root specified in the spec file can be overridden. RPM will set the build root (and therefore, the value of $RPM_BUILD_ROOT) to one of the following values:

- The value of buildroot in the spec file
- The value of buildroot in an rpmrc file
- The value following the --buildroot option on the command line

Because of this, it's important that the spec file and the makefile be written in such a way that no assumptions about the build root are made. The main issue is that the build root must not be hard-coded anywhere. Always use the `RPM_BUILD_ROOT` environment variable!

Another issue to keep in mind is cleaning up after the build. Once software builds and is packaged successfully, it's probably no longer necessary to leave the build root in place. Therefore, it's a good idea to include the necessary commands in the spec file's `%clean` section. Here's an example:

```
%clean
rm -rf $RPM_BUILD_ROOT
```

Since RPM executes the `%clean` section after the binary package has been created, it's the perfect place to delete the build root tree. In this example, that's exactly what we're doing. We're also doing the right thing by using `RPM_BUILD_ROOT` instead of a hard-coded path.

The last issue to keep in mind relates to the `%clean` section we just created. At the start of the chapter, we mentioned that it's not a good idea to define a build root of `/`. The `%clean` section is why: If the build root were set to `/`, the `%clean` section would blow away your root filesystem! Keep in mind that this can bite you, even if the package's spec file doesn't specify `/` as a build root. It's possible to use the `--buildroot` option to specify a dangerous build root, too:

```
# rpm -ba --buildroot / cdplayer-1.0.spec
```

But for all the possible hazards using build roots can pose for the careless, it's the only way to prevent a build from disrupting the operation of certain packages on the build system. And for the person wanting to build packages without root access, it's the first of three steps necessary to accomplish the task. The next step is to direct RPM to build the software in a directory other than RPM's default one.

16.2. Having RPM Use a Different Build Area

While RPM's build root requires a certain amount of spec file and makefile tweaking in order to get it working properly, directing RPM to perform the build in a different directory is a snap. The hardest part is to create the directories RPM will use during the build process.

16.2.1. Setting Up a Build Area

RPM's build area consists of five directories in the top level:

- The `BUILD` directory is where the software is unpacked and built.
- The `RPMS` directory is where the newly created binary package files are written.
- The `SOURCES` directory contains the original sources, patches, and icon files.
- The `SPECS` directory contains the spec files for each package to be built.
- The `SRPMS` directory is where the newly created source package files are written.

The description of the RPMS directory is missing one key point. Since the binary package files are specific to an architecture, the directory actually contains one or more subdirectories, one for each architecture. It is in these subdirectories that RPM will write the binary package files.

Let's start by creating the directories. We can even do it with one command:

```
% pwd
/home/ed
% mkdir mybuild\
? mybuild/BUILD\
? mybuild/RPMS\
? mybuild/RPMS/i386\
? mybuild/SOURCES\
? mybuild/SPECS\
? mybuild/SRPMS
%
```

That's all there is to it. You might have noticed that we created a subdirectory to RPMS called i386. This is the architecture-specific subdirectory for Intel x86-based systems, which is our sample build system.

The next step in getting RPM to use a different build area is telling RPM where the new build area is. And it's almost as easy as creating the build area itself.

16.2.2. Directing RPM to Use the New Build Area

All that's required to get RPM to start using the new build area is to define an alternate value for topdir in an rpmrc file. For the nonroot user, this means putting the following line in a file called .rpmrc, located in your home directory:

```
topdir: <path>
```

By replacing *<path>* with the path to the new build area's top-level directory, RPM will attempt to use it the next time a build is performed. Using our newly created build area as an example, we'll set topdir to /home/ed/mybuild:

```
topdir: /home/ed/mybuild
```

That's all there is to it. Now it's time to try a build.

16.2.3. Performing a Build in a New Build Area

In the following example, a nonroot user attempts to build the cdplayer package in a personal build area. If the user has modified rpmrc file entries to change the default build area, the command used to start the build is just like the one used by a root user. Otherwise, the --buildroot option will need to be used:

```
% cd /home/ed/mybuild/SPECS
% rpm -ba --buildroot /home/ed/mybuildroot cdplayer-1.0.spec
* Package: cdplayer
```

```
+ umask 022
Executing: %prep
+ cd /home/ed/mybuild/BUILD
+ cd /home/ed/mybuild/BUILD
+ rm -rf cdplayer-1.0
+ gzip -dc /home/ed/mybuild/SOURCES/cdplayer-1.0.tgz
+ tar -xvvf -
drwxrwxr-x root/users 0 Aug 20 20:58 1996 cdplayer-1.0/
-rw-r--r-- root/users 17982 Nov 10 01:10 1995 cdplayer-1.0/COPYING
...
+ cd /home/ed/mybuild/BUILD/cdplayer-1.0
+ chmod -R a+rX,g-w,o-w .
+ exit 0
Executing: %build
+ cd /home/ed/mybuild/BUILD
+ cd cdplayer-1.0
+ make
gcc -Wall -O2 -c -I/usr/include/ncurses cdp.c
...
Executing: %install
+ cd /home/ed/mybuild/BUILD
+ make ROOT=/home/ed/mybuildroot/cdplayer install
install -m 755 -o 0 -g 0 -d /home/ed/mybuildroot/cdplayer/usr/local/bin/
install: /home/ed/mybuildroot/cdplayer: Operation not permitted
install: /home/ed/mybuildroot/cdplayer/usr: Operation not permitted
install: /home/ed/mybuildroot/cdplayer/usr/local: Operation not permitted
install: /home/ed/mybuildroot/cdplayer/usr/local/bin: Operation not permitted
install: /home/ed/mybuildroot/cdplayer/usr/local/bin/: Operation not permitted
make: *** [install] Error 1
Bad exit status
%
```

Things started out pretty well. The %prep section of the spec file unpacked the sources into the new build area, as did the %build section. The build was proceeding normally in the user-specified build area, and root access was not required. In the %install section, however, things started to fall apart. What happened?

Take a look at that install command. The two options, -o 0 and -g 0, dictate that the directories to be created in the build root are to be owned by the root account. Since the user performing this build did not have root access, the install failed, and rightly so.

Okay, let's remove the offending options and see where that gets us. Here's the install section of the makefile after our modifications:

```
install: cdp cdp.1.Z
install -m 755 -d $(ROOT)/usr/local/bin/
install -m 755 cdp $(ROOT)/usr/local/bin/cdp
rm -f $(ROOT)/usr/local/bin/cdplay
ln -s ./cdp $(ROOT)/usr/local/bin/cdplay
install -m 755 -d $(ROOT)/usr/local/man/man1/
install -m 755 cdp.1 $(ROOT)/usr/local/man/man1/cdp.1
```

We'll spare you having to read through another build, but this time it completed successfully. Now, let's put our sysadmin hat on and install the newly built package:

```
# rpm -ivh cdplayer-1.0-1.i386.rpm
cdplayer ##################################################
#
```

Well, that was easy enough. Let's take a look at some of the files and make sure everything looks okay. We know there are some files installed in /usr/local/bin, so let's check those:

```
# ls -al /usr/local/bin
-rwxr-xr-x 1 ed ed 40739 Sep 13 20:16 cdp*
lrwxrwxrwx 1 ed ed 47 Sep 13 20:34 cdplay -> ./cdp*
#
```

Looks pretty good. Wait a minute! What's up with the owner and group? The answer is simple: User ed ran the build, which executed the makefile, which ran install, which created the files. Since ed created the files, they are owned by him.

This brings up an interesting point. Software must be installed with very specific file ownership and permissions. But a nonroot user can't create files that are owned by anyone other than himself or herself. What is a nonroot user to do?

16.3. Specifying File Attributes

In cases where the package builder cannot create the files to be packaged with the proper ownership and permissions, the %attr macro can be used to make things right.

16.3.1. %attr: How Does It Work?

The %attr macro has the following format:

```
%attr(<mode>, <user>, <group>) <file>
```

- ■ *<mode>* is represented in traditional numeric fashion.
- ■ *<user>* is specified by the login name of the user. Numeric UIDs are not used, for reasons we'll explore in a moment.
- ■ *<group>* is specified by the group's name, as entered in /etc/group. Numeric GIDs are not used, either. Yes, we'll be discussing that, too!
- ■ *<file>* represents the file. Shell-style globbing is supported.

There are a couple other wrinkles to using the %attr macro. If a particular file attribute doesn't need to be specified, that attribute can be replaced with a dash (-), and %attr will not change it. Say, for instance, that a package's files are installed with the permissions correctly set, as they almost always are. Instead of having to go to the trouble of entering the permissions for each and every file, each file can have the same %attr:

```
%attr(-, root, root)
```

This works for user and group specifications, as well.

The other wrinkle is that although we've been showing the three file attributes separated by commas, in reality they could be separated by spaces as well. Whichever delimiter you choose, it pays to be consistent throughout a spec file.

Let's fix up cdplayer with a liberal sprinkling of %attrs. Here's what the %files list looks like after we've had our way with it:

```
%files
%attr(-, root, root) %doc README
%attr(4755, root, root) /usr/local/bin/cdp
%attr(-, root, root) /usr/local/bin/cdplay
%attr(-, root, rot) /usr/local/man/man1/cdp.1
```

A couple points are worth noting here. The line for README shows that multiple macros can be used on a line—in this case, one to set file attributes and one to mark the file as being documentation. The %attr for /usr/local/bin/cdp declares the file to be setuid root. If it sends a shiver down your spine to know that anybody can create a package that will run setuid root when installed on your system, good! Just because RPM makes it easy to install software doesn't mean that you should blindly install every package you find.

A single RPM command can quickly point out areas of potential problems and should be issued on any package file whose creators you don't trust:

```
% rpm -qlvp ../RPMS/i386/cdplayer-1.0-1.i386.rpm
drwxr-xr-x- root root 1024 Sep 13 20:16 /usr/doc/cdplayer-1.0-1
-rw-r--r-- root root 1085 Nov 10 01:10 /usr/doc/cdplayer-1.0-1/README
-rwsr-xr-x- root root 40739 Sep 13 21:32 /usr/local/bin/cdp
lrwxrwxrwx- root root 47 Sep 13 21:32 /usr/local/bin/cdplay -> ./cdp
-rwxr-xr-x- root root 4550 Sep 13 21:32 /usr/local/man/man1/cdp.1
%
```

Sure enough. There's that setuid root file. In this case we trust the package builder, so let's install it:

```
# rpm -ivh cdplayer-1.0-1.i386.rpm
cdplayer #################################################
group rot does not exist - using root
#
```

What's this about group rot? Looking back at the rpm -qlvp output, you can see that /usr/local/man/man1/cdp.1 has a bogus group. Looking back even further, it's there in the %attr for that file. Must have been a typo. We could pretend that RPM used advanced artificial intelligence technology to come to the same conclusion as we did and made the appropriate change, but, in reality, RPM simply used the only group identifier it could count on: root. RPM will do the same thing if it can't resolve a user specification.

Let's look at some of the files the package installed, including that worrisome setuid root file:

```
# ls /usr/local/bin
total 558
-rwsr-xr-x  1 root    root        40739 Sep 13 21:32 cdp*
lrwxrwxrwx  1 root    root           47 Sep 13 21:36 cdplay -> ./cdp*
#
```

RPM did just what it was supposed to: It gave the files the attributes specified by the %attr macros.

16.3.2. Betcha Thought We Forgot

At the start of this section, we mentioned that the %attr macro wouldn't accept numeric UIDs or GIDs, and we promised to explain why. The reason is simply that, even if a package requires a certain user or group to own the package's files, the user may not have the same UID/GID from system to system. Wasn't that simple?

17

Adding PGP Signatures to a Package

In this chapter, we'll explore the steps required to add a digital signature to a package using the software known as Pretty Good Privacy, or PGP. If you've used PGP before, you probably know everything you'll need to start signing packages in short order.

On the other hand, if you feel you need a bit more information on PGP before starting, see Appendix G, "An Introduction to PGP," for a brief introduction. When you feel comfortable with PGP, come on back and learn how easy signing packages is.

17.1. Why Sign a Package?

The reason for signing a package is to provide authentication. With a signed package, it's possible for your user community to verify that the package they have was in your possession at some time and has not been changed since then. That "not changed" part is also a good reason to sign your packages, because digital signatures are a very robust way to guard against any modifications to the package.

Of course, as with anything else in life, adding a digital signature to a package isn't an ironclad guarantee that everything is right with the package, but it's about as sure a thing as humans can make it.

17.2. Getting Ready to Sign

Okay, we've convinced you that signing packages is a good idea. Now we've got to make sure PGP and RPM are up to the task. As you might imagine, there are two parts to this process: one for PGP, and one for RPM. Let's get PGP ready first.

17.2.1. Preparing PGP: Creating a Key Pair

There is really very little to be done to PGP, assuming it's been installed properly. The only thing required is to generate a key pair. As mentioned in our mini-primer on PGP, the key pair consists of a secret key and a public key. In terms of signing packages, you will use your secret key to do the actual signing. Anyone interested in checking your signature will need your public key.

Creating a key pair is quite simple. All that's required is to issue a `pgp -kg` command, enter some information, and create some random bits. Here's a sample key-generating session:

```
# pgp -kg
Pretty Good Privacy(tm) 2.6.3a - Public-key encryption for the masses.
(c) 1990-96 Philip Zimmermann, Phil's Pretty Good Software. 1996-03-04
Uses the RSAREF(tm) Toolkit, which is copyright RSA Data Security, Inc.
Distributed by the Massachusetts Institute of Technology.
Export of this software may be restricted by the U.S. government.
Current time: 1996/10/31 00:42 GMT
```

```
Pick your RSA key size:
1) 512 bits- Low commercial grade, fast but less secure
2) 768 bits- High commercial grade, medium speed, good security
3) 1024 bits- "Military" grade, slow, highest security

Choose 1, 2, or 3, or enter desired number of bits: 3
Generating an RSA key with a 1024-bit modulus.

You need a user ID for your public key. The desired form for this
user ID is your name, followed by your E-mail address enclosed in
<angle brackets>, if you have an E-mail address.
For example: John Q. Smith <12345.6789@compuserve.com>
Enter a user ID for your public key:

Example Key for RPM Book
You need a pass phrase to protect your RSA secret key.
Your pass phrase can be any sentence or phrase and may have many
words, spaces, punctuation, or any other printable characters.

Enter pass phrase: <passphrase> (Not echoed)
Enter same pass phrase again: <passphrase> (Still not echoed)

Note that key generation is a lengthy process.

We need to generate 952 random bits. This is done by measuring the
time intervals between your keystrokes. Please enter some random text
on your keyboard until you hear the beep:

(Many random characters were entered)

0 * -Enough, thank you.
........................................
.............................****  ...****
Pass phrase is good. Just a moment....
Key signature certificate added.
Key generation completed.
#
```

Let's review each of the times PGP required information. The first thing PGP needed to know was the key size we wanted. Depending on your level of paranoia, simply choose an appropriate key size. In our example, we chose the "They're out to get me" key size of 1,024 bits.

Next, we needed to choose a user ID for the key. The user ID should be descriptive and should also include sufficient information for someone to contact you. We entered `Example Key for RPM Book`, which goes against this suggestion but is sufficient for the purposes of our example.

After entering a user ID, we needed to add a passphrase. The passphrase is used to protect your secret key, so it should be something difficult for someone else to guess. It should also be memorable for you, because if you forget your passphrase, you won't be able to use your secret key! I entered a couple words and numbers, put together in such a way that no one could ever guess I typed `rpm2kool4words`....Oops!

The passphrase is entered twice to ensure that no typing mistakes were made. PGP also performs some cursory checks on the passphrase, ensuring that the phrase is at least somewhat secure.

Finally comes the strangest part of the key-generation process: creating random bits. This is done by measuring the time between keystrokes. The secret here is to not hold down a key so that it auto-repeats and to not wait several seconds between keystrokes. Simply start typing anything (even nonsense text) until PGP tells you you've typed enough.

After generating enough random bits, PGP takes a minute or so to create the key pair. Assuming that everything completed successfully, you'll see an ending message similar to the one shown in this example. You'll also find, in a subdirectory of your login directory called `.pgp`, the following files:

```
# ls -al ~ /.pgp
total 6
drwxr-xr-x    2 root     root         1024 Oct 30 19:44 .
drwxr-xr-x    5 root     root         1024 Oct 30 19:44 ..
-rw------    1 root     root          176 Oct 30 19:44 pubring.bak
-rw------    1 root     root          331 Oct 30 19:44 pubring.pgp
-rw------    1 root     root          408 Oct 30 19:44 randseed.bin
-rw------    1 root     root          509 Oct 30 19:44 secring.pgp
#
```

Those of you interested in learning exactly what each file is can consult any of the fine books on PGP. For the purposes of signing packages, all you need to know is where these files are located.

That's it! Now it's time to configure RPM to use your newly generated key.

17.2.2. Preparing RPM

RPM's configuration process is quite straightforward. It simply consists of adding a few `rpmrc` entries in a file of your choice. For more information on `rpmrc` files in general, see Appendix B, "The `rpmrc` File."

The entries that need to be added to an `rpmrc` file are

■   `signature`

■   `pgp_name`

■   `pgp_path`

Let's check out the entries:

■   `signature`—The `signature` entry is used to select the type of signature that RPM is to use. At the time this book is being written, the only legal value is `pgp`. So you would enter

    `signature: pgp`

■ pgp_name—The pgp_name entry gives RPM the user ID of the key it is to sign packages with. In our key-generation example, the user ID of the key we created was Example Key for RPM Book, so this is what our entry should look like:

pgp_name: Example Key for RPM Book

■ pgp_path—The pgp_path entry is used to define the path to the directory where the keys are kept. This entry is not needed if the environment variable PGPPATH has been defined. In our example, we didn't move them from PGP's default location, which is in the subdirectory .pgp, off the user's login directory. Because we generated the key as root, our path is /root/.pgp. Therefore, our entry would look like this:

pgp_path: /root/.pgp

And that's it. Now it's time to sign some packages.

17.3. Signing Packages

There are three different ways to sign a package:

■ Sign the package at build time.

■ Replace the signature on an already-existing package.

■ Add a signature to an already-existing package.

Let's take a look at each one, starting with build time signing.

17.3.1. --sign: Sign a Package at Build Time

The --sign option is used to sign a package as it is being built. When this option is added to an RPM build command, RPM will ask for your PGP passphrase. If the passphrase is correct, the build will proceed. If not, the build stops immediately.

Here's an example of --sign in action:

```
# rpm -ba --sign blather-7.9.spec
Enter pass phrase: <passphrase> (Not echoed)

Pass phrase is good.
* Package: blather
...
Binary Packaging: blather-7.9-1
Finding dependencies...
...
Generating signature: 1002
Wrote: /usr/src/redhat/RPMS/i386/blather-7.9-1.i386.rpm
...
Source Packaging: blather-7.9-1
...
Generating signature: 1002
Wrote: /usr/src/redhat/SRPMS/blather-7.9-1.src.rpm
#
```

Once the passphrase is entered, there's very little that is different from a normal build. The only obvious difference is the `Generating signature` message in both the binary and source packaging sections. The number following the message indicates that the signature added was created using PGP. (The list of possible signature types can be found in the RPM sources, specifically `signature.h`, in RPM's `lib` subdirectory.)

Notice that since RPM only signs the source and binary package files, only the `-bb` and `-ba` options make any sense when used with `--sign`. This is due to the fact that only the `-bb` and `-ba` options create package files.

If we issue a quick signature check using RPM's `--checksig` option, we can see that there is, in fact, a PGP signature present:

```
# rpm --checksig blather-7.9-1.i386.rpm
blather-7.9-1.i386.rpm: size pgp md5 OK
#
```

It's clear that, in addition to the usual size and MD5 signatures, the package has a PGP signature.

17.3.1.1. Multiple Builds? No Problem!

You might be wondering how the `--sign` option will work if more than one package is to be built. Do you have to enter the passphrase for every single package you build? The answer is no, as long as you build the packages with a single RPM command. Here's an example:

```
# rpm -ba --sign b*.spec
Enter pass phrase: <passphrase> (Not echoed)

Pass phrase is good.
* Package: blather
...
Binary Packaging: blather-7.9-1
...
Generating signature: 1002
Wrote: /usr/src/redhat/RPMS/i386/blather-7.9-1.i386.rpm
...
Source Packaging: blather-7.9-1
...
Generating signature: 1002
Wrote: /usr/src/redhat/SRPMS/blather-7.9-1.src.rpm
...
* Package: bother
...
Binary Packaging: bother-3.5-1
...
Generating signature: 1002
Wrote: /usr/src/redhat/RPMS/i386/bother-3.5-1.i386.rpm
...
Source Packaging: bother-3.5-1
...
Generating signature: 1002
Wrote: /usr/src/redhat/SRPMS/bother-3.5-1.src.rpm
#
```

Using the --sign option makes it as easy to sign one package as it is to sign 100. But what happens if you need to change your public key? Will you need to rebuild every single one of your packages just to update the signature? No, because there's an easy way out that we'll explore in the next section.

17.3.2. --resign: **Replace a Package's Signature(s)**

As mentioned at the end of the previous section, from time to time it may be necessary to change your public key. Certainly this would be necessary if your key's security were compromised, but other, more mundane situations might require this.

Fortunately, RPM has an option that permits you to replace the signature on an already-built package with a new one. The option is called --resign. Here's an example of its use:

```
# rpm --resign blather-7.9-1.i386.rpm
Enter pass phrase: <passphrase> (Not echoed)

Pass phrase is good.
blather-7.9-1.i386.rpm:
#
```

While the output is not as exciting as a package build, the --resign option can be a lifesaver if you need to change a package's signature and you don't want to rebuild.

As you might have guessed, the --resign option works properly on multiple package files:

```
# rpm --resign b*.rpm
Enter pass phrase: <passphrase> (Not echoed)

Pass phrase is good.
blather-7.9-1.i386.rpm:
bother-3.5-1.i386.rpm:
#
```

17.3.2.1. There Are Limits, However...

Unfortunately, older package files cannot be re-signed. The package file must be in version 3 format, at least. If you attempt to re-sign a package that is too old, here's what you'll see:

```
# rpm --resign blah.rpm
Enter pass phrase: <passphrase> (Not echoed)

Pass phrase is good.
blah.rpm:
blah.rpm: Can't re-sign v2.0 RPM
#
```

Not sure what version your package files are in? Just use the file command to check:

```
# file blather-7.9-1.i386.rpm
blather-7.9-1.i386.rpm: RPM v3 bin i386 blather-7.9-1
#
```

The v3 in file's output indicates the package file format.

17.3.3. --addsign: Add a Signature to a Package

The --addsign option, as the name suggests, is used to add another signature to the package. It's pretty easy to see why someone would want to have a package that had been signed by the package builders. But what reason would there be for adding a signature to a package?

One reason to have more than one signature on a package would be to provide a means of documenting the path of ownership from the package builder to the end user.

As an example, one division of a company creates a package and signs it with the division's key. The company's headquarters then checks the package's signature and adds the corporate signature to the package, in essence stating that the signed package it received is authentic.

Continuing the example, the doubly signed package makes its way to a retailer. The retailer checks the package's signatures and, when they check out, adds its signature to the package.

The package now makes its way to a company that wants to deploy the package. After checking every signature on the package, it knows that it is an authentic copy, unchanged since it was first created. Depending on the deploying company's internal controls, it may choose to add its own signature, thereby reassuring its employees that the package has received its corporate blessing.

After this lengthy example, the actual output from the --addsign option is a bit anticlimactic:

```
# rpm --addsign blather-7.9-1.i386.rpm
Enter pass phrase: <passphrase> (Not echoed)

Pass phrase is good.
blather-7.9-1.i386.rpm:
#
```

If we check the signatures of this package, we'll be able to see the multiple signatures:

```
# rpm --checksig blather-7.9-1.i386.rpm
blather-7.9-1.i386.rpm: size pgp pgp md5 OK
#
```

The two pgps in --checksig's output clearly show that the package has been signed twice.

17.3.3.1. A Few Caveats

As with the --resign option, the --addsign option cannot do its magic on pre-version 3 package files:

```
# rpm --addsign blah.rpm
Enter pass phrase: <passphrase> (Not echoed)

Pass phrase is good.
blah.rpm:
blah.rpm: Can't re-sign v2.0 RPM
#
```

Okay, the error message may not be 100% accurate, but you get the idea.

Another thing to be aware of is that the `--addsign` option does not check for multiple identical signatures. Although it doesn't make much sense to do so, RPM will happily let you add the same signature as many times as you'd like:

```
# rpm --addsig blather-7.9-1.i386.rpm
Enter pass phrase: <passphrase> (Not echoed)

Pass phrase is good.
blather-7.9-1.i386.rpm:
# rpm --addsig blather-7.9-1.i386.rpm
Enter pass phrase: <passphrase> (Not echoed)

Pass phrase is good.
blather-7.9-1.i386.rpm:
# rpm --addsig blather-7.9-1.i386.rpm
Enter pass phrase: <passphrase> (Not echoed)

Pass phrase is good.
blather-7.9-1.i386.rpm:
# rpm --addsig blather-7.9-1.i386.rpm
Enter pass phrase: <passphrase> (Not echoed)

Pass phrase is good.
blather-7.9-1.i386.rpm:
# rpm --checksig blather-7.9-1.i386.rpm
blather-7.9-1.i386.rpm: size pgp pgp pgp pgp md5 OK
#
```

As you can see from `--checksig`'s output, the package now has four identical signatures. Maybe this is the digital equivalent of pressing down extra-hard while writing your name.

18

Creating Subpackages

In this chapter, we will explore one of RPM's more interesting capabilities: the capability to create subpackages.

18.1. What Are Subpackages?

Very simply put, a *subpackage* is one of several package files created from a single spec file. RPM has the ability to create a main package, along with one or more subpackages. Subpackages can also be created without the main package. It's all up to the package builder.

18.2. Why Are Subpackages Needed?

If all the software in the world followed the usual "one source, one binary" structure, there would be no need for subpackages. After all, RPM handles the building and packaging of a program into a single package file just fine.

But software doesn't always conform to this simplistic structure. It's not unusual for software to support two or more different modes of operation. A client/server program, for example, comes in two flavors: a client and a server.

And it can get more complicated than that. Sometimes software relies on another program so completely that the two cannot be built separately. The result is often several packages.

Although it is certainly possible that some convoluted procedure could be devised to force these kinds of software into a single-package structure, it makes more sense to let RPM manage the creation of subpackages. Why? From the package builder's viewpoint, the main reason to use subpackages is to eliminate any duplication of effort.

When using subpackages, there's no need to maintain separate spec files and endure the resulting headaches when new versions of the software become available. By keeping everything in one spec file, new software versions can be quickly integrated, and every related subpackage can be rebuilt with a single command.

But that's enough of the preliminaries. Let's see how subpackages are created.

18.3. Our Sample Spec File: Subpackages Galore!

Throughout this chapter, we'll be constructing a spec file that will consist of a number of subpackages. Let's start by listing the spec file's requirements:

- The main package name is to be foo.
- The version is to be 2.7.

■ There are three subpackages:

  ■ The server subpackage, to be called `foo-server`

  ■ The client subpackage, to be called `foo-client`

  ■ The `baz` development library subpackage, to be called `bazlib`

■ The `bazlib` subpackage has a version 5.6.

■ Each subpackage will have its own `summary` and `description` tags.

Every spec file starts with a preamble. In this case, the preamble will contain the following tags:

```
Name: foo
Version: 2.7
Release: 1
Source: foo-2.7.tgz
CopyRight: probably not
Summary: The foo app, and the baz library needed to build it
Group: bogus/junque
%description
This is the long description of the foo app, and the baz library needed to
build it...
```

As you can see, there's nothing different here: This is an ordinary spec file so far. Let's delve into things a bit more and see what we'll need to add to this spec file to create the subpackages we require.

18.4. Spec File Changes for Subpackages

The creation of subpackages is based strictly on the contents of the spec file. This doesn't mean that you'll have to learn an entirely new set of tags, conditionals, and directives in order to create subpackages, however. In fact, you'll only need to learn one.

The primary change to a spec file is structural and starts with the definition of a preamble for each subpackage.

18.4.1. The Subpackage's Preamble

When we introduced RPM package building in Chapter 10, "The Basics of Developing with RPM," we said that every spec file contains a preamble. The preamble contains a variety of tags that define all sorts of information about the package. In a single-package situation, the preamble must be at the start of the spec file. The spec file we're creating will have one there, too.

When you're creating a spec file that will build subpackages, each subpackage also needs a preamble of its own. These subpreambles need only define information for the subpackage when that information differs from what is defined in the main preamble. For example, if we wanted to define an installation prefix for a subpackage, we would add the appropriate `prefix` tag to that subpackage's preamble. That subpackage would then be relocatable.

In a single-package spec file, nothing explicitly identifies the preamble other than its position at the top of the file. For subpackages, however, we need to be a bit more explicit. So we use the %package directive to identify the preamble for each subpackage.

18.4.1.1. The %package **Directive**

The %package directive actually performs two functions. As mentioned, it is used to denote the start of a subpackage's preamble. It also plays a role in forming the subpackage's name. For example, let's say the main preamble contains the following name tag:

```
name: foo
```

Later in the spec file, there is a %package directive:

```
%package bar
```

This would result in the name of the subpackage being foo-bar.

In this way, it's easy to see the relationship of the subpackage to the main package (or to other subpackages, for that matter). Of course, this naming convention might not be appropriate in every case. So there is an option to the %package directive for just this circumstance.

18.4.1.2. Adding -n **to the** %package **Directive**

The -n option is used to change the final name of a subpackage from *mainpackage-subpackage* to *subpackage*. Let's modify the %package directive in our earlier example to be

```
%package -n bar
```

The result is that the subpackage name would be bar instead of foo-bar.

18.4.1.3. Updating Our Spec File

Let's apply some of our newly found knowledge to the spec file we're writing. Here's the list of subpackages we need to create:

- The server subpackage, to be called foo-server
- The client subpackage, to be called foo-client
- The baz development library subpackage, to be called bazlib

Since our package name is foo, and since the %package directive creates subpackage names by prepending the package name, the %package directives for the foo-server and foo-client subpackages would be written as

```
%package server
```

and

```
%package client
```

Since the baz library's package name is not to start with foo, we need to use the -n option on its %package directive:

```
%package -n bazlib
```

Our requirements further state that foo-server and foo-client are to have the same version as the main package.

One of the time-saving aspects of using subpackages is that there is no need to duplicate information for each subpackage if it is already defined in the main package. Therefore, since the main package's preamble has a version tag defining the version as 2.7, the two subpackages that lack a version tag in their preambles will simply inherit the main package's version definition.

Since the bazlib subpackage's preamble contains a version tag, it must have its own unique version.

In addition, each subpackage must have its own summary tag.

So, based on these requirements, our spec file now looks like this:

```
Name: foo
Version: 2.7
Release: 1
Source: foo-2.7.tgz
CopyRight: probably not
Summary: The foo app, and the baz library needed to build it
Group: bogus/junque
%description
This is the long description of the foo app, and the baz library needed to
build it...

%package server
Summary: The foo server

%package client
Summary: The foo client

%package -n bazlib
Version: 5.6
Summary: The baz library
```

We can see the subpackage structure starting to appear now.

18.4.1.4. Required Tags in Subpackages

There are a few more tags we should add to the subpackages in our sample spec file. In fact, if these tags are not present, RPM will issue a most impressive warning:

```
# rpm -ba foo-2.7.spec
Package: foo
Package:  foo-server
Field must be present : Description
Field must be present : Group
```

```
Package:  foo-client
Field must be present : Description
Field must be present : Group
Package: bazlib
Field must be present : Description
Field must be present : Group

Spec file check failed!!
Tell rpm-list@redhat.com if this is incorrect.
#
```

Our spec file is incomplete. The bottom line is that each subpackage *must* have these three tags:

- The %description tag
- The group tag
- The summary tag

It's easy to see that the first two tags are required, but what about summary? Well, we lucked out on that one: We already included a summary for each subpackage in our sample spec file.

Let's take a look at the %description tag first.

18.4.1.5. The %description Tag

As you've probably noticed, the %description tag differs from other tags. First of all, it starts with a percent sign, making it look similar to a directive. Second, its data can span multiple lines. The third difference is that the %description tag must include the name of the subpackage it describes. This is done by appending the subpackage name to the %description tag itself. So, given these %package directives:

```
%package server
%package client
%package -n bazlib
```

our %description tags would start with

```
%description server
%description client
%description -n bazlib
```

Notice that we've included the -n option in the %description tag for bazlib. This was intentional, as it makes the name completely unambiguous.

18.4.1.6. Our Spec File So Far

Okay, let's take a look at the spec file after we've added the appropriate %descriptions, along with group tags for each subpackage:

```
Name: foo
Version: 2.7
Release: 1
```

```
Source: foo-2.7.tgz
CopyRight: probably not
Summary: The foo app, and the baz library needed to build it
Group: bogus/junque
%description
This is the long description of the foo app, and the baz library needed to
build it...

%package server
Summary: The foo server
Group: bogus/junque
%description server
This is the long description for the foo server...

%package client
Summary: The foo client
Group: bogus/junque
%description client
This is the long description for the foo client...

%package -n bazlib
Version: 5.6
Summary: The baz library
Group: bogus/junque
%description -n bazlib
This is the long description for the bazlib...
```

Let's take a look at what we've done. We've created a main preamble as we normally would. We then created three additional preambles, each starting with a %package directive. Finally, we added a few tags to the subpackage preambles.

But what about version tags? Aren't the server and client subpackages missing them?

Not really. Remember that if a subpackage is missing a given tag, it will inherit the value of that tag from the main preamble. We're well on our way to having a complete spec file, but we aren't quite there yet.

Let's continue by looking at the next part of the spec file that changes when building subpackages.

18.4.2. The %files List

In an ordinary single-package spec file, the %files list is used to determine which files are actually going to be packaged. It is no different when building subpackages. What *is* different is that there must be a %files list for each subpackage.

Since each %files list must be associated with a particular %package directive, we simply label each %files list with the name of the subpackage, as specified by each %package directive. Going back to our example, our %package lines were

```
%package server
%package client
%package -n bazlib
```

Therefore, our `%files` lists should start with

```
%files server
%files client
%files -n bazlib
```

In addition, we need the main package's `%files` list, which remains unnamed:

```
%files
```

The contents of each `%files` list is dictated entirely by the software's requirements. If, for example, a certain file needs to be packaged in more than one package, it's perfectly all right to include the filename in more than one list.

18.4.2.1. Controlling Packages with the `%files` List

The `%files` list wields considerable power over subpackages. It's even possible to prevent a package from being created by using the `%files` list. But is there a reason you'd want to go to the trouble of setting up subpackages, only to keep one from being created?

Actually, there is. Take, for example, the case where client/server–based software is to be packaged. Certainly, it makes sense to create two subpackages: one for the client and one for the server. But what about the main package? Is there any need for it?

Quite often there's no need for a main package. In those cases, removing the main `%files` list entirely will result in no main package being built.

18.4.2.2. A Point Worth Noting

Keep in mind that an empty `%files` list (that is, a `%files` list that contains no files) is *not* the same as not having a `%files` list at all. As noted previously, entirely removing a `%files` list results in RPM not creating that package. However, if RPM comes across a `%files` list with no files, it will happily create an empty package file.

This feature (which also works with subpackage `%files` lists) comes in handy when used in concert with conditionals. If a `%files` list is enclosed by a conditional, the package will be created (or not) based on the evaluation of the conditional.

18.4.2.3. Our Spec File So Far

Okay, let's update our sample spec file. Here's what it looks like after adding each of the subpackages' `%files` lists:

```
Name: foo
Version: 2.7
Release: 1
Source: foo-2.7.tgz
CopyRight: probably not
```

```
Summary: The foo app, and the baz library needed to build it
Group: bogus/junque
%description
This is the long description of the foo app, and the baz library needed to
build it...
%package server
Summary: The foo server
Group: bogus/junque

%package client
Summary: The foo client
Group: bogus/junque

%package -n bazlib
Version: 5.6
Summary: The baz library
Group: bogus/junque


%files
/usr/local/foo-file

%files server
/usr/local/server-file

%files client
/usr/local/client-file

%files -n bazlib
/usr/local/bazlib-file
```

As you can see, we've added `%files` lists for

- The main **foo** package
- The `foo-server` subpackage
- The `foo-client` subpackage
- The `bazlib` subpackage

Each package contains a single file. (Hey, we said it was a simple example!) If there was no need for a main package, we could simply remove the unnamed `%files` list. Keep in mind that even if you do not create a main package, the tags defined in the main package's preamble *will* appear somewhere—specifically, in the source package file.

Let's look at the last subpackage-specific part of the spec file: the install and erase time scripts.

18.4.3. Install and Erase Time Scripts

The install and erase time scripts, `%pre`, `%preun`, `%post`, and `%postun`, can all be named using exactly the same method as was used for the other subpackage-specific sections of the spec file. The script used during package verification, `%verifyscript`, can be made package specific as well. Using the subpackage structure from our sample spec file, we would end up with script definitions like this:

- ■ `%pre server`
- ■ `%postun client`
- ■ `%preun -n bazlib`
- ■ `%verifyscript client`

Other than the change in naming, there's only one thing to be aware of when creating scripts for subpackages. It's important that you consider the possibility of scripts from various subpackages interacting with each other. Of course, this is simply good script-writing practice, even if the packages involved are not related.

18.4.3.1. Back at the Spec File

Here we've added some scripts to our spec file. So that our example doesn't get too complex, we've just added preinstall scripts for each package:

```
Name: foo
Version: 2.7
Release: 1
Source: foo-2.7.tgz
CopyRight: probably not
Summary: The foo app, and the baz library needed to build it
Group: bogus/junque
%description
This is the long description of the foo app, and the baz library needed to
build it...

%package server
Summary: The foo server
Group: bogus/junque
%description server
This is the long description for the foo server...

%package client
Summary: The foo client
Group: bogus/junque
%description client
This is the long description for the foo client...

%package -n bazlib
Version: 5.6
Summary: The baz library
Group: bogus/junque
%description -n bazlib
This is the long description for the bazlib...
```

```
%pre
echo "This is the foo package preinstall script"

%pre server
echo "This is the foo-server subpackage preinstall script"
```

```
%pre client
echo "This is the foo-client subpackage preinstall script"

%pre -n bazlib
echo "This is the bazlib subpackage preinstall script"

%files
/usr/local/foo-file

%files server
/usr/local/server-file

%files client
/usr/local/client-file

%files -n bazlib
/usr/local/bazlib-file
```

As preinstall scripts go, these don't do very much. But they will allow us to see how subpackage-specific scripts can be defined.

Those of you who have built packages probably realize that our spec file is missing something. Let's add that part now.

18.5. Build-Time Scripts: Unchanged for Subpackages

Although creating subpackages changes the general structure of the spec file, there's one section that doesn't change: the build-time scripts. This means there is only one set of `%prep`, `%build`, and `%install` scripts in any spec file.

Of course, even if RPM doesn't require any changes to these scripts, you still might need to make some subpackage-related changes to them. Normally these changes are related to doing whatever is required to get all the software unpacked, built, and installed. For example, if packaging client/server software, the software for both the client and the server must be unpacked, and then both the client and server binaries must be built and installed.

18.5.1. Our Spec File: One Last Look

Let's add some build time scripts and take a final look at the spec file:

```
Name: foo
Version: 2.7
Release: 1
Source: foo-2.7.tgz
CopyRight: probably not
Summary: The foo app, and the baz library needed to build it
Group: bogus/junque
%description
```

```
This is the long description of the foo app, and the baz library needed to
build it...

%package server
Summary: The foo server
Group: bogus/junque
%description server
This is the long description for the foo server...

%package client
Summary: The foo client
Group: bogus/junque
%description client
This is the long description for the foo client...

%package -n bazlib
Version: 5.6
Summary: The baz library
Group: bogus/junque
%description -n bazlib
This is the long description for the bazlib...

%prep
%setup

%build
make

%install
make install

%pre
echo "This is the foo package preinstall script"

%pre server
echo "This is the foo-server subpackage preinstall script"

#%pre client
echo "This is the foo-client subpackage preinstall script"

%pre -n bazlib
echo "This is the bazlib subpackage preinstall script"

%files
/usr/local/foo-file

%files server
/usr/local/server-file

%files client
/usr/local/client-file

%files -n bazlib
/usr/local/bazlib-file
```

As you can see, the build time scripts are about as simple as they can be. This is the advantage to making up an example. A more real-world spec file would undoubtedly have more interesting scripts.

18.6. Building Subpackages

Now it's time to give our sample spec file a try. The build process is not that much different from that of a single-package spec file:

```
# rpm -ba foo-2.7.spec
Package: foo
Package: foo-server
Package: foo-client
Package: bazlib
...
Executing: %prep
...
Executing: %build
...
Executing: %install
...
Executing: special doc
+ cd /usr/src/redhat/BUILD
+ cd foo-2.7
+ DOCDIR=//usr/doc/foo-2.7-1
+ DOCDIR=//usr/doc/foo-server-2.7-1
+ DOCDIR=//usr/doc/foo-client-2.7-1
+ DOCDIR=//usr/doc/bazlib-5.6-1
+ exit 0
Binary Packaging: foo-2.7-1
Finding dependencies...
usr/local/foo-file
1 block
Generating signature: 0
Wrote: /usr/src/redhat/RPMS/i386/foo-2.7-1.i386.rpm
Binary Packaging: foo-server-2.7-1
Finding dependencies...
usr/local/server-file
1 block
Generating signature: 0
Wrote: /usr/src/redhat/RPMS/i386/foo-server-2.7-1.i386.
rpm Binary Packaging: foo-client-2.7-1
Finding dependencies...
usr/local/client-file
1 block
Generating signature: 0
Wrote: /usr/src/redhat/RPMS/i386/foo-client-2.7-1.i386.rpm
Binary Packaging: bazlib-5.6-1
Finding dependencies...
usr/local/bazlib-file
1 block
Generating signature: 0
Wrote: /usr/src/redhat/RPMS/i386/bazlib-5.6-1.i386.rpm
...
Source Packaging: foo-2.7-1
foo-2.7.spec
foo-2.7.tgz
4 blocks
Generating signature: 0
Wrote: /usr/src/redhat/SRPMS/foo-2.7-1.src.rpm
#
```

Starting at the top, we start the build with the usual command. Immediately following the command, RPM indicates that four packages are to be built from this spec file. The %prep, %build, and %install scripts then execute as usual.

Next, RPM executes its special doc internal script, even though we haven't declared any files to be documentation. It's worth noting, however, that the DOCDIR environment variables show that if the spec file *had* declared some of the files as documentation, RPM would have created the appropriate documentation directories for each of the packages.

At this point, RPM creates the binary packages. As you can see, each package contains the file defined in its %files list.

Finally, the source package file is created. It contains the spec file and the original sources, just like any other source package.

One spec file. One set of sources. One build command. Four packages (five, if you count the source package). All in all, a pretty good deal, isn't it?

18.6.1. Giving Subpackages the Once-Over

Let's take a look at our newly created packages. As with any other package, each subpackage should be tested by being installed on a system that has not had that software installed before. In this section, we'll point out how subpackages differ from their nonsubpackaged counterparts.

First, let's just look at each package's information:

```
# rpm -qip foo-2.7-1.i386.rpm
Name        : foo                    Distribution: (none)
Version     : 2.7                        Vendor: (none)
Release     : 1                      Build Date: Wed Nov 06 13:33:37 1996
Install date: (none)                 Build Host: foonly.rpm.org
Group       : bogus/junque          Source RPM: foo-2.7-1.src.rpm
Size        : 35
Summary     : The foo app, and the baz library needed to build it
Description :
This is the long description of the foo app, and the baz library needed to
build it...


# rpm -qip foo-server-2.7-1.i386.rpm
Name        : foo-server             Distribution: (none)
Version     : 2.7                        Vendor: (none)
Release     : 1                      Build Date: Wed Nov 06 13:33:37 1996
Install date: (none)                 Build Host: foonly.rpm.org
Group       : bogus/junque          Source RPM: foo-2.7-1.src.rpm
Size        : 42
Summary     : The foo server
Description :
This is the long description for the foo server...
```

```
# rpm -qip foo-client-2.7-1.i386.rpm
Name        : foo-client      Distribution: (none)
Version     : 2.7                   Vendor: (none)
Release     : 1               Build Date: Wed Nov 06 13:33:37 1996
Install date: (none)          Build Host: foonly.rpm.org
Group       : bogus/junque    Source RPM: foo-2.7-1.src.rpm
Size        : 42
Summary     : The foo client
Description :
This is the long description for the foo client...


# rpm -qip bazlib-5.6-1.i386.rpm
Name        : bazlib          Distribution: (none)
Version     : 5.6                   Vendor: (none)
Release     : 1               Build Date: Wed Nov 06 13:33:37 1996
Install date: (none)          Build Host: foonly.rpm.org
Group       : bogus/junque    Source RPM: foo-2.7-1.src.rpm
Size        : 38
Summary     : The baz library
Description :
This is the long description for the bazlib...
#
```

Here we've used RPM's query capability to display a list of summary information for each package. A few points are worth noting.

First, each package lists foo-2.7-1.src.rpm as its source package file. This is the only way to tell if two package files were created from the same set of sources. Trying to use a package's name as an indicator is futile, as the bazlib package shows us.

The next thing to notice is that the summaries and descriptions for each package are specific to that package. Since these tags were placed and named according to each package, this should be no surprise.

Finally, we can see that each package's version has been either inherited from the main package's preamble or, as in the case of the bazlib package, the main package's version has been overridden by a version tag added to bazlib's preamble.

If we look at the source package's information, we see that its information has been taken entirely from the main package's set of tags:

```
# rpm -qip foo-2.7-1.src.rpm
Name        : foo             Distribution: (none)
Version     : 2.7                   Vendor: (none)
Release     : 1               Build Date: Wed Nov 06 13:33:37 1996
Install date: (none)          Build Host: foonly.rpm.org
Group       : bogus/junque    Source RPM: (none)
Size        : 1415
Summary     : The foo app, and the baz library needed to build it
Description :
This is the long description of the foo app, and the baz library needed to
build it...
#
```

It's easy to see that if there were no %files list for the main package, and therefore, no main package, the tags in the main preamble would still be used in the source package. This is why RPM enforces the requirement that the main preamble contain copyright, %description, and group tags. So, here's a word to the wise: Don't put something stupid in the main preamble's %description just to satisfy RPM. Your witty saying will be immortalized for all time in every source package you distribute. (Yes, the author found out about this the hard way!)

18.6.1.1. Verifying Subpackage-Specific Install and Erase Scripts

The easiest way to verify that the %pre scripts we defined for each package were actually used is to simply install each package:

```
# rpm -Uvh foo-2.7-1.i386.rpm
foo                       This is the foo package preinstall script
#################################################


# rpm -Uvh foo-server-2.7-1.i386.rpm
foo-server                This is the foo-server subpackage preinstall script
#################################################


# rpm -Uvh foo-client-2.7-1.i386.rpm
foo-client                This is the foo-client subpackage preinstall script
#################################################


# rpm -Uvh bazlib-5.6-1.i386.rpm
bazlib                    This is the bazlib subpackage preinstall script
#################################################
#
```

As expected, the unique %pre script for each package has been included. Of course, if we hadn't wanted to actually install the packages, we could have used RPM's --scripts option to display the scripts:

```
# rpm -qp --scripts foo-2.7-1.i386.rpm
preinstall script:
echo "This is the foo-server subpackage preinstall script"

postinstall script:
(none)
preuninstall script:
(none)
postuninstall script:
(none)
verify script:
(none)
#
```

This approach might be a bit safer, particularly if installing the newly built package would disrupt operations on your build system.

19

Building Packages for Multiple Architectures and Operating Systems

While RPM certainly makes packaging software as easy as possible, it doesn't stop there. RPM gives you the tools you need to build a package on different types of computers. More importantly, RPM makes it possible to build packages on different types of computers using a single spec file. Those of you who have developed software for different computers know the importance of maintaining a single set of sources. RPM lets you continue that practice through the package-building phase.

Before we get into RPM's capabilities, let's quickly review what is involved in developing software for different types of computer systems.

19.1. Architectures and Operating Systems: A Primer

From a software engineering standpoint, there are only two major differences between any two computer systems:

- The architecture implemented by the computer's hardware
- The system software running on the computer

The first difference is built into the computer. The architecture is the manner in which the computer system was designed. It includes the number and type of registers present in the processor, the number of machine instructions, what operations they perform, and so on. For example, every PC today, no matter who built it, is based on the Intel x86 architecture.

The second difference is more under our control. The operating system is software that controls how the system operates. Different operating systems have different methods of storing information on disk, different ways of implementing functions used by programs, and different hardware requirements.

As far as package building is concerned, two systems with the same architecture running two different operating systems are as different as two systems with different architectures running the same operating system. In the first case, the software being packaged for the different operating systems will differ due to the differences between the operating systems. In the second case, the software being packaged for different architectures will differ due to the underlying differences in hardware. (This is a somewhat simplistic view of the matter; it's common for incompatibilities to crop up between two different implementations of the same operating system on different architectures.)

RPM supports differences in architecture and operating system equally. If there is a tag, rpmrc file entry, or conditional that is used to support architectural differences, there is a corresponding tag, entry, or conditional that supports operating system differences.

19.1.1. Let's Just Call Them Platforms

In order to keep the duplication in this chapter to a minimum, we'll refer to a computer of a given architecture running a given operating system as a *platform*. If another system differs in either aspect, it is considered a different platform.

Okay, now that we've gotten through the preliminaries, let's look at RPM's multiplatform capabilities.

19.2. What Does RPM Do to Make Multiplatform Packaging Easier?

As we mentioned, RPM supports multiplatform package building through a set of tags, `rpmrc` file entries, and conditionals. None of these tools is difficult to use. In fact, the hardest part of multiplatform package building is figuring out how the software needs to be changed to support different platforms.

Let's take a look at each multiplatform tool RPM provides.

19.2.1. Automatic Detection of the Build Platform

The first thing necessary for easy multiplatform package building is to identify which platform the package is to be built for. Except in the fairly esoteric case of cross-compilation, the *build platform* is the platform on which the package is built. RPM does this for you automatically, although it can be overridden at build time.

19.2.2. Automatic Detection of the Install Platform

The other important platform in package building is the platform on which the package is to be installed. Here again, RPM does this for you, although it's possible to override this when the package is installed.

But there is more to multiplatform package building than simply being able to determine the platform during package building and installation. The next component in multiplatform package building is a set of platform-dependent tags.

19.2.3. Platform-Dependent Tags

RPM uses a number of tags that control which platforms can build a package. These tags make it easier for the package builder to build multiple packages automatically since the tags keep RPM from attempting to build packages that are incompatible with the build platform.

19.2.4. Platform-Dependent Conditionals

Whereas the platform-dependent tags provide a crude level of multiplatform control (that is, the package will be built or not, depending on the tags and the build platform), RPM's platform-dependent conditionals provide a much finer level of control. By using these conditionals, it's possible to excise those parts of the spec file that are specific to another platform and replace them with one or more lines that are compatible with the build platform.

Now that you have a basic idea of RPM's multiplatform support features, let's take a more in-depth look at each one.

19.3. Build and Install Platform Detection

As mentioned earlier, the first step to multiplatform package building is to identify the build platform. This is done by matching information from the build system's uname output against a number of rpmrc file entries.

Normally, it's not necessary to worry too much about the following rpmrc file entries because RPM comes with a set of entries that support all platforms that currently run RPM. However, when adding support for new platforms, it will be necessary to use the following entries to add support for the new build platform.

19.3.1. Platform-Specific `rpmrc` Entries

Normally, the file /usr/lib/rpmrc contains the following rpmrc file entries. They can be over-ridden by entries in /etc/rpmrc or ~ /.rpmrc. This is discussed more completely in Appendix B, "The rpmrc File."

Because each entry type is available in both architecture and operating system flavors, we'll just use *xxx* in place of arch and os in the following descriptions.

19.3.1.1. *xxx*_canon: Define Canonical Platform Name and Number

The *xxx*_canon entry is used to convert information obtained from the system running RPM into a canonical name and number that RPM will use internally. Here's the format:

*xxx*_canon:*<label>*: *<string> <value>*

<label> is compared against information from uname(2). If a match is found, *<string>* is used by RPM as the canonical name, and *<value>* is used as a unique numeric value. Here are two examples:

```
arch_canon: sun4: sparc 3
os_canon: Linux: Linux 1
```

The arch_canon tag here is used to define the canonical architecture information for Sun Microsystems's SPARC architecture. In this case, the output from uname is compared against sun4. If there's a match, the canonical architecture name is set to sparc, and the architecture number is set to 3.

The os_canon tag here is used to define the canonical operating system information for the Linux operating system. In this case, the output from uname is compared against Linux. If there's a match, the canonical operating system name is set to Linux, and the operating system number is set to 1.

This description is not 100% complete—there is an additional step performed during the time RPM gets the system information from uname and compares it against a canonical name. Let's look at the rpmrc file entry that comes into play during this intermediate step.

19.3.1.2. buildxxxtranslate: Define Build Platform

The buildxxxtranslate entry is used to define the build platform information. Specifically, these entries are used to create a table that maps information from uname to the appropriate architecture/operating system name.

The buildxxxtranslate entry looks like this:

```
buildxxxtranslate:<label>: <string>
```

<label> is compared against information from uname(2). If a match is found, <string> is used by RPM as the build platform information after it has been processed by xxx_canon. Here are two examples:

```
buildarchtranslate: i586: i386
buildostranslate: Linux: Linux
```

The buildarchtranslate tag shown here is used to define the build architecture for an Intel Pentium (or i586, as it's shown here) processor. Any Pentium-based system will, by default, build packages for the Intel 80386 (or i386) architecture.

The buildostranslate tag shown here is used to define the build operating system for systems running the Linux operating system. In this case, the build operating system remains unchanged.

19.3.1.3. xxx_compat: Define Compatible Architectures

The xxx_compat entry is used to define which architectures and operating systems are compatible with one another. It is used at install time only. The format of the entry is

```
xxx_compat:<label>: <list>
```

The <label> is a name string as defined by an xxx_canon entry. The <list> following it consists of one or more names, also defined by arch_canon. If there is more than one name in the list, the names should be separated by a space.

The names in the list are considered compatible to the name specified in the label.

The following `arch_compat` lines illustrate how a family of upwardly compatible architectures may be represented. For example, if the build architecture was defined as i586, the compatible architectures would be i486 and i386. However, if the build system were an i486, the only compatible architecture would be an i386.

While the `os_compat` line shown here is entirely fictional, its purpose would be to declare AIX compatible with Linux:

```
arch_compat: i586: i486
arch_compat: i486: i386
os_compat: Linux: AIX
```

If only it were that simple....

19.3.2. Overriding Platform Information at Build Time

By using the `rpmrc` file entries discussed in the preceding section, RPM usually makes the right decisions in selecting the build and install platforms. However, there might be times when RPM's selections aren't the best. Normally the circumstances are unusual, as in the case of cross-compiling software. In these cases, it is nice to have an easy way of overriding the build time architecture and operating system.

The `--buildarch` and `--buildos` options can be used to set the build time architecture and operating system rather than relying on RPM's automatic detection capabilities. These options are added to a normal RPM build command. One important point to remember is that although RPM does try to find the specified architecture name, it does no checking as to the sanity of the entered architecture or operating system. For example, if you enter an entirely fictional operating system, RPM will issue a warning message, but then happily build a package for it.

Why? Wouldn't it make more sense for RPM to perform some sort of sanity check? In a word, no. One of RPM's main design goals was to never get in the way of the package builder. If someone has a need to override his build platform information, he should know what he's doing and what the full implications of his actions are.

Bottom line: Unless you know why you need to use `--buildarch` or `--buildos`, you probably don't need to use them.

19.3.3. Overriding Platform Information at Install Time

It's also possible to direct RPM to ignore platform information while a package is being installed. The `--ignorearch` and `--ignoreos` options, when added to any install or upgrade command, will direct RPM to proceed with the install or upgrade, even if the package's platform doesn't match the install platform.

Dangerous? Yes. But it can be indispensable in certain circumstances. As with the ability to override platform information at build time, unless you know why you need to use `--ignorearch` or `--ignoreos`, you probably don't need to use them.

19.4. `optflags`: The Other `rpmrc` File Entry

While the `optflags` entry doesn't play a part in determining the build or install platform, it does play a role in multiplatform package building. The `optflags` entry is used to define a standard set of options that can be used during the build process, specifically during compilation.

The `optflags` entry looks like this:

```
optflags:<architecture> <value>
```

For example, assume that the following `optflags` entries were placed in an `rpmrc` file:

```
optflags: i386 -O2 -m486 -fno-strength-reduce
optflags: sparc -O2
```

If RPM were running on an Intel 80386-compatible architecture, the `optflags` value would be set to `-O2 -m486 -fno-strength-reduce`. If, however, RPM were running on a Sun SPARC-based system, `optflags` would be set to `-O2`.

This entry sets the `RPM_OPT_FLAGS` environment variable, which can be used in the `%prep`, `%build`, and `%install` scripts.

19.5. Platform-Dependent Tags

Once RPM has determined the build platform's information, that information can be used in the build process. The first way this information can be used is to determine whether a given package should be built on a given platform. This is done through the use of four tags (discussed in the following sections) that can be added to a spec file.

There can be many reasons to do this. For example, the software may not build correctly on a given platform. Or the software may be platform specific, such that packaging the software on any other platform, while technologically possible, would really make no sense.

The real world is not always so clear cut, so there might even be cases where a package should be built on, say, three different platforms, but no others. By carefully using the tags described in the following sections, any conceivable situation can be covered.

As with the `rpmrc` file entries we've already discussed, there are identical tags for architecture and operating system, so we'll discuss them together.

19.5.1. The excludexxx Tags

excludexxx tags are used to direct RPM to ensure that the package does not attempt to build on the excluded platforms. One or more platforms may be specified after the excludexxx tags, separated by either spaces or commas. Here are two examples:

```
ExcludeArch: sparc alpha
ExcludeOS: Irix
```

The first line prevents systems based on the Sun SPARC and Digital Alpha/AXP architectures from attempting to build the package. The second line ensures that the package will not be built for the Silicon Graphics operating system Irix.

If a build is attempted on an excluded architecture or operating system, the following message will be displayed, and the build will fail:

```
# rpm -ba cdplayer-1.0.spec
Arch mismatch!
cdplayer-1.0.spec doesn't build on this architecture
#
```

excludexxx tags are meant to explicitly prevent a finite set of architectures or operating systems from building a package. If your goal is to ensure that a package will build on only *one* architecture, you should use the exclusivexxx tags.

19.5.2. The exclusivexxx Tags

exclusivexxx tags are used to direct RPM to only build the package on the specified platforms. These tags ensure that in the future no brand-new platform will mistakenly attempt to build the package. RPM will build the package on the specified platforms only.

The syntax of the exclusivexxx tags is identical to that of excludexxx:

```
ExclusiveArch: sparc alpha
ExclusiveOS: Irix
```

In the first line, the package will only build on a Sun SPARC or Digital Alpha/AXP system. In the second, the package will only be built on the Irix operating system.

exclusivexxx tags are meant to explicitly allow a finite set of architectures or operating systems to build a package. If your goal is to ensure that a package will *not* build on a specific platform, you should use the excludexxx tag.

19.6. Platform-Dependent Conditionals

Of course, the control exerted by the excludexxx and exclusivexxx tags over package building is often too coarse. There may be packages, for example, that would build just fine on another platform, if only you could substitute a platform-specific patch file or change some paths in the %files list.

The key to exerting this kind of platform-specific control in the spec file is to use RPM's conditionals. The conditionals provide a general-purpose means of constructing a platform-specific version of the spec file during the actual build process.

19.6.1. Common Features of All Conditionals

A few things are common to each conditional, so let's discuss them first. The first thing is that conditionals are block structured. The second is that conditionals can be nested. Finally, conditionals can span any part of the spec file.

19.6.1.1. Conditionals Are Block Structured

Every conditional is block structured—in other words, the conditional begins at a certain point within the spec file and continues some number of lines until it is ended. This forms a block that will be used or ignored, depending on the platform the conditional is checking for as well as the build platform itself.

Every conditional starts with a line beginning with `%if` and is followed by one of four platform-related conditions. Every conditional ends with a line containing `%endif`.

Ignoring the platform-related conditions for a moment, here's an example of a conditional block:

```
%ifos Linux
Summary: This is a package for the Linux operating system
%endif
```

It's a one-line block, but a block nonetheless.

There's also another style of conditional block. As before, it starts with `%if` and ends with `%endif`. But there's something new in the middle:

```
%ifos Linux
Summary: This is a package for the Linux operating system
%else
Summary: This is a package for some other operating system
%endif
```

Here we've replaced one summary tag with another.

19.6.1.2. Conditionals Can Be Nested

Conditionals can be nested—that is, the block formed by one conditional can enclose another conditional. Here's an example:

```
%ifarch i386

echo "This is an i386"

%ifos Linux
echo "This is a Linux system"
```

```
%else
echo "This is not a Linux system"
%endif

%else

echo "This is not an i386"

%endif
```

In this example, the first conditional block formed by the `%ifarch i386` line contains a complete `%ifos...%else...%endif` conditional. Therefore, if the build system were Intel based, the `%ifos` conditional would be tested. If the build system were not Intel based, the `%ifos` conditional would not be tested.

19.6.1.3. Conditionals Can Cross Spec File Sections

The next thing each conditional has in common is that there is no limit to the number of lines a conditional block can contain. You could enclose the entire spec file within a conditional. But it's much better to use conditionals to insert only the appropriate platform-specific contents.

Now that we have the basics out of the way, let's take a look at each of the conditionals and see how they work.

19.6.2. %ifxxx

The `%ifxxx` conditionals are used to control the inclusion of a block as long as the platform-dependent information is true. Here is an example:

```
%ifarch i386 alpha
```

In this case, the block following the conditional would be included only if the build architecture were `i386` or `alpha`.

Here's another example:

```
%ifos Linux
```

This example would include the block following the conditional only if the operating system were `Linux`.

19.6.3. %ifnxxx

The `%ifnxxx` conditionals are used to control the inclusion of a block as long as the platform-dependent information is *not* true. Here is an example:

```
%ifnarch i386 alpha
```

In this case, the block following the conditional would be included only if the build architecture were not i386 or alpha.

Here's another example:

```
%ifnos Linux
```

This example would include the block following the conditional only if the operating system were not Linux.

19.7. Hints and Kinks

There isn't much in the way of hard-and-fast rules when it comes to multiplatform package building. But in general, the following uses of RPM's multiplatform capabilities seem to work the best:

- The exclude*xxx* and exclusive*xxx* tags are best used when it's known that there's no reason for the package to be built on specific architectures.
- The %if*xxx* and %ifn*xxx* conditionals are most likely to be used in the following areas:
  - Controlling the inclusion of %patch macros for platform-specific patches.
  - Setting up platform-specific initialization prior to building the software.
  - Tailoring the %files list when the software creates platform-specific files.

Given that some software is more easily ported to different platforms than others, this list is far from complete. If there's one thing to remember about multiplatform package building, it's to not be afraid to experiment!

20

Real-World
Package Building

In Chapter 11, "Building Packages: A Simple Example," we packaged a fairly simple application. Since our goal was to introduce package building, we kept things as simple as possible. However, things aren't always that simple in the real world.

In this chapter, we'll package a more complex application that will call on most of RPM's capabilities. We'll start with a general overview of the application and end with a completed package, just as you would if you were tasked with packaging an application that you'd not seen before.

So without further ado, let's meet amanda....

20.1. An Overview of Amanda

Amanda is a network backup utility. The name *amanda* stands for Advanced Maryland Automatic Network Disk Archiver. If the word Maryland seems somewhat incongruous, it helps to realize that the program was developed at the University of Maryland by James Da Silva and has subsequently been enhanced by many people around the world.

The sources are available at `ftp.cs.umd.edu`, in the `/pub/amanda` directory. At the time of this writing, the latest version of amanda is version 2.3.0. Therefore, it should come as no surprise that the amanda source `tar` file is called `amanda-2.3.0.tar.gz`.

As with most network-centric applications, amanda has a server component and a client component. An amanda server controls how the various client systems are backed up to the server's tape drive. Each amanda client uses the operating system's native `dump` utility to perform the actual backup, which is then compressed and sent to the server. A server can back itself up simply by having the client software installed and configured, just like any other client system.

The software builds with `make`, and most customization is done in two `.h` files in the `config` subdirectory. A fair amount of documentation is available in the `doc` subdirectory. All in all, amanda is a typical non-trivial application.

Amanda can be built on several UNIX-based operating systems. In this chapter, we'll build and package amanda for Red Hat Linux version 4.0.

20.2. Initial Building Without RPM

Because amanda can be built on numerous platforms, there needs to be some initial customization when first building the software. Since customization implies that mistakes will be made, we'll start off by building amanda without any involvement on the part of RPM.

But before we can build amanda, we have to get it and unpack it.

20.2.1. Setting Up a Test Build Area

As already mentioned, the home FTP site for amanda is `ftp.cs.umd.edu`. The sources are in `/pub/amanda`.

After getting the sources, it's necessary to unpack them. We'll unpack them into RPM's SOURCES directory so we can keep all our work in one place:

```
# tar zxvf amanda-2.3.0.tar.gz
amanda-2.3.0/
amanda-2.3.0/COPYRIGHT
amanda-2.3.0/Makefile
amanda-2.3.0/README
...
amanda-2.3.0/man/amtape.8
amanda-2.3.0/tools/
amanda-2.3.0/tools/munge
#
```

As we saw, the sources unpacked into a directory called `amanda-2.3.0`. Let's rename that directory to `amanda-2.3.0-orig` and unpack the sources again:

```
# ls
total 177
drwxr-xr-x 11 adm games 1024 May 19 1996 amanda-2.3.0/
-rw-r--r-- 1 root root 178646 Nov 20 10:42 amanda-2.3.0.tar.gz
# mv amanda-2.3.0 amanda-2.3.0-orig
# tar zxvf amanda-2.3.0.tar.gz
amanda-2.3.0/
amanda-2.3.0/COPYRIGHT
amanda-2.3.0/Makefile
amanda-2.3.0/README
...
amanda-2.3.0/man/amtape.8
amanda-2.3.0/tools/
amanda-2.3.0/tools/munge
# ls
total 178
drwxr-xr-x 11 adm games 1024 May 19 1996 amanda-2.3.0/
drwxr-xr-x 11 adm games 1024 May 19 1996 amanda-2.3.0-orig/
-rw-r--r-- 1 root root 178646 Nov 20 10:42 amanda-2.3.0.tar.gz
#
```

Now why did we do that? The reason lies in the fact that we will undoubtedly need to make changes to the original sources in order to get amanda to build on Linux. We'll do all our hacking in the `amanda-2.3.0` directory and leave the `amanda-2.3.0-orig` directory untouched.

Since one of RPM's design features is to build packages from the original, unmodified sources, the changes we'll make will need to be kept as a set of patches. The `amanda-2.3.0-orig` directory will let us issue a simple recursive `diff` command to create our patches when the time comes.

Now that our sources are unpacked, it's time to work on building the software.

20.2.2. Getting Software to Build

Looking at the docs/INSTALL file, we find that the steps required to get amanda configured and ready to build are actually fairly simple. The first step is to modify tools/munge to point to cpp, the C preprocessor.

Amanda uses cpp to create makefiles containing the appropriate configuration information. This approach is a bit unusual, but not unheard of. In munge, we find the following section:

```
# Customize CPP to point to your system's C preprocessor.

# if cpp is on your path:
CPP=cpp

# if cpp is not on your path, try one of these:
# CPP=/lib/cpp                    # traditional
# CPP=/usr/lib/cpp                # also traditional
# CPP=/usr/ccs/lib/cpp           # Solaris 2.x
```

Since cpp exists in /lib on Red Hat Linux, we need to change this part of munge to

```
# Customize CPP to point to your system's C preprocessor.

# if cpp is on your path:
#CPP=cpp

# if cpp is not on your path, try one of these:
CPP=/lib/cpp                     # traditional
# CPP=/usr/lib/cpp                # also traditional
# CPP=/usr/ccs/lib/cpp           # Solaris 2.x
```

Next, we need to take a look in config/ and create two files:

- config.h, which will contain platform-specific configuration information
- options.h, which will contain site-specific configuration information

There are a number of sample config.h files for a number of different platforms. There is a Linux-specific version, so we copy that file to config.h and review it. After a few changes to reflect our Red Hat Linux environment, it's ready. Now let's turn our attention to options.h.

In the case of options.h, there's only one sample file: options.h-vanilla. As the name implies, this is a basic file that contains a series of #defines that configure amanda for a typical environment. We'll need to make a few changes:

- Define the paths to common utility programs.
- Keep the programs from being named with the suffix -2.3.0.
- Define the directories where the programs should be installed.

While the first change is pretty much standard fare for anyone used to building software, the last two changes are really due to RPM. With RPM, there's no need to name the programs with a version-specific name, as RPM can easily upgrade to a new version and even downgrade back if the new version doesn't work as well. The default paths amanda uses segregate the files so that they can be easily maintained. With RPM, there's no need to do this because every file installed by RPM gets written into the database. In addition, Red Hat Linux systems adhere to the File System Standard, so any package destined for Red Hat systems should really be FSSTND compliant, too. Fortunately for us, amanda was written to make these types of changes easy. But even if we had to hack an installation script, RPM would pick up the changes as part of its patch handling.

We'll spare you the usual discovery of typos, incompatibilities, and the resulting rebuilds. After an undisclosed number of iterations, our config.h and options.h files are perfect. Amanda now builds:

```
# make
Making all in common-src
make[1]: Entering directory '/usr/src/redhat/SOURCES/amanda-2.3.0/common-src'
...
make[1]: Leaving directory '/usr/src/redhat/SOURCES/amanda-2.3.0/man'
#
```

As noted, amanda is constructed so that most of the time changes will be necessary only in tools/munge and in the two files in config. Our situation was no different—after all was said and done, that was all we needed to hack.

20.2.3. Installing and Testing

As we all know, just because software builds doesn't mean that it's ready for prime time. It's necessary to test it first. In order to test amanda, we need to install it. Amanda's makefile has an install target, so let's use that to get started. We'll also get a copy of the output because we'll need that later:

```
# make install
Making install in common-src
...
make[1]: Entering directory '/usr/src/redhat/SOURCES/amanda-2.3.0/client-src'
Installing Amanda client-side programs:
install -c -o bin amandad /usr/lib/amanda
install -c -o bin sendsize /usr/lib/amanda
install -c -o bin calcsize /usr/lib/amanda
install -c -o bin sendbackup-dump /usr/lib/amanda
install -c -o bin sendbackup-gnutar /usr/lib/amanda
install -c -o bin runtar /usr/lib/amanda
install -c -o bin selfcheck /usr/lib/amanda
Setting permissions for setuid-root client programs:
(cd /usr/lib/amanda ; chown root calcsize; chmod u+s calcsize)
(cd /usr/lib/amanda ; chown root runtar; chmod u+s runtar)
...
Making install in server-src
Installing Amanda libexec programs:
install -c -o bin taper /usr/lib/amanda
install -c -o bin dumper /usr/lib/amanda
install -c -o bin driver /usr/lib/amanda
install -c -o bin planner /usr/lib/amanda
install -c -o bin reporter /usr/lib/amanda
install -c -o bin getconf /usr/lib/amanda
```

```
Setting permissions for setuid-root libexec programs:
(cd /usr/lib/amanda ; chown root dumper; chmod u+s dumper)
(cd /usr/lib/amanda ; chown root planner; chmod u+s planner)
Installing Amanda user programs:
install -c -o bin amrestore /usr/sbin
install -c -o bin amadmin /usr/sbin
install -c -o bin amflush /usr/sbin
install -c -o bin amlabel /usr/sbin
install -c -o bin amcheck /usr/sbin
install -c -o bin amdump /usr/sbin
install -c -o bin amcleanup /usr/sbin
install -c -o bin amtape /usr/sbin
Setting permissions for setuid-root user programs:
(cd /usr/sbin ; chown root amcheck; chmod u+s amcheck)
...
Installing Amanda changer libexec programs:
install -c -o bin chg-generic /usr/lib/amanda
...
Installing Amanda man pages:
install -c -o bin amanda.8 /usr/man/man8
install -c -o bin amadmin.8 /usr/man/man8
install -c -o bin amcheck.8 /usr/man/man8
install -c -o bin amcleanup.8 /usr/man/man8
install -c -o bin amdump.8 /usr/man/man8
install -c -o bin amflush.8 /usr/man/man8
install -c -o bin amlabel.8 /usr/man/man8
install -c -o bin amrestore.8 /usr/man/man8
install -c -o bin amtape.8 /usr/man/man8
...
#
```

Okay, no major problems there. Amanda does require a bit of additional effort to get everything running, though. Looking at docs/INSTALL, we follow the steps to get amanda running on our test system as both a client and a server. As we perform each step, we note it for future reference.

For the client:

1. Set up an ~/.rhosts file, allowing the server to connect.

2. Make the disk device files readable by the client.

3. Make /etc/dumpdates readable and writable by the client.

4. Put an amanda entry in /etc/services.

5. Put an amanda entry in /etc/inetd.conf.

6. Issue a kill -HUP on inetd.

For the server:

1. Create a directory to hold the server configuration files.

2. Modify the provided sample configuration files to suit our site.

3. Add crontab entries to run amanda nightly.

4. Put an amanda entry in /etc/services.

Once everything is ready, we run a few tests. Everything performs flawlessly. (Well, eventually it does!) Looks like we've got a good build. Let's start getting RPM involved.

20.3. Initial Building with RPM

Now that amanda has been configured, built, and is operational on our build system, it's time to have RPM take over each of these tasks. The first task is to have RPM make the necessary changes to the original sources. To do that, RPM needs a patch file.

20.3.1. Generating Patches

The `amanda-2.3.0` directory tree is where we did all our work building amanda. We need to take all the work we've done in that directory tree and compare it against the original sources contained in the `amanda-2.3.0-orig` directory tree. But before we do that, we need to clean things up a bit.

20.3.1.1. Cleaning Up the Test Build Area

Looking through our work tree, it has all sorts of junk in it: emacs save files, object files, and the executable programs. In order to generate a clean set of patches, all these extraneous files must go. Looking over amanda's makefiles, there is a clean target that should take care of most of the junk:

```
# make clean
Making clean in common-src
...
rm -f *~ *.o *.a genversion version.c Makefile.out
...
Making clean in client-src
...
rm -f amandad sendsize calcsize sendbackup-dump
sendbackup-gnutar runtar selfcheck *~ *.o Makefile.out
...
Making clean in server-src
...
rm -f amrestore amadmin amflush amlabel amcheck amdump
amcleanup amtape taper dumper driver planner reporter
getconf *~ *.o Makefile.out
...
Making clean in changer-src
...
rm -f chg-generic *~ *.o Makefile.out
...
Making clean in man
...
rm -f *~ Makefile.out
...
#
```

Looking in the tools and config directories where we did all our work, we see that there are still emacs save files there. A bit of studying confirms that the makefiles don't bother to clean these two directories. That's a nice touch because a make clean won't wipe out old copies of the config files, giving you a chance to go back to them in case you've botched something. However, in our case, we're sure we won't need the save files, so out they go:

```
# cd /usr/src/redhat/SOURCES/amanda-2.3.0
# find . -name "* " -exec rm -vf \;
./config/config.h
./config/options.h
./tools/munge
#
```

We let find take a look at the whole directory tree, just in case there was something still out there that we'd forgotten about. As you can see, the only save files are from the three files we've been working on.

You'll note that we've left our modified munge file, as well as the config.h and options.h files we so carefully crafted. That's intentional, as we want to make sure those changes are applied when RPM patches the sources. Everything looks pretty clean, so it's time to make the patches.

20.3.1.2. Actually Generating Patches

This step is actually pretty anticlimactic:

```
# diff -uNr amanda-2.3.0-orig/ amanda-2.3.0/ > amanda-2.3.0-linux.patch
#
```

With that one command, we've compared each file in the untouched directory tree (amanda-2.3.0-orig) with the directory tree we've been working in (amanda-2.3.0). If we've done our homework, the only things in the patch file should be related to the files we've changed. Let's take a look through it to make sure:

```
# cd /usr/src/redhat/SOURCES
# cat amanda-2.3.0-linux.patch
diff -uNr amanda-2.3.0-orig/config/config.h amanda-2.3.0/config/config.h
--- amanda-2.3.0-orig/config/config.h Wed Dec 31 19:00:00 1969
+++ amanda-2.3.0/config/config.h Sat Nov 16 16:22:47 1996
@@ -0,0 +1,52 @@
...
diff -uNr amanda-2.3.0-orig/config/options.h amanda-2.3.0/config/options.h
--- amanda-2.3.0-orig/config/options.h Wed Dec 31 19:00:00 1969
+++ amanda-2.3.0/config/options.h Sat Nov 16 17:08:57 1996
@@ -0,0 +1,211 @@
...
diff -uNr amanda-2.3.0-orig/tools/munge amanda-2.3.0/tools/munge
--- amanda-2.3.0-orig/tools/munge Sun May 19 22:11:25 1996
+++ amanda-2.3.0/tools/munge Sat Nov 16 16:23:50 1996
@@ -35,10 +35,10 @@
# Customize CPP to point to your system's C preprocessor.

# if cpp is on your path:
-CPP=cpp
+# CPP=cpp
```

```
# if cpp is not on your path, try one of these:
-# CPP=/lib/cpp                # traditional
+CPP=/lib/cpp                 # traditional
# CPP=/usr/lib/cpp            # also traditional
# CPP=/usr/ccs/lib/cpp        # Solaris 2.x
#
```

The patch file contains complete copies of our config.h and options.h files, followed by the changes we've made to munge. Looks good! Time to hand this grunt work over to RPM.

20.3.2. Making a First-Cut Spec File

Since amanda comes in two parts, it's obvious that we'll need to use subpackages: one for the client software and one for the server. Given that, and the fact that the first part of any spec file consists of tags that are easily filled in, let's sit down and fill in the blanks, tag-wise:

```
Summary: Amanda Network Backup System
Name: amanda
Version: 2.3.08
Release: 1
Group: System/Backup
Copyright: BSD-like, but see COPYRIGHT file for details
Packager: Edward C. Bailey <bailey@rpm.org>
URL: http://www.cs.umd.edu/projects/amanda/
Source: ftp://ftp.cs.umd.edu/pub/amanda/amanda-2.3.0.tar.gz
Patch: amanda-2.3.0-linux.patch
%description
Amanda is a client/server backup system. It uses standard tape
devices and networking, so all you need is any working tape drive
and a network. You can use it for local backups as well.
```

That part was pretty easy. We set the package's release number to 1. We'll undoubtedly be changing that as we continue work on the spec file. You'll notice that we've included a URL tag line; the uniform resource locator there points to the home page for the amanda project, making it easier for the user to get additional information on amanda.

The Source tag here includes the name of the original source tar file and is preceded by the URL pointing to the file's primary location. Again, this makes it easy for the user to grab a copy of the sources from the software's "birthplace."

Finally, the patch file that we've just created gets a line of its own on the Patch tag line.

Next, let's take a look at the tags for our two subpackages. Let's start with the client:

```
%package client
Summary: Client-side Amanda package
Group: System/Backup
Requires: dump
%description client
The Amanda Network Backup system contains software necessary to
automatically perform backups across a network. Amanda consists of
two packages -- a client (this package), and a server:
```

```
The client package enable a network-capable system to have its
filesystems backed up by a system running the Amanda server.

NOTE: In order for a system to perform backups of itself, install both
the client and server packages!
```

The %package directive names the package. Because we wanted the subpackages to be named amanda-<something>, we didn't use the -n option. This means our client subpackage will be called amanda-client, just as we wanted. RPM requires unique summary, %description, and group tags for each subpackage, so we've included them. Of course, it would be a good idea even if RPM didn't require them—we've used the tags to provide client-specific information.

The requires tag is the only other tag in the client subpackage. Because amanda uses dump on the client system, we included this tag so that RPM will ensure that the dump package is present on client systems.

Next, let's take a look at the tags for the server subpackage:

```
%package server
Summary: Server-side Amanda package
Group: System/Backup
%description server
The Amanda Network Backup system contains software necessary to
automatically perform backups across a network. Amanda consists of
two package -- a client, and a server (this package):

The server package enables a network-capable system to control one
or more Amanda client systems performing backups. The server system
will direct all backups to a locally attached tape drive. Therefore,
the server system requires a tape drive.

NOTE: In order for a system to perform backups of itself, install both
the client and server packages!
```

No surprises here, really. You'll note that the server subpackage has no requires tag for the dump package. The reason for that is due to a design decision we've made. Since amanda is comprised of a client and a server component, in order for the server system to perform backups of itself, the client component must be installed. Since we've already made the client subpackage require dump, we've already covered the bases.

Since an amanda server cannot back itself up without the client software, why don't we have the server subpackage require the client subpackage? Well, that could be done, but the fact of the matter is that there are cases where an amanda server won't need to back itself up. So the server subpackage needs no package requirements.

20.3.2.1. Adding the Build-Time Scripts

Next we need to add the build-time scripts. There's really not much to them:

```
%prep
%setup
```

```
%build
make

%install
make install
```

The `%prep` script consists of one line containing the simplest flavor of `%setup` macro. Since we only need `%setup` to unpack one set of sources, there are no options we need to add.

The `%build` script is just as simple, with the single `make` command required to build amanda.

Finally, the `%install` script maintains our singe-line trend for build-time scripts. Here a simple `make install` will put all the files where they need to be for RPM to package them.

20.3.2.2. Adding `%files` Lists

The last part of our initial attempt at a spec file is a `%files` list for each package the spec file will build. Because we're planning on a client and a server subpackage, we'll need two `%files` lists. For the time being, we'll just add the `%files` lines; we'll be adding the actual filenames later:

```
%files client

%file server
```

There's certainly more to come, but this is enough to get us started. And the first thing we want RPM to do is to unpack the amanda sources.

20.3.3. Getting the Original Sources Unpacked

In keeping with a step-by-step approach, RPM has an option that let's us stop the build process after the `%prep` script has run. Let's give the `-bp` option a try and see how things look:

```
# rpm -bp amanda-2.3.0.spec
* Package: amanda
* Package: amanda-client
* Package: amanda-server
+ umask 022
+ echo Executing: %prep
Executing: %prep
+ cd /usr/src/redhat/BUILD
+ cd /usr/src/redhat/BUILD
+ rm -rf amanda-2.3.0
+ gzip -dc /usr/src/redhat/SOURCES/amanda-2.3.0.tar.gz
+ tar -xvvf -
drwxr-xr-x 3/20              0 May 19 22:10 1996 amanda-2.3.0/
-rw-r--r-- 3/20           1389 May 19 22:11 1996 amanda-2.3.0/COPYRIGHT
-rw-r--r-- 3/20           1958 May 19 22:11 1996 amanda-2.3.0/Makefile
-rw-r--r-- 3/20          11036 May 19 22:11 1996 amanda-2.3.0/README
...
-rw-r--r-- 3/20           2010 May 19 22:11 1996 amanda-2.3.0/man/amtape.8
drwxr-xr-x 3/20              0 May 19 22:11 1996 amanda-2.3.0/tools/
-rwxr-xr-x 3/20           2437 May 19 22:11 1996 amanda-2.3.0/tools/munge
+ [ 0 -ne 0 ]
+ cd amanda-2.3.0
```

```
+ cd /usr/src/redhat/BUILD/amanda-2.3.0
+ chown -R root.root .
+ chmod -R a+rX,g-w,o-w .
+ exit 0
#
```

By looking at the output, it would be pretty hard to miss the fact that the sources were un-packed. If we look in RPM's default build area (/usr/src/redhat/BUILD), we'll see an amanda directory tree:

```
# cd /usr/src/redhat/BUILD/
# ls -l
total 3
drwxr-xr-x 11 root root 1024 May 19 1996 amanda-2.3.0
#
```

After a quick look around, it seems like the sources were unpacked properly. But wait—where are our carefully crafted configuration files in config? Why isn't tools/munge modified?

20.3.4. Getting Patches Properly Applied

Ah, perhaps our %prep script was a bit too simple. We need to apply our patch. So let's add two things to our spec file:

■ A patch tag line pointing to our patch file

■ A %patch macro in our %prep script

Easy enough. At the top of the spec file, along with the other tags, let's add

```
Patch: amanda-2.3.0-linux.patch
```

Then we'll make our %prep script look like this:

```
%prep
%setup
%patch -p 1
```

There, that should do it. Let's give that -bp option another try:

```
# rpm -bp amanda-2.3.0.spec
* Package: amanda
* Package: amanda-client
* Package: amanda-server
+ umask 022
+ echo Executing: %prep
Executing: %prep
+ cd /usr/src/redhat/BUILD
+ cd /usr/src/redhat/BUILD
+ rm -rf amanda-2.3.0
+ gzip -dc /usr/src/redhat/SOURCES/amanda-2.3.0.tar.gz
+ tar -xvvf -
drwxr-xr-x 3/20           0 May 19 22:10 1996 amanda-2.3.0/
-rw-r--r-- 3/20        1389 May 19 22:11 1996 amanda-2.3.0/COPYRIGHT
-rw-r--r-- 3/20        1958 May 19 22:11 1996 amanda-2.3.0/Makefile
-rw-r--r-- 3/20       11036 May 19 22:11 1996 amanda-2.3.0/README
```

```
...
-rw-r--r-- 3/20            2010 May 19 22:11 1996 amanda-2.3.0/man/amtape.8
drwxr-xr-x 3/20               0 May 19 22:11 1996 amanda-2.3.0/tools/
-rwxr-xr-x 3/20 2437            May 19 22:11 1996 amanda-2.3.0/tools/munge
+ [ 0 -ne 0 ]
+ cd amanda-2.3.0
+ cd /usr/src/redhat/BUILD/amanda-2.3.0
+ chown -R root.root .
+ chmod -R a+rX,g-w,o-w .
+ echo Patch #0:
Patch #0:
+ patch -p1 -s
+ exit 0
#
```

Not much difference, until the very end, where we see the patch being applied. Let's take a look into the build area and see if our configuration files are there:

```
# cd /usr/src/redhat/BUILD/amanda-2.3.0/config
# ls -l
total 58
-rw-r--r--   1 root     root        7518 May 19  1996  config-common.h
-rw-r--r--   1 root     root        1846 Nov 20 20:46 config.h
-rw-r--r--   1 root     root        2081 May 19  1996  config.h-aix
-rw-r--r--   1 root     root        1690 May 19  1996  config.h-bsdi1
...
-rw-r--r--   1 root     root        1830 May 19  1996  config.h-ultrix4
-rw-r--r--   1 root     root           0 Nov 20 20:46 config.h.orig
-rw-r--r--   1 root     root        7196 Nov 20 20:46 options.h
-rw-r--r--   1 root     root        7236 May 19  1996  options.h-vanilla
-rw-r--r--   1 root     root           0 Nov 20 20:46 options.h.orig
#
```

Much better. Those zero-length .orig files are a dead giveaway that patch has been here, as are the dates on config.h and options.h. In the tools directory, munge has been modified, too. These sources are ready for building!

20.3.5. Letting RPM Do the Building

We know that the sources are ready. We know that the %build script is ready. There shouldn't be much in the way of surprises if we let RPM build amanda. Let's use the -bc option to stop things after the %build script completes:

```
# rpm -bc amanda-2.3.0.spec
* Package: amanda
* Package: amanda-client
* Package: amanda-server
...
echo Executing: %build
Executing: %build
+ cd /usr/src/redhat/BUILD
+ cd amanda-2.3.0
+ make
Making all in common-src
make[1]: Entering directory '/usr/src/redhat/BUILD/amanda-2.3.0/common-src'
```

```
../tools/munge Makefile.in Makefile.out
make[2]: Entering directory '/usr/src/redhat/BUILD/amanda-2.3.0/common-src'
cc -g -I. -I../config -c error.c -o error.o
cc -g -I. -I../config -c alloc.c -o alloc.o
...
Making all in man
make[1]: Entering directory '/usr/src/redhat/BUILD/amanda-2.3.0/man'
../tools/munge Makefile.in Makefile.out
make[2]: Entering directory '/usr/src/redhat/BUILD/amanda-2.3.0/man'
make[2]: Nothing to be done for 'all'.
make[2]: Leaving directory '/usr/src/redhat/BUILD/amanda-2.3.0/man'
make[1]: Leaving directory '/usr/src/redhat/BUILD/amanda-2.3.0/man'
+ exit 0
#
```

As we thought, no surprises. A quick look through the build area shows a full assortment of
binaries, all ready to be installed. So it seems that the most natural thing to do next would be
to let RPM install amanda.

20.3.6. Letting RPM Do the Installing

And that's just what we're going to do! Our %install script has the necessary make install
command, so let's give it a shot:

```
# rpm -bi amanda-2.3.0.spec
* Package: amanda
* Package: amanda-client
* Package: amanda-server
...
echo Executing: %build
Executing: %build
+ cd /usr/src/redhat/BUILD
+ cd amanda-2.3.0
+ make
Making all in common-src
make[1]: Entering directory '/usr/src/redhat/BUILD/amanda-2.3.0/common-src'
../tools/munge Makefile.in Makefile.out
make[2]: Entering directory '/usr/src/redhat/BUILD/amanda-2.3.0/common-src'
cc -g -I. -I../config -c error.c -o error.o
cc -g -I. -I../config -c alloc.c -o alloc.o
...
+ umask 022
+ echo Executing: %install
Executing: %install
+ cd /usr/src/redhat/BUILD
+ cd amanda-2.3.0
+ make install
Making install in common-src
make[1]: Entering directory '/usr/src/redhat/BUILD/amanda-2.3.0/common-src'
...
install -c -o bin amrestore.8 /usr/man/man8
install -c -o bin amtape.8 /usr/man/man8
make[2]: Leaving directory '/usr/src/redhat/BUILD/amanda-2.3.0/man'
make[1]: Leaving directory '/usr/src/redhat/BUILD/amanda-2.3.0/man'
+ exit 0
+ umask 022
```

```
+ echo Executing: special doc
Executing: special doc
+ cd /usr/src/redhat/BUILD
+ cd amanda-2.3.0
+ DOCDIR=//usr/doc/amanda-2.3.0-1
+ DOCDIR=//usr/doc/amanda-client-2.3.0-1
+ DOCDIR=//usr/doc/amanda-server-2.3.0-1
+ exit 0
#
```

Everything looks pretty good. At this point, the amanda software, built by RPM, has been installed on the build system. Since we performed all the configuration steps before, when we were manually building amanda, everything should still be configured properly to test this new build. (Of course, if the process of installing the software changed some necessary config files, they would have to be redone, but in this case it didn't happen.) So why don't we give the new binaries a try?

20.3.7. Testing RPM's Handiwork

After a quick double-check to ensure that all the configuration steps were still in place from our manual build, we reran our tests. No problems were found. It's time to build some packages!

20.4. Package Building

Okay, let's go for broke and tell RPM to do the works, including the creation of the binary and source packages:

```
# rpm -ba amanda-2.3.0.spec
* Package: amanda
* Package: amanda-client
* Package: amanda-server
...
echo Executing: %build
Executing: %build
+ cd /usr/src/redhat/BUILD
+ cd amanda-2.3.0
+ make
Making all in common-src
...
+ echo Executing: %install
Executing: %install
+ cd /usr/src/redhat/BUILD
+ cd amanda-2.3.0
+ make install
Making install in common-src
...
+ echo Executing: special doc
Executing: special doc
...
Binary Packaging: amanda-client-2.3.0-1
```

```
Finding dependencies...
Requires (1): dump
1 block
Generating signature: 0
Wrote: /usr/src/redhat/RPMS/i386/amanda-client-2.3.0-1.i386.rpm
Binary Packaging: amanda-server-2.3.0-1
Finding dependencies...
1 block
Generating signature: 0
Wrote: /usr/src/redhat/RPMS/i386/amanda-server-2.3.0-1.i386.rpm
+ umask 022
+ echo Executing: %clean
Executing: %clean
+ cd /usr/src/redhat/BUILD
+ cd amanda-2.3.0
+ exit 0
Source Packaging: amanda-2.3.0-1
amanda-2.3.0.spec
amanda-2.3.0-linux.patch
amanda-2.3.0.tar.gz
374 blocks
Generating signature: 0
Wrote: /usr/src/redhat/SRPMS/amanda-2.3.0-1.src.rpm
#
```

Great! Let's take a look at our handiwork:

```
# cd /usr/src/redhat/RPMS/i386/
# ls -l
total 2
-rw-r--r-- 1 root root 1246 Nov 20 21:19 amanda-client-2.3.0-1.i386.rpm
-rw-r--r-- 1 root root 1308 Nov 20 21:19 amanda-server-2.3.0-1.i386.rpm
#
rpm-first-look
```

Hmmm, those binary packages look sort of small. We'd better see what's in there:

```
# rpm -qilp amanda-*-1.i386.rpm
Name : amanda-client                  Distribution: (none)
Version : 2.3.0                             Vendor: (none)
Release : 1                             Build Date: Wed Nov 20 21:19:44 1996
Install date: (none)                    Build Host: moocow.rpm.org
Group : System/Backup                   Source RPM: amanda-2.3.0-1.src.rpm
Size : 0
Summary : Client-side Amanda package
Description :
The Amanda Network Backup system contains software necessary to
automatically perform backups across a network. Amanda consists of
two packages -- a client (this package), and a server:

The client package enable a network-capable system to have its
filesystems backed up by a system running the Amanda server.

NOTE: In order for a system to perform backups of itself, install both
the client and server packages!
(contains no files)
```

```
Name : amanda-server          Distribution: (none)
Version : 2.3.0                     Vendor: (none)
Release : 1                     Build Date: Wed Nov 20 21:19:44 1996
Install date: (none)            Build Host: moocow.rpm.org
Group : System/Backup           Source RPM: amanda-2.3.0-1.src.rpm
Size : 0
Summary : Server-side Amanda package
Description :
The Amanda Network Backup system contains software necessary to
automatically perform backups across a network. Amanda consists of
two package -- a client, and a server (this package):

The server package enables a network-capable system to control one
or more Amanda client systems performing backups. The server system
will direct all backups to a locally attached tape drive. Therefore,
the server system requires a tape drive.

NOTE: In order for a system to perform backups of itself, install both
the client and server packages!
(contains no files)

#
```

What do they mean, (`contains no files`)? The spec file has perfectly good `%files` lists....

Oops.

20.4.1. Creating the `%files` List

Everything was going so smoothly, we forgot that the `%files` lists were going to need files. No problem; we just need to put the filenames in there, and we'll be all set. But is it really that easy?

20.4.1.1. How to Find the Installed Files

Luckily, it's not too bad. Since we saved the output from our first `make install`, we can see the filenames as they're installed. Of course, it's important to make sure the install output is valid. Fortunately for us, amanda didn't require much fiddling by the time we got it built and tested. If it had, we would have had to get more recent output from the installation phase.

It's time for more decisions. We have one list of installed files and two `%files` lists. It would be silly to put all the files in both `%files` lists, so we have to decide which file goes where.

This is where experience with the software really pays off, because the wrong decision made here can result in awkward, ill-featured packages. Here's the `%files` list we came up with for the client subpackage:

```
%files client
/usr/lib/amanda/amandad
/usr/lib/amanda/sendsize
/usr/lib/amanda/calcsize
/usr/lib/amanda/sendbackup-dump
/usr/lib/amanda/selfcheck
```

```
/usr/lib/amanda/sendbackup-gnutar
/usr/lib/amanda/runtar
README
COPYRIGHT
docs/INSTALL
docs/SYSTEM.NOTES
docs/WHATS.NEW
```

The files in /usr/lib/amanda are all the client-side amanda programs, so that part was easy. The remaining files are part of the original source archive. Amanda doesn't install them, but they contain information that users should see.

Realizing that RPM can't package these files specified as they are, let's leave the client %files list for a moment and check out the list for the server subpackage:

```
%files server
/usr/sbin/amadmin
/usr/sbin/amcheck
/usr/sbin/amcleanup
/usr/sbin/amdump
/usr/sbin/amflush
/usr/sbin/amlabel
/usr/sbin/amrestore
/usr/sbin/amtape
/usr/lib/amanda/taper
/usr/lib/amanda/dumper
/usr/lib/amanda/driver
/usr/lib/amanda/planner
/usr/lib/amanda/reporter
/usr/lib/amanda/getconf
/usr/lib/amanda/chg-generic
/usr/man/man8/amanda.8
/usr/man/man8/amadmin.8
/usr/man/man8/amcheck.8
/usr/man/man8/amcleanup.8
/usr/man/man8/amdump.8
/usr/man/man8/amflush.8
/usr/man/man8/amlabel.8
/usr/man/man8/amrestore.8
/usr/man/man8/amtape.8
README
COPYRIGHT
docs/INSTALL
docs/KERBEROS
docs/SUNOS4.BUG
docs/SYSTEM.NOTES
docs/TAPE.CHANGERS
docs/WHATS.NEW
docs/MULTITAPE
example
```

The files in /usr/sbin are programs that will be run by the amanda administrator in order to perform backups and restores. The files in /usr/lib/amanda are the server-side programs that do the actual work during backups. Following that are a number of man pages: one for each program to be run by the amanda administrator, and one with an overview of amanda.

Bringing up the rear are a number of files that are not installed, but would be handy for the amanda administrator to have available. There is some overlap with the files that will be part of the client subpackage, but the additional files here discuss features that would interest only amanda administrators. Included here is the example subdirectory, which contains a few sample configuration files for the amanda server.

As in the client %files list, these last files can't be packaged by RPM as we've listed them. We need to use a few more of RPM's tricks to get them packaged.

20.4.1.2. Applying Directives

Since we'd like the client subpackage to include those files that are not normally installed, and since the files are documentation, let's use the %doc directive on them. That will accomplish two things:

■ When the client subpackage is installed, it will direct RPM to place them in a package-specific directory in /usr/doc.

■ It will tag the files as being documentation, making it possible for users to easily track down the documentation with a simple rpm -qd command.

In the course of looking over the %files lists, it becomes apparent that the directory /usr/lib/ amanda will contain only files from the two amanda subpackages. If the subpackages are erased, the directory will remain, which won't hurt anything, but it isn't as neat as it could be. But if we add the directory to the list, RPM will automatically package every file in the directory. Because the files in that directory are part of both the client and the server subpackages, we'll need to use the %dir directive to instruct RPM to package only the directory.

After these changes, here's what the client %files list looks like now:

```
%files client
%dir /usr/lib/amanda/
/usr/lib/amanda/amandad
/usr/lib/amanda/sendsize
/usr/lib/amanda/calcsize
/usr/lib/amanda/sendbackup-dump
/usr/lib/amanda/selfcheck
/usr/lib/amanda/sendbackup-gnutar
/usr/lib/amanda/runtar
%doc README
%doc COPYRIGHT
%doc docs/INSTALL
%doc docs/SYSTEM.NOTES
%doc docs/WHATS.NEW
```

We've also applied the same directives to the server %files list:

```
%files server
/usr/sbin/amadmin
/usr/sbin/amcheck
/usr/sbin/amcleanup
/usr/sbin/amdump
```

```
/usr/sbin/amflush
/usr/sbin/amlabel
/usr/sbin/amrestore
/usr/sbin/amtape
%dir /usr/lib/amanda/
/usr/lib/amanda/taper
/usr/lib/amanda/dumper
/usr/lib/amanda/driver
/usr/lib/amanda/planner
/usr/lib/amanda/reporter
/usr/lib/amanda/getconf
/usr/lib/amanda/chg-generic
/usr/man/man8/amanda.8
/usr/man/man8/amadmin.8
/usr/man/man8/amcheck.8
/usr/man/man8/amcleanup.8
/usr/man/man8/amdump.8
/usr/man/man8/amflush.8
/usr/man/man8/amlabel.8
/usr/man/man8/amrestore.8
/usr/man/man8/amtape.8
%doc README
%doc COPYRIGHT
%doc docs/INSTALL
%doc docs/KERBEROS
%doc docs/SUNOS4.BUG
%doc docs/SYSTEM.NOTES
%doc docs/TAPE.CHANGERS
%doc docs/WHATS.NEW
%doc docs/MULTITAPE
%doc example
```

You'll note that we neglected to use the %doc directive on the man page files. The reason is that RPM automatically tags any file destined for /usr/man as documentation. Now our spec file has a complete set of tags, the two subpackages are defined, it has build-time scripts that work, and now, %files lists for each subpackage. Why don't we try that build again?

```
# rpm -ba amanda-2.3.0.spec
* Package: amanda
* Package: amanda-client
* Package: amanda-server
...
echo Executing: %build
Executing: %build
+ cd /usr/src/redhat/BUILD
+ cd amanda-2.3.0
+ make
Making all in common-src
...
+ echo Executing: %install
Executing: %install
+ cd /usr/src/redhat/BUILD
+ cd amanda-2.3.0
+ make install
Making install in common-src
...
+ echo Executing: special doc
Executing: special doc
```

```
...
Binary Packaging: amanda-client-2.3.0-6
Finding dependencies...
Requires (3): libc.so.5 libdb.so.2 dump
usr/doc/amanda-client-2.3.0-6
usr/doc/amanda-client-2.3.0-6/COPYRIGHT
usr/doc/amanda-client-2.3.0-6/INSTALL
...
usr/lib/amanda/sendbackup-gnutar
usr/lib/amanda/sendsize
1453 blocks
Generating signature: 0
Wrote: /usr/src/redhat/RPMS/i386/amanda-client-2.3.0-6.i386.rpm
Binary Packaging: amanda-server-2.3.0-6
Finding dependencies...
Requires (2): libc.so.5 libdb.so.2
usr/doc/amanda-server-2.3.0-6
usr/doc/amanda-server-2.3.0-6/COPYRIGHT
usr/doc/amanda-server-2.3.0-6/INSTALL
...
usr/sbin/amrestore
usr/sbin/amtape
3404 blocks
Generating signature: 0
Wrote: /usr/src/redhat/RPMS/i386/amanda-server-2.3.0-6.i386.rpm
...
Source Packaging: amanda-2.3.0-6
amanda-2.3.0.spec
amanda-2.3.0-linux.patch
amanda-rpm-instructions.tar.gz
amanda-2.3.0.tar.gz
393 blocks
Generating signature: 0
Wrote: /usr/src/redhat/SRPMS/amanda-2.3.0-6.src.rpm
#
```

If we take a quick look at the client and server subpackages, we find that, sure enough, this time they contain files:

```
# cd /usr/src/redhat/RPMS/i386/
# ls -l amanda-*
-rw-r--r-- 1 root root 211409 Nov 21 15:56 amanda-client-2.3.0-1.i386.rpm
-rw-r--r-- 1 root root 512814 Nov 21 15:57 amanda-server-2.3.0-1.i386.rpm
# rpm -qilp amanda-*
Name         : amanda-client    Distribution: (none)
Version      : 2.3.0                  Vendor: (none)
Release      : 1                  Build Date: Thu Nov 21 15:55:59 1996
Install date: (none)             Build Host: moocow.rpm.org
Group        : System/Backup     Source RPM: amanda-2.3.0-1.src.rpm
Size         : 737101
Summary      : Client-side Amanda package
Description :
The Amanda Network Backup system contains software necessary to
automatically perform backups across a network. Amanda consists of
two packages -- a client (this package), and a server:

The client package enable a network-capable system to have its
filesystems backed up by a system running the Amanda server.
```

```
NOTE: In order for a system to perform backups of itself, install both
the client and server packages!

/usr/doc/amanda-client-2.3.0-1
/usr/doc/amanda-client-2.3.0-1/COPYRIGHT
/usr/doc/amanda-client-2.3.0-1/INSTALL
...
/usr/lib/amanda/sendbackup-gnutar
/usr/lib/amanda/sendsize

Name        : amanda-server    Distribution: (none)
Version     : 2.3.0                  Vendor: (none)
Release     : 1                  Build Date: Thu Nov 21 15:55:59 1996
Install date: (none)            Build Host: moocow.rpm.org
Group       : System/Backup     Source RPM: amanda-2.3.0-1.src.rpm
Size        : 1733825
Summary     : Server-side Amanda package
Description :
The Amanda Network Backup system contains software necessary to
automatically perform backups across a network. Amanda consists of
two package -- a client, and a server (this package):

The server package enables a network-capable system to control one
or more Amanda client systems performing backups. The server system
will direct all backups to a locally attached tape drive. Therefore,
the server system requires a tape drive.

NOTE: In order for a system to perform backups of itself, install both
the client and server packages!

/usr/doc/amanda-server-2.3.0-1
/usr/doc/amanda-server-2.3.0-1/COPYRIGHT
/usr/doc/amanda-server-2.3.0-1/INSTALL
...
/usr/sbin/amrestore
/usr/sbin/amtape
#
```

We're finally ready to test these packages!

20.4.2. Testing Those First Packages

The system we've built the packages on already has amanda installed. This is due to the build process itself. However, we can install the new packages on top of the already-existing files:

```
# cd /usr/src/redhat/RPMS/i386
# rpm -ivh amanda-*-1.i386.rpm
amanda-client ###########################################
amanda-server ###########################################
#
```

Running some tests, it looks like everything is running well. But back in Chapter 11, specifically in section 11.5.2, we mentioned that it is possible to install a newly built package on the build system and not realize that the package is missing files. Well, there's another reason installing the package on the build system for testing is a bad idea. Let's bring our packages to a different system, test them there, and see what happens.

20.4.2.1. Installing the Package on a Different System

Looks like we're almost through. Let's install the packages on another system that has not previously run amanda, and test it there:

```
# rpm -ivh amanda-*-1.i386.rpm
amanda-client ##################################################
amanda-server ##################################################
#
```

The install went smoothly enough, but testing did not. Why? Nothing was set up! The server configuration files, the `inetd.conf` entry for the client—everything was missing. If we stop and think about it for a moment, it makes sense: We had gone through all those steps on the build system, but none of those steps can be packaged as files.

After following the steps in the installation instructions, everything works. While we could expect users to do most of the grunt work associated with getting amanda configured, RPM does have the capability to run scripts when packages are installed and erased. Why don't we use that feature to make life easier for our users?

20.4.3. Finishing Touches

At this point in the build process, we're on the home stretch. The software builds correctly and is packaged. It's time to stop looking at things from a "build the software" perspective, and time to starting looking at things from a "package the software" point of view.

The difference lies in looking at the packages from the user's perspective. Does the package install easily, or does it require a lot of effort to make it operative? When the package is removed, does it clean up after itself, or does it leave bits and pieces strewn throughout the filesystem?

Let's put a bit more effort into this spec file and make life easier on our users.

20.4.3.1. Creating Install Scripts

When it comes to needing postinstallation configuration, amanda certainly is no slouch! We'll work on the client first. Let's look at a section of the script we wrote, comment on it, and move on:

```
%post client

# See if they've installed amanda before...
# If they have, none of this should be necessary...

if [ "$1" = 1 ];
then
```

First, we start the script with a %post statement and indicate that this script is for the client subpackage. As the comments indicate, we only want to perform the following tasks if this is the first time the client subpackage has been installed. To do this, we use the first and only argument passed to the script. It is a number indicating how many instances of this package will be installed after the current installation is complete.

If the argument is equal to 1, no other instances of the client subpackage are presently installed and this one is the first. Let's continue:

```
# Set disk devices so that bin can read them
# (This is actually done on Red Hat Linux; only need to add bin to
# group disk)

if grep "^disk::.*bin" /etc/group > /dev/null
then
 true
else

# If there are any members in group disk, add bin after a comma...
 sed -e 's/\(^disk::[0-9]\{1,\}:.\{1,\}\)/\1,bin/' /etc/group > /etc/group.tmp

# If there are no members in group disk, add bin...
 sed -e 's/\(^disk::[0-9]\{1,\}:$\)/\1bin/' /etc/group.tmp > /etc/group

# clean up!
 rm -f /etc/group.tmp
fi
```

One of amanda's requirements is that the user ID running the dumps on the client needs to be able to read from every disk's device file. The folks at Red Hat have done half the work for us by creating a group disk and giving that group read/write access to every disk device. Since our dumpuser is bin, we only need to add bin to the disk group. Two lines of sed, and we're done!

The next section is related to the last. It also focuses on making sure bin can access everything it needs while doing backups:

```
# Also set /etc/dumpdates to be writable by group disk

chgrp disk /etc/dumpdates
chmod g+w /etc/dumpdates
```

Since amanda uses dump to obtain the backups, and since dump keeps track of the backups in /etc/dumpdates, it's only natural that bin will need read/write access to the file. In a perfect world, /etc/dumpdates would have already been set to allow group disk to read and write, but we had to do it ourselves. It's not a big problem, though.

Next, we need to create the appropriate network-related entries so that amanda clients can communicate with amanda servers and vice versa:

```
# Add amanda line to /etc/services

if grep "^amanda" /etc/services >/dev/null
then
```

```
 true
else
 echo "amanda 10080/udp # Added by package amanda-client" >>/etc/services
fi
```

By using `grep` to look for lines that begin with the letters `amanda`, we can easily see whether `/etc/services` is already configured properly. If it isn't, we simply append a line to the end.

We also added a comment so that sysadmins will know where the entry came from and either take our word for it or issue an `rpm -q --scripts amanda-client` command and see for themselves. We did it all on one line because it makes the script simpler.

Let's look at the rest of the network-related part of this script:

```
# Add amanda line to /etc/inetd.conf

if grep "^amanda" /etc/inetd.conf >/dev/null
then
 true
else
 echo "amanda dgram udp wait bin /usr/lib/amanda/amandad amandad
# added by package amanda-client" >>/etc/inetd.conf

# Kick inetd

if [ -f /var/run/inetd.pid ];
then
 kill -HUP 'cat /var/run/inetd.pid'
fi
fi
fi
```

Here, we've used the same approach to add an entry to `/etc/inetd.conf`. We then send a hangup signal to `inetd` so the change will take effect, and we're done!

Oh, and that last `fi` at the end? That's to close the `if [ "$1" = 1 ]` at the start of the script. Now let's look at the server's postinstall script:

```
%post server
# See if they've installed amanda before...

if [ "$1" = 1 ];
then

# Add amanda line to /etc/services

if grep "^amanda" /etc/services >/dev/null
then
 true
else
 echo "amanda 10080/udp # Added by package amanda-server">>/etc/services
fi

fi
```

That was short! And this huge difference brings up a good point about writing install scripts: It's important to understand what you as the package builder should do for the users, and what they should do for themselves.

In the case of the client package, every one of the steps performed by the postinstall script was something that a fairly knowledgeable user could have done. But all these steps have one thing in common. No matter how the user configures amanda, these steps will never change. And given the nature of client/server applications, there's a good chance that many more amanda client packages will be installed than amanda servers. Would you like to be tasked with installing this package on 20 systems and performing each of the steps we've automated 20 times? We thought not.

There is one step we did not automate for the client package: the creation of an .rhosts file. Since this file must contain the name of the amanda server, we have no way of knowing what the file should look like. Therefore, that's one step we can't automate.

The server's postinstall script is so short because there's little else that can be automated. The other steps required to set up an amanda server include the following:

1. Choosing a configuration name, which requires user input.
2. Creating a directory to hold the server configuration files, named according to the configuration name, which depends on the first step.
3. Modifying sample configuration files to suit the site, which requires user input.
4. Adding crontab entries to run amanda nightly, which requires user input.

Since every step depends on the user making decisions, the best way to handle them is to not handle them at all. Let the user do it!

20.4.3.2. Creating Uninstall Scripts

Where there are install scripts, there are uninstall scripts. While there is no ironclad rule to that effect, it is a good practice. Following this practice, we have an uninstall script for the client package, and one for the server. Let's take the client first:

```
%postun client

# First, see if we're the last amanda-client package on the system...
# If not, then we don't need to do this stuff...

if [ "$1" = 0 ];
then
```

As before, we start out with a declaration of the type of script this is and which subpackage it is for. Following that, we have an if statement similar to the one we used in the install scripts, save one difference. Here, we're comparing the argument against zero. The reason is that we are trying to see whether there will be zero instances of this package after the uninstall is complete. If this is the case, the remainder of the script needs to be run, since there are no other amanda client packages left.

Next, we remove `bin` from the `disk` group:

```
# First, get rid of bin from the disk group...

if grep "^disk::.*bin" /etc/group > /dev/null
then

# Nuke bin at the end of the line...
 sed -e 's/\(^disk::[0-9]\{1,\}:.\{1,\}\),bin$/\1/' /etc/group> /etc/group.tmp

# Nuke bin on the line by itself...
 sed -e 's/\(^disk::[0-9]\{1,\}:\)bin$/\1/' /etc/group.tmp> /etc/group1.tmp

# Nuke bin in the middle of the line...
 sed -e 's/\(^disk::[0-9]\{1,\}:.\{1,\}\),bin,\(.\{1,\}\)/\1,\2/'/etc/group1.tmp >
/etc/group2.tmp

# Nuke bin at the start of the line...
 sed -e 's/\(^disk::[0-9]\{1,\}:\)bin,\(.\{1,\}\)/\1\2/'/etc/group2.tmp > /etc/
group

# Clean up after ourselves...
 rm -f /etc/group.tmp /etc/group1.tmp /etc/group2.tmp
fi
```

No surprises there. Continuing our uninstall, we start on the network-related tasks:

```
# Next, lose the amanda line in /etc/services...
# We only want to do this if the server package isn't installed
# Look for /usr/sbin/amdump, and leave it if there...

if [ ! -f /usr/sbin/amdump ];
then

 if grep "^amanda" /etc/services > /dev/null
 then
  grep -v "^amanda" /etc/services > /etc/services.tmp
  mv -f /etc/services.tmp /etc/services
 fi
fi
```

That's odd. Why are we looking for a file from the server package? If you look back at the install scripts for the client and server packages, you'll find that the one thing they have in common is that both the client and the server require the same entry in /etc/services.

If an amanda server is going to back itself up, it also needs the amanda client software.

Therefore, both subpackages need to add an entry to /etc/services. But what if one of the packages is removed? Perhaps the server is being demoted to a client, or maybe the server is no longer going to be backed up using amanda. In these cases, the entry in /etc/services must stay. So, in the case of the client, we look for a file from the server subpackage, and if it's there, we leave the entry alone.

Granted, this is a somewhat unsightly way to see whether a certain package is installed. Some of you are probably even saying, "Why can't RPM be used? Just do an `rpm -q amanda-server`, and decide what to do based on that." And that would be the best way to do it, except for one small point: Only one invocation of RPM can run at any given time.

Since RPM is running to perform the uninstall, if the uninstall script were to attempt to run RPM again, it would fail. The reason it would fail is because only one copy of RPM can access the database at a time. So we are stuck with our unsightly friend.

Continuing the network-related uninstall tasks…

```
# Finally, the amanda entry in /etc/inetd.conf

if grep "^amanda" /etc/inetd.conf > /dev/null
then
 grep -v "^amanda" /etc/inetd.conf > /etc/inetd.conf.tmp
 mv -f /etc/inetd.conf.tmp /etc/inetd.conf

# Kick inetd

 if [ -f /var/run/inetd.pid ];
 then
  kill -HUP 'cat /var/run/inetd.pid'
 fi
fi


fi
```

Here, we're using grep's capability to return lines that don't match the search string, in order to remove every trace of amanda from /etc/inetd.conf. After issuing a HUP on inetd, we're done.

On to the server. If you've been noticing a pattern between the various scripts, you won't be disappointed here:

```
%postun server

# See if we're the last server package on the system...
# If not, we don't need to do any of this stuff...

if [ "$1" = 0 ];
then

# Lose the amanda line in /etc/services...
# We only want to do this if the client package isn't installed
# Look for /usr/lib/amandad, and leave it if there...

if [ ! -f /usr/lib/amanda/amandad ];
then

  if grep "^amanda" /etc/services > /dev/null
  then
   grep -v "^amanda" /etc/services > /etc/services.tmp
   mv -f /etc/services.tmp /etc/services
  fi
 fi
fi
```

By now, the opening if statement is an old friend. As you might have expected, we are verifying whether the client package is installed by looking for a file from that package. If the client package isn't there, the entry is removed from /etc/services. And that is that.

Obviously, these scripts must be carefully tested. In the case of amanda, because the two subpackages have some measure of interdependency, it's necessary to try different sequences of installing and erasing the two packages to make sure the /etc/services logic works properly in all cases.

After a bit of testing, our install and uninstall scripts pass with flying colors. From a technological standpoint, the client and server subpackages are ready to go.

20.4.3.3. Bits and Pieces

However, just because a package has been properly built and installs and can be erased without problems doesn't mean that the package-builder's job is done. It's necessary to look at each newly built package from the user's perspective. Does the package contain everything users needs in order to deploy it effectively? Or will users need to fiddle with it, guessing as they go?

In the case of our amanda packages, it was obvious that some additional documentation was required so that the user would know what needed to be done to finalize the installation. Simply directing the user to the standard amanda documentation wasn't the right solution, either. Many of the steps outlined in the INSTALL document had already been done by the postinstall scripts. No, an interim document was required. Two, actually: one for the client, and one for the server.

So two files were created, one to be added to each subpackage. The question was, how to do it? Essentially, there were two options:

- Put the files in the amanda directory tree that had been used to perform the initial builds and generate a new patch file
- Create a tar file containing the two files, and modify the spec file to unpack the documentation into the amanda directory tree
- Drop the files directly into the amanda directory tree without using tar

Since the second approach was more interesting, that's the approach we chose. It required an additional source tag in the spec file:

```
Source1: amanda-rpm-instructions.tar.gz
```

Also required was an additional %setup macro in the %prep script:

```
%setup -T -D -a 1
```

While the %setup macro might look intimidating, it wasn't that hard to construct. Here's what each option means:

-T—Do not perform the default archive unpacking.

-D—Do not delete the directory before unpacking.

-a 1—Unpack the archive specified by the source1 tag after changing directories.

Finally, two additions to the %files lists were required, one for the client:

```
%doc amanda-client.README
```

and one for the server:

```
%doc amanda-server.README
```

At this point, the packages are complete. Certainly there is software out there that doesn't require this level of effort to package. Just as certainly there is software that is much more of a challenge.

21

A Guide to the RPM
Library API

In this chapter, we'll explore the functions used internally by RPM. These functions are available for anyone to use, making it possible to add RPM functionality to new and existing programs. Rather than continually refer to "the RPM library" throughout this chapter, we'll use the name of the library's main include file—rpmlib.

21.1. An Overview of rpmlib

A number of files make up rpmlib. First and foremost, of course, is the rpmlib library, `librpm.a`. This library contains all the functions required to implement all the basic functions contained in RPM.

The remaining files define the various data structures, parameters, and symbols used by rpmlib:

- `rpmlib.h`
- `dbindex.h`
- `header.h`

In general, `rpmlib.h` will always be required. When using rpmlib's header-related functions, `header.h` will be required, while the database-related functions will require `dbindex.h`. As each function is described in this chapter, we'll provide the function's prototype as well as the `#include` statements the function requires.

21.2. rpmlib Functions

There are more than 60 different functions in rpmlib. The tasks they perform range from low-level database record traversal to high-level package manipulation. We've grouped the functions into different categories for easy reference.

21.2.1. Error Handling

The functions in this section perform rpmlib's basic error handling. All error handling centers on the use of specific status codes. The status codes are defined in `rpmlib.h` and are of the form `RPMERR_xxx`, where *xxx* is the name of the error.

21.2.1.1. `rpmErrorCode()`—Return Error Code

This function returns the error code set by the last rpmlib function that failed. It should only be used in an error callback function defined by `rpmErrorSetCallBack()`:

```
#include <rpm/rpmlib.h>

int rpmErrorCode(void);
```

21.2.1.2. `rpmErrorString()`—Return Error String

This function returns the error string set by the last rpmlib function that failed. It should only be used in an error callback function defined by `rpmErrorSetCallBack()`:

```
#include <rpm/rpmlib.h>

char *rpmErrorString(void);
```

21.2.1.3. `rpmErrorSetCallback()`—Set Error CallBack Function

This function sets the current error callback function to the error callback function passed to it. The previous error callback function is returned:

```
#include <rpm/rpmlib.h>

rpmErrorCallBackType rpmErrorSetCallback(rpmErrorCallBackType);
```

21.2.2. Getting Package Information

The functions described in this section are used to obtain information about a package file.

Note that most information is returned in the form of a `Header` structure. This data structure is widely used throughout rpmlib. We will discuss more header-related functions in sections 21.2.13 and 21.2.14.

21.2.2.1. `rpmReadPackageInfo()`—Read Package Information

Given an open package on fd, read in the header and signature:

```
#include <rpm/rpmlib.h>
#include <rpm/header.h>

int rpmReadPackageInfo(int fd,
                       Header * signatures,
                       Header * hdr);
```

This function operates as expected, with both socket and pipe file descriptors passed as `fd`. It is safe to use on nonseekable `fds`. When the function returns, `fd` is left positioned at the start of the package's archive section.

If either `signatures` or `hdr` is `NULL`, information for the `NULL` parameter will not be passed back to the caller. Otherwise, `signatures` and `hdr` will return the package's signatures and header, respectively.

This function returns the following status values:

  `0`—Success

  `1`—Bad magic numbers found in package

  `2`—Other error

21.2.2.2. `rpmReadPackageHeader()`—Read Package Header

Given an open package on `fd`, read in the header:

```
#include <rpm/rpmlib.h>
#include <rpm/header.h>

int rpmReadPackageHeader(int fd,
                         Header * hdr,
                         int * isSource,
                         int * major,
                         int * minor);
```

This function operates as expected, with both socket and pipe file descriptors passed as `fd`. It is safe on nonseekable `fd`s. When the function returns, `fd` is left positioned at the start of the package's archive section.

If `hdr`, `isSource`, `major`, or `minor` is `NULL`, information for the `NULL` parameter(s) will not be passed back to the caller. Otherwise, they will return the package's header (`hdr`), information on whether the package is a source package file (`isSource`), and the package format's major and minor revision number (`major` and `minor`, respectively).

This function returns the following status values:

> `0`—Success
>
> `1`—Bad magic numbers found in package
>
> `2`—Other error

21.2.3. Variable Manipulation

The following functions are used to get, set, and interpret RPM's internal variables. The variables are set according to various pieces of system information, as well as from `rpmrc` files. They control various aspects of RPM's operation.

The variables have symbolic names in the form `RPMVAR_xxx`, where *xxx* is the name of the variable. All variable names are defined in `rpmlib.h`.

21.2.3.1. `rpmGetVar()`—Return Value of RPM Variable

This function returns the value of the variable specified in `var`:

```
#include <rpm/rpmlib.h>

char *rpmGetVar(int var);
```

On error, the function returns `NULL`.

21.2.3.2. `rpmGetBooleanVar()`—Return Boolean Value of RPM Variable

This function looks up the variable specified in `var` and returns 0 or 1, depending on the variable's value:

```
#include <rpm/rpmlib.h>

int rpmGetBooleanVar(int var);
```

On error, the function returns 0.

21.2.3.3. `rpmSetVar()`—Set Value of RPM Variable

This function sets the variable specified in `var` to the value passed in `val`. It is also possible for `val` to be NULL:

```
#include <rpm/rpmlib.h>

void rpmSetVar(int var,
               char *val);
```

21.2.4. `rpmrc`-Related Information

The functions in this section are all related to `rpmrc` information—the `rpmrc` files as well as the variables set from those files. This information also includes the architecture and operating system information based on `rpmrc` file entries.

21.2.4.1. `rpmReadConfigFiles()`—Read `rpmrc` Files

This function:

```
#include <rpm/rpmlib.h>

int rpmReadConfigFiles(char * file,
                       char * arch,
                       char * os,
                       int building);
```

reads `rpmrc` files according to the following rules:

- Always read `/usr/lib/rpmrc`.
- If file is specified, read it.
- If file is not specified, read `/etc/rpmrc` and `~/.rpmrc`.

Every `rpmrc` file entry is used with `rpmSetVar()` to set the appropriate RPM variable. Part of the normal `rpmrc` file processing also includes setting the architecture and operating system variables for the system executing this function. These default settings can be overridden by entering architecture and/or operating system information in `arch` and `os`, respectively. This information will still go through the normal `rpmrc` translation process.

The building argument should be set to 1 only if a package is being built when this function is called. Since most rpmlib-based applications will probably not duplicate RPM's package-building capabilities, building should normally be set to 0.

21.2.4.2. rpmGetOsName()—Return Operating System Name

This function returns the name of the operating system, as determined by rpmlib's normal rpmrc file processing:

```
#include <rpm/rpmlib.h>

char *rpmGetOsName(void);
```

21.2.4.3. rpmGetArchName()—Return Architecture Name

This function returns the name of the architecture, as determined by rpmlib's normal rpmrc file processing:

```
#include <rpm/rpmlib.h>

char *rpmGetArchName(void);
```

21.2.4.4. rpmShowRC()—Print All rpmrc-Derived Variables

This function writes all variable names and their values to the file f. It always returns 0:

```
#include <rpm/rpmlib.h>

int rpmShowRC(FILE *f);
```

21.2.4.5. rpmArchScore()—Return Architecture Compatibility Score

This function returns the level of compatibility between the architecture whose name is specified in arch and the current architecture. Returns 0 if the two architectures are incompatible. The smaller the number returned, the more compatible the two architectures are:

```
#include <rpm/rpmlib.h>

int rpmArchScore(char * arch);
```

21.2.4.6. rpmOsScore()—Return Operating System Compatibility Score

This function returns the level of compatibility between the operating system whose name is specified in os and the current operating system. Returns 0 if the two operating systems are incompatible. The smaller the number returned, the more compatible the two operating systems are:

```
#include <rpm/rpmlib.h>

int rpmOsScore(char * os);
```

21.2.5. RPM Database Manipulation

The functions in this section perform the basic operations on the RPM database. This includes opening and closing the database, as well as creating the database. A function also exists to rebuild a database that has been corrupted.

Every function that accesses the RPM database in some fashion makes use of the rpmdb structure. This structure is used as a handle to refer to a particular RPM database.

21.2.5.1. rpmdbOpen()—Open RPM Database

This function opens the RPM database located in RPMVAR_DBPATH, returning the rpmdb structure dbp. If root is specified, it is prepended to RPMVAR_DBPATH prior to opening. The mode and perms parameters are identical to open(2)'s flags and mode parameters, respectively:

```
#include <rpm/rpmlib.h>

int rpmdbOpen(char * root,
              rpmdb * dbp,
              int mode,
              int perms);
```

The function returns 1 on error, and 0 on success.

21.2.5.2. rpmdbClose()—Close RPM Database

This function closes the RPM database specified by the rpmdb structure db. The db structure is also freed:

```
#include <rpm/rpmlib.h>

void rpmdbClose(rpmdb db);
```

21.2.5.3. rpmdbInit()—Create RPM Database

This function creates a new RPM database to be located in RPMVAR_DBPATH. If the database already exists, it is left unchanged. If root is specified, it is prepended to RPMVAR_DBPATH prior to creation. The perms parameter is identical to open(2)'s mode parameter:

```
#include <rpm/rpmlib.h>

int rpmdbInit(char * root,
              int perms);
```

The function returns 1 on error, and 0 on success.

21.2.5.4. `rpmdbRebuild()`—Rebuild RPM Database

This function rebuilds the RPM database located in RPMVAR_DBPATH. If root is specified, it is prepended to RPMVAR_DBPATH prior to rebuilding:

```
#include <rpm/rpmlib.h>

int rpmdbRebuild(char * root);
```

The function returns 1 on error, and 0 on success.

21.2.6. RPM Database Traversal

The following functions are used to traverse the RPM database. Also described in this section is a function to retrieve a database record by its record number.

Note that database records are returned in the form of a Header structure. This data structure is widely used throughout rpmlib. We will discuss more header-related functions in sections 21.2.13 and 21.2.14.

21.2.6.1. `rpmdbFirstRecNum()`—Begin RPM Database Traversal

This function returns the record number of the first record in the database specified by db:

```
#include <rpm/rpmlib.h>

unsigned int rpmdbFirstRecNum(rpmdb db);
```

On error, it returns 0.

21.2.6.2. `rpmdbNextRecNum()`—Traverse to Next RPM Database Record

This function returns the record number of the record following the record number passed in lastOffset, in the database specified by db:

```
#include <rpm/rpmlib.h>

unsigned int rpmdbNextRecNum(rpmdb db,
                             unsigned int lastOffset);
```

On error, this function returns 0.

21.2.6.3. `rpmdbGetRecord()`—Return Record from RPM Database

This function returns the record at the record number specified by offset from the database specified by db:

```
#include <rpm/rpmlib.h>

Header rpmdbGetRecord(rpmdb db,
                      unsigned int offset);
```

This function returns NULL on error.

21.2.7. RPM Database Search

The functions in this section search the various parts of the RPM database. They all return a structure of type dbiIndexSet, which contains the records that match the search term. Here is the definition of the structure, as found in <rpm/dbindex.h>:

```
typedef struct {
    dbiIndexRecord * recs;
    int count;
} dbiIndexSet;
```

Each dbiIndexRecord is also defined in <rpm/dbindex.h>, as follows:

```
typedef struct {
    unsigned int recOffset;
    unsigned int fileNumber;
} dbiIndexRecord;
```

The recOffset element is the offset of the record from the start of the database file. The fileNumber element is only used by rpmdbFindByFile().

Keep in mind that the rpmdbFind*xxx*() search functions each return dbiIndexSet structures, which must be freed with dbiFreeIndexRecord() when no longer needed.

21.2.7.1. dbiFreeIndexRecord()—Free Database Index

This function frees the database index set specified by set:

```
#include <rpm/rpmlib.h>
#include <rpm/dbindex.h>

void dbiFreeIndexRecord(dbiIndexSet set);
```

21.2.7.2. rpmdbFindByFile()—Search RPM Database by File

This function searches the RPM database specified by db for the package that owns the file specified by filespec. It returns matching records in matches:

```
#include <rpm/rpmlib.h>
#include <rpm/dbindex.h>

int rpmdbFindByFile(rpmdb db,
                    char * filespec,
        dbiIndexSet * matches);
```

This function returns the following status values:

-1—An error occurred while reading a database record.

0—The search completed normally.

1—The search term was not found.

21.2.7.3. rpmdbFindByGroup()—Search RPM Database by Group

This function searches the RPM database specified by db for the packages that are members of the group specified by group. It returns matching records in matches:

```
#include <rpm/rpmlib.h>
#include <rpm/dbindex.h>

int rpmdbFindByGroup(rpmdb db,
                     char * group,
                     dbiIndexSet * matches);
```

This function returns the following status values:

-1—An error occurred while reading a database record.

0—The search completed normally.

1—The search term was not found.

21.2.7.4. rpmdbFindPackage()—Search RPM Database by Package

This function searches the RPM database specified by db for the packages with the package name (not label) specified by name. It returns matching records in matches:

```
#include <rpm/rpmlib.h>
#include <rpm/dbindex.h>

int rpmdbFindPackage(rpmdb db,
                     char * name,
                     dbiIndexSet * matches);
```

This function returns the following status values:

-1—An error occurred while reading a database record.

0—The search completed normally.

1—The search term was not found.

21.2.7.5. rpmdbFindByProvides()—Search RPM Database by Provides

This function searches the RPM database specified by db for the packages that make available the provides information specified by provides. It returns matching records in matches:

```
#include <rpm/rpmlib.h>
#include <rpm/dbindex.h>

int rpmdbFindByProvides(rpmdb db,
                        char * provides,
                        dbiIndexSet * matches);
```

This function returns the following status values:

-1—An error occurred while reading a database record.

0—The search completed normally.

1—The search term was not found.

21.2.7.6. rpmdbFindByRequiredBy()—Search RPM Database by Requires

This function searches the RPM database specified by db for the packages that need the requires information specified by requires. It returns matching records in matches:

```
#include <rpm/rpmlib.h>
#include <rpm/dbindex.h>

int rpmdbFindByRequiredBy(rpmdb db,
                          char * requires,
                          dbiIndexSet * matches);
```

This function returns the following status values:

-1—An error occurred while reading a database record.

0—The search completed normally.

1—The search term was not found.

21.2.7.7. rpmdbFindByConflicts()—Search RPM Database by Conflicts

This function searches the RPM database specified by db for the packages that conflict with the conflicts information specified by conflicts. It returns matching records in matches:

```
#include <rpm/rpmlib.h>
#include <rpm/dbindex.h>

int rpmdbFindByConflicts(rpmdb db,
                         char * conflicts,
                         dbiIndexSet * matches);
```

This function returns the following status values:

-1—An error occurred while reading a database record.

0—The search completed normally.

1—The search term was not found.

21.2.8. Package Manipulation

The functions described in this section perform the operations most RPM users are familiar with. Functions that install and erase packages are here, along with a few related, lower-level support functions.

21.2.8.1. `rpmInstallSourcePackage()`—Install Source Package File

This function installs the source package file specified by `fd`:

```
#include <rpm/rpmlib.h>

int rpmInstallSourcePackage(char * root,
                            int fd,
                            char ** specFile,
                            rpmNotifyFunction notify,
                            char * labelFormat);
```

If `root` is not `NULL`, it is prepended to the variables `RPMVAR_SOURCEDIR` and `RPMVAR_SPECDIR` prior to the actual installation. If `specFile` is not `NULL`, the complete path and filename of the just-installed spec file are returned.

The `notify` parameter is used to specify a progress-tracking function that will be called during the installation. See section 21.2.8.3 for more information on this parameter.

The `labelFormat` parameter can be used to specify how the package label should be formatted. It is used when printing the package label (once the package install is ready to proceed). If `labelFormat` is `NULL`, the package label is not printed.

This function returns the following status values:

> 0—The source package was installed successfully.
>
> 1—The source package file contained incorrect magic numbers.
>
> 2—Another type of error occurred.

21.2.8.2. `rpmInstallPackage()`—Install Binary Package File

This function installs the binary package specified by `fd`:

```
#include <rpm/rpmlib.h>

int rpmInstallPackage(char * rootdir,
                      rpmdb db,
                      int fd,
                      char * prefix,
                      int flags,
                      rpmNotifyFunction notify,
                      char * labelFormat,
                      char * netsharedPath);
```

If a path is specified in `rootdir`, the package will be installed with that path acting as the root directory. If a path is specified in `prefix`, it will be used as the prefix for relocatable packages. The RPM database specified by `db` is updated to reflect the newly installed package.

The `flags` parameter is used to control the installation behavior. The flags are defined in `rpmlib.h` and take the form `RPMINSTALL_xxx`, where *xxx* is the name of the flag.

The following flags are currently defined:

- RPMINSTALL_REPLACEPKG—Install the package even if it is already installed.
- RPMINSTALL_REPLACEFILES—Install the package even if it will replace files owned by another package.
- RPMINSTALL_TEST—Perform all install-time checks, but do not actually install the package.
- RPMINSTALL_UPGRADE—Install the package, and remove all older versions of the package.
- RPMINSTALL_UPGRADETOOLD—Install the package, even if the package is an older version of an already-installed package.
- RPMINSTALL_NODOCS—Do not install the package's documentation files.
- RPMINSTALL_NOSCRIPTS—Do not execute the package's install- and erase-time (in the case of an upgrade) scripts.
- RPMINSTALL_NOARCH—Do not perform architecture-compatibility tests.
- RPMINSTALL_NOOS—Do not perform operating system–compatibility tests.

The notify parameter is used to specify a progress-tracking–function that will be called during the installation. See section 21.2.8.3 for more information on this parameter.

The labelFormat parameter can be used to specify how the package label should be formatted. This information is used when printing the package label once the package install is ready to proceed. If labelFormat is NULL, the package label is not printed.

The netsharedPath parameter is used to specify that part of the local filesystem that is shared with other systems. If there is more than one path that is shared, the paths should be separated with a colon.

This function returns the following status values:

  0—The binary package was installed successfully.

  1—The binary package file contained incorrect magic numbers.

  2—Another type of error occurred.

21.2.8.3. rpmNotifyFunction()—Track Package Installation Progress

A function can be passed to rpmInstallSourcePackage or rpmInstallPackage via the notify parameter:

```
#include <rpm/rpmlib.h>

typedef void (*rpmNotifyFunction)(const unsigned long amount,
                                  const unsigned long total);
```

The function will be called at regular intervals during the installation, and will have two parameters passed to it:

- amount—The number of bytes of the install that have been completed so far.
- total—The total number of bytes that will be installed.

This function permits the creation of a dynamically updating progress meter during package installation.

21.2.8.4. rpmRemovePackage()—Remove Installed Package

This function removes the package at record number offset in the RPM database specified by db:

```
#include <rpm/rpmlib.h>

int rpmRemovePackage(char * root,
                     rpmdb db,
                     unsigned int offset,
                     int flags);
```

If root is specified, it is used as the path to a directory that will serve as the root directory while the package is being removed.

The flags parameter is used to control the package removal behavior. The flags that may be passed are defined in rpmlib.h and are in the form RPMUNINSTALL*xxx* , where *xxx* is the name of the flag.

The following flags are currently defined:

- RPMUNINSTALL_TEST—Perform all erase-time checks, but do not actually remove the package.
- RPMUNINSTALL_NOSCRIPTS—Do not execute the package's erase-time scripts.

This function returns the following status values:

0—The package was removed successfully.

1—The package removal failed.

21.2.9. Package and File Verification

The functions in this section perform the verification operations necessary to ensure that the files comprising a package have not been modified since they were installed.

Verification takes place on three distinct levels:

- On the file-by-file level
- On a package-wide level, through the use of the %verifyscript verification script
- On an interpackage level, through RPM's normal dependency processing

The first two types of verification are performed by functions described in this section. The functions that implement dependency-related verification are covered in section 21.2.10.

21.2.9.1. `rpmVerifyFile()`—Verify File

This function verifies the `filenum`th file from the package whose header is `h`:

```
#include <rpm/rpmlib.h>
#include <rpm/header.h>

int rpmVerifyFile(char * root,
                  Header h,
                  int filenum,
                  int * result);
```

If `root` is specified, it is used as the path to a directory that will serve as the root directory while the file is being verified. The results of the file verification are returned in `result` and consist of a number of flags. Each flag that is set indicates a verification failure.

The flags are defined in `rpmlib.h` and are in the form `RPMVERIFY_xxx`, where *xxx* is the name of the data that failed verification.

This function returns 0 on success, and 1 on failure.

21.2.9.2. `rpmVerifyScript()`—Execute Package's `%verifyscript` Verification Script

This function executes the `%verifyscript` verification script for the package whose header is `h`. `err` must contain a valid file descriptor. If `rpmIsVerbose()` returns `true`, the `%verifyscript` verification script will direct all status messages to `err`:

```
#include <rpm/rpmlib.h>
#include <rpm/header.h>

int rpmVerifyScript(char * root,
                    Header h,
                    int err);
```

This function returns 0 on success, and 1 on failure.

21.2.10. Dependency-Related Operations

The functions in this section are used to perform the various dependency-related operations supported by rpmlib.

Dependency processing is entirely separate from normal package-based operations. The package installation and removal functions do not perform any dependency processing themselves. Therefore, dependency processing is somewhat different from other aspects of rpmlib's operation.

Dependency processing centers around the rpmDependencies data structure. The operations that are to be performed against the RPM database (adding, removing, and upgrading packages) are performed against this data structure, using the functions that are described in this section. These functions simply populate the data structure according to the operation being performed. They do not perform the actual operation on the package. This is an important point to keep in mind.

Once the data structure has been completely populated, a dependency check function is called to determine if there are any dependency-related problems. The result is a structure of dependency conflicts. This structure, rpmDependencyConflict, is defined in rpmlib.h.

Note that it is necessary to free both the conflicts structure and the rpmDependencies structure when they are no longer needed. However, free() should not be used—special functions for this are provided and are discussed in this section.

21.2.10.1. rpmdepDependencies()—Create a New Dependency Data Structure

This function returns an initialized rpmDependencies structure. The dependency checking to be done will be based on the RPM database specified in the db parameter. If this parameter is NULL, the dependency checking will be done as if an empty RPM database were being used:

```
#include <rpm/rpmlib.h>

rpmDependencies rpmdepDependencies(rpmdb db);
```

21.2.10.2. rpmdepAddPackage()—Add a Package Install to the Dependency Data Structure

This function adds the installation of the package whose header is h to the rpmDependencies data structure, rpmdep:

```
#include <rpm/rpmlib.h>
#include <rpm/header.h>

void rpmdepAddPackage(rpmDependencies rpmdep,
                      Header h);
```

21.2.10.3. rpmdepUpgradePackage()—Add a Package Upgrade to the Dependency Data Structure

This function adds the upgrading of the package whose header is h to the rpmDependencies data structure, rpmdep. It is similar to rpmdepAddPackage(), but older versions of the package are removed:

```
#include <rpm/rpmlib.h>
#include <rpm/header.h>
```

```
void rpmdepUpgradePackage(rpmDependencies rpmdep,
                          Header h);
```

21.2.10.4. rpmdepRemovePackage()—Add a Package Removal to the Dependency Data Structure

This function adds the removal of the package whose RPM database offset is dboffset to the rpmDependencies data structure, rpmdep:

```
#include <rpm/rpmlib.h>

void rpmdepRemovePackage(rpmDependencies rpmdep,
                         int dboffset);
```

21.2.10.5. rpmdepAvailablePackage()—Add an Available Package to the Dependency Data Structure

This function adds the package whose header is h to the rpmDependencies structure, rpmdep:

```
#include <rpm/rpmlib.h>
#include <rpm/header.h>

void rpmdepAvailablePackage(rpmDependencies rpmdep,
                            Header h,
                            void * key);
```

The key parameter can be anything that uniquely identifies the package being added. It will be returned as part of the rpmDependencyConflict structure returned by rpmdepCheck(), specifically in that structure's suggestedPackage element.

21.2.10.6. rpmdepCheck()—Perform a Dependency Check

This function performs a dependency check on the rpmDependencies structure rpmdep. It returns an array of size numConflicts, pointed to by conflicts:

```
#include <rpm/rpmlib.h>

int rpmdepCheck(rpmDependencies rpmdep,
                struct rpmDependencyConflict ** conflicts,
                int * numConflicts);
```

This function returns 0 on success, and 1 on error.

21.2.10.7. rpmdepFreeConflicts()—Free Results of rpmdepCheck()

This function frees the dependency conflict information of size numConflicts that is pointed to by conflicts:

```
#include <rpm/rpmlib.h>

void rpmdepFreeConflicts(struct rpmDependencyConflict * conflicts,
                         int numConflicts);
```

21.2.10.8. rpmdepDone()—Free a Dependency Data Structure

This function frees the rpmDependencies structure pointed to by rpmdep:

```
#include <rpm/rpmlib.h>

void rpmdepDone(rpmDependencies rpmdep);
```

21.2.11. Diagnostic Output Control

The functions in this section are used to control the amount of diagnostic output produced by other rpmlib functions. The rpmlib library can produce a wealth of diagnostic output, making it easy to see what is going on at any given time.

There are several different verbosity levels defined in rpmlib.h. Their symbolic names are in the form RPMMESS_*xxx*, where *xxx* is the name of the verbosity level. Note that the numeric values of the verbosity levels increase with a decrease in verbosity.

Unless otherwise set, the default verbosity level is RPMMESS_NORMAL.

21.2.11.1. rpmIncreaseVerbosity()—Increase Verbosity Level

This function is used to increase the current verbosity level by one:

```
#include <rpm/rpmlib.h>

void rpmIncreaseVerbosity(void);
```

21.2.11.2. rpmSetVerbosity()—Set Verbosity Level

This function is used to set the current verbosity level to level. Note that no range checking is done to level:

```
#include <rpm/rpmlib.h>

void rpmSetVerbosity(int level);
```

21.2.11.3. rpmGetVerbosity()—Return Verbosity Level

This function returns the current verbosity level:

```
#include <rpm/rpmlib.h>

int rpmGetVerbosity(void);
```

21.2.11.4. rpmIsVerbose()—Check Verbosity Level

This function checks the current verbosity level and returns 1 if the current level is set to RPMMESS_VERBOSE or a level of higher verbosity. Otherwise, it returns 0:

```
#include <rpm/rpmlib.h>

int rpmIsVerbose(void);
```

21.2.11.5. rpmIsDebug()—Check Debug Level

This function checks the current verbosity level and returns 1 if the current level is set to RPMMESS_DEBUG or a level of higher verbosity. Otherwise, it returns 0:

```
#include <rpm/rpmlib.h>

int rpmIsDebug(void);
```

21.2.12. Signature Verification

The functions in this section deal with the verification of package signatures. A package file may contain more than one type of signature. For example, a package may contain a signature that contains the package's size, as well as a signature that contains cryptographically derived data that can be used to prove the package's origin.

Each type of signature has its own tag value. These tag values are defined in rpmlib.h and are in the form RPMSIGTAG_*xxx*, where *xxx* is the type of signature.

21.2.12.1. rpmVerifySignature()—Verify a Package File's Signature

This function verifies the signature of the package pointed to by file. The result of the verification is stored in result, in a format suitable for printing:

```
#include <rpm/rpmlib.h>

int rpmVerifySignature(char *file,
                       int_32 sigTag,
                       void *sig,
                       int count,
                       char *result);
```

The sigTag parameter specifies the type of signature to be checked. The sig parameter specifies the signature against which the package is to be verified. The count parameter specifies the size of the signature; at present, this parameter is only used for PGP-based signatures.

This function returns the following values:

- ■ RPMSIG_OK—The signature verified correctly.
- ■ RPMSIG_UNKNOWN—The signature type is unknown.
- ■ RPMSIG_BAD—The signature did not verify correctly.
- ■ RPMSIG_NOKEY—The key required to check this signature is not available.

21.2.12.2. `rpmFreeSignature()`—Free Signature Read by `rpmReadPackageInfo()`

This function frees the signature `h`:

```
#include <rpm/rpmlib.h>
#include <rpm/header.h>

void rpmFreeSignature(Header h);
```

21.2.13. Header Manipulation

The header is one of the key data structures in rpmlib. The functions in this section perform basic manipulations of the header.

The header is actually a data structure. It is not necessary to fully understand the actual data structure, but it is necessary to understand the basic concepts on which the header is based.

The header serves as a kind of miniature database. It can be searched for specific information, which can then be retrieved easily. As in a database, the information contained in the header can be of varying sizes.

21.2.13.1. `headerRead()`—Read a Header

This function reads a header from file `fd`, converting it from network byte order to the host system's byte order:

```
#include <rpm/rpmlib.h>
#include <rpm/header.h>

Header headerRead(int fd,
                  int magicp);
```

If `magicp` is defined to be `HEADER_MAGIC_YES`, `headerRead()` will expect header magic numbers and will return an error if they are not present. Likewise, if `magicp` is defined to be `HEADER_MAGIC_NO`, `headerRead()` will not check the header's magic numbers and will return an error if they are present.

On error, this function returns `NULL`.

21.2.13.2. `headerWrite()`—Write a Header

This function writes the header `h` to the file `fd`, converting it from host byte order to network byte order. If `magicp` is defined to be `HEADER_MAGIC_YES`, `headerWrite()` will add the appropriate magic numbers to the header being written. If `magicp` is defined to be `HEADER_MAGIC_NO`, `headerWrite()` will not include magic numbers:

```
#include <rpm/rpmlib.h>
#include <rpm/header.h>
```

```
void headerWrite(int fd,
                 Header h,
                 int magicp);
```

21.2.13.3. headerCopy()—Copy a Header

This function returns a copy of header h:

```
#include <rpm/rpmlib.h>
#include <rpm/header.h>

Header headerCopy(Header h);
```

21.2.13.4. headerSizeof()—Calculate a Header's Size

This function returns the number of bytes the header h takes up on disk. Note that in versions of RPM prior to 2.3.3, this function also changes the location of the data in the header. The result is that pointers from headerGetEntry() will no longer be valid. Therefore, any pointers acquired before calling headerSizeof() should be discarded:

```
#include <rpm/rpmlib.h>
#include <rpm/header.h>

unsigned int headerSizeof(Header h,
                          int magicp);
```

21.2.13.5. headerNew()—Create a New Header

This function returns a new header.

```
#include <rpm/rpmlib.h>
#include <rpm/header.h>

Header headerNew(void);
```

21.2.13.6. headerFree()—Deallocate a Header

This function deallocates the header specified by h:

```
#include <rpm/rpmlib.h>
#include <rpm/header.h>

void headerFree(Header h);
```

21.2.13.7. headerDump()—Print Header Structure in Human-Readable Form

This function prints the structure of the header h to the file f. If the flags parameter is defined to be HEADER_DUMP_INLINE, the header's data is also printed:

```
#include <rpm/rpmlib.h>
#include <rpm/header.h>

void headerDump(Header h,
                FILE *f,
                int flags);
```

21.2.14. Header Entry Manipulation

The functions in this section provide the basic operations necessary to manipulate header entries. The following header entry types are currently defined:

- RPM_NULL_TYPE—This type is not used.
- RPM_CHAR_TYPE—The entry contains a single character.
- RPM_INT8_TYPE—The entry contains an 8-bit integer.
- RPM_INT16_TYPE—The entry contains a 16-bit integer.
- RPM_INT32_TYPE—The entry contains a 32-bit integer.
- RPM_INT64_TYPE—The entry contains a 64-bit integer.
- RPM_STRING_TYPE—The entry contains a null-terminated character string.
- RPM_BIN_TYPE—The entry contains binary data that will not be interpreted by rpmlib.
- RPM_STRING_ARRAY_TYPE—The entry contains an array of null-terminated strings.

21.2.14.1. headerGetEntry()—Get Entry from Header

This function retrieves the entry matching tag from header h:

```
#include <rpm/rpmlib.h>
#include <rpm/header.h>

int headerGetEntry(Header h,
                   int_32 tag,
                   int_32 *type,
                   void **p,
                   int_32 *c);
```

The type of the entry is returned in type, a pointer to the data is returned in p, and the size of the data is returned in c. Both type and c may be NULL, in which case that data will not be returned. Note that if the entry type is RPM_STRING_ARRAY_TYPE, you must issue a free() on p when done with the data.

This function returns 1 on success, and 0 on failure.

21.2.14.2. headerAddEntry()—Add Entry to Header

This function adds a new entry to the header h:

```
#include <rpm/rpmlib.h>
#include <rpm/header.h>

int headerAddEntry(Header h,
                   int_32 tag,
                   int_32 type,
                   void *p,
                   int_32 c);
```

The entry's tag is specified by the tag parameter, and the entry's type is specified by the type parameter.

The entry's data is pointed to by p, and the size of the data is specified by c. This function always returns 1.

> **NOTE**
>
> In versions of RPM prior to 2.3.3, headerAddEntry() will only work successfully with headers produced by headerCopy() and headerNew(). In particular, headerAddEntry() is not supported when used to add entries to a header produced by headerRead(). Later versions of RPM lift this restriction.

21.2.14.3. headerIsEntry()—Determine if Entry Is in Header

This function returns 1 if an entry with tag tag is present in header h. If the tag is not present, this function returns 0:

```
#include <rpm/rpmlib.h>
#include <rpm/header.h>

int headerIsEntry(Header h,
                  int_32 tag);
```

21.2.15. Header Iterator Support

Iterators are used as a means to step from entry to entry, through an entire header. The functions in this section are used to create, use, and free iterators.

21.2.15.1. headerInitIterator()—Create an Iterator

This function returns a newly created iterator for the header h:

```
#include <rpm/rpmlib.h>
#include <rpm/header.h>

HeaderIterator headerInitIterator(Header h);
```

21.2.15.2. headerNextIterator()—Step to the Next Entry

This function steps to the next entry in the header specified when the iterator iter was created with headerInitIterator():

```
#include <rpm/rpmlib.h>
#include <rpm/header.h>

int headerNextIterator(HeaderIterator iter,
                       int_32 *tag,
                       int_32 *type,
                       void **p,
                       int_32 *c);
```

The next entry's tag, type, data, and size are returned in tag, type, p, and c, respectively. Note that if the entry type is RPM_STRING_ARRAY_TYPE, you must issue a free() on p when done with the data.

This function returns 1 if successful, and 0 if there are no more entries in the header.

21.2.15.3. headerFreeIterator()—Free an Iterator

This function frees the resources used by the iterator iter:

```
#include <rpm/rpmlib.h>
#include <rpm/header.h>

void headerFreeIterator(HeaderIterator iter);
```

21.3. Sample Code

In this section, we'll study sample programs that make use of rpmlib to perform an assortment of commonly required operations. We'll intersperse sections of code with a running commentary to minimize page turning.

21.3.1. Example #1

In this example, we'll use a number of rpmlib's header-manipulation functions.

Here we've included rpmlib.h, which is necessary for all programs that use rpmlib:

```
#include <errno.h>
#include <fcntl.h>
#include <stdio.h>
#include <unistd.h>
#include <string.h>

#include <rpm/rpmlib.h>
```

Here we've defined the program's storage. Note in particular the HeaderIterator, Header, and int_32 data types:

```
void main(int argc, char ** argv)
{
  HeaderIterator iter;
    Header h, sig;
    int_32 itertag, type, count;
    void **p = NULL;
    char *blather;
    char * name;

    int fd, stat;
```

Standard stuff here. The first argument is supposed to be an RPM package file. It is opened here. If there is no argument on the command line, the program will use stdin instead:

```
if (argc == 1) {
    fd = 0;
} else {
    fd = open(argv[1], O_RDONLY, 0644);
}

if (fd < 0) {
    perror("open");
    exit(1);
}
```

Here things start to get interesting! The signature and headers are read from the package file that was just opened. Notice in the preceding code that we've defined sig and h to be of type Header. That means we can use rpmlib's header-related functions on them. After a little bit of error checking, it's time to move on....

```
stat = rpmReadPackageInfo(fd, &sig, &h);
if (stat) {
  fprintf(stderr,
          "rpmReadPackageInfo error status: %d\n%s\n",
          stat, strerror(errno));
    exit(stat);
}
```

Now that we have the package's header, we get the package name (specified by the RPMTAG_NAME in the call to headerGetEntry). Next, we see if the package has preinstall (RPMTAG_PREIN) or postinstall (RPMTAG_POSTIN) scripts. If it does, we print out a message, along with the package name:

```
headerGetEntry(h, RPMTAG_NAME, &type, (void **) &name, &count);

if (headerIsEntry(h, RPMTAG_PREIN)) {
    printf("There is a preinstall script for %s\n", name);
}

if (headerIsEntry(h, RPMTAG_POSTIN)) {
    printf("There is a postinstall script for %s\n", name);
}
```

Turning to the other Header structure we've read, we print out the package's signatures in human-readable form. When we're done, we free the block of signatures:

```
printf("Dumping signatures...\n");
headerDump(sig, stdout, 1);

rpmFreeSignature(sig);
```

Here we set up an iterator for the package's header. This will allow us to step through each entry in the header:

```
printf("Iterating through the header...\n");

iter = headerInitIterator(h);
```

This loop uses `headerNextIterator()` to return each entry's tag, type, data, and size. By using a `switch` statement on the tag, we can perform different operations on each type of entry in the header:

```
while (headerNextIterator(iter, &itertag, &type, p, &count)) {
  switch (itertag) {
  case RPMTAG_SUMMARY:
    blather = *p;
    printf("The Summary: %s\n", blather);
    break;
  case RPMTAG_FILENAMES:
    printf("There are %d files in this package\n", count);
    break;
}
```

This is the housecleaning section of the program. First we free the iterator that we've been using, and finally the header itself:

```
}

headerFreeIterator(iter);

headerFree(h);

}
```

Running this program on a package gives us the following output:

```
# ./dump amanda-client-2.3.0-2.i386.rpm
There is a postinstall script for amanda-client
Dumping signatures...
Entry count: 2
Data count : 20

            CT  TAG              TYPE        OFSET       COUNT
Entry    : 000 (1000)NAME        INT32_TYPE  0x00000000 00000001
      Data: 000 0x00029f5d (171869)
Entry    : 001 (1003)SERIAL      BIN_TYPE    0x00000004 00000016
      Data: 000 27 01 f9 97 d8 2c 36 40
      Data: 008 c6 4a 91 45 32 13 d1 62
Iterating through the header...
The Summary: Client-side Amanda package
There are 11 files in this package
#
```

21.3.2. Example #2

This example delves a bit more into the database-related side of rpmlib. After initializing rpmlib's variables by reading the appropriate `rpmrc` files, the code traverses the database records, looking for a specific package. That package's header is then dumped in its entirety.

As before, this is the normal way of including all of rpmlib's definitions:

```
#include <errno.h>
#include <fcntl.h>
#include <stdio.h>
#include <string.h>
```

```
#include <unistd.h>
#include <stdlib.h>

#include <rpm/rpmlib.h>
```

Here are the data declarations. Note the declaration of db; this is how we will be accessing the RPM database:

```
void main(int argc, char ** argv)
{
Header h;
int offset;
int dspBlockNum = 0;                    /* default to all */
int blockNum = 0;
int_32 type, count;
char * name;
rpmdb db;
```

Before opening the RPM database, it's necessary to know where the database resides. This information is stored in rpmrc files, which are read by rpmReadConfigFiles(). To show that this function is really doing its job, we retrieve the RPM database path before and after the rpmrc files are read. Note that we test the return value of rpmGetVar(RPM_DBPATH) and, if it is null, we insert (none) in the printf() output. This prevents possible core dumps if no database path has been set; and besides, it's more user friendly:

```
printf("The database path is: %s\n",
    rpmGetVar(RPMVAR_DBPATH) ? rpmGetVar(RPM_DBPATH) : "(none)");

rpmReadConfigFiles(NULL, NULL, NULL, 0);

printf("The database path is: %s\n",
    rpmGetVar(RPMVAR_DBPATH) ? rpmGetVar(RPM_DBPATH) : "(none)");
```

Here we're opening the RPM database and doing some cursory error checking to make sure we should continue:

```
if (rpmdbOpen("", &db, O_RDONLY, 0644) != 0) {
    fprintf(stderr, "cannot open /var/lib/rpm/packages.rpm\n");
    exit(1);
}
```

We get the offset of the first database record:

```
offset = rpmdbFirstRecNum(db);
```

Here we start a while loop based on the record offset. As long as there is a non-zero offset (meaning that there is still an available record), we get the record. If there's a problem getting the record, we exit:

```
while (offset) {

    h = rpmdbGetRecord(db, offset);
    if (!h) {
            fprintf(stderr, "headerRead failed\n");
    exit(1);
            }
```

Next, we get the package name entry from the record and compare it with the name of the package we're interested in. If it matches, we dump the contents of the entire record:

```
headerGetEntry(h, RPMTAG_NAME, &type, (void **) &name, &count);
if (strcmp(name, argv[1]) == 0)
  headerDump(h, stdout, 1);
```

At the end of the loop, we free the record and get the offset to the next record:

```
headerFree(h);

offset = rpmdbNextRecNum(db, offset);
}
```

At the end, we close the database and exit:

```
rpmdbClose(db);
}
```

Here's the program's output, edited for brevity (notice that the database path changes from (null) to /var/lib/rpm after the rpmrc files are read):

```
# ./showdb amanda-client
The database path is: (null)
The database path is: /var/lib/rpm
Entry count: 37
Data count : 5219


            CT  TAG               TYPE             OFSET     COUNT
Entry     : 000 (1000)NAME        STRING_TYPE      0x00000000 00000001
      Data: 000 amanda-client
Entry     : 001 (1001)VERSION     STRING_TYPE      0x0000000e 00000001
      Data: 000 2.3.0
Entry     : 002 (1002)RELEASE     STRING_TYPE      0x00000014 00000001
      Data: 000 7
Entry     : 003 (1004)SUMMARY     STRING_TYPE      0x00000016 00000001
      Data: 000 Client-side Amanda package
Entry     : 004 (1005)DESCRIPTION STRING_TYPE      0x00000031 00000001
...
Entry     : 017 (1027)FILENAMES   STRING_ARRAY_TYPE 0x00000df3 00000015
      Data: 000 /usr/doc/amanda-client-2.3.0-7
      Data: 001 /usr/doc/amanda-client-2.3.0-7/COPYRIGHT
      Data: 002 /usr/doc/amanda-client-2.3.0-7/INSTALL
      Data: 003 /usr/doc/amanda-client-2.3.0-7/README
      Data: 004 /usr/doc/amanda-client-2.3.0-7/SYSTEM.NOTES
      Data: 005 /usr/doc/amanda-client-2.3.0-7/WHATS.NEW
      Data: 006 /usr/doc/amanda-client-2.3.0-7/amanda-client.README
...
Entry     : 034 (1049)REQUIRENAME STRING_ARRAY_TYPE 0x0000141c 00000006
      Data: 000 libc.so.5
      Data: 001 libdb.so.2
      Data: 002 grep
      Data: 003 sed
      Data: 004 NetKit-B
      Data: 005 dump
...
#
```

As you can see, everything that you could possibly want to know about an installed package is available using this method.

21.3.3. Example #3

This example is similar in function to the previous one, except that it uses rpmlib's search functions to find the desired package record. Here we include rpmlib's definitions:

```
#include <errno.h>
#include <fcntl.h>
#include <stdio.h>
#include <string.h>
#include <unistd.h>
#include <stdlib.h>

#include <rpm/rpmlib.h>
```

Here are the storage declarations:

```
void main(int argc, char ** argv)
{
    Header h;
    int stat;
    rpmdb db;
    dbiIndexSet matches;
```

In this section, we do some argument processing, process the rpmrc files, and open the RPM database:

```
if (argc != 2) {
    fprintf(stderr, "showdb2 <search term>\n");
    exit(1);
}

rpmReadConfigFiles(NULL, NULL, NULL, 0);

if (rpmdbOpen("", &db, O_RDONLY, 0644) != 0) {
    fprintf(stderr, "cannot open /var/lib/rpm/packages.rpm\n");
    exit(1);
}
```

In this section, we use rpmdbFindPackage() to search for the desired package:

```
stat = rpmdbFindPackage(db, argv[1], &matches);
printf("Status is: %d\n", stat);
if (stat == 0) {
  if (matches.count) {
    printf("Number of matches: %d\n", matches.count);
    h = rpmdbGetRecord(db, matches.recs[0].recOffset);
    if (h) headerDump(h, stdout, 1);
    headerFree(h);
    dbiFreeIndexRecord(matches);
  }
}
```

After checking for successful status, the count of matching package records is checked. If there is at least one match, the first matching record is retrieved and dumped. Note that there could be more than one match. Although this example doesn't dump more than the first matching record, it would be simple to access all matches by stepping through the matches.recs array.

Once we're done with the record, we free it, as well as the list of matching records:

```
    rpmdbClose(db);
}
```

The last thing we do before exiting is close the database. Here's some sample output from the program (note the successful status and the number of matches printed before the dump):

```
# ./showdb2 rpm
Status is: 0
Number of matches: 1
Entry count: 37
Data count : 2920

            CT  TAG              TYPE              OFSET      COUNT
Entry    : 000 (1000)NAME        STRING_TYPE       0x00000000 00000001
    Data: 000 rpm
Entry    : 001 (1001)VERSION     STRING_TYPE       0x00000004 00000001
    Data: 000 2.2.9
Entry    : 002 (1002)RELEASE     STRING_TYPE       0x0000000a 00000001
    Data: 000 1
Entry    : 003 (1004)SUMMARY     STRING_TYPE       0x0000000c 00000001
    Data: 000 Red Hat Package Manager
...
Entry    : 034 (1049)REQUIRENAME STRING_ARRAY_TYPE 0x00000b40 00000003
    Data: 000 libz.so.1
    Data: 001 libdb.so.2
    Data: 002 libc.so.5
Entry    : 035 (1050)REQUIREVERSION STRING_ARRAY_TYPE 0x00000b5f 00000003
    Data: 000
    Data: 001
    Data: 002
Entry    : 036 (1064)RPMVERSION  STRING_TYPE       0x00000b62 00000001
    Data: 000 2.2.9
#
```

III

Appendixes

The Format of the RPM File

A.1. The RPM File-Naming Convention

Although RPM will run just as well if a package file has been renamed, when the packages are created during RPM's build process, they follow this specific naming convention:

`name-version-release.architecture.rpm`

In this convention

- ■ `name` is a name describing the packaged software.
- ■ `version` is the version of the packaged software.
- ■ `release` is the number of times this version of the software has been packaged.
- ■ `architecture` is a shorthand name describing the type of computer hardware the packaged software is meant to run on. It may also be the string `src`, or `nosrc`. Both of these strings indicate that the file is an RPM source package. The `nosrc` string means that the file contains only package building files, while the `src` string means that the file contains the necessary package building files and the software's source code.

A few notes are in order. Normally, the package name is taken verbatim from the packaged software's name. Occasionally, this approach won't work—usually this occurs when the software is split into multiple subpackages, each supporting a different set of functions. An example of this situation is the way `ncurses` was packaged on Red Hat Linux. The package incorporating the `ncurses` basic functionality was called `ncurses`, while the package incorporating those parts of `ncurses`'s program development functionality was named `ncurses-devel`.

The version number is normally taken verbatim from the package's version. The only restriction placed on the version is that it cannot contain a dash (-).

The release can be thought of as the package's version. Traditionally it is a number, starting at 1, that shows how many times the packaged software, at a given version, has been built. This is tradition and not a restriction, however. As with the version number, the only restriction is that dashes are not allowed.

The architecture specifier is a string that indicates what hardware the package has been built for. There are a number of architectures defined:

- ■ `i386`—The Intel x86 family of microprocessors, starting with the 80386
- ■ `alpha`—The Digital Alpha/AXP series of microprocessors
- ■ `sparc`—Sun Microsystem's SPARC series of chips
- ■ `mips`—MIPS Technologies' processors
- ■ `ppc`—The Power PC microprocessor family
- ■ `m68k`—Motorola's 68000 series of CISC microprocessors
- ■ `SGI`—Equivalent to `MIPS`

This list will almost certainly change. For the most up-to-date list, refer to the file /usr/lib/ rpmrc. It contains information used internally by RPM, including a list of architectures and equivalent code numbers.

A.2. The RPM File Format

While the following details concerning the actual format of an RPM package file were accurate at the time this was written, three points should be kept in mind:

- The file format is subject to change.
- If a package file is to be manipulated somehow, you are strongly urged to use the appropriate rpmlib routines to access the package file. Why? See the previous point!
- This appendix describes the most recent version of the RPM file format: version 3. The file(1) utility can be used to see a package's file format version.

With those caveats out of the way, let's take a look inside an RPM file...

A.2.1. Parts of an RPM File

Every RPM package file can be divided into four distinct sections:

- The lead
- The signature
- The header
- The archive

Package files are written to disk in network byte order. If required, RPM will automatically convert to host byte order when the package file is read. Let's take a look at each section, starting with the lead.

A.2.1.1. The Lead

The lead is the first part of an RPM package file. In previous versions of RPM, it was used to store information used internally by RPM. Today, however, the lead's sole purpose is to make it easy to identify an RPM package file. For example, the file(1) command uses the lead. (Refer to section A.4 for a discussion on identifying RPM package files with the file command.) All the information contained in the lead has been duplicated or superseded by information contained in the header. (The header is discussed in section A.2.1.3.)

RPM defines a C structure that describes the lead:

```
struct rpmlead {
    unsigned char magic[4];
    unsigned char major, minor;
```

```
        short type;
        short archnum;
        char name[66];
        short osnum;
        short signature_type;
        char reserved[16];
} ;
```

Let's take a look at an actual package file and examine the various pieces of data that make up the lead. In the following display, the number to the left of the colon is the byte offset, in hexadecimal, from the start of the file. The eight groups of four characters show the hex value of the bytes in the file—2 bytes per group of four characters. Finally, the characters on the right show the ASCII values of the data bytes. When a data byte's value results in a non-printable character, a dot (.) is inserted instead. Here are the first 32 bytes of a package file—in this case, the package file `rpm-2.2.1-1.i386.rpm`:

```
00000000: edab eedb 0300 0000 0001 7270 6d2d 322e ..........rpm-2.
00000010: 322e 312d 3100 0000 0000 0000 0000 0000 2.1-1...........
```

The first 4 bytes (`edab eedb`) are the magic values that identify the file as an RPM package file. Both the `file` command and RPM use these magic numbers to determine whether a file is legitimate.

The next 2 bytes (`0300`) indicate the RPM file format version. In this case, the file's major version number is 3, and the minor version number is 0. Versions of RPM later than 2.1 create version 3.0 package files.

The next 2 bytes (`0000`) determine what type of RPM file the file is. There are presently two types defined:

- Binary package file (type=`0000`)
- Source package file (type=`0001`)

In this case, the file is a binary package file.

The next 2 bytes (`0001`) are used to store the architecture that the package was built for. In this case, the number 1 refers to the i386 architecture. (Note that the architecture used internally by RPM is actually stored in the header. This value is strictly for `file(1)`'s use.) In the case of a source package file, these two bytes should be ignored, as source packages are not built for a specific architecture.

The next 66 bytes (starting with `7270 6d2d`) contain the name of the package. The name must end with a null byte, which leaves 65 bytes for RPM's usual *name-version-release*–style name. In this case, we can read the name from the right side of the output:

```
rpm-2.2.1-1
```

Since the name `rpm-2.2.1-1` is shorter than the 65 bytes allocated for the name, the leftover bytes are filled with nulls.

Skipping past the space allocated for the name, we see 2 bytes (0001):

```
00000040: 0000 0000 0000 0000 0000 0000 0001 0005  ...............
00000050: 0400 0000 24e1 ffbf 6bb3 0008 00e6 ffbf  ....$...k.......
```

These bytes represent the operating system for which this package was built. In this case, 1 equals Linux. As with the architecture-to-number translations, the operating system and corresponding code numbers can be found in the file, /usr/lib/rpmrc.

The next two bytes (0005) indicate the type of signature used in the file. A type 5 signature is new to version 3 RPM files. The signature appears next in the file, but we need to discuss an additional detail before exploring the signature.

A.2.1.1.1. Wanted: A New RPM Data Structure

By looking at the C structure that defines the lead, and matching it with the bytes in an actual package file, it's trivial to extract the data from the lead. From a programming standpoint, it's also easy to manipulate data in the lead; it's simply a matter of using the element names from the structure. But there's a problem. And because of that problem, the lead is no longer used internally by RPM.

A.2.1.1.1.1. The Lead: An Abandoned Data Structure

What's the problem, and why is the lead no longer used by RPM? The answer to these questions is a single word: inflexibility. The technique of defining a C structure to access data in a file just isn't very flexible. Let's look at an example.

Flip back to the lead's C structure on page 349. Say, for example, that some software comes along, and it has a long name. A very long name. A name so long, in fact, that the 66 bytes defined in the structure element name just couldn't hold it.

What can we do? Well, we could certainly change the structure such that the name element would be 100 bytes long. But once a new version of RPM is created using this new structure, we have two problems:

- Any package file created with the new version of RPM wouldn't be able to read older package formats.
- Any older version of RPM would be unable to install packages created with the newer version of RPM.

Not a very good situation! Ideally, we would like to somehow eliminate the requirement that the format of the data written to a package file be engraved in granite. We should be able to do the following things, all without losing compatibility with existing versions of RPM:

- Add extra data to the file format
- Change the size of existing data
- Reorder the data

Sounds like a big problem, but there's a solution.

A.2.1.1.1.1.1. Is There a Solution?

The solution is to standardize the method by which information is retrieved from a file. This is done by creating a well-defined data structure that contains easily searched information about the data, and then physically separating that information from the data.

When the data is required, it is found by using the easily searched information, which points to the data itself. The benefits are that the data can be placed anywhere in the file, and that the format of the data itself can change.

A.2.1.1.1.1.2. The Solution: The Header Structure

The header structure is RPM's solution to the problem of easily manipulating information in a standard way. The header structure's sole purpose in life is to contain zero or more pieces of data. A file can have more than one header structure in it. In fact, an RPM package file has two—the signature and the header. It was from this header that the header structure got its name.

There are three sections to each header structure. The first section is known as the *header structure header*. The header structure header is used to identify the start of a header structure, its size, and the number of data items it contains.

Following the header structure header is an area called the *index*. The index contains one or more index entries. Each index entry contains information about, and a pointer to, a specific data item.

After the index comes the *store*. It is in the store that the data items are kept. The data in the store is packed together as closely as possible. The order in which the data is stored is immaterial—a far cry from the C structure used in the lead.

A.2.1.1.1.1.3. The Header Structure in Depth

Let's take a more in-depth look at the actual format of a header structure, starting with the header structure header.

A.2.1.1.1.1.4. The Header Structure Header

The header structure header always starts with a 3-byte magic number: 8e ad e8. Following this is a 1-byte version number. Next are 4 bytes that are reserved for future expansion. After the reserved bytes is a 4-byte number that indicates how many index entries exist in this header structure, followed by another 4-byte number indicating how many bytes of data are part of the header structure.

A.2.1.1.1.1.5. The Index Entry

The header structure's index is made up of zero or more index entries. Each entry is 16 bytes long. The first 4 bytes contain a *tag*—a numeric value that identifies what type of data is pointed to by the entry. The tag values change according to the header structure's position in the RPM file. A list of the actual tag values, and what they represent, is included in section A.2.1.3.2.

Following the tag is a 4-byte *type*, which is a numeric value that describes the format of the data pointed to by the entry. The types and their values do not change from header structure to header structure. Here is the current list:

- NULL = 0
- CHAR = 1
- INT8 = 2
- INT16 = 3
- INT32 = 4
- INT64 = 5
- STRING = 6
- BIN = 7
- STRING_ARRAY = 8

A few of the data types might need some clarification. The STRING data type is simply a null-terminated string, while the STRING_ARRAY is a collection of strings. Finally, the BIN data type is a collection of binary data. This is normally used to identify data that is longer than an INT but is not a printable STRING.

Next is a 4-byte *offset* that contains the position of the data, relative to the beginning of the store. We'll talk about the store in just a moment.

Finally, there is a 4-byte *count* that contains the number of data items pointed to by the index entry. There are a few wrinkles to the meaning of the count, and they center around the STRING and STRING_ARRAY data types. STRING data always has a count of 1, while STRING_ARRAY data has a count equal to the number of strings contained in the store.

A.2.1.1.1.1.6. The Store

The *store* is where the data contained in the header structure is stored. Depending on the data type being stored, there are some details that should be kept in mind:

- For STRING data, each string is terminated with a null byte.
- For INT data, each integer is stored at the natural boundary for its type. A 64-bit INT is stored on an 8-byte boundary, a 16-bit INT is stored on a 2-byte boundary, and so on.
- All data is in network byte order.

With all these details out of the way, let's take a look at the signature.

A.2.1.2. The Signature

The signature section follows the lead in the RPM package file. It contains information that can be used to verify the integrity and, optionally, the authenticity of the majority of the package file. The signature is implemented as a header structure.

You probably noticed our use of the word *majority*. The information in the signature header structure is based on the contents of the package file's header and archive only. The data in the lead and the signature header structure is not included when the signature information is created, nor is it part of any subsequent checks based on that information.

While that omission might seem to be a weakness in RPM's design, it really isn't. In the case of the lead, since it is used only for easy identification of package files, any changes made to that part of the file would, at worst, leave the file in such a state that RPM wouldn't recognize it as a valid package file. Likewise, any changes to the signature header structure would make it impossible to verify the file's integrity, since the signature information would have been changed from its original value.

A.2.1.2.1. Analyzing the Signature Area

Using our newfound knowledge of header structures, let's take a look at the signatures in `rpm-2.2.1-1.i386.rpm`:

```
00000060: 8ead e801 0000 0000 0000 0003 0000 00ac ................
```

The first 3 bytes (`8ead e8`) contain the magic number for the start of the header structure. The next byte (`01`) is the header structure's version.

As we discussed earlier, the next 4 bytes (`0000 0000`) are reserved. The 4 bytes after that (`0000 0003`) represent the number of index entries in the signature section, namely, three. Following that are 4 bytes (`0000 00ac`) that indicate how many bytes of data are stored in the signature. The hex value `00ac`, when converted to decimal, means the store is 172 bytes long.

Following the first 16 bytes is the index. Each of the three index entries in this header structure consists of four 32-bit integers, in the following order:

- Tag
- Type
- Offset
- Count

Let's take a look at the first index entry:

```
00000070: 0000 03e8 0000 0004 0000 0000 0000 0001 ................
```

The tag consists of the first 4 bytes (`0000 03e8`), which is 1,000 when translated from hex. Looking in the RPM source directory, at the file `lib/signature.h`, we find the following tag definitions:

```
#define SIGTAG_SIZE         1000
#define SIGTAG_MD5          1001
#define SIGTAG_PGP          1002
```

So the tag we are studying is for a size signature. Let's continue.

The next 4 bytes (0000 0004) contain the data type. As we saw earlier, data type 4 means that the data stored for this index entry is a 32-bit integer. Skipping the next 4 bytes for a moment, the last 4 bytes (0000 0001) are the number of 32-bit integers pointed to by this index entry.

Now let's go back to the 4 bytes prior to the count (0000 0000). This number is the offset, in bytes, at which the size signature is located. It has a value of zero, but the question is, 0 bytes from what? The answer, although it doesn't do us much good, is that the offset is calculated from the start of the store. So first we must find where the store begins, and we can do that by performing a simple calculation.

First, go back to the start of the signature section. We've made a copy here so you won't need to flip from page to page:

```
00000060: 8ead e801 0000 0000 0000 0003 0000 00ac ...............
```

After the magic, the version, and the 4 reserved bytes, there are the number of index entries (0000 0003). Since we know that each index entry is 16 bytes long (4 for the tag, 4 for the type, 4 for the offset, and 4 for the count), we can multiply the number of entries (3) by the number of bytes in each entry (16) and obtain the total size of the index, which is 48 in decimal, or 30 in hex. Since the first index entry starts at hex offset 70, we can simply add hex 30 to hex 70, and get, in hex, offset a0. So let's skip down to offset a0 and see what's there:

```
000000a0: 0004 4c4f b025 b097 1597 0132 df35 d169 ..LO.%.....2.5.i
```

If we've done our math correctly, the first 4 bytes (0004 4c4f) should represent the size of this file. Converting to decimal, this is 281,679. Let's take a look at the size of the actual file:

```
# ls -al rpm-2.2.1-1.i386.rpm
-rw-rw-r-- 1 ed ed (282015) Jul 21 16:05 rpm-2.2.1-1.i386.rpm
#
```

Hmmm, something's not right. Or is it? It looks like we're short by 336 bytes, or in hex, 150. Interesting how that's a nice round hex number, isn't it? For now, let's continue through the remainder of the index entries, and see if hex 150 pops up elsewhere.

Here's the next index entry. It has a tag of decimal 1001, which is an MD5 checksum. It is type 7, which is the BIN data type, it is 16 bytes long, and its data starts 4 bytes after the beginning of the store:

```
00000080: 0000 03e9 0000 0007 0000 0004 0000 0010 ...............
```

And here's the data. It starts with b025 (Remember that offset of four!) and ends on the second line with 5375. This is a 128-bit MD5 checksum of the package file's header and archive sections:

```
000000a0: 0004 4c4f b025 b097 1597 0132 df35 d169 ..LO.%.....2.5.i
000000b0: 329c 5375 8900 9503 0500 31ed 6390 a520 2.Su......1.c..
```

Okay, let's jump back to the last index entry:

```
00000090: 0000 03ea 0000 0007 0000 0014 0000 0098 ...............
```

It has a tag value of 03ea (1002 in decimal—a PGP signature block) and is also a BIN data type. The data starts 20 decimal bytes from the start of the data area, which would put it at file offset b4 (in hex). It's a biggie—152 bytes long! Here's the data, starting with 8900:

```
000000b0: 329c 5375 8900 9503 0500 31ed 6390 a520  2.Su......1.c..
000000c0: e8f1 cba2 9bf9 0101 437b 0400 9c8e 0ad4  ........C{......
000000d0: 3790 364e dfb0 9a8a 22b5 b0b3 dc30 4c6f  7.6N...."....0Lo
000000e0: 91b8 c150 704e 2c64 d88a 8fca 18ab 5b6f  ...PpN,d......[o
000000f0: f041 ebc8 d18a 01c9 3601 66f0 9ddd e956  .A......6.f....V
00000100: 3142 61b3 b1da 8494 6bef 9c19 4574 c49f  1Ba.....k...Et..
00000110: ee17 35e1 d105 fb68 0ce6 715a 60f1 c660  ..5....h..qZ'..'
00000120: 279f 0306 28ed 0ba0 0855 9e82 2b1c 2ede  '...(....U..+...
00000130: e8e3 5090 6260 0b3c ba04 69a9 2573 1bbb  ..P.b'.<..i.%s..
00000140: 5b65 4de1 b1d2 c07f 8afa 4a9b 0000 0000  [eM.......J.....
```

It ends with the bytes 4a9b. This is a 1,216-bit PGP signature block. It is also the end of the signature section. There are 4 null bytes following the last data item in order to round the size out so that it ends on an 8-byte boundary. This means that the offset of the next section starts at offset 150, in hex. Say, wasn't the size in the size signature off by 150 hex? Yes, the size in the signature is the size of the file—minus the size of the lead and the signature sections.

A.2.1.3. The Header

The header section contains all available information about the package. Entries such as the package's name, version, and file list are contained in the header. Like the signature section, the header is in header structure format. Unlike the signature, which has only three possible tag types, the header has more than 60 different tags. (The list of currently defined tags appears in section A.2.1.3.2.) Be aware that the list of tags changes frequently; the definitive list appears in the RPM sources in lib/rpmlib.h.

A.2.1.3.1. Analyzing the Header

The easiest way to find the start of the header is to look for the second header structure by scanning for its magic number (8ead e8). The 16 bytes, starting with the magic, are the header structure's header. They follow the same format as the header in the signature's header structure:

```
00000150: 8ead e801 0000 0000 0000 0021 0000 09d3  ...........!....
```

As before, the byte following the magic identifies this header structure as being in version 1 format. Following the 4 reserved bytes, we find the count of entries stored in the header (0000 0021). Converting to decimal, we find that there are 33 entries in the header. The next 4 bytes (0000 09d3), converted to decimal, tell us that there are 2,515 bytes of data in the store.

Since the header is a header structure just like the signature, we know that the next 16 bytes are the first index entry:

```
00000160: 0000 03e8 0000 0006 0000 0000 0000 0001  ................
```

The first 4 bytes (`0000 03e8`) are the tag, which is the tag for the package name. The next 4 bytes indicate that the data is type 6, or a null-terminated string. There's an offset of 0 in the next 4 bytes, meaning that the data for this tag is first in the store. Finally, the last 4 bytes (`0000 0001`) show that the data count is 1, which is the only legal value for data of type `STRING`.

To find the data, we need to take the offset from the start of the first index entry in the header (160) and add in the count of index entries (21) multiplied by the size of an index entry (10). Doing the math (all the values shown are in hex, remember!), we arrive at the offset to the store, hex 370. Since the offset for this particular index entry is 0, the data should start at offset 370:

```
00000370: 7270 6d00 322e 322e 3100 3100 5265 6420 rpm.2.2.1.1.Red
```

Since the data type for this entry is a null-terminated string, we need to keep reading bytes until we reach a byte whose numeric value is 0. We find the bytes `72`, `70`, `6d`, and `00`—a null. Looking at the ASCII display on the right, we find that the bytes form the string `rpm`, which is the name of this package.

Now for a slightly more complicated example. Let's look at the following index entry:

```
00000250: 0000 0403 0000 0008 0000 0199 0000 0018 ................
```

Tag 403 means that this entry is a list of filenames. The data type 8, or `STRING_ARRAY`, seems to bear this out. From the previous example, we found that the data area for the header began at offset 370. Adding the offset to the first filename (`199`) gives us 509. Finally, the count of 18 hex means that there should be 24 null-terminated strings containing filenames:

```
00000500: 696e 6974 6462 0a0a 002f 6269 6e2f 7270 initdb.../bin/rp
00000510: 6d00 2f65 7463 2f72 706d 7263 002f 7573 m./etc/rpmrc./us
```

The byte at offset 509 is `2f`—a slash (`/`). Reading up to the first null byte, we find that the first filename is `/bin/rpm`, followed by `/etc/rpmrc`. This continues on for 22 more filenames.

There are many more tags we could decode, but they are all done in the same manner.

A.2.1.3.2. Header Tag Listing

The following list shows the tags available, along with their defined values, for use in the header:

```
#define RPMTAG_NAME                    1000
#define RPMTAG_VERSION                 1001
#define RPMTAG_RELEASE                 1002
#define RPMTAG_SERIAL                  1003
#define RPMTAG_SUMMARY                 1004
#define RPMTAG_DESCRIPTION             1005
#define RPMTAG_BUILDTIME               1006
#define RPMTAG_BUILDHOST               1007
#define RPMTAG_INSTALLTIME             1008
#define RPMTAG_SIZE                    1009
#define RPMTAG_DISTRIBUTION            1010
#define RPMTAG_VENDOR                  1011
#define RPMTAG_GIF                     1012
```

```
#define RPMTAG_XPM                  1013
#define RPMTAG_COPYRIGHT            1014
#define RPMTAG_PACKAGER             1015
#define RPMTAG_GROUP                1016
#define RPMTAG_CHANGELOG            1017
#define RPMTAG_SOURCE               1018
#define RPMTAG_PATCH                1019
#define RPMTAG_URL                  1020
#define RPMTAG_OS                   1021
#define RPMTAG_ARCH                 1022
#define RPMTAG_PREIN                1023
#define RPMTAG_POSTIN               1024
#define RPMTAG_PREUN                1025
#define RPMTAG_POSTUN               1026
#define RPMTAG_FILENAMES            1027
#define RPMTAG_FILESIZES            1028
#define RPMTAG_FILESTATES           1029
#define RPMTAG_FILEMODES            1030
#define RPMTAG_FILEUIDS             1031
#define RPMTAG_FILEGIDS             1032
#define RPMTAG_FILERDEVS            1033
#define RPMTAG_FILEMTIMES           1034
#define RPMTAG_FILEMD5S             1035
#define RPMTAG_FILELINKTOS          1036
#define RPMTAG_FILEFLAGS            1037
#define RPMTAG_ROOT                 1038
#define RPMTAG_FILEUSERNAME         1039
#define RPMTAG_FILEGROUPNAME        1040
#define RPMTAG_EXCLUDE              1041 /* not used */
#define RPMTAG_EXCLUSIVE            1042 /* not used */
#define RPMTAG_ICON                 1043
#define RPMTAG_SOURCERPM            1044
#define RPMTAG_FILEVERIFYFLAGS      1045
#define RPMTAG_ARCHIVESIZE          1046
#define RPMTAG_PROVIDES             1047
#define RPMTAG_REQUIREFLAGS         1048
#define RPMTAG_REQUIRENAME          1049
#define RPMTAG_REQUIREVERSION       1050
#define RPMTAG_NOSOURCE             1051
#define RPMTAG_NOPATCH              1052
#define RPMTAG_CONFLICTFLAGS        1053
#define RPMTAG_CONFLICTNAME         1054
#define RPMTAG_CONFLICTVERSION      1055
#define RPMTAG_DEFAULTPREFIX        1056
#define RPMTAG_BUILDROOT            1057
#define RPMTAG_INSTALLPREFIX        1058
#define RPMTAG_EXCLUDEARCH          1059
#define RPMTAG_EXCLUDEOS            1060
#define RPMTAG_EXCLUSIVEARCH        1061
#define RPMTAG_EXCLUSIVEOS          1062
#define RPMTAG_AUTOREQPROV          1063 /* used internally by build */
#define RPMTAG_RPMVERSION           1064
#define RPMTAG_TRIGGERSCRIPTS       1065
#define RPMTAG_TRIGGERNAME          1066
#define RPMTAG_TRIGGERVERSION       1067
#define RPMTAG_TRIGGERFLAGS         1068
#define RPMTAG_TRIGGERINDEX         1069
#define RPMTAG_VERIFYSCRIPT         1079
```

This list is current as of version 2.3 of RPM. For the most up-to-date version, look in the file lib/rpmlib.h in the latest version of the RPM sources.

A.2.1.3.2. The Archive

Following the header section is the archive. The archive holds the actual files that comprise the package. The archive is compressed using GNU zip. We can verify this if we look at the start of the archive:

```
00000d40: 0000 001f 8b08 0000 0000 0002 03ec fd7b ..............{
00000d50: 7c13 d516 388e 4e92 691b 4a20 010a 1428 |...8.N.i.J ...(
```

In this example, the archive starts at offset d43. According to the contents of /usr/lib/magic, the first 2 bytes of a gzipped file should be 1f8b, which is, in fact, what we see. The following byte (08) is the flag used by GNU zip to indicate the file has been compressed with gzip's deflation method. The eighth byte has a value of 02, which means that the archive has been compressed using gzip's maximum compression setting. The following byte contains a code indicating the operating system under which the archive was compressed. A 03 in this byte indicates that the compression ran under a UNIX-like operating system.

The remainder of the RPM package file is the compressed archive. After the archive is uncompressed, it is an ordinary cpio archive in SVR4 format with a CRC checksum.

A.3. Tools for Studying RPM Files

In the tools directory packaged with the RPM sources are a number of small programs that use the RPM library to extract the various sections of a package file. Normally used by the RPM developers for debugging purposes, these tools can also be used to make it easier to understand the RPM package file format. Here is a list of the programs and what they do:

- rpmlead—Extracts the lead section from a package file
- rpmsignature—Extracts the signature section from a package file
- rpmheader—Extracts the header from a package file
- rpmarchive—Extracts the archive from a package file
- dump—Displays a header structure in an easily readable format

The first four programs take an RPM package file as their input. The package file can be read either from standard input or by including the filename on the command line. In either case, the programs write to standard output. Here is how rpmlead can be used to display the lead from a package file:

```
# rpmlead foo.rpm | od -x
0000000 abed dbee 0003 0000 0100 7072 2d6d 2e32
0000020 2e32 2d31 0031 0000 0000 0000 0000 0000
0000040 0000 0000 0000 0000 0000 0000 0000 0000
```

```
0000100 0000 0000 0000 0000 0000 0000 0100 0500
0000120 0004 0000 e124 bfff b36b 0800 e600 bfff
0000140
#
```

Since each of these programs can also act as a filter, the following command is equivalent to the preceding one:

```
# cat foo.rpm ¦ rpmlead ¦ od -x
0000000 abed dbee 0003 0000 0100 7072 2d6d 2e32
0000020 2e32 2d31 0031 0000 0000 0000 0000 0000
0000040 0000 0000 0000 0000 0000 0000 0000 0000

0000100 0000 0000 0000 0000 0000 0000 0100 0500
0000120 0004 0000 e124 bfff b36b 0800 e600 bfff
0000140
#
```

The dump program is used in conjunction with rpmsignature or rpmheader. It makes decoding header structures a snap:

```
# rpmsignature foo.rpm ¦ dump
Entry count: 3
Data count : 172

              CT  TAG                  TYPE          OFSET        COUNT
Entry      : 000 (1000)NAME            INT32_TYPE    0x00000000 00000001
      Data: 000 0x00044c4f (281679)
Entry      : 001 (1001)VERSION         BIN_TYPE      0x00000004 00000016
      Data: 000 b0 25 b0 97 15 97 01 32
      Data: 008 df 35 d1 69 32 9c 53 75
Entry      : 002 (1002)RELEASE         BIN_TYPE      0x00000014 00000152
      Data: 000 89 00 95 03 05 00 31 ed
      Data: 008 63 90 a5 20 e8 f1 cb a2
      Data: 016 9b f9 01 01 43 7b 04 00
      Data: 024 9c 8e 0a d4 37 90 36 4e
      Data: 032 df b0 9a 8a 22 b5 b0 b3
      Data: 040 dc 30 4c 6f 91 b8 c1 50
      Data: 048 70 4e 2c 64 d8 8a 8f ca
      Data: 056 18 ab 5b 6f f0 41 eb c8
      Data: 064 d1 8a 01 c9 36 01 66 f0
      Data: 072 9d dd e9 56 31 42 61 b3
      Data: 080 b1 da 84 94 6b ef 9c 19
      Data: 088 45 74 c4 9f ee 17 35 e1
      Data: 096 d1 05 fb 68 0c e6 71 5a
      Data: 104 60 f1 c6 60 27 9f 03 06
      Data: 112 28 ed 0b a0 08 55 9e 82
      Data: 120 2b 1c 2e de e8 e3 50 90
      Data: 128 62 60 0b 3c ba 04 69 a9
      Data: 136 25 73 1b bb 5b 65 4d e1
      Data: 144 b1 d2 c0 7f 8a fa 4a 9b
#
```

One aspect of dump worth noting is that it is optimized for decoding the header section of a package file. When used with rpmsignature, it displays the tag names used in the header instead of the signature tag names. The data is displayed properly in either case, however.

A.4. Identifying RPM Files with the file(1) Command

The magic file on most UNIX-like systems today should have the necessary information to identify RPM files. But in case your system doesn't, the following information can be added to the file:

```
#--------------------------------------------------------------------
#
# RPM: file(1) magic for Red Hat Packages
#
0         beshort         0xedab
>2        beshort         0xeedb          RPM
>>4       byte            x               v%d
>>6       beshort         0               bin
>>6       beshort         1               src
>>8       beshort         1               i386
>>8       beshort         2               Alpha
>>8       beshort         3               Sparc
>>8       beshort         4               MIPS
>>8       beshort         5               PowerPC
>>8       beshort         6               68000
>>8       beshort         7               SGI
>>10      string          x               %s
```

The output of the file command is succinct:

```
# file baz
baz: RPM v3 bin i386 vlock-1.0-2
#
```

In this case, the file called baz is a version 3 format RPM file containing release 2 of version 1.0 of the vlock package, which has been built for the Intel x86 architecture.

B

The rpmrc File

The rpmrc file is used to control RPM's actions. The file's entries have an effect on nearly every aspect of RPM's operations. Here, we describe in more detail the rpmrc files, as well as the command used to show how RPM interprets the files.

B.1. Using the --showrc Option

As we'll see in a moment, RPM can read more than one rpmrc file, and each file can contain nearly 30 different types of entries. This can make it difficult to determine what values RPM is actually using.

Luckily, there's an option that can be used to help make sense of it all. The --showrc option displays the value for each of the entries. The output is divided into two sections:

- Architecture and operating system values
- rpmrc values

The architecture and operating system values define the architecture and operating system on which RPM is running. These values define the environment for both building and installing packages. They also define which architectures and operating systems are compatible with each other.

The rpmrc values define many aspects of RPM's operation. These values range from the path to RPM's database to the name of the person listed as having built the package.

Here's an example of --showrc's output:

```
# rpm --showrc
ARCHITECTURE AND OS:
build arch            : i386
build os              : Linux
install arch          : i486
install os            : Linux
compatible arch list  : i486 i386
compatible os list    : Linux
RPMRC VALUES:
builddir              : /usr/src/redhat/BUILD
buildroot             : (not set)
cpiobin               : cpio
dbpath                : /var/lib/rpm
defaultdocdir         : /usr/doc
distribution          : (not set)
excludedocs           : (not set)
ftpport               : (not set)
ftpproxy              : (not set)
messagelevel          : (not set)
netsharedpath         : (not set)
optflags              : -O2 -m486 -fno-strength-reduce
packager              : (not set)
pgp_name              : (not set)
```

```
pgp_path            : (not set)
require_distribution : (not set)
require_icon        : (not set)
require_vendor      : (not set)
root                : (not set)
rpmdir              : /usr/src/redhat/RPMS
signature           : none
sourcedir           : /usr/src/redhat/SOURCES
specdir             : /usr/src/redhat/SPECS
srcrpmdir           : /usr/src/redhat/SRPMS
timecheck           : (not set)
tmppath             : /var/tmp
topdir              : /usr/src/redhat
vendor              : (not set)
#
```

As you can see, the --showrc option clearly displays the values RPM will use. --showrc can also be used with the --rcfile option, which makes it easy to see the effect of specifying a different rpmrc file.

B.2. Different Places an rpmrc File Resides

RPM looks for rpmrc files in four places:

- In /usr/lib/, for a file called rpmrc
- In /etc/, for a file called rpmrc
- In a file called .rpmrc in the user's login directory
- In a file specified by the --rcfile option, if the option is present on the command line

The first three files are read in the order listed, such that if a given rpmrc entry is present in each file, the value of the entry read last is the one used by RPM. This means, for example, that an entry in .rpmrc in the user's login directory will always override the same entry in /etc/rpmrc. Likewise, an entry in /etc/rpmrc will always override the same entry in /usr/lib/rpmrc.

If the --rcfile option is used, then only /usr/lib/rpmrc and the file following the --rcfile option are read, in that order. The /usr/lib/rpmrc file is always read first. This cannot be changed.

Let's look at each of these files, starting with /usr/lib/rpmrc.

B.2.1. /usr/lib/rpmrc

The file /usr/lib/rpmrc is always read. It contains information that RPM uses to set some default values. *This file should never be modified!* Doing so may cause RPM to operate incorrectly.

After this stern warning, we should note that it's perfectly all right to look at it. Here it is, in fact:

```
###############################################################
# Default values, often overridden in /etc/rpmrc

dbpath: /var/lib/rpm
topdir: /usr/src/redhat
tmppath: /var/tmp
cpiobin: cpio
defaultdocdir: /usr/doc

###############################################################

# Please send new entries to rpm-list@redhat.com

###############################################################
# Values for RPM_OPT_FLAGS for various platforms

optflags: i386 -O2 -m486 -fno-strength-reduce
optflags: alpha -O2
optflags: sparc -O2
optflags: m68k -O2 -fomit-frame-pointer

###############################################################
# Canonical arch names and numbers

arch_canon: i986: i986 1
arch_canon: i886: i886 1
arch_canon: i786: i786 1
arch_canon: i686: i686 1
arch_canon: i586: i586 1
arch_canon: i486: i486 1
arch_canon: i386: i386 1
arch_canon: alpha: alpha 2
arch_canon:  sparc: sparc 3
arch_canon:  sun4: sparc 3
arch_canon:  sun4m: sparc 3
arch_canon:  sun4c: sparc 3
# This is really a place holder for MIPS.
arch_canon: mips: mips 4
arch_canon: ppc: ppc 5
# This is really a place holder for 68000
arch_canon: m68k: m68k 6
# This is wrong. We really need globbing in here :-(
arch_canon: IP: sgi 7
arch_canon:     IP22: sgi     7

arch_canon:    9000/712:      hppa1.1 9

arch_canon:    sun4u: usparc  10

###############################################################
# Canonical OS names and numbers
```

```
os_canon: Linux: Linux 1
os_canon: IRIX: Irix 2
# This is wrong
os_canon: SunOS5: solaris 3
os_canon: SunOS4: SunOS 4

os_canon:        AmigaOS: AmigaOS 5
os_canon:            AIX: AIX      5
os_canon:          HP-UX: hpux10   6
os_canon:           OSF1: osf1     7
os_canon:         FreeBSD: FreeBSD 8

#############################################################
# For a given uname().machine, the default build arch

buildarchtranslate: osfmach3_i986: i386
buildarchtranslate: osfmach3_i886: i386
buildarchtranslate: osfmach3_i786: i386
buildarchtranslate: osfmach3_i686: i386
buildarchtranslate: osfmach3_i586: i386
buildarchtranslate: osfmach3_i486: i386
buildarchtranslate: osfmach3_i386: i386

buildarchtranslate: i986: i386
buildarchtranslate: i886: i386
buildarchtranslate: i786: i386
buildarchtranslate: i686: i386
buildarchtranslate: i586: i386
buildarchtranslate: i486: i386
buildarchtranslate: i386: i386

buildarchtranslate: osfmach3_ppc: ppc

#############################################################
# Architecture compatibility

arch_compat: alpha: axp

arch_compat: i986: i886
arch_compat: i886: i786
arch_compat: i786: i686
arch_compat: i686: i586
arch_compat: i586: i486
arch_compat: i486: i386

arch_compat: osfmach3_i986: i986 osfmach3_i886
arch_compat: osfmach3_i886: i886 osfmach3_i786
arch_compat: osfmach3_i786: i786 osfmach3_i686
arch_compat: osfmach3_i686: i686 osfmach3_i586
arch_compat: osfmach3_i586: i586 osfmach3_i486
arch_compat: osfmach3_i486: i486 osfmach3_i386
arch_compat: osfmach3_i386: i486

arch_compat: osfmach3_ppc: ppc

arch_compat: usparc: sparc
```

Quite a bunch of stuff, isn't it? With the exception of the first five lines, which indicate where several important directories and programs are located, the remainder of this file contains rpmrc entries that are related to RPM's architecture and operating system processing. As you might imagine, any tinkering here will probably not be very productive, so leave any modifications here to the RPM developers.

Next, we have /etc/rpmrc.

B.2.2. /etc/rpmrc

The file /etc/rpmrc, unlike /usr/lib/rpmrc, is fair game for modifications and additions. In fact, /etc/rpmrc isn't created by default, so its contents are entirely up to you. It's the perfect place to keep rpmrc entries of a systemwide or global nature.

The vendor entry is a great example of a good candidate for inclusion in /etc/rpmrc. In most cases, a particular system is dedicated to building packages for one vendor. In these instances, setting the vendor entry in /etc/rpmrc is best.

Next in the hierarchy is a file named .rpmrc, which resides in the user's login directory.

B.2.3. .rpmrc in the User's Login Directory

As you might imagine, a file called .rpmrc in a user's login directory is only going to be read by that user when he or she runs RPM. Like /etc/rpmrc, this file is not created by default, but it can contain the same rpmrc entries as the other files. The packager entry, which should contain the name and contact information for the person who built the package, is an appropriate candidate for ~/.rpmrc.

B.2.4. File Specified by the --rcfile Option

The --rcfile option is best used only when a totally different RPM configuration is desired for one or two packages. Since the only other rpmrc file read is /usr/lib/rpmrc with its low-level default settings, the file specified with the --rcfile option will have to be more comprehensive than either /etc/rpmrc or ~/.rpmrc.

B.3. rpmrc File Syntax

As you might have surmised from the sample file we briefly reviewed, the basic syntax of an rpmrc file entry is

```
<name>:<value>
```

The <name> part of the entry is not case sensitive, so any capitalization is acceptable. The colon separating the name from its value must immediately follow the name. No spaces are allowed here. The formatting requirements on the value side of the entry vary from value to value and are discussed along with each entry.

B.4. rpmrc File Entries

In this section, we discuss the various entries that can be used in each of the rpmrc files.

B.4.1. arch_canon

The arch_canon entry is used to define a table of architecture names and their associated numbers. These canonical architecture names and numbers are then used internally by RPM whenever architecture-specific processing takes place. This entry's format is

```
arch_canon:<label>: <string> <value>
```

<label> is compared against information from uname(2) after it's been translated using the appropriate buildarchtranslate entry. If a match is found, *<string>* is used by RPM to reference the system's architecture. When building a binary package, RPM uses *<string>* as part of the package's filename, for instance.

<value> is a numeric value RPM uses internally to identify the architecture. For example, this number is written in the header of each package file so that the file command can identify the architecture for which the package was built.

B.4.2. os_canon

The os_canon entry is used to define a table of operating system names and their associated numbers. These canonical operating system names and numbers are then used internally by RPM whenever operating system–specific processing takes place. This entry's format is

```
os_canon:<label>: <string> <value>
```

The *<label>* is compared against information from uname(2) after it's been translated using the appropriate buildostranslate entry. (The buildostranslate rpmrc file entry is discussed in section B.4.4.) If a match is found, *<string>* is used by RPM to reference the operating system.

The *<value>* is a numeric value used to uniquely identify the operating system.

B.4.3. buildarchtranslate

The buildarchtranslate entry is used in the process of defining the architecture that RPM will use as the build architecture. As the name implies, it is used to translate the raw information returned from uname(2) to the canonical architecture defined by arch canon.

The format of the `buildarchtranslate` entry is slightly different from most other `rpmrc` file entries. Instead of the usual `<name>:<value>` format, the `buildarchtranslate` entry looks like this:

```
buildarchtranslate:<label>: <string>
```

The `<label>` is compared against information from `uname(2)`. If a match is found, then `<string>` is used by RPM to define the build architecture.

B.4.4. `buildostranslate`

The `buildostranslate` entry is used in the process of defining the operating system RPM will use as the build operating system. As the name implies, it is used to translate the raw information returned by `uname(2)` to the canonical operating system defined by `os_canon`.

The format of the `buildostranslate` entry is slightly different from most other `rpmrc` file entries. Instead of the usual `<name>:<value>` format, the `buildostranslate` entry looks like this:

```
buildostranslate:<label>: <string>
```

`<label>` is compared against information from `uname(2)`. If a match is found, `<string>` is used by RPM to define the build operating system.

B.4.5. `arch_compat`

The `arch_compat` entry is used to define which architectures are compatible with one another. This information is used when packages are installed; in this way, RPM can determine whether a given package file is compatible with the system. The format of the entry is

```
arch_compat:<label>: <list>
```

`<label>` is an architecture string, as defined by an `arch_canon` entry. `<list>` following it consists of one or more architectures, also defined by `arch_canon`. If there is more than one architecture in the list, they should be separated by a space.

The architectures in the list are considered compatible to the architecture specified in the label.

B.4.6. `os_compat`

Default value: (operating system specific)

The `os_compat` entry is used to define which operating systems are compatible with one another. This information is used when packages are installed; in this way, RPM can determine whether a given package file is compatible with the system. The format of the entry is

```
<name>:<label>: <list>
```

`<label>` is an operating system string, as defined by an os_canon entry. `<list>` following it consists of one or more operating systems, also defined by os_canon. If there is more than one operating system in the list, they should be separated by a space.

The operating systems in the list are considered compatible to the operating system specified in the label.

B.4.7. builddir

Default value: (`topdir`)/`BUILD`

The `builddir` entry is used to define the path to the directory in which RPM will build packages. Its default value is taken from the value of the `topdir` entry, with /`BUILD` appended to it. Note that if you redefine `builddir`, you'll need to specify a complete path.

B.4.8. buildroot

Default value: (none)

The `buildroot` entry defines the path used as the root directory during the install phase of a package build. For more information on using build roots, see Chapter 16, "Making a Package That Can Build Anywhere," specifically section 16.1.

B.4.9. cpiobin

Default value: `cpio`

The `cpiobin` entry is used to define the name (and optionally, the path) of the `cpio` program. RPM uses `cpio` to perform a variety of functions, and needs to know where the program can be found.

B.4.10. dbpath

Default value: /`var`/`lib`/`rpm`

The `dbpath` entry is used to define the directory in which the RPM database files are stored. It can be overridden by using the `--dbpath` option on the RPM command line.

B.4.11. defaultdocdir

Default value: /`usr`/`doc`

The `defaultdocdir` entry is used to define the directory in which RPM will store documentation for all installed packages. It is used only during builds to support the `%doc` directive.

B.4.12. distribution

Default value: (none)

The distribution entry is used to define the distribution for each package. The distribution can also be set by adding the distribution tag to a particular spec file. The distribution tag in the spec file overrides the distribution rpmrc file entry.

B.4.13. excludedocs

Default value: 0

The excludedocs entry is used to control if documentation should be written to disk when a package is installed. By default, documentation is installed; however, this can be overridden by setting the value of excludedocs to 1. Note also that the --excludedocs and --includedocs options can be added to the RPM command line to override the excludedocs entry's behavior. For more information on the --excludedocs and --includedocs options, please refer to Chapter 2, "Using RPM to Install Packages."

B.4.14. ftpport

Default value: (none)

The ftpport entry is used to define the port RPM should use when manipulating package files via FTP. See Chapter 2 for more information on how FTP ports are used by RPM.

B.4.15. ftpproxy

Default value: (none)

The ftpproxy entry is used to define the hostname of the FTP proxy system RPM should use when manipulating package files via FTP. See Chapter 2 for more information on how FTP proxy systems are used by RPM.

B.4.16. messagelevel

Default value: 3

The messagelevel entry is used to define the desired verbosity level. Levels less than 3 produce greater amounts of output, while levels greater than 3 produce less output.

B.4.17. netsharedpath

Default value: (none)

The netsharedpath entry is used to define one or more paths that, on the local system, are shared with other systems. If more than one path is specified, they must be separated with colons.

B.4.18. optflags

Default value: (architecture specific)

The optflags entry is used to define a standard set of options that can be used during the build process, specifically during compilation.

The format of the optflags entry is slightly different from most other rpmrc file entries. Instead of the usual *<name>*:*<value>* format, the optflags entry looks like this:

```
optflags:<architecture> <value>
```

For example, assume the following optflags entries were placed in an rpmrc file:

```
optflags: i386 -O2 -m486 -fno-strength-reduce
optflags: sparc -O2
```

If RPM was running on an Intel 80386–compatible architecture, the optflags value would be set to -O2 -m486 -fno-strength-reduce. If, however, RPM was running on a Sun SPARC–based system, optflags would be set to -O2.

This entry sets the RPM_OPT_FLAGS environment variable, which can be used in the %prep, %build, and %install scripts.

B.4.19. packager

Default value: (none)

The packager entry is used to define the name and contact information for the individual responsible for building the package. The contact information is traditionally defined in the following format:

```
packager:Erik Troan <ewt@redhat.com>
```

B.4.20. pgp_name

Default value: (none)

The pgp_name entry is used to define the name of the PGP public key that will be used to sign each package built. The value is not case sensitive, but the key name entered here must match the actual key name in every other aspect.

For more information on signing packages with PGP, please read Chapter 17, "Adding PGP Signatures to a Package."

B.4.21. pgp_path

Default value: (none)

The pgp_path entry is used to point to a directory containing PGP keyring files. These files will be searched for the public key specified by the pgp_name entry.

For more information on signing packages with PGP, see Chapter 17.

B.4.22. require_distribution

Default value: 0

The require_distribution entry is used to direct RPM to require that every package built must contain distribution information. The default value directs RPM to not enforce this requirement. If the entry has a non-zero value, RPM will only build packages that define a distribution.

B.4.23. require_icon

Default value: 0

The require_icon entry is used to direct RPM to require that every package built must contain an icon. The default value directs RPM to not enforce this requirement. If the entry has a non-zero value, RPM will only build packages that contain an icon.

B.4.24. require_vendor

Default value: 0

The require_vendor entry is used to direct RPM to require that every package built must contain vendor information. The default value directs RPM to not enforce this requirement. If the entry has a non-zero value, RPM will only build packages that define a vendor.

B.4.25. rpmdir

Default value: (topdir)/RPMS

The rpmdir entry is used to define the path to the directory in which RPM will write binary package files. Its default value is taken from the value of the topdir entry, with /RPMS appended to it. Note that if you redefine rpmdir, you'll need to specify a complete path. RPM will automatically add an architecture-specific directory to the end of the path. For example, on an Intel-based system, the actual path would be

/usr/src/redhat/RPMS/i386

B.4.26. signature

Default value: (none)

The signature entry is used to define the type of signature that is to be added to each package built. At the present time, only signatures from PGP are supported. Therefore, the only acceptable value is pgp.

For more information on signing packages with PGP, see Chapter 17.

B.4.27. sourcedir

Default value: (topdir)/SOURCES

The sourcedir entry is used to define the path to the directory in which RPM will look for sources. Its default value is taken from the value of the topdir entry, with /SOURCES appended to it. Note that if you redefine sourcedir, you'll need to specify a complete path.

B.4.28. specdir

Default value: (topdir)/SPECS

The specdir entry is used to define the path to the directory in which RPM will look for spec files. Its default value is taken from the value of the topdir entry, with /SPECS appended to it. Note that if you redefine specdir, you'll need to specify a complete path.

B.4.29. srcrpmdir

Default value: (topdir)/SRPMS

The srcrpmdir entry is used to define the path to the directory in which RPM will write source package files. Its default value is taken from the value of the topdir entry, with /SRPMS appended to it. Note that if you redefine srcrpmdir, you'll need to specify a complete path.

B.4.30. timecheck

Default value: (none)

The timecheck entry is used to define the default number of seconds to apply to the --timecheck option when building packages. For more information on the --timecheck option, please see Chapter 12, "rpm -b Command Reference."

B.4.31. tmppath

Default value: /var/tmp

The `tmpdir` entry is used to define a path to the directory that RPM will use for temporary work space. This normally consists of temporary scripts that are used during the build process. It should be set to an absolute path (that is, starting with /).

B.4.32. topdir

Default value: `/usr/src/redhat`

The `topdir` entry is used to define the path to the top-level directory in RPM's build directory tree. It should be set to an absolute path (that is, starting with /). The following entries base their default values on the value of `topdir`:

- builddir
- rpmdir
- sourcedir
- specdir
- srcrpmdir

B.4.33. vendor

Default value: (none)

The `vendor` entry is used to define the name of the organization that is responsible for distributing the packaged software. Normally, this would be the name of a business or other such entity.

C

Concise RPM Command Reference

C.1. Global Options

The following options can be used in any of RPM's modes:

- `--quiet`—Print as little output as possible.
- `-v`—Be a little more verbose.
- `-vv`—Be incredibly verbose (for debugging).
- `--root <dir>`—Use `<dir>` as the top-level directory.
- `--dbpath <dir>`—Use `<dir>` as the directory for the database.
- `--rcfile <file>`—Use `<file>` instead of `/etc/rpmrc` and `$HOME/.rpmrc`.

C.2. Informational Options

The following options are used to display information about RPM:

Format: `rpm <option>`

- `--version`—Print the version of RPM being used.
- `--help`—Print a help message.
- `--showrc`—Show rcfile information.
- `--querytags`—List the tags that can be used with `--queryformat`.

C.3. Query Mode

RPM's query mode is used to display information about packages.

Format: `rpm --query <options>`

            or

            `rpm -q <options>`

C.3.1. Package Specification Options for Query Mode

No more than one of the following options may be present in every query command. They are used to select the source of the information to be displayed. Where plus signs appear, more than one item may be included, separated by a space:

- `<packagename>`—Query the named package.
- `-a`—Query all packages.
- `-f <file>+`—Query package owning `<file>`.

- -g *<group>*+—Query packages with group *<group>*.
- -p *<packagefile>*+—Query (uninstalled) package *<packagefile>*.
- --whatprovides *<i>*—Query packages that provide *<i>* capability.
- --whatrequires *<i>*—Query packages that require *<i>* capability.

C.3.2. Information Selection Options for Query Mode

One or more of the following options may be added to any query command. They are used to select what information RPM will display. If no information-selection option is present on the command line, RPM will simply display the applicable package label(s):

- -i—Display package information.
- -l—Display package file list.
- -s—Show file states (implies -l).
- -d—List only documentation files (implies -l).
- -c—List only configuration files (implies -l).
- --dump—Show all available information for each file (must be used with -l, -c, or -d).
- --provides—List capabilities that the package provides.
- --requires, -R—List capabilities that the package requires.
- --scripts—Print the various (un)install, verification scripts.
- --queryformat *<s>*—Use *<s>* as the header format (implies -i).
- --qf *<s>*—Shorthand for --queryformat.

C.4. Verify Mode

RPM's verification mode is used to ensure that a package is still installed properly:

Format: rpm --verify *<options>*

or

rpm -V *<options>*

or

rpm -y *<options>*

C.4.1. Options for Verify Mode

The following options can be used on any verify command:

- ■ `--nodeps`—Do not verify package dependencies.
- ■ `--nofiles`—Do not verify file attributes.
- ■ `--noscripts`—Do not execute the package's verification script.

C.5. Install Mode

RPM's installation mode is used to install packages.

Format: `rpm --install` *`<packagefile>`*

          or

          `rpm -i` *`<packagefile>`*

C.5.1. Options for Install Mode

The following options can be used on any install command:

- ■ `-h, --hash`—Print hash marks as package installs (good with `-v`).
- ■ `--prefix` *`<dir>`*—Relocate the package to *`<dir>`*, if relocatable.
- ■ `--excludedocs`—Do not install documentation.
- ■ `--force`—Shorthand for `--replacepkgs` and `--replacefiles`.
- ■ `--ignorearch`—Do not verify package architecture.
- ■ `--ignoreos`—Do not verify package operating system.
- ■ `--includedocs`—Install documentation.
- ■ `--nodeps`—Do not check package dependencies.
- ■ `--noscripts`—Do not execute any installation scripts.
- ■ `--percent`—Print percentages as package installs.
- ■ `--replacefiles`—Install even if the package replaces installed files.
- ■ `--replacepkgs`—Reinstall if the package is already present.
- ■ `--test`—Do not install, but tell whether it would work.

C.6. Upgrade Mode

RPM's upgrade mode is used to upgrade packages.

Format: `rpm --upgrade <packagefile>`

            or

            `rpm -U <packagefile>`

C.6.1. Options for Upgrade Mode

The following options can be used on any upgrade command:

- ■ `-h, --hash`—Print hash marks as package installs (good with `-v`).
- `--prefix <dir>`—Relocate the package to `<dir>`, if relocatable.
- `--excludedocs`—Do not install documentation.
- `--force`—Shorthand for `--replacepkgs`, `--replacefiles`, and `--oldpackage`.
- `--ignorearch`—Do not verify package architecture.
- `--ignoreos`—Do not verify package operating system.
- `--includedocs`—Install documentation.
- ■ `--nodeps`—Do not verify package dependencies.
- ■ `--noscripts`—Do not execute any installation scripts.
- `--percent`—Print percentages as package installs.
- ■ `--replacefiles`—Install even if the package replaces installed files.
- ■ `--replacepkgs`—Reinstall if the package is already present.
- `--test`—Do not install, but tell whether it would work.
- `--oldpackage`—Upgrade to an old version of the package (`--force` on upgrades does this automatically).

C.7. Erase Mode

RPM's erase mode is used to erase previously installed packages.

Format: `rpm --erase <package>`

            or

            `rpm -e <package>`

C.7.1. Options for Erase Mode

The following options can be used on any erase command:

- `--nodeps`—Do not verify package dependencies.
- `--noscripts`—Do not execute any installation scripts.

C.8. Build Mode

RPM's build mode is used to build packages.

Format: `rpm -b<stage> <options> <specfile>`

(Note that `-vv` is the default for all build mode commands.)

C.8.1. Build Mode Stages

One of the following stages must follow the `-b` option:

- `p`—Prep (unpack sources and apply patches).
- `l`—List check (do some cursory checks on `%files`).
- `c`—Compile (prep and compile).
- `i`—Install (prep, compile, install).
- `b`—Binary package (prep, compile, install, package).
- `a`—Binary/source package (prep, compile, install, package).

C.8.2. Options for Build Mode

The following options can be used on any build command:

- `--short-circuit`—Skip straight to specified stage (only for `c` and `i`).
- `--clean`—Remove build tree when done.
- `--sign`—Generate PGP signature.
- `--buildroot <s>`—Use `<s>` as the build root.
- `--buildarch <s>`—Use `<s>` as the build architecture.
- `--buildos <s>`—Use `<s>` as the build operating system.
- `--test`—Do not execute any stages.
- `--timecheck <s>`—Set the time check to `<s>` seconds (`0` disables it).

C.9. Rebuild Mode

RPM's rebuild mode is used to rebuild packages from a source package file. The source archives, patches, and icons that comprise the source package are removed after the binary package is built. Rebuild mode implies `--clean`.

Format: `rpm --rebuild <options> <source-package>`

(Note that `-vv` is the default for all rebuild mode commands.)

C.9.1. Options for Rebuild Mode

Only the global options may be used.

C.10. Recompile Mode

RPM's recompile mode is used to recompile software from a source package file. Unlike `--rebuild`, no binary package is created.

Format: `rpm --recompile <options> <source-package>`

Note that `-vv` is the default for all recompile mode commands.

C.10.1. Options for Recompile Mode

Only the global options may be used.

C.11. Resign Mode

RPM's resign mode is used to replace a package's signature with a new one.

Format: `rpm --resign <options> <packagefile>+`

C.11.1. Options for Resign Mode

Only the global options may be used.

C.12. Add Signature Mode

RPM's add signature mode is used to add a signature to a package.

Format: `rpm --addsign <options> <packagefile>+`

C.12.1. Options for Add Signature Mode

Only the global options may be used.

C.13. Check Signature Mode

RPM's check signature mode is used to verify a package's signature.

Format: `rpm --checksig <options> <packagefile>+`

        or

        `rpm -K <options> <packagefile>+`

C.13.1. Options for Check Signature Mode

The following option can be used on any check signature command:

■ `--nopgp`—Skip any PGP signatures (size and MD5 only).

C.14. Initialize Database Mode

RPM's initialize database mode is used to create a new RPM database.

Format: `rpm --initdb <options>`

C.14.1. Options for Initialize Database Mode

Only the global options may be used.

C.15. Rebuild Database Mode

RPM's rebuild database mode is used to rebuild an RPM database.

Format: `rpm --rebuilddb <options>`

C.15.1. Options to Rebuild Database Mode

Only the global options may be used.

D

Available Tags for
--queryformat

The following tags are all the ones defined at the time this book was written. For the latest list of available `queryformat` tags, issue the following command:

```
rpm --querytags
```

Keep in mind that the list of tags produced by the `--querytags` option is the complete list of all tags used by RPM internally (for instance, during package builds). Because of this, some tags do not produce meaningful output when used in a `--queryformat` format string.

D.1. List of `--queryformat` Tags

For every tag in this section, there can be as many as three different pieces of information:

■ A short description of the tag.

■ Whether the data specified by the tag is an array, and, if so, how many members are present in the array.

■ What modifiers can be used with the tag.

The NAME Tag

The NAME tag is used to display the name of the package.

Array: No

Used with modifiers: N/A

The VERSION Tag

The VERSION tag is used to display the version of the packaged software.

Array: No

Used with modifiers: N/A

The RELEASE Tag

The RELEASE tag is used to display the release number of the package.

Array: No

Used with modifiers: N/A

The SERIAL Tag

The SERIAL tag is used to display the serial number of the package.

Array: No

Used with modifiers: N/A

The SUMMARY Tag

The SUMMARY tag is used to display a one-line summation of the packaged software.

Array: No

Used with modifiers: N/A

The DESCRIPTION Tag

The DESCRIPTION tag is used to display a detailed summation of the packaged software.

Array: No

Used with modifiers: N/A

The BUILDTIME Tag

The BUILDTIME tag is used to display the time and date the package was created.

Array: No

Used with modifiers: :date

The BUILDHOST Tag

The BUILDHOST tag is used to display the hostname of the system that built the package.

Array: No

Used with modifiers: N/A

The INSTALLTIME Tag

The INSTALLTIME tag is used to display the time and date the package was installed.

Array: No

Used with modifiers: :date

The SIZE Tag

The SIZE tag is used to display the total size, in bytes, of every file installed by this package.

Array: No

Used with modifiers: N/A

The DISTRIBUTION Tag

The DISTRIBUTION tag is used to display the distribution this package is a part of.

Array: No

Used with modifiers: N/A

The VENDOR Tag

The VENDOR tag is used to display the organization responsible for marketing the package.

Array: No

Used with modifiers: N/A

The GIF Tag

The GIF tag is not available for use with --queryformat.

The XPM Tag

The XPM tag is not available for use with --queryformat.

The COPYRIGHT Tag

The COPYRIGHT tag is used to display the copyright terms of the package.

Array: No

Used with modifiers: N/A

The PACKAGER Tag

The PACKAGER tag is used to display the person or persons responsible for creating the package.

Array: No

Used with modifiers: N/A

The GROUP Tag

The GROUP tag is used to display the group to which the package belongs.

Array: No

Used with modifiers: N/A

The CHANGELOG Tag

The CHANGELOG tag is reserved for a future version of RPM.

The SOURCE Tag

The SOURCE tag is used to display the source archives contained in the source package file.

Array: Yes (Size: One entry per source)

Used with modifiers: N/A

The PATCH Tag

The PATCH tag is used to display the patch files contained in the source package file.

Array: Yes (Size: One entry per patch)

Used with modifiers: N/A

The URL Tag

The URL tag is used to display the uniform resource locator that points to additional information about the packaged software.

Array: No

Used with modifiers: N/A

The OS Tag

The OS tag is used to display the operating system for which the package was built.

Array: No

Used with modifiers: N/A

The ARCH Tag

The ARCH tag is used to display the architecture for which the package was built.

Array: No

Used with modifiers: N/A

The PREIN Tag

The PREIN tag is used to display the package's preinstall script.

Array: No

Used with modifiers: N/A

The POSTIN Tag

The POSTIN tag is used to display the package's postinstall script.

Array: No

Used with modifiers: N/A

The PREUN Tag

The PREUN tag is used to display the package's preuninstall script.

Array: No

Used with modifiers: N/A

The POSTUN Tag

The POSTUN tag is used to display the package's postuninstall script.

Array: No

Used with modifiers: N/A

The FILENAMES Tag

The FILENAMES tag is used to display the names of the files that comprise the package.

Array: Yes (Size: One entry per file)

Used with modifiers: N/A

The FILESIZES Tag

The FILESIZES tag is used to display the size, in bytes, of each of the files that comprise the package.

Array: Yes (Size: One entry per file)

Used with modifiers: N/A

The FILESTATES Tag

The FILESTATES tag is used to display the state of each of the files that comprise the package.

Array: Yes (Size: One entry per file)

Used with modifiers: N/A

Since there is no modifier to display the file states in human-readable form, it will be necessary to manually interpret the flag values, based on the RPMFILE_STATE_*xxx* #defines contained in rpmlib.h. This file is part of the rpm-devel package and is also present in the RPM source package.

The FILEMODES Tag

The FILEMODES tag is used to display the permissions of each of the files that comprise the package.

Array: Yes (Size: One entry per file)

Used with modifiers: :perms

The FILEUIDS Tag

The FILEUIDS tag is used to display the user ID, in numeric form, of each of the files that comprise the package.

Array: Yes (Size: One entry per file)

Used with modifiers: N/A

The FILEGIDS Tag

The FILEGIDS tag is used to display the group ID, in numeric form, of each of the files that comprise the package.

Array: Yes (Size: One entry per file)

Used with modifiers: N/A

The FILERDEVS Tag

The FILERDEVS tag is used to display the major and minor numbers for each of the files that comprise the package. It will only be non-zero for device special files.

Array: Yes (Size: One entry per file)

Used with modifiers: N/A

The FILEMTIMES Tag

The FILEMTIMES tag is used to display the modification time and date for each of the files that comprise the package.

Array: Yes (Size: One entry per file)

Used with modifiers: :date

The FILEMD5S Tag

The FILEMD5S tag is used to display the MD5 checksum for each of the files that comprise the package.

Array: Yes (Size: One entry per file)

Used with modifiers: N/A

The FILELINKTOS Tag

The FILELINKTOS tag is used to display the link string for symlinks.

Array: Yes (Size: One entry per file)

Used with modifiers: N/A

The FILEFLAGS Tag

The FILEFLAGS tag is used to indicate whether the files that comprise the package have been flagged as being documentation or configuration.

Array: Yes (Size: One entry per file)

Used with modifiers: :fflags

The ROOT Tag

The ROOT tag is not available for use with --queryformat.

The FILEUSERNAME Tag

The FILEUSERNAME tag is used to display the owner, in alphanumeric form, of each of the files that comprise the package.

Array: No

Used with modifiers: N/A

The FILEGROUPNAME Tag

The FILEGROUPNAME tag is used to display the group, in alphanumeric form, of each of the files that comprise the package.

Array: Yes (Size: One entry per file)

Used with modifiers: N/A

The EXCLUDE Tag

The EXCLUDE tag is deprecated and should no longer be used.

The EXCLUSIVE Tag

The EXCLUSIVE tag is deprecated and should no longer be used.

The ICON Tag

The ICON tag is not available for use with --queryformat.

The SOURCERPM Tag

The SOURCERPM tag is used to display the name of the source package from which this binary package was built.

Array: No

Used with modifiers: N/A

The FILEVERIFYFLAGS Tag

The FILEVERIFYFLAGS tag is used to display the numeric value of the file verification flags for each of the files that comprise the package.

Array: Yes (Size: One entry per file)

Used with modifiers: N/A

Since there is no modifier to display the verification flags in human-readable form, it will be necessary to manually interpret the flag values based on the RPMVERIFY_*xxx* #defines contained in rpmlib.h. This file is part of the rpm-devel package and is also present in the RPM source package.

The ARCHIVESIZE Tag

The ARCHIVESIZE tag is used to display the size, in bytes, of the archive portion of the original package file.

Array: No

Used with modifiers: N/A

The PROVIDES Tag

The PROVIDES tag is used to display the capabilities the package provides.

Array: Yes (Size: One entry per provide)

Used with modifiers: N/A

The REQUIREFLAGS Tag

The REQUIREFLAGS tag is used to display the requirement flags for each capability the package requires.

Array: Yes (Size: One entry per require)

Used with modifiers: `:depflags`

The REQUIRENAME Tag

The REQUIRENAME tag is used to display the capabilities the package requires.

Array: Yes (Size: One entry per require)

Used with modifiers: N/A

The REQUIREVERSION Tag

The REQUIREVERSION tag is used to display the version-related aspect of each capability the package requires.

Array: Yes (Size: One entry per require)

Used with modifiers: N/A

The NOSOURCE Tag

The NOSOURCE tag is used to display the source archives that are not contained in the source package file.

Array: Yes (Size: One entry per nosource)

Used with modifiers: N/A

The NOPATCH Tag

The NOPATCH tag is used to display the patch files that are not contained in the source package file.

Array: Yes (Size: One entry per nopatch)

Used with modifiers: N/A

The CONFLICTFLAGS Tag

The CONFLICTFLAGS tag is used to display the conflict flags for each capability the package conflicts with.

Array: Yes (Size: One entry per conflict)

Used with modifiers: :depflags

The CONFLICTNAME Tag

The CONFLICTNAME tag is used to display the capabilities that the package conflicts with.

Array: Yes (Size: One entry per conflict)

Used with modifiers: N/A

The CONFLICTVERSION Tag

The CONFLICTVERSION tag is used to display the version-related aspect of each capability the package conflicts with.

Array: Yes (Size: One entry per conflict)

Used with modifiers: N/A

The DEFAULTPREFIX Tag

The DEFAULTPREFIX tag is used to display the path that will, by default, be used to install a relocatable package.

Array: No

Used with modifiers: N/A

The BUILDROOT Tag

The BUILDROOT tag is not available for use with --queryformat.

The INSTALLPREFIX Tag

The INSTALLPREFIX tag is used to display the actual path used when a relocatable package was installed.

Array: No

Used with modifiers: N/A

The EXCLUDEARCH Tag

The EXCLUDEARCH tag is used to display the architectures that should not install this package.

Array: Yes (Size: One entry per excludearch)

Used with modifiers: N/A

The EXCLUDEOS Tag

The EXCLUDEOS tag is used to display the operating systems that should not install this package.

Array: Yes (Size: One entry per excludeos)

Used with modifiers: N/A

The EXCLUSIVEARCH Tag

The EXCLUSIVEARCH tag is used to display the architectures that are the only ones that should install this package.

Array: Yes (Size: One entry per exclusivearch)

Used with modifiers: N/A

The EXCLUSIVEOS Tag

The EXCLUSIVEOS tag is used to display the operating systems that are the only ones that should install this package.

Array: Yes (Size: One entry per exclusiveos)

Used with modifiers: N/A

The AUTOREQPROV Tag

The AUTOREQPROV tag is not available for use with `--queryformat`.

The RPMVERSION Tag

The RPMVERSION tag is used to display the version of RPM that was used to build the package.

Array: No

Used with modifiers: N/A

The TRIGGERSCRIPTS Tag

The TRIGGERSCRIPTS tag is reserved for a future version of RPM.

The TRIGGERNAME Tag

The TRIGGERNAME tag is reserved for a future version of RPM.

The TRIGGERVERSION Tag

The TRIGGERVERSION tag is reserved for a future version of RPM.

The TRIGGERFLAGS Tag

The TRIGGERFLAGS tag is reserved for a future version of RPM.

The TRIGGERINDEX Tag

The TRIGGERINDEX tag is reserved for a future version of RPM.

The VERIFYSCRIPT Tag

The VERIFYSCRIPT tag is used to display the script to be used for package verification.

Array: No

Used with modifiers: N/A

E

Concise Spec File Reference

E.1. Comments

Comments are a way to make RPM ignore a line in the spec file. To create a comment, enter a pound sign (#) at the start of the line. Any text following the comment character will be ignored by RPM:

```
# This is the spec file for playmidi 2.3...
```

Comments can be placed in any section of the spec file.

For more information, see section 13.1 in Chapter 13, "Inside the Spec File."

E.2. The Preamble

The preamble contains information that will be displayed when users request information about the package.

E.2.1. Package-Naming Tags

Package-naming tags are used to define the parts of the package's label. For more information about these tags, see section 13.2.1.

E.2.1.1. The name Tag

The name tag is used to define the name of the software being packaged:

```
Name: cdplayer
```

E.2.1.2. The version Tag

The version tag defines the version of the software being packaged:

```
Version: 1.2
```

E.2.1.3. The release Tag

The release tag can be thought of as the package's version:

```
Release: 5
```

E.2.2. Descriptive Tags

Descriptive tags are used to define various types of information about the package. For more information about these tags, see section 13.2.2.

E.2.2.1. The %description Tag

The %description tag is used to define an in-depth description of the packaged software. In the descriptive text, a space in the first column indicates that that line of text should be presented to users as is, with no formatting done by RPM. Blank lines in the descriptive text denote paragraphs:

```
%description
 It slices!
 It dices!
 It's a CD player app that can't be beat.

By using the resonant frequency of the CD itself, it is able to simulate
20X oversampling. This leads to sound quality that cannot be equaled with
more mundane software...
```

You can make the %description tag specific to a particular subpackage by adding the subpackage name and, optionally, the -n option:

```
%description bar
```

```
%description -n bar
```

The subpackage name and the usage of the -n option must match those defined with the %package directive.

E.2.2.2. The summary Tag

The summary tag is used to define a one-line description of the packaged software:

```
Summary: A CD player app that rocks!
```

E.2.2.3. The copyright Tag

The copyright tag is used to define the copyright terms applicable to the software being packaged:

```
Copyright: GPL
```

E.2.2.4. The distribution Tag

The distribution tag is used to define a group of packages of which this package is a part:

```
Distribution: Doors '95
```

E.2.2.5. The icon Tag

The icon tag is used to name a file containing an icon representing the packaged software:

```
Icon: foo.xpm
```

The file may be in either GIF or XPM format, although XPM is preferred. In either case, the background of the icon should be transparent.

E.2.2.6. The `vendor` Tag

The `vendor` tag is used to define the name of the entity that is responsible for packaging the software:

```
Vendor: White Socks Software, Inc.
```

E.2.2.7. The `url` Tag

The `url` tag is used to define a uniform resource locator that can be used to obtain additional information about the packaged software:

```
URL: http://www.gnomovision.com/cdplayer.html
```

E.2.2.8. The `group` Tag

The `group` tag is used to group packages together by the types of functionality they provide:

```
Group: Applications/Editors
```

E.2.2.9. The `packager` Tag

The `packager` tag is used to hold the name and contact information for the person or persons who built the package:

```
Packager: Fred Foonly <fred@gnomovision.com>
```

E.2.3. Dependency Tags

Dependency tags are used to define a package's dependency-related requirements. For more information about these tags, see section 13.2.3.

E.2.3.1. The `provides` Tag

The `provides` tag is used to specify a "virtual package" that the packaged software makes available when it is installed:

```
Provides: module-info
```

E.2.3.2. The `requires` Tag

The `requires` tag is used to make RPM aware that the package needs to have certain capabilities available in order to operate properly:

```
Requires: playmidi
```

A version may be specified, following the package specification. The following comparison operators may be placed between the package and version: <, >, =, >=, and <=. Here's an example:

```
Requires: playmidi >= 2.3
```

If the `requires` tag needs to perform a comparison against a serial number defined with the serial tag, the proper format would be

```
Requires: playmidi =S 4
```

E.2.3.3. The `serial` Tag

The `serial` tag is used to define a serial number for a package:

```
Serial: 4
```

This is only necessary if RPM is unable to determine the ordering of a package's version numbers.

E.2.3.4. The `conflicts` Tag

The `conflicts` tag is used to make RPM aware that the package is not compatible with other packages:

```
Conflicts: playmidi
```

A version may be specified, following the package specification. The following comparison operators may be placed between the package and version: <, >, =, >=, and <=. Here's an example:

```
Conflicts: playmidi >= 2.3
```

If the `conflicts` tag needs to perform a comparison against a serial number defined with the serial tag, the proper format would be

```
Conflicts: playmidi =S 4
```

E.2.3.5. The `autoreqprov` Tag

The `autoreqprov` tag is used to control the automatic dependency processing performed when the package is being built. To disable automatic dependency processing, add the following line:

```
AutoReqProv: no
```

(The number 0 may be used instead of no.) Although RPM defaults to performing automatic dependency processing, the effect of the `autoreqprov` tag can be reversed by changing no to yes. (The number 1 may be used instead of yes.)

E.2.4. Architecture- and Operating System–Specific Tags

These tags are used to control RPM's behavior when the package is built on different platforms. For more information about these tags, see section 13.2.4.

E.2.4.1. The excludearch Tag

The excludearch tag is used to direct RPM to ensure that the package does not attempt to build on the excluded architecture(s):

```
ExcludeArch: sparc alpha
```

E.2.4.2. The exclusivearch Tag

The exclusivearch tag is used to direct RPM to ensure the package is only built on the specified architecture(s):

```
ExclusiveArch: sparc alpha
```

E.2.4.3. The excludeos Tag

The excludeos tag is used to direct RPM to ensure that the package does not attempt to build on the excluded operating system(s):

```
ExcludeOS: linux irix
```

E.2.4.4. The exclusiveos Tag

The exclusiveos tag is used to denote which operating system(s) should be exclusively permitted to build the package:

```
ExclusiveOS: linux
```

E.2.5. Directory-Related Tags

Directory-related tags are used to define certain directory-related aspects of RPM's operation. For more information about these tags, see section 13.2.5.

E.2.5.1. The prefix Tag

The prefix tag is used to define part of the path RPM will use when installing the package's files:

```
Prefix: /opt
```

The prefix can be redefined by the user when the package is installed, thereby changing where the package is installed.

E.2.5.2. The buildroot Tag

The buildroot tag is used to define an alternate build root, where the software will be installed during the build process:

```
BuildRoot: /tmp/cdplayer
```

E.2.6. Source and Patch Tags

The source and patch tags are used to define the names of the files that contain the package's source code, and patches. For more information about these tags see section 13.2.6 in Chapter 13.

E.2.6.1. The source Tag

The source tag is used to define the filename of the sources to be packaged:

```
Source0: ftp://ftp.gnomovision.com/pub/cdplayer-1.0.tgz
Source1: foo.tgz
```

When there is more than one source tag in a spec file, each one must be numbered so it is unique, starting with the number 0. When there is only one tag, it does not need to be numbered. By convention, the source filename is usually preceded by a URL pointing to the location of the original sources, but RPM does not require this.

E.2.6.2. The nosource Tag

The nosource tag is used to make RPM aware that one or more source files should be excluded from the source package file:

```
NoSource: 0, 3
```

The tag is followed by one or more numbers. The numbers correspond to the numbers following the source tags that are to be excluded from packaging.

E.2.6.3. The patch Tag

The patch tag is used to define the name of a patch file to be applied to the package's sources:

```
Patch: cdp-0.33-fsstnd.patch
```

When there is more than one patch tag in a spec file, each one must be numbered so it is unique, starting with the number 0. When there is only one tag, it does not need to be numbered.

E.2.6.4. The nopatch Tag

The nopatch tag is used to make RPM aware that one or more patch files should be excluded from the source package file:

```
NoPatch: 2 3
```

The tag is followed by one or more numbers. The numbers correspond to the numbers following the patch tags that are to be excluded from packaging.

E.3. Scripts

Scripts are used by RPM to perform processing at various times.

E.3.1. Build Time Scripts

Every build time script has the following environment variables defined:

- RPM_SOURCE_DIR
- RPM_BUILD_DIR
- RPM_DOC_DIR
- RPM_OPT_FLAGS
- RPM_ARCH
- RPM_OS
- RPM_ROOT_DIR
- RPM_BUILD_ROOT
- RPM_PACKAGE_NAME
- RPM_PACKAGE_VERSION
- RPM_PACKAGE_RELEASE

For more information on these environment variables and build time scripts, see section 13.3.1 in Chapter 13.

E.3.1.1. The %prep Script

The %prep script is the first script RPM executes during a build:

%prep

As the name implies, it is normally used to prepare the sources for building. The commands in the script can be any valid sh commands.

E.3.1.2. The %build Script

The %build script is the second script RPM executes during a build:

%build

As the name implies, it is normally used to build the software. The commands in the script can be any valid sh commands.

E.3.1.3. The %install Script

The %install script is the third script RPM executes during a build:

```
%install
```

As the name implies, it is normally used to install the software. The commands in the script can be any valid sh commands.

E.3.1.4. The %clean Script

The %clean script, as the name implies, is used to clean up the software's build directory tree:

```
%clean
```

RPM will normally do this for you, but in certain cases (most notably in those packages that use a build root) you'll need to include a %clean script. The commands in the script can be any valid sh commands.

E.3.2. Install and Erase Time Scripts

Install time and erase time scripts are executed whenever the package is installed or erased, respectively. Each script can consist of any valid sh commands.

You can make each of the following scripts specific to a particular subpackage by adding the subpackage name and, optionally, the -n option:

```
%post bar
```

```
%preun -n bar
```

The subpackage name and usage of the -n option must match those defined with the %package directive.

Each script has the following environment variable defined:

■ RPM_INSTALL_PREFIX

For more information on this environment variable and the associated scripts, see section 13.3.2 in Chapter 13.

E.3.2.1. The %pre Script

The %pre script executes just before the package is to be installed:

```
%pre
```

E.3.2.2. The %post Script

The %post script executes just after the package is to be installed:

```
%post
```

E.3.2.3. The %preun Script

The %preun script executes just before the package is to be erased:

```
%preun
```

E.3.2.4. The %postun Script

The %postun script executes just after the package is to be erased:

```
%postun
```

E.3.3. Verification Scripts

Verification scripts are executed when an installed package is to be verified.

E.3.3.1. The %verifyscript Script

The %verifyscript script executes whenever the package is verified using RPM's -V option. The script can consist of any valid sh commands.

For more information, see section 13.3.3 in Chapter 13.

E.4. Macros

Macros are used to simplify certain types of repetitive operations.

E.4.1. The %setup Macro

The %setup macro is used to unpack the original sources in preparation for the build. It is used in the %prep script:

```
%prep
%setup
```

For more information about the %setup macro and the related options described in this section, see section 13.4.1 in Chapter 13.

E.4.1.1. The -n <name> Option

The -n option is used to set the name of the software's build directory:

```
%setup -n cd-player
```

This is necessary only when the source archive unpacks into a directory named other than *<name>-<version>*.

E.4.1.2. The -c Option

The -c option is used to direct %setup to create the top-level build directory before unpacking the sources:

```
%setup -c
```

E.4.1.3. The -D Option

The -D option is used to direct %setup to not delete the build directory prior to unpacking the sources:

```
%setup -D -T -b 3
```

This option is used when more than one source archive is to be unpacked into the build directory, normally with the -b or -a option.

E.4.1.4. The -T Option

The -T option is used to direct %setup to not perform the default unpacking of the source archive specified by the first source tag. It is used with the -a or -b options:

```
%setup -D -T -a 1
```

E.4.1.5. The -b <*n*> Option

The -b option is used to direct %setup to unpack the source archive specified on the *n*th source tag line before changing directories into the build directory:

```
%setup -D -T -b 2
```

E.4.1.6. The -a <*n*> Option

The -a option is used to direct %setup to unpack the source archive specified on the *n*th source tag line after changing directories into the build directory:

```
%setup -D -T -a 5
```

E.4.2. The %patch Macro

The %patch macro, as its name implies, is used to apply patches to the unpacked sources. With no additional options specified, it will apply the patch file specified by the patch (or patch0) tag:

```
%patch
```

When there is more than one patch tag line in a spec file, they can be specified by appending the number of the patch tag to the %patch macro name itself:

```
%patch2
```

For more information about the `patch` tag and the related options described in this section, see section 13.4.2 in Chapter 13.

E.4.2.1. The `-P` *<n>* Option

The `-P` option is another method of applying a specific patch. The number from the `patch` tag follows the `-P` option. The following `%patch` macros both apply the patch specified on the `patch2` tag line:

```
%patch -P 2
%patch2
```

E.4.2.2. The `-p<#>` Option

The `-p` option is sent directly to the `patch` command. It is followed by a number that specifies the number of leading slashes (and the directories in between) to strip from any filenames present in the patch file:

```
%patch -p2
```

E.4.2.3. The `-b` *<name>* Option

When the `patch` command is used to apply a patch, unmodified copies of the files patched are renamed to end with the extension `.orig`. The `-b` option is used to change the extension used by `patch`:

```
%patch -b .fsstnd
```

E.4.2.4. The `%patch` `-E` Option

The `-E` option is sent directly to the `patch` command. It is used to direct `patch` to remove any empty files after the patches have been applied.

```
%patch -E
```

E.5. The `%files` List

The `%files` list indicates which files on the build system are to be packaged. The list consists of one file per line:

```
%files
/etc/foo.conf
/sbin/foo
/usr/bin/foocmd
```

If a directory is specified, by default all files and subdirectories will be packaged.

You can make the `%files` list specific to a particular subpackage by adding the subpackage name and, optionally, the `-n` option:

```
%files bar
```

```
%files -n bar
```

The subpackage name and the usage of the `-n` option must match those defined with the `%package` directive.

The `%files` list can also use the contents of a file as the list of files to be packaged. This is done by using the `-f` option, which is then followed by a filename:

```
%files -f files.list
```

For more information, see section 13.5 in Chapter 13.

E.6. Directives for the `%files` List

The directives outlined in the following sections are used to modify various attributes of one or more entries in the `%files` list.

E.6.1. File-Related Directives

The directives outlined in the following sections modify `%files` list entries that are files. For more information about these directives, see section 13.6.1.

E.6.1.1. The `%doc` Directive

The `%doc` directive flags the filename(s) that follow it as being documentation:

```
%doc README
```

E.6.1.2. The `%config` Directive

The `%config` directive is used to flag the specified file as being a configuration file:

```
%config /etc/fstab
```

E.6.1.3. The `%attr` Directive

The `%attr` directive is used to permit RPM to directly control a file's permissions and ownership. It is normally used when non-root users build packages. The `%attr` directive has the following format:

```
%attr(<mode>, <user>, <group>) file
```

The user and group identifiers must be non-numeric. Attributes that do not need to be set by `%attr` may be replaced with a dash:

```
%attr(755, root, -) foo.bar
```

E.6.1.4. The `%verify` Directive

The `%verify` directive is used to control which of nine different file attributes are to be verified by RPM. The attributes are

- `owner`—The file's owner.
- `group`—The file's group.
- `mode`—The file's mode.
- `md5`—The file's MD5 checksum.
- `size`—The file's size.
- `maj`—The file's major number.
- `min`—The file's minor number.
- `symlink`—The file's symbolic link string.
- `mtime`—The file's modification time.

One or more of these attributes may be listed in each `%verify` directive:

```
%verify(mode md5 size maj min symlink mtime) /dev/ttyS0
```

If the keyword not precedes the list of attributes, every attribute except those listed will be verified.

E.6.2. Directory-Related Directives

The directives outlined in the following sections modify `%files` list entries that are directories. For more information about these directives, see section 13.6.2 in Chapter 13.

E.6.2.1. The `%docdir` Directive

The `%docdir` directive is used to add the specified directory to RPM's internal list of directories containing documentation. When a directory is added to this list, every file packaged in this directory (and any subdirectories) will automatically be marked as documentation.

E.6.2.2. The `%dir` Directive

The `%dir` directive is used to direct RPM to package only the directory itself, regardless of what files may reside in the directory at the time the package is created:

```
%dir /usr/blather
```

E.7. The %package Directive

The %package directive is used to control the creation of subpackages. The subpackage name is derived from the first name tag in the spec file, followed by the name specified after the %package directive. Therefore, if the first name tag is

```
Name: foo
```

and a subpackage is defined with the following %package directive:

```
%package bar
```

the subpackage name will be foo-bar.

For more information on this package and its options, see section 13.7 in Chapter 13.

E.7.1. The %package -n Option

The -n option is used to change how RPM derives the subpackage name. When the -n option is used, the name following the %package directive becomes the complete subpackage name. Therefore, if a subpackage is defined with the following %package directive:

```
%package -n bar
```

the subpackage name will be bar.

E.8. Conditionals

The %if*xxx* conditionals are used to begin a section of the spec file that is specific to a particular architecture or operating system. They are followed by one or more architecture or operating system specifiers, each separated by commas or whitespace.

Conditionals may be nested within other conditionals, provided that the inner conditional is completely enclosed by the outer conditional. For more information about conditionals, see section 13.8 in Chapter 13.

E.8.1. The %ifarch Conditional

If the build system's architecture is specified, the part of the spec file following the %ifarch but before an %else or %endif will be used during the build:

```
%ifarch i386 sparc
```

E.8.2. The `%ifnarch` Conditional

If the build system's architecture is specified, the part of the spec file following the `%ifarch` but before an `%else` or `%endif` will not be used during the build:

```
%ifnarch i386 sparc
```

E.8.3. The `%ifos` Conditional

If the build system is running one of the specified operating systems, the part of the spec file following the `%ifos` but before an `%else` or `%endif` will be used during the build:

```
%ifos linux
```

E.8.4. The `%ifnos` Conditional

If the build system is running one of the specified operating systems, the part of the spec file following the `%ifnos` but before an `%else` or `%endif` will not be used during the build:

```
%ifnos linux
```

E.8.5. The `%else` Conditional

The `%else` conditional is placed between an `%if` conditional of some persuasion and an `%endif`. It is used to create two blocks of spec file statements, only one of which will be used in any given case:

```
%ifarch alpha
make RPM_OPT_FLAGS="$RPM_OPT_FLAGS -I ."
%else
make RPM_OPT_FLAGS="$RPM_OPT_FLAGS"
%endif
```

E.8.6. The `%endif` Conditional

An `%endif` is used to end a conditional block of spec file statements. The `%endif` is always needed after a conditional; otherwise, the build will fail:

```
%ifarch i386
make INTELFLAG=-DINTEL
%endif
```

F

RPM-Related Resources

There are a number of resources available to help you with RPM, over and above the RPM man page and this book. Here are some pointers to them.

F.1. Where to Get RPM

Perhaps before asking where you can get RPM, it might be better to see if RPM is already installed on your system. If you have Red Hat Linux on your system, it's there already. But be sure to check on other operating systems; people are porting RPM to different operating systems every day, and it just might be there waiting for you.

Here's a quick way to see if RPM is installed on your system:

```
% rpm --version
RPM version 2.3
%
```

If this command doesn't work, it might be that your path doesn't include the directory where RPM resides. Check the usual binary directories before declaring RPM a no-show!

F.1.1. FTP Sites

If you can't find RPM on your system, you'll have to grab a copy by FTP. RPM can be found practically anywhere Red Hat Linux is available. While the most obvious site, `ftp.redhat.com`, is certainly an option, it might not be your best choice. For one thing, it can be very busy. For another, unless your link to the Internet is near Red Hat's sprawling development campus in Durham, North Carolina, there's probably an FTP site closer to you.

Here is a list of sites that mirror Red Hat Software's main FTP site. Be aware that this list changes frequently, so don't be surprised if a particular site no longer mirrors Red Hat or has moved from the paths listed here (an up-to-date copy of the list of mirror sites is always available on `ftp.redhat.com`, in the file MIRRORS):

FTP Site	*Directory*
sunsite.doc.ic.ac.uk	/packages/linux/redhat
ftp.mpi-sb.mpg.de	/pub/linux/mirror/ftp.redhat.com
ftp.jate.u-szeged.hu	/pub/linux/redhat
ftp.ibp.fr	/pub/linux/distributions/redhat
ftp.gwdg.de	/pub/linux/install/redhat
ftp.msu.ru	/pub/Linux/Redhat
ftp.sgg.ru	/mirror/redhat
sunsite.mff.cuni.cz	/OS/Linux/Distributions/Redhat
ftp.ton.tut.fi	/pub/Linux/Redhat
ftp.funet.fi	/pub/Linux/images/Redhat

FTP Site	*Directory*
sunsite.icm.edu.pl	/pub/Linux/redhat
ftp.arch.pwr.proc.pl	/mirror/linux/redhat
ftp.rhi.hi.is	/pub/linux/Redhat
ftp.nvg.unit.no	/pub/linux/redhat
ftp.pk.edu.pl	/pub/linux/redhat
ftp.nluug.nl	/pub/os/Linux/distr/Redhat
dutepp0.et.tudelft.nl	/pub/Unix/Linux/Distributions/redhat
ftp.iol.ie	/pub/Unix/Linux/distributions/Redhat
sunsite.auc.dk	/pub/os/linux/redhat
ftp.tku.edu.tw	/Unix/Linux/Redhat
ftp.cs.us.es	/pub/Linux/redhat
ftp.is.co.za	/linux/distributions/redhat
ftp.dstc.edu.au	/pub/linux-redhat
ftp.lab.kdd.co.jp	/OS/Linux/packages/redhat
sunsite.ust.hk	/pub/Linux/distributions/redhat
ftp.sunsite.dcc.uchile.cl	/pub/OS/linux/redhat
ftp.interpath.net	/pub/linux/redhat
schlitz.cae.wisc.edu	/pub/Linux/Redhat
ftp.wownet.net	/LINUX/redhat
ftp.engr.uark.edu	/pub/linux/redhat
ftp.infomagic.com	/pub/mirrors/linux/Redhat
ftp.wgs.com	/pub/linux/redhat
ftp.drcdrom.com	/pub/linux-redhat
ftp.hkstar.com	/pub/Linux/redhat
ftp.pht.com	/pub/linux/redhat
linux.ucs.indiana.edu	/pub/linux/redhat
ftp.uoknor.edu	/linux/redhat
ftp.cc.gatech.edu	/pub/linux/distributions/redhat
uiarchive.cso.uiuc.edu	/pub/systems/linux/distributions/redhat
ftp.caldera.com	/pub/mirrors/redhat
ftp.cms.uncwil.edu	/linux/redhat
ftp.wilmington.net	/linux/redhat
sunsite.unc.edu	/pub/Linux/distributions/redhat
gatekeeper.dec.com	/pub/linux/redhat
ftp.rge.com	/pub/systems/linux/redhat
linuxwww.db.erau.edu	/pub/linux/distrib/redhat
ftp.eit.com	/pub/mirrors/redhat
ftp.real-time.com	/pub/redhat

Red Hat Software has also set up an FTP site meant specifically for RPM. It's available at ftp.rpm.org and contains all present and past versions of RPM.

F.1.2. What Do I Need?

Once you find a nearby site with RPM and the directory where it's kept, you'll notice a variety of files, all starting with rpm. What are they? Which ones do you need? Here's a representative list, along with the ways in which each file would be used:

```
ftp> ls
200 PORT command successful.
150 Opening ASCII mode data connection for /bin/ls.
total 2689
drwxr-xr-x  6 root 97      2048 Jul 18 10:04 .
drwxr-xr-x  6 root 97      1024 Aug  2 10:09 ..
lrwxrwxrwx  1 root root      23 Jan 22  1996 RPM-HOWTO.ps ->
                                      ../../docs/RPM-HOWTO.ps
lrwxrwxrwx  1 root root      24 Jan 22  1996 RPM-HOWTO.txt ->
                                      ../../docs/RPM-HOWTO.txt
-rw-rw-r--  1 root 97     59239 Jan 20 1996 paper.ps.gz
-rw-r--r--  1 root 97    365319 Jul 18 06:05 rpm-2.2.2-1.axp.rpm
-rw-rw-r--  1 root 97    278620 Jul 18 06:05 rpm-2.2.2-1.i386.cpio.gz
-rw-r--r--  1 root 97    282015 Jul 18 06:05 rpm-2.2.2-1.i386.rpm
-rw-r--r--  1 root 97    279855 Jul 18 06:05 rpm-2.2.2-1.sparc.rpm
-rw-r--r--  1 root 97    359354 Jul 18 06:05 rpm-2.2.2-1.src.rpm
-rw-rw-r--  1 root 97    356943 Jul 18 06:05 rpm-2.2.2.tar.gz
-rw-r--r--  1 root 97    122157 Jul 18 06:05 rpm-devel-2.2.2-1.axp.rpm
-rw-r--r--  1 root 97     51132 Jul 18 06:05 rpm-devel-2.2.2-1.i386.rpm
-rw-r--r--  1 root 97     54470 Jul 18 06:05 rpm-devel-2.2.2-1.sparc.rpm
-rw-r--r--  1 root 97     35504 May  1 04:28 rpmbuild.ps.gz
226 Transfer complete.
ftp>
```

Although the version numbers may change, the types of files kept in this directory will not. The files RPM-HOWTO, paper.ps.gz, and rpmbuild.ps.gz contain a variety of information concerning RPM. As such, they are valuable sources of supplemental information. The remaining files contain RPM, packaged for various architectures and in source form. We'll look at them, grouped according to their contents. Here's the first group of files:

```
-rw-r--r-- 1 root 97 365319 Jul 18 06:05 rpm-2.2.2-1.axp.rpm
-rw-r--r-- 1 root 97 282015 Jul 18 06:05 rpm-2.2.2-1.i386.rpm
-rw-r--r-- 1 root 97 279855 Jul 18 06:05 rpm-2.2.2-1.sparc.rpm
```

These files are the binary package files for RPM version 2.2.2, release 1, on the Digital Alpha, the Intel 386/486/Pentium, and the Sun SPARC. Note that the version number will change in time, but the other parts of the file-naming convention won't. As binary package files, they must be installed using RPM. So if you don't have RPM yet, they won't do you much good.

If your goal is to install RPM on one of these systems, it might be a good idea to copy the appropriate binary package. That way, once you have RPM running, you can reinstall it with the --force option to ensure that RPM is properly installed and configured.

Let's look at the next file:

```
-rw-r--r-- 1 root 97 359354 Jul 18 06:05 rpm-2.2.2-1.src.rpm
```

This is the source package file for RPM version 2.2.2, release 1. Like the binary packages, the source package requires RPM to install; therefore, it cannot be used to perform an initial install of RPM. Let's see what else is here:

```
-rw-r--r-- 1 root 97 122157 Jul 18 06:05 rpm-devel-2.2.2-1.axp.rpm
-rw-r--r-- 1 root 97 51132 Jul 18 06:05 rpm-devel-2.2.2-1.i386.rpm
-rw-r--r-- 1 root 97 54470 Jul 18 06:05 rpm-devel-2.2.2-1.sparc.rpm
```

These files are binary package files that contain the rpm-devel subpackage. The rpm-devel package contains header files and the RPM library and is used for developing programs that can perform RPM-related functions. These files cannot be used to get RPM running. That leaves two files:

```
-rw-rw-r-- 1 root 97 278620 Jul 18 06:05 rpm-2.2.2-1.i386.cpio.gz
-rw-rw-r-- 1 root 97 356943 Jul 18 06:05 rpm-2.2.2.tar.gz
```

The first file is a gzipped cpio archive of the files comprising RPM. After you uncompress the file, cpio can be used to extract the files and place them on your system. Note, however, that there is a cpio archive for the i386 architecture only. To extract the files, issue the following command:

```
# zcat file.cpio.gz | (cd / ; cpio --extract)
```

When you're actually issuing the command, file.cpio.gz should be replaced with the actual name of the cpio archive.

Note that the archive should be extracted using GNU cpio version 2.4.1 or greater. It may also be necessary to issue the following command prior to using RPM:

```
# mkdir /var/lib/rpm
```

The last file, rpm-2.2.2.tar.gz, contains the sources for RPM. Using it, you can build RPM from scratch. This is the most involved option, but it is the only choice for people interested in porting RPM to a new architecture.

F.2. Where to Talk About RPM

As much as we've tried to make this book a comprehensive reference for RPM, there are going to be times when you'll need additional help. The best way to connect with others who use RPM is to try one of the mailing lists listed in the following sections.

F.2.1. The `rpm-list` Mailing List

Red Hat Software, Inc., maintains a mailing list specifically for RPM. To subscribe to the list, it's necessary to send a mail message to

`rpm-list-request@redhat.com`

On the message's subject line, place the word `subscribe`. After a short delay, you should receive an automated response with general information about the mailing list.

To send messages to the list, address them to

`rpm-list@redhat.com`

As with other online forums, it's advisable to lurk for a while before sending anything to the list. That way, you'll be able to see what types of questions are acceptable for the list. Let the list's name be your guide; if the message you want to send doesn't have anything to do with RPM, you shouldn't send it to `rpm-list`!

In general, the flavor of `rpm-list` is a bit biased toward RPM's development, building packages, and issues surrounding the porting of RPM to other systems. If your question is more along the lines of "How do I use RPM to install new software?" consider reviewing the first half of this book and lurking on `rpm-list` a while first.

F.2.2. The `redhat-list` Mailing List

The `redhat-list` mailing list is meant to serve as a forum for users of Red Hat Software's Linux operating system. If your question concerns the use of RPM on Red Hat Linux, `redhat-list` is a good place to start. To subscribe, send a message to

`redhat-list-request@redhat.com`

On the message's subject line, place the word `subscribe`. After a short delay, you should receive an automated response with general information about the mailing list. As with `rpm-list`, it's best to lurk for a while before posting to the list.

To send messages to the list, address them to

`redhat-list@redhat.com`

F.2.3. The `redhat-digest` Mailing List

Some people might find the number of messages on `redhat-list` more than they can handle. However, there is a digest version of the list available. Each digest consists of one or more messages sent to `redhat-list`. The digest is sent out when the collected messages reach a certain size. Therefore, a digest might have one very long message or 20 smaller ones. In either case, you'll have the collected knowledge of the Red Hat Software development team and their many customers, delivered in one message.

To subscribe to `redhat-digest`, send a message to

`redhat-digest-request@redhat.com`

On the message's subject line, place the word `subscribe`. After a short delay, you should receive an automated response with general information about the mailing list.

To send messages to the list, address them to

`redhat-list@redhat.com`

As always, observe proper netiquette—lurk before you leap!

F.3. RPM on the World Wide Web

Up-to-date information on RPM can always be found at the RPM Web site:

`http://www.rpm.org/`

The site is completely dedicated to RPM, which makes finding things a snap. You can also try Red Hat Software's Web site:

`http://www.redhat.com/`

This site's content changes frequently, so it's impossible to specify an exact URL for RPM information. However, the site is very well run and always has a comprehensive table of contents as well as a search engine.

F.4. RPM's License

RPM is licensed under the GNU General Public License or, as it's more commonly called, the GPL. If you're not familiar with the GPL, it would be worthwhile to spend a few minutes looking it over. The purpose of the GPL is to ensure that GPLed software remains freely available.

"Freely available" doesn't necessarily mean at no cost, although GPLed software is often available by anonymous FTP. The idea behind the GPL is to make it impossible for anyone to take GPLed code and make it proprietary. But enough preliminaries! The best way to understand the GPL is to read it:

GNU GENERAL PUBLIC LICENSE

Version 2, June 1991

Copyright © 1989, 1991
Free Software Foundation, Inc.
675 Mass Ave, Cambridge, MA 02139, USA
Everyone is permitted to copy and distribute verbatim copies of this license document, but changing it is not allowed.

Preamble

The licenses for most software are designed to take away your freedom to share and change it. By contrast, the GNU General Public License is intended to guarantee your freedom to share and change free software—to make sure the software is free for all its users. This General Public License applies to most of the Free Software Foundation's software and to any other program whose authors commit to using it. (Some other Free Software Foundation software is covered by the GNU Library General Public License instead.) You can apply it to your programs, too.

When we speak of free software, we are referring to freedom, not price. Our General Public Licenses are designed to make sure that you have the freedom to distribute copies of free software (and charge for this service if you wish), that you receive source code or can get it if you want it, that you can change the software or use pieces of it in new free programs; and that you know you can do these things.

To protect your rights, we need to make restrictions that forbid anyone to deny you these rights or to ask you to surrender the rights. These restrictions translate to certain responsibilities for you if you distribute copies of the software, or if you modify it.

For example, if you distribute copies of such a program, whether gratis or for a fee, you must give the recipients all the rights that you have. You must make sure that they, too, receive or can get the source code. And you must show them these terms so they know their rights.

We protect your rights with two steps:

1. copyright the software, and
2. offer you this license which gives you legal permission to copy, distribute and/or modify the software.

Also, for each author's protection and ours, we want to make certain that everyone understands that there is no warranty for this free software. If the software is modified by someone else and passed on, we want its recipients to know that what they have is not the original, so that any problems introduced by others will not reflect on the original authors' reputations.

Finally, any free program is threatened constantly by software patents. We wish to avoid the danger that redistributors of a free program will individually obtain patent licenses, in effect making the program proprietary. To prevent this, we have made it clear that any patent must be licensed for everyone's free use or not licensed at all.

The precise terms and conditions for copying, distribution and modification follow.

GNU General Public License

TERMS AND CONDITIONS FOR COPYING, DISTRIBUTION AND MODIFICATION

0. This License applies to any program or other work which contains a notice placed by the copyright holder saying it may be distributed under the terms of this General Public License. The "Program," below, refers to any such program or work, and a "work based on the Program" means either the Program or any derivative work under copyright law: that is to say, a work containing the Program or a portion of it, either verbatim or with modifications and/or translated into another language. (Hereinafter, translation is included without limitation in the term "modification".) Each licensee is addressed as "you".

    Activities other than copying, distribution and modification are not covered by this License; they are outside its scope. The act of running the Program is not restricted, and the output from the Program is covered only if its contents constitute a work based on the Program (independent of having been made by running the Program). Whether that is true depends on what the Program does.

1. You may copy and distribute verbatim copies of the Program's source code as you receive it, in any medium, provided that you conspicuously and appropriately publish on each copy an appropriate copyright notice and disclaimer of warranty; keep intact all the notices that refer to this License and to the absence of any warranty; and give any other recipients of the Program a copy of this License along with the Program.

    You may charge a fee for the physical act of transferring a copy, and you may at your option offer warranty protection in exchange for a fee.

2. You may modify your copy or copies of the Program or any portion of it, thus forming a work based on the Program, and copy and distribute such modifications or work under the terms of Section 1 above, provided that you also meet all of these conditions:

    (a) You must cause the modified files to carry prominent notices stating that you changed the files and the date of any change.

    (b) You must cause any work that you distribute or publish, that in whole or in part contains or is derived from the Program or any part thereof, to be licensed as a whole at no charge to all third parties under the terms of this License.

    (c) If the modified program normally reads commands interactively when run, you must cause it, when started running for such interactive use in the most ordinary way, to print or display an announcement including an appropriate copyright notice and a notice that there is no warranty (or else, saying that you provide a warranty) and that users may redistribute the program under these conditions, and telling the user how to view a copy of this License. (Exception: if the Program itself is interactive but does not normally print such an announcement, your work based on the Program is not required to print an announcement.)

These requirements apply to the modified work as a whole. If identifiable sections of that work are not derived from the Program, and can be reasonably considered independent and separate works in themselves, then this License, and its terms, do not apply to those sections when you distribute them as separate works. But when you distribute the same sections as part of a whole which is a work based on the Program, the distribution of the whole must be on the terms of this License, whose permissions for other licensees extend to the entire whole, and thus to each and every part regardless of who wrote it.

Thus, it is not the intent of this section to claim rights or contest your rights to work written entirely by you; rather, the intent is to exercise the right to control the distribution of derivative or collective works based on the Program.

In addition, mere aggregation of another work not based on the Program with the Program (or with a work based on the Program) on a volume of a storage or distribution medium does not bring the other work under the scope of this License.

3. You may copy and distribute the Program (or a work based on it, under Section 2) in object code or executable form under the terms of Sections 1 and 2 above provided that you also do one of the following:

   (a) Accompany it with the complete corresponding machine-readable source code, which must be distributed under the terms of Sections 1 and 2 above on a medium customarily used for software interchange; or,

   (b) Accompany it with a written offer, valid for at least three years, to give any third party, for a charge no more than your cost of physically performing source distribution, a complete machine-readable copy of the corresponding source code, to be distributed under the terms of Sections 1 and 2 above on a medium customarily used for software interchange; or,

   (c) Accompany it with the information you received as to the offer to distribute corresponding source code. (This alternative is allowed only for noncommercial distribution and only if you received the program in object code or executable form with such an offer, in accord with Subsection b above.)

   The source code for a work means the preferred form of the work for making modifications to it. For an executable work, complete source code means all the source code for all modules it contains, plus any associated interface definition files, plus the scripts used to control compilation and installation of the executable. However, as a special exception, the source code distributed need not include anything that is normally distributed (in either source or binary form) with the major components (compiler, kernel, and so on) of the operating system on which the executable runs, unless that component itself accompanies the executable.

If distribution of executable or object code is made by offering access to copy from a designated place, then offering equivalent access to copy the source code from the same place counts as distribution of the source code, even though third parties are not compelled to copy the source along with the object code.

4. You may not copy, modify, sublicense, or distribute the Program except as expressly provided under this License. Any attempt otherwise to copy, modify, sublicense or distribute the Program is void, and will automatically terminate your rights under this License. However, parties who have received copies, or rights, from you under this License will not have their licenses terminated so long as such parties remain in full compliance.

5. You are not required to accept this License, since you have not signed it. However, nothing else grants you permission to modify or distribute the Program or its derivative works. These actions are prohibited by law if you do not accept this License. Therefore, by modifying or distributing the Program (or any work based on the Program), you indicate your acceptance of this License to do so, and all its terms and conditions for copying, distributing or modifying the Program or works based on it.

6. Each time you redistribute the Program (or any work based on the Program), the recipient automatically receives a license from the original licensor to copy, distribute or modify the Program subject to these terms and conditions. You may not impose any further restrictions on the recipients' exercise of the rights granted herein. You are not responsible for enforcing compliance by third parties to this License.

7. If, as a consequence of a court judgment or allegation of patent infringement or for any other reason (not limited to patent issues), conditions are imposed on you (whether by court order, agreement or otherwise) that contradict the conditions of this License, they do not excuse you from the conditions of this License. If you cannot distribute so as to satisfy simultaneously your obligations under this License and any other pertinent obligations, then as a consequence you may not distribute the Program at all. For example, if a patent license would not permit royalty-free redistribution of the Program by all those who receive copies directly or indirectly through you, then the only way you could satisfy both it and this License would be to refrain entirely from distribution of the Program.

   If any portion of this section is held invalid or unenforceable under any particular circumstance, the balance of the section is intended to apply and the section as a whole is intended to apply in other circumstances.

   It is not the purpose of this section to induce you to infringe any patents or other property right claims or to contest validity of any such claims; this section has the sole purpose of protecting the integrity of the free software distribution system, which is implemented by public license practices. Many people have made generous contributions to the wide range of software distributed through that system in reliance on consistent application of that system; it is up to the author/donor to decide if he or she is willing to distribute software through any other system and a licensee cannot impose that choice.

This section is intended to make thoroughly clear what is believed to be a consequence of the rest of this License.

8. If the distribution and/or use of the Program is restricted in certain countries either by patents or by copyrighted interfaces, the original copyright holder who places the Program under this License may add an explicit geographical distribution limitation excluding those countries, so that distribution is permitted only in or among countries not thus excluded. In such case, this License incorporates the limitation as if written in the body of this License.

9. The Free Software Foundation may publish revised and/or new versions of the General Public License from time to time. Such new versions will be similar in spirit to the present version, but may differ in detail to address new problems or concerns.

   Each version is given a distinguishing version number. If the Program specifies a version number of this License which applies to it and "any later version", you have the option of following the terms and conditions either of that version or of any later version published by the Free Software Foundation. If the Program does not specify a version number of this License, you may choose any version ever published by the Free Software Foundation.

10. If you wish to incorporate parts of the Program into other free programs whose distribution conditions are different, write to the author to ask for permission. For software which is copyrighted by the Free Software Foundation, write to the Free Software Foundation; we sometimes make exceptions for this. Our decision will be guided by the two goals of preserving the free status of all derivatives of our free software and of promoting the sharing and reuse of software generally.

NO WARRANTY

11. BECAUSE THE PROGRAM IS LICENSED FREE OF CHARGE, THERE IS NO WARRANTY FOR THE PROGRAM, TO THE EXTENT PERMITTED BY APPLICABLE LAW. EXCEPT WHEN OTHERWISE STATED IN WRITING THE COPYRIGHT HOLDERS AND/OR OTHER PARTIES PROVIDE THE PROGRAM "AS IS" WITHOUT WARRANTY OF ANY KIND, EITHER EXPRESSED OR IMPLIED, INCLUDING, BUT NOT LIMITED TO, THE IMPLIED WARRANTIES OF MERCHANTABILITY AND FITNESS FOR A PARTICULAR PURPOSE. THE ENTIRE RISK AS TO THE QUALITY AND PERFORMANCE OF THE PROGRAM IS WITH YOU. SHOULD THE PROGRAM PROVE DEFECTIVE, YOU ASSUME THE COST OF ALL NECESSARY SERVICING, REPAIR OR CORRECTION.

12. IN NO EVENT UNLESS REQUIRED BY APPLICABLE LAW OR AGREED TO IN WRITING WILL ANY COPYRIGHT HOLDER, OR ANY OTHER PARTY WHO MAY MODIFY AND/OR REDISTRIBUTE THE PROGRAM AS PERMITTED ABOVE, BE LIABLE TO YOU FOR DAMAGES, INCLUDING ANY GENERAL, SPECIAL, INCIDENTAL OR CONSEQUENTIAL DAMAGES ARISING OUT OF THE USE OR INABILITY TO USE THE PROGRAM (INCLUDING BUT NOT LIMITED TO LOSS OF DATA OR DATA BEING RENDERED INACCURATE OR LOSSES SUSTAINED BY YOU OR THIRD PARTIES OR A FAILURE OF THE PROGRAM TO OPERATE WITH ANY OTHER PROGRAMS), EVEN IF SUCH HOLDER OR OTHER PARTY HAS BEEN ADVISED OF THE POSSIBILITY OF SUCH DAMAGES.

END OF TERMS AND CONDITIONS

How to Apply These Terms to Your New Programs

If you develop a new program, and you want it to be of the greatest possible use to the public, the best way to achieve this is to make it free software which everyone can redistribute and change under these terms.

To do so, attach the following notices to the program. It is safest to attach them to the start of each source file to most effectively convey the exclusion of warranty; and each file should have at least the "copyright" line and a pointer to where the full notice is found.

```
< one line to give the program name and a brief idea of what it does. >

              Copyright c 19yy < name of author >
This program is free software; you can redistribute it and/or
modify it under the terms of the GNU General Public License as
published by the Free Software Foundation; either version 2 of
the License, or (at your option) any later version.

This program is distributed in the hope that it will be useful,
but WITHOUT ANY WARRANTY; without even the implied warranty of
MERCHANTABILITY or FITNESS FOR A PARTICULAR PURPOSE. See the GNU
General Public License for more details.

You should have received a copy of the GNU General Public License
along with this program; if not, write to the Free Software
Foundation, Inc., 675 Mass Ave, Cambridge, MA 02139, USA.
```

Also add information on how to contact you by electronic and paper mail.

If the program is interactive, make it output a short notice like this when it starts in an interactive mode:

```
Gnomovision version 69, Copyright c 19yy name of author
```

```
Gnomovision comes with ABSOLUTELY NO WARRANTY; for details type
"show w". This is free software, and you are welcome to
redistribute it under certain conditions; type "show c" for details.
```

The hypothetical commands "show w" and "show c" should show the appropriate parts of the General Public License. Of course, the commands you use may be called something other than "show w" and "show c"; they could even be mouse-clicks or menu items—whatever suits your program.

You should also get your employer (if you work as a programmer) or your school, if any, to sign a "copyright disclaimer" for the program, if necessary. Here is a sample; alter the names:

Yoyodyne, Inc., hereby disclaims all copyright interest in the program 'Gnomovision' (which makes passes at compilers) written by James Hacker.

<signature of Ty Coon> , 1 April 1989
Ty Coon, President of Vice

This General Public License does not permit incorporating your program into proprietary programs. If your program is a subroutine library, you may consider it more useful to permit linking proprietary applications with the library. If this is what you want to do, use the GNU Library General Public License instead of this License.

G

An Introduction to PGP

Assuming you're not the curious type and haven't flipped your way back here, you are probably here looking for some information on the program known as Pretty Good Privacy, or PGP.

G.1. PGP: Privacy for Regular People

PGP, or Pretty Good Privacy, is a program that is intended to help make electronic mail more secure. It does this by using a sophisticated technique known as public key encryption.

If you find yourself wondering what electronic mail and making information unreadable by spies have to do with RPM, you have a good point. However, although PGP's claim to fame is the handling of e-mail in total privacy, it has some other tricks up its sleeve.

G.1.1. Keys Your Locksmith Wouldn't Understand

As mentioned earlier, PGP uses public key encryption to do some of its magic. You might guess from the name that this type of encryption involves keys of some sort. But, as you might imagine, these are not keys that you can copy at the local hardware store. They are numbers—really large numbers. Here's what a key might look like (when we say that keys are numbers, we aren't lying even though the sample key doesn't look like a number; it has been processed so that it can be concisely displayed using only printable characters):

```
----BEGIN PGP PUBLIC KEY BLOCK----
Version: 2.6.2
```

```
mQCNAzEpXjUAAAEEAKG4/V9oUSiDc9wIge6Bmg6erDGCLzmFyioAho8kDIJSrcmi
F9qTdPq+fj726pgW1iSb0Y7syZn9Y2lgQm5HkPODfNi8eWyTFSxbr8ygosLRClTP
xqHVhtInGrfZNLoSpv1LdWOme0yOpOQJnghdOMzKXpgf5g84vaUg6PHLopv5AAUR
tCpSZWQgSGF0IFNvZnR3YXJlLCBJbmMuIDxyZWRoYXRAcmVkaGF0LmNvbT6JAFUD
BRAxc0xcKO2uixUx6ZEBAQOfAfsGwmueeH3WcjngsAoZyremvyV3Q8C1YmY1EZC9
SWkQxdRKe7n2PY/WiA82Mvc+op1XGTkmqByvxM9Ax/dXh+peiQCVAwUQMXL7xiIS
axFDcvLNAQH5PAP/TdAOyVcuDkXfOPjN/TIjqKRPRt7k6Fm/ameRvzSqB0fMVHEE
5iZKi55Ep1AkBJ3wX257hvduZ/9juKSJjQNuW/FxcHazPU+7yLZmf27xIq7E0ihW
8zz9JNFWSA9+8vlCMBYwdP1a+DzVdwjbJcnOu3/Z/aCY2lYi9U45PzmtU8iJAJUD
BRAxU9GUGXO+IyM0cSUBAbWfA/9+lVfqcpFYkJIV4HuV5niVv7LW4ywxW/SftqCM
lXDXdJdoDbrvLtVYIGWeGwJ6bES6CoQiQjiW7/WaC3BY9ZITQE4hWOPQADzOnZPQ
fdkIIxuIUAUnU/YarasqvxCs5v/TygfWUTPLPSP+MqGqJcDF2UHXCiNAHrItse9M
h7etkYkAdQMFEDEp61/Nq6IpInoskQEB538C+wSIaCNNDOGx1xS5E2tClXRwMYf0
ymuKXs/srvIUjOO7xuIH4K7qcSSdI4eUwuXy6w5tWWR3xZ/XiygcLtKMi2IZIq0j
wmFq7MEk+Xp8MN7Icawkqj1/1p0p4EwKKkIU64kAlQMFEDEp6pZEcVNogr/H7QEB
jp4D/iblfiCzVTA5QhGeWOj1rRxWzohMvnngn29IJgdnN3zuQXB1/lbVV3zYciRH
NyvpynfcTcgORHNpAIxXDaZ7sd48/v7hHLarcR5kxuY0T75XOTGOKTOlFvb4XmcY
HZR2wSWSBteKezB5uK47A6uhwtvPokV0Owk9xPmBV+LPXkW4
=pnqV
----END PGP PUBLIC KEY BLOCK----
```

PGP uses two different types of keys: public and private. The *public key*, as its name suggests, can be shared with anyone. The key shown above is, in fact, a public key. The *private key*, as its name suggests, should be kept a secret. PGP creates keys in pairs—one private and one public. A key pair must remain a pair; if one is lost, the other by itself is useless. Why? Because the two keys have an interesting property that can be exploited in two ways:

■ A message encrypted by a given public key can only be decrypted with the corresponding private key.

■ A message encrypted by a given private key can only be decrypted with the corresponding public key.

In the case of sending messages in total privacy, the key pairs are used in the first manner. It allows two people to exchange private messages without first exchanging any "secret codes." The only requirement is that each know the other's public key.

However, for RPM, the second method is the important one. Let's say a company needs to send you a document and you'd like to make sure it really did come from them. If the company first encrypted the file with its private key and sent it to you, you would have an encrypted file you couldn't read.

Or could you? If you have the company's public key, you should be able to decrypt it. In fact, if you can't, you can be sure that the message you received did not come from them! (Or at least that it didn't make it to you unchanged.)

It is this feature that is used by RPM. By using PGP's public key encryption, it is possible to not only prove that a package file came from a certain person or persons, but also that it was not changed somewhere along the line.

G.1.2. Are RPM Packages Encrypted?

In a word, no. Rather than being encrypted, RPM package files possess *digital signatures*. This is a way of using encryption to attach a signature (again, basically a large number) to some information, such that

■ The signature cannot be separated from the information. Any attempt to verify the signature against any other information will fail.

■ The signature can only be produced by one private key.

In the case of RPM, the information being signed is the contents of the .rpm file itself.

A digital signature is just like a regular signature. It doesn't obscure the contents of the document being signed; it just provides a method of determining the authenticity of a document. Here is an example of a digital signature turned into printable text:

```
----BEGIN PGP SIGNATURE----
Version: 2.6.3a
Charset: noconv

iQCVAwUBMXVGMFIa2NdXHZJZAQFe4AQAz0FZrHdH8o+zkIvcI/4ABg4gfE7cG0xE
Z2J9GVWD2zi4tG+s1+IWEY6Ae17kx925JKrzF4Ti2upAwTN2Pnb/x0G8WJQVKQzP
mZcD+XNnAaYCqFz8iIuAFVLchYeWj1Pqxxq0weGCtjQIrpzrmGxV7xXzK0jus+6V
rML3TxQSwdA=
=T9Mc
----END PGP SIGNATURE----
```

G.1.3. Do All RPM Packages Have Digital Signatures?

Again, no. In a perfect world, every `.rpm` file would be signed. However, RPM has no formal requirement that this be the case. There is also no requirement that you do anything special with a signed `.rpm` file. Think of it as an extra feature that you can take advantage of, or not—it's strictly your choice.

G.1.4. So Much to Cover, So Little Time

PGP has a wealth of features, 99% of which we will not cover in this book. For more information on the basics of encryption, see *Applied Cryptography*, by Bruce Schneier, which contains a wealth of information on the subject. For more details on PGP specifically, O'Reilly's *PGP: Pretty Good Privacy* by Simson Garfinkel is an excellent reference.

If you'd rather surf the Net, use your favorite World Wide Web index to hunt for `crypto` or `PGP`, and you'll be in business.

G.2. Installing PGP for RPM's Use

To use RPM's PGP-related capabilities, you'll need to have PGP installed on your system. If it's installed already, you should be able to flip to the chapters on verifying package signatures and signing packages and be in business in a matter of minutes. Otherwise, read on for a thumbnail sketch of what's required to install PGP.

G.2.1. Obtaining PGP

The first step in being able to verify `.rpm` files is to get a copy of PGP. Unfortunately, this is not quite as simple as it might sound. The reason is that PGP is very controversial stuff.

Why the controversy? It centers on PGP's primary mission: to provide a means of communicating with others in complete privacy. As we've discussed, PGP uses encryption to provide this privacy. Good encryption. Very good encryption. Encryption so good, it appears that some of the world's governments consider PGP a threat to their national security.

G.2.1.1. Know Your Laws!

Various countries have differing stands on the use of "strong encryption" products such as PGP. In some countries, possession of encryption software is strictly forbidden. Other countries attempt to control the flow of encryption technology into (or out of) their countries. It is vital that you know your country's laws, lest you find yourself in prison, or possibly in front of a firing squad!

G.2.1.2. Patent/Licensing Issues Surrounding PGP

Over and above PGP's legal status, there are other aspects to PGP that people living in the U.S. and Canada should keep in mind:

■ PGP is free—for noncommercial use only. If you are going to use PGP for business purposes, you should look into getting a commercial copy. PGP is marketed in the United States by

Pretty Good Privacy, Inc.
2121 S. El Camino Real
Suite 902
San Mateo, CA 94403
Phone: 415-572-0430
Fax: 415-572-1932
`http://www.pgp.com/`

■ Part of the software that comprises PGP is protected by several U.S. patents. Versions of PGP approved for use in the United States contain a licensed version of this software, known as RSAREF, which includes a patent license that allows the use of the software in noncommercial settings only. Commercial use of the technology contained in RSAREF requires a separate license. This is one reason there are restrictions on the commercial use of PGP in the United States and Canada.

While people outside the United States and Canada can use RSAREF-based PGP, they will probably choose the so-called international version. This version replaces RSAREF with software known as MPILIB. MPILIB is, in general, faster than RSAREF, but it cannot legally be used in the United States or Canada.

To summarize, if you are using PGP for commercial purposes in the United States or Canada, you'll need to purchase it. Otherwise, people living in the United States or Canada should use a version of PGP incorporating RSAREF. People in other countries can use any version of PGP they desire, although they'll probably choose the MPILIB-based international version. (Note that there are no commercial restrictions regarding PGP in countries other than the United States and Canada.)

G.2.1.3. Getting RSAREF-Based PGP

The official source for the latest version of PGP based on RSAREF is the Massachusetts Institute of Technology. Due to the restrictions on the export of encryption technology, the process is somewhat convoluted. The easiest way to obtain PGP from the official MIT archive is to use the World Wide Web. Point your Web browser to

`http://web.mit.edu/network/pgp.html`

Simply follow the steps, and you'll have the necessary software on your system in no time.

There is a more cumbersome method that doesn't use the Web. It involves first using anonymous FTP to obtain several files of instructions and license agreements. You will then be directed to use telnet to obtain the name of a temporary FTP directory containing the PGP software. Finally, you can use anonymous FTP to retrieve the software. To start this process, FTP to

`net-dist.mit.edu`

and then change the directory to

`/pub/PGP`

Obtain a copy of the file README and follow the instructions in it exactly.

If all this seems like too much trouble, there is another alternative. You can find copies of PGP on just about any BBS, FTP, or Web site advertising freely available software. Be aware, however, that Floyd's Storm Door and BBS Company may not be as trustworthy a place as MIT to obtain encryption software. It's really a question of how paranoid you are.

G.2.1.4. Outside the United States and Canada

For people living in other countries, it is much easier to find PGP (depending on the legality of encryption software, of course). Try any of the places you'd normally look for free software. Keep in mind, however, that you shouldn't download PGP from any sites in the U.S. Doing so is considered an "export" of munitions, and can get the people responsible for the site in deep trouble. Wherever you eventually get PGP, since the patents that complicate matters for the United States do not apply abroad, you'll probably end up with the international version of PGP.

G.2.2. Building PGP

Building PGP is mostly a matter of following instructions. However, users of ELF-based Linux distributions (such as Red Hat Linux) will find that PGP will not build. The problem, according to the PGP FAQ, is that two files do not properly handle the C preprocessor directives that affect support for ELF. The changes are to two files: `80386.S` and `zmatch.S`. Near the beginning of each, you'll find either an `#ifndef` or an `#ifdef` for SYSV. If you find

`#ifndef SYSV`

it should be changed to read

`#if !defined(SYSV) && !defined(__ELF__)`

If you find

`#ifdef SYSV`

it should be changed to read

`#if defined(SYSV) || defined(____ELF____)`

After you make these changes, PGP should build with no problems.

G.2.3. Ready to Go!

After building and installing PGP, you're ready to start using RPM's package-signature capabilities. If your primary interest is in checking the signatures on packages built by someone else, see Chapter 7, "Using RPM to Verify Package Files," which will tell you everything you need to know.

On the other hand, if you are a package builder and would like to start signing packages, see Chapter 17, "Adding PGP Signatures to a Package," and it will have you signing packages in no time.

I

Index

Symbols

%attr file directive, 196, 399
%attr macro, 233-235
%build build-time script, 394
%build script, 287-288
%build section, 130
%clean build-time script, 395
%clean section, 132
%config file directive, 196, 399
%description tag, 252, 389
%dir directive tag, 293, 400
%doc directive tag, 220, 293-294
%doc file directive, 195, 399
%docdir directives, 400
%docdir directory directive, 197-199
%else conditional, 203, 402
%endif conditional, 203, 402
%files list, 131, 194, 254, 398
  %doc directive tag, 220, 294
  adding to spec file, 285
  checking, 146-148
  clients, 292-293, 304
  creating, 291
  directives, 194
    %attr, 196, 399
    %dir, 199, 400
    %doc, 195, 399
    %docdir, 198, 400
    %verify, 196, 400
    -f <file>, 200
    config, 196
  directory-related, 197
  file directives (%config), 399
  files, locating, 291-293
  packages, 254
  prefix tag, 217
  restrictions, 218
  servers, 292-293, 304
  subpackages, 253
%if.xxx conditional, 272
%ifarch conditional, 202, 401
%ifn.xxx conditional, 272
%ifnarch conditional, 202, 402
%ifnos conditional, 203, 402

%ifos conditional, 203, 402
%install build-time script, 395
%install script, 288-289
%install section, 130
%package directive, 200
  -n option, 201, 250, 401
%patch macros, 286
  -b option, 398
  -E option, 398
  -P option, 398
%post install scripts, 395
%postum erase-time script, 396
%pre installation scripts, 395
%prep, 141
%prep build-time script, 394
%prep script, 129, 286
%preun erase-time script, 396
%setup macro, 396
  -a option, 397
  -b option, 397
  -c option, 397
  -D option, 397
  -n option, 396
  -T option, 397
%verify file directive, 196, 400
%verifyscript script, 396
%verifyscript verification-time script, 183

A

-a %setup macro option, 397
absolute symlinks, 217, 223
accessing
  ftp ports, 34
  help, 104
  read/write, 298
  RPM database, 42
adding
  %files list to spec file, 285
  build-time scripts, 284
  directories, 197
  disclaimers to downloaded software, 415
  entries to headers, 326

packages
  dependency processing, 320
  signatures, 241, 244
  signatures to packages, 152, 373
--addsign command, 373
--addsign signature command option, 244-245
alpha architecture, 338
amanda
  %files list, 285
  backups, 292, 298
  building, 287-288
  cleaning, 281-282
  clients, 280, 284, 297-298
    backups, 276
    dump utility, 276
  configuration, 278-279
  dumps, 298
  files
    clients, 292
    configuration, 299
  ftp site, 276-277
  installation, 279-280, 285, 288-289
  patches, 277, 281-283
  restores, 292
  scripts, 298
    build-time, 284
    installation, 297
  servers, 284, 298
    .rhosts files, 300
    backups, 276
    configuration names, 300
    postinstall scripts, 300
  sources, unpacking, 277
  spec file, 283
  subpackages, 284
  testing, 277, 303
  uninstallation, 300-302
  user IDs, 298
applications
  porting to multiple operating systems, 116
  upgrading, 116
Applied Cryptography, 420
arch canon rpmrc file entry, 359
arch compat entry, 360

ARCH query tag, 73, 379
architecture, 354
 alpha, 338
 compatibility, 35, 267, 310,
  360
 conditionals
  %if.xxx, 272
  nested, 271
 detection logic, overriding,
  151
 files
  conditional, 201
  naming, 338
 i386, 338
 m68k, 338
 mips, 338
 multiple (support), 10
 name, 310
 packages, building, 172-173
 ppc, 338
 RPM version 1, 10
 SGI, 338
 sparc, 338
 spec files, 202-203
 tags (exclusive xxx), 270
 verification, overriding, 35
architecture, 172, 264
 conditionals (%ifn.xxx), 272
 multiple, 8, 161
 packages, building, 201
 tags
  excludearch, 172, 392
  exclusivearch, 173, 392
 see also hardware; platforms
archives
 compression, 349
 cpio, 105
 files, extracting, 106
 packages, 349
 source files, unpacking, 186
ARCHIVESIZE - -
 queryformat tag, 382
arguments, 298
 erase-time scripts, 181
 install scripts, 181
array iterators, 71-72
attributes (files), 91, 196-197,
 233-234, 400
authentication (packages)
 digital signatures, 14
 signatures, 238

automatic dependencies,
 206-209
 autoreqprov tag, 209
 scripts, 207-208
automatic handling (configuration files), 9
automatic packages, building,
 116
AUTOREQPROV - -
 queryformat tag, 385
autoreqprov dependency tag,
 171, 391
autoreqprov tag, 209

B

-b %patch macro option, 398
-b %setup macro option, 397
backups, 292, 298
 amanda (read/write access),
  298
 clients, 276
 file extensions (patch%
  macros), 193
bazlib subpackage, 249
BIN header structure value,
 343
binary files
 directories, 364
 installation, 316
 package files, 108-109, 123,
  135
binary packages, 116, 145,
 289-291, 340
 creating, 162
 files, 157
 installation, 406
 queries, 62
block structures (conditionals), 271
BOGUS distribution, 9
Boolean values, 309
Bourne again shell, restoring,
 43
- -buildarch <arch> rpm -b
 command option, 151
- -buildarch rpm -b command
 option, 372
build command
 - -rebuild, 161-162
 - -recompile, 160-161
 - -sign option, 241-242

- -buildos <os> rpm -b
 command option, 152
- -buildos rpm -b command
 option, 372
build platform, 265
build root, 156, 229
- -buildroot <path> rpm -b
 command option, 155
- -buildroot rpm -b command
 option, 156-157, 372
- -buildroot rpm-b command
 option, 157
build roots, 226-227
 alternate, 227
 cleaning, 230
 configuration, 230-231
 default, 226
 selecting, 227
build sections, 122
build system (packages), 137
build xxx translate rpmrc file,
 267
build% build-time script, 180
build-time package signatures,
 241
build-time scripts, 178, 284
 %build, 180, 394
 %clean, 180, 395
 %install, 180, 395
 %prep, 179, 394
 environmental variables,
  179, 394
 subpackages, 257
buildarchtranslate entry, 359
builddir entry, 361
BUILDHOST - -queryformat
 tag, 377
building
 amanda, 287-288
 databases, 374
 packages, 115-116,
  132-136, 140, 143-144,
  201, 303, 372
  %build, 142
  %build section, 130
  %files list, 131,
   147-148
  checking, 146
  %install section, 130
  %prep, 141

%prep script, 129
architecture, 172-173
binary files, 145
build root, 229
build roots, 226-227,
   231-232
build trees, 142
date, 14
dedicated systems, 226
detection logic, 151-152
directories, selecting,
   230-232
directory structure, 126
directory trees, removing,
   154
files, cleaning, 132
inputs, 120-122
installation scrips, 298
installation scripts,
   298-300
length, 140
location, 230-232
macros, 130
multiple, 242
operating system, 173
output, 133
outputs, 123
permissions, 142
platforms, overriding, 268
public keys, 95
relocatable, 219
root directory (alternate),
   155-157
RPM, 123
scripts (uninstallation),
   300
shortcuts, 149-150
signatures, 152,
   241-242
source package files, 135
source packages, 146
sources, 127
spec file preamble, 127
status, 372
terminating, 132, 136
testing, 153-154
third-party, 114-115
time, 14
time options, 365

troubleshooting, 136
uninstallation scripts,
   301-302
PGP, 422
subpackages, 201, 259-260
buildostranslate entry, 360
BUILDROOT - -queryformat
tag, 384
buildroot directory tag, 174,
392
buildroot entry, 361
buildroot tag, overriding, 174
builds, testing, 154
BUILDTIME - -queryformat
tag, 377

C

-c %setup macro option, 396
C preprocessor directives
(PGP), 422
C structures, 339
capabilities
   packages
      libraries, 213
      provided, 65, 213
      provides tag, 213
      queries, 65-66
      required, 65-66, 213
      sonames, 213
   provided, 206
   required, 209
carriage control escape
sequences, 69
CHANGELOG - -queryformat
tag, 378
changing directories, 185, 188
CHAR header structure value,
343
- -checksig command, 374
   see also rpm -K command
checksum
   configuration files, 117
   current files, 48
   files
      current, 48-49
      new, 48-49
      original, 48-49

MD5
   configuration files,
      47-48
   verification, 82
new files, 48
original files, 48
upgrades, 47-49
- -clean rpm -b command
option, 154-155, 372
clean% build-time script, 180
cleaning
   amanda, 281-282
   build roots, 230
   directory trees, 180
   files, 132
client subpackage, 249
clients
   %files list, 292-293, 304
   amanda, 280, 284, 298
   backups, 276
   directives, 293
   packages, 300
   servers, 280, 295
   subpackages, 250, 293, 295
closing databases, 311
command options
   build (- -sign), 241-242
   global, 368
   informational, 368
   pkg1...pkgN, 54
   rpm -b
      - - buildarch, 372
      - - buildarch <arch>, 151
      - - buildos, 152, 372
      - - buildroot, 155-157,
         372
      - - clean, 154-155, 372
      - - noscripts, 372
      - - quiet, 159
      - - rcfile <rcfile>, 160
      rpm -ba, 145-146
      rpm -bb, 144
      rpm -bc, 142-143
      rpm -bi, 143-144
      rpm -bl, 146-148
      rpm -bp, 141
      - - short-circuit,
         149-150, 372
      - - sign, 152, 372
      - - test, 153, 372

- -*timecheck, 372*
- -*timecheck <secs>, 158*
-*vv, 159*
rpm -e
  - -*dbpath <path>, 38, 42*
  - -*nodeps, 38, 41, 372*
  rcfile <rcfile>, 38, 42
  root <path>, 38, 42
  - -*test, 18, 38-41*
  -*vv, 38-40*
rpm -i
  - -*dbpath <path>, 18, 34*
  - -*excludedocs, 18, 30, 370*
  - -*force, 18, 30, 370*
  - -*ftpport <port>, 18, 34*
  - -*ftpproxy <host>, 18, 34*
  - -*hash, 18, 22, 370*
  - -*ignorearch, 370*
  - -*ignoreos, 18, 35, 370*
  - -*ignorereach, 18, 35*
  - -*includedocs, 18, 31, 370*
  - -*nodeps, 18, 29, 370*
  - -*noscripts, 18, 32, 370*
  - -*percent, 18, 33, 370*
  - -*prefix, 18, 31-32, 370*
  - -*rcfile <rcfile>, 18, 33*
  - -*replacefiles, 18, 25-29, 370*
  - -*replacepkgs, 18, 24-25, 370*
  - -*root <path>, 18, 33*
  - -*test, 18, 23-24, 370*
  -*v, 18, 22*
  -*vv, 18, 23*
rpm -K
  - -*nopgp, 94, 99*
  rcfile <rcfile>, 94, 100
  - -*vv, 94, 100*
  -*v, 94-97*
rpm -K command
  - -*rcfile <rcfile>, 94, 100*
  - -*vv, 94, 100*
rpm -noscripts, 38, 41-42
rpm -q
  - -*dump, 369*
  - -*provides, 369*
  - -*queryformat, 369*
  - -*requires, 369*

- -*scripts, 369*
- -*whatprovides, 369*
rpm -U
  - -*prefix, 371*
rpm -U
  - -*dbpath <path>, 46*
  - -*excludedocs, 46, 371*
  - -*force, 46, 51, 371*
  - -*ftpport <port>, 46*
  - -*ftpproxy <host>, 46*
  - -*hash, 46, 371*
  - -*ignorearch, 46*
  - -*ignoreos, 46, 371*
  - -*includedocs, 46, 371*
  - -*nodeps, 46, 371*
  - -*noscripts, 46, 51-52, 371*
  - -*oldpackage, 46, 50-51, 371*
  - -*percent, 46, 371*
  - -*prefix <path>, 46*
  - -*rcfile <rcfile>, 46*
  - -*replacefiles, 46, 371*
  - -*replacepkgs, 46, 371*
  - -*root <path>, 46*
  - -*test, 46, 371*
  -*v, 46*
  -*vv, 46*
rpm -V
  - -*dbpath, 90*
  - -*nodeps, 87, 370*
  - -*nofiles, 88, 370*
  - -*noscripts, 88, 370*
  - -*rcfile, 90*
  - -*root, 90*
  rpm -Va, 85
  rpm -Vf, 86
  rpm -Vg, 87
  rpm -Vp, 86
  rpm -Vv, 89
  rpm -Vvv, 89
signature
  - -*addsign, 244-245*
  - -*resign, 243*
command parameters
  rpm -e, 38
  rpm -K, 94
commands
  - -addsign, 373
  - -checksig, 374

- -·*initdb, 374*
- -·*rebuild, 373*
- -·*rebuilddb, 374*
- -·*recompile, 373*
- -·*resign, 373*
build
  - -*rebuild, 161-162*
  - -*recompile, 160-161*
file(1), 339, 351
grep, 57
output, 104, 159
rpm -e, 38, 43
rpm -K, 94-96, 374
rpm -U, 47, 50
rpm2cpio, 105
syntax (build-related), 160
comment lines, 129
  creating, 164
  ignoring, 164
  spec file, 388
commercial use (PGP), 421
comparing source trees, 121
comparison operators' version requirements, 210
compatibility, 206
  architecture, 35, 267, 310, 360
  libraries, 60, 171
  operating systems, 35, 310, 360
  packages (queries), 60
  software versions, 341
  updated software, 341
compression
  archives, 349
  patch files, 194
  qzip, 194
conditional files, 201
conditionals, 201
  %else, 203, 402
  %endif, 203, 402
  %if.xxx, 272
  %ifarch, 202, 401
  %ifn.xxx, 272
  %ifnarch, 202, 402
  %ifnos, 203, 402
  %ifos, 203, 402
  block structures, 271-272
  nested, 271
  platform-dependent, 266
  structure, 271

config file, 221
config.h configuration file, 278
configuration
  amanda, 278-279
  build roots, 230-231
  defaults, 160
  files, 116, 299-300
  packages, 114, 182
configuration files, 81, 196
  automatic handling (RPM version 1), 9
  checksums, 117
  config.h, 278
  conflicts, 26-27
  defaults, 90
  listing, 64
  maintaining, 43
  MD5 checksums, 47-48
  modifications, saving, 117
  monitoring, 7
  options.h, 278
  packages
    erasing, 43
    listing, 63
  platforms, 278
  restoring, 26-27
  sites, 278
  software installation, 19
  upgrades, 47-49
  verification, 81
CONFLICTFLAGS - - queryformat tag, 384
CONFLICTNAME - - queryformat tag, 384
conflicts
  dependency, 321
  files, 25-28
  packages, 211
    in databases, 315
    installation, 170
  software installation, 19
conflicts dependency tag, 170, 391
CONFLICTVERSION - - queryformat tag, 384
conventions (package labels), 13
conversion packages (cpio archives), 105

copying
  headers, 325
  software, 411-413
COPYRIGHT - - queryformat tags, 378
copyright descriptive tag, 167, 389
copyrights, 128, 167, 410
count (4-byte), 343
cpio archives (package conversion), 105
cpiobin entry, 361
creating
  %files list, 131
  binary packages, 145, 162
  comment lines, 164
  databases, 103-104, 311, 374
  directories, 185
  documentation files, 195
  headers, 325
  installation scripts, 298-299
  iterators, 327
  key pairs, 238-239
  packages (relocation), 219
  patches, 121, 277
  PMS, 7
  source packages, 146
  top-level directories, 180
cross-platform
  hardware, 172
  packages, building, 12
current files, 48-49
customizing package queries, 68
  escape sequences, 69
  field width, 70
  justification, 70
  literal text, 69-73
  readable data, 70-71
  tags, 70, 73-74

D

data
  4-byte count, 343
  4-byte offset, 343
  index entries, 342
  integer, 343

packages, 307
  queries, 61-62
  viewing, 7, 121
readable, 70-71
storing, 342-343
string, 343
database manipulation functions
  rpmdbClose( ), 311
  rpmdbInit( ), 311
  rpmdbOpen( ), 311
  rpmdbRebuild( ), 312
database search functions
  dbiFreeIndexRecord( ), 313
  rpmdbFindByConflicts( ), 315
  rpmdbFindByFile( ), 313
  rpmdbFindByGroup( ), 314
  rpmdbFindByProvides( ), 314
  rpmdbFindByRequired By( ), 315
  rpmdbFindPackage( ), 314
database traversal functions
  rpmdbFirst RecNum( ), 312
  rpmdbGetRecord( ), 312
  rpmdbNextRecNum( ), 312
databases, 90, 331
  building, 374
  closing, 311
  creating, 103-104, 311, 374
  files
    listing, 66-67
    locating, 58
    monitoring, 117
  groups, locating, 314
  index sets, 313
  locating, 34, 331
  opening, 311
  packages, 313-315
  paths, editing, 42
  queries, 8, 10
  rebuilding, 312
  records
    locating, 330, 333
    numbers, 312
  root directories, 74
  RPM, accessing, 42
  RPM version 1, 10
  storing, 361

date (packages), 14
dbiFreeIndexRecord( )
  database search function,
  313
dbindex.h file, 306
- -dbpath <path> rpm -e
  command option, 38, 42
- -dbpath <path> rpm -i
  command option, 18, 34
- -dbpath <path> rpm -U
  command option, 46
- -dbpath <path> rpm -V
  command option, 90
dbpath entry, 361
deallocation (headers), 325
decoding headers, 350
decompression
  qzip, 194
  tar files, 121
decryption (PGP), 419
dedicated systems, 226
defaults
  build roots, 226
  path prefixes, 223
  settings, 75
  source files (archived), 186
defaultdocdir entry, 361
DEFAULTPREFIX
  - -queryformat tag, 384
defaults
  configuration, 160
  configuration files, 90
  files, 33, 42, 100
deleting directories, 186
dependencies
  automatic, 206-209
  conflicts tag, 211
  manual (requires tag), 209
  packages, 41, 60, 213
    capabilities, 206
    virtual, 212
  provides tag, 212
  requires tag (version
    requirements), 210
  version numbers, 210
  versions (comparison
    operators), 210
dependency checks, 19, 321

dependency conflicts, 321
dependency functions
  rpmdepAddPackage( ), 320
  rpmdepAvailablePackage( ),
    321
  rpmdepCheck( ), 321
  rpmdepDependencies( ),
    320
  rpmdepDone( ), 322
  rpmdepFreeConflicts( ), 321
  rpmdepRemovePackage( ),
    321
  rpmdepUpgradePackage( ),
    320
dependency processing, 320
  automatic, 171
  checking, 320
  disabling, 209
  packages, adding, 320
  verification, disabling, 87
dependency tags
  autoreqprov, 171, 391
  conflicts, 170, 391
  provides, 169, 390
  requires, 170, 390
  serial, 170, 391
dependent files, installation,
  29
description, 129
DESCRIPTION
  - -queryformat tag, 377
description tags (summary),
  389
description% tag, 166
descriptions (packages), 261
descriptive tags
  %description, 166, 389
  copyright, 167, 389
  distribution, 167, 389
  group, 168
  icon, 168, 389
  packager, 169
  summary, 167
  url, 168, 390
  vendor, 168, 390
detection (install platform),
  265
detection logic, overriding,
  151-152

diagnostic control functions
  rpmGetVerbosity( ), 322
  rpmIncreaseVerbosity( ),
    322
  rpmIsDebug( ), 323
  rpmIsVerbose( ), 322
  rpmSetVerbosity( ), 322
diagnostic output (verbosity),
  322
digital signatures, 419
  package authentication, 14
directive tags
  %dir, 293
  %doc, 293-294
  group, 390
  packager, 390
directives
  %files list, 194
    clients, 293
    servers, 293
  %package, 200, 250
  %packages, 201
  C preprocessors, 422
  directories
    %dir, 199, 400
    %docdir, 197-198, 400
    -f <file>, 200
  file-related, 196
  files, 399
directories, 361
  adding, 197
  binary files, 364
  build roots, 226-227
  changing, 185, 188
  creating, 180, 185
  deleting, 186
  directives
    %dir, 400
    %docdir, 197-199, 400
    -f <file>, 200
  documentation, 198
  files, locating, 58
  naming, 185
  paths, 241, 365-366
  root, 33, 42, 74, 90, 361
  selecting (build areas),
    230-232
  source files, unpacking, 186
  structure, 126
  subdirectories, 199

subpackages, erasing, 293
tools, 349
top-level, 180, 189-190, 366
trees, cleaning, 180
directory tags
buildroot, 174, 392
prefix, 174, 392
directory trees, removing, 154
disabling
automatic dependency
processing, 171, 209
scripts (preinstall), 32
scriptspost, 32
verification, 87-88
**disclaimers, adding to
downloaded software, 415**
discussion groups
redhat-digest mailing list,
408
redhat-list mailing list, 408
rpm-list mailing list, 408
technical support, 408
**disk devices (files), reading,
298**
disks (packages), writing, 339
displaying
files (ftp sites), 406-407
packages, 169, 368-369
verification output, 96
distributing
software, 411-413
source code, 411
distribution, 128
packages (queries), 62
**DISTRIBUTION
- -queryformat tag, 377**
**distribution descriptive tag,
167, 389**
distribution entry, 362
distribution information, 364
documentation
directories, 197-198
filenames, 195
files, 131, 293
creating, 195
installation, 30-31, 157
listing, 64

packages (queries), 63
writing to disk, 362
downloading
PGP, 421-422
software, 415
**- -dump rpm -q command
option, 369**
dump tool, 349
dump utility, 276

E

-E %patch macro option, 398
execution, 51-52
e-mail
PGP, 418
security, 418
editing databases, 42
Elf-based Linux, 422
Emacs verification, 98
encryption
PGP, 420
private key, 418
public key, 418
software, 420
entries
adding to headers, 326
headers, 326
networks, 298
entry manipulation functions
headerAddEntry( ), 326
headerGetEntry( ), 326
headerIsEntry( ), 327
environmental variables, 394
build-time scripts, 179
install scripts (RPM
INSTALL PREFIX), 181
- -erase command, 372
see also rpm -e command
erase-time scripts, 181-182
%postun, 183, 256, 396
%preun, 183, 256, 396
arguments, 181
erasing
packages, 6, 38-40, 183,
318, 321, 371
configuration files, 43
dependencies, 41
older versions, 47
testing, 40-41
subpackages, 293

error codes, 306
error handling functions
rpmErrorCode( ), 306
rpmErrorSetCallback( ), 307
rpmErrorString( ), 307
errors (functions), 307
**escape sequences (carriage
control), 69**
**EXCLUDE - -queryformat
tag, 382**
exclude.xxx tag, 270
**- -excludedocs rpm -i
command option, 18, 30,
370**
**- -excludedocs rpm -U
command option, 46, 371**
**EXCLUDEARCH
- -queryformat tag, 385**
**excludearch architecture tag,
172, 392**
excludedocs entry, 362
**EXCLUDEOS - -queryformat
tag, 385**
**excludeos operating system
tag, 173, 392**
excluding
architecture from package
building, 172-173
patches from packages, 177
source files from packages,
176-177
subdirectories from
packages, 199
**EXCLUSIVE - -queryformat
tag, 382**
exclusive xxx tag, 270
**EXCLUSIVEARCH
- -queryformat tag, 385**
**exclusivearch architecture tag,
173, 392**
**EXCLUSIVEOS
- -queryformat tag, 385**
**exclusiveos operating system
tag, 173**
executing %prep, 141
execution
postuninstall scripts,
preventing, 42

preuninstall scripts,
preventing, 42
scripts, 122
extracting files, 107
packages, 106

F

**-f <file> directory directive,
200**
file directives
%attr, 196, 399
%config, 196, 399
%doc, 195
%verify, 196
file(1) command, 339, 351
file1.rpm...fileN.rpm
command parameter, 94
rpm -i parameter, 18
rpm -U command param-
eter, 46
**FILEFLAGS - -queryformat
tag, 381**
**FILEGIDS - -queryformat
tag, 380**
**FILEGROUPNAME
- -queryformat tag, 382**
**FILELINKTOS
- -queryformat tag, 381**
**FILEMD5S - -queryformat
tag, 381**
**FILEMODES - -queryformat
tag, 380**
**FILEMTIMES - -queryformat
tag, 381**
filenames
documentation, 195
package labels, 13
patch% macros, 192
patches, 177
paths, 200
**FILENAMES - -queryformat
tag, 380**
FILENAMES query tag, 73
**FILERDEVS - -queryformat
tag, 381**
files
.rpm, *see* packages
attributes, 91, 196-197,
233-234, 400

cleaning, 132
configuration, 9, 81, 116,
196, 299
checksums, 117
conflicts, 26-27
defaults, 90
listing, 64
MD5 checksums, 48
modifications, 117
monitoring, 7
packages, 43
software installation, 19
conflicts, 25-28
current, 48
default, 75
defaults, 33, 42, 100
dependent (installation), 29
directives, 399
documentation, 131, 293
creating, 195
installation, 30, 157
installaton, 31
listing, 64
extensions (backups), 193
extracting, 107
format, 349
formats, 339
RPM version 1, 10
versions, 339
ftp sites, displaying, 406-407
group IDs, 196
listing, 66-67, 106
locating, 57-58, 291-293
MD5 checksums, 48-49
monitoring, 117
naming, 13, 338
original (checksums), 48
output, removing, 193
overwriting, 25-26
packages
binary, 108, 123
extracting, 106
group specificiation, 14
installation, 14
listing, 62
MD5 checksum, 14
names, 14
net shared paths, 65
netsharedpath rpmrc, 65
normal, 64

owners, 14
permissions, 14
queries, 57-59, 64
size, 14
source, 107-108
sources, 123
status, 64-65
verification, 94
patch compression, 194
queries, 57-59, 117
reading disk devices, 298
replacing (installation),
28-29
restoring, 7
rpmlib
dbindex.h, 306
header.h, 306, 328
rpmlib.h, 306, 328
rpmrc, 309
options, 354-355
servers, 295
sharing, 64
software installation, 19
source, 292
spec, 121-122
%files list, 194
architecture, 202
conditional, 203
conditionals, 201-203
directives, 199-201
user IDs, 196
variables (writing), 310
verification, 86, 318-319
disabling, 88
file ownership, 82
groups, 82
major number, 83
MD5 checksum, 82
minor number, 83
modes, 82
modification time, 83
size, 82
symlinks, 83
**FILESIZES - -queryformat
tag, 380**
FILESIZES query tag, 73
**FILESTATES - -queryformat
tag, 380**
**FILEUIDS - -queryformat
tag, 380**

FILEUSERNAME - -
   queryformat tag, 382
FILEVERIFYFLAGS - -
   queryformat tag, 382
find-provides script, 208
find-requires script, 207
flags (binary files), 316
- -force rpm -i command
   option, 18, 30, 370
- -force rpm -U command
   option, 46, 51, 371
forcing
   installation, 30
   upgrades, 51
formats
   files, 339, 349
      RPM version 1, 10
      versions, 339
   software, 114
   spec files, 121-122
free software, 410
freeing iterator resources, 328
- -ftpport <port>
   rpm -i command option, 18,
      34
   rpm -U command option,
      46
- -ftpproxy <host>
   rpm -i command option, 18,
      34
   rpm -U command option,
      46
ftp
   ports, 34
   servers
      PGP, 422
      proxies, 34
   sites
      amanda, 276-277
      displaying files, 406-407
      installation, 406-407
      technical support,
         404-406
ftpport entry, 362
ftpproxy entry, 362
functions
   database manipulation,
      311-312
   database search, 313-315
   database transversal, 312
   dependency, 320-322

diagnostic control, 322
entry manipulation,
      326-327
error handling, 306-307
errors, 307
header manipulation,
      324-325
iterator, 327-328
package data, 307-308
package manipulation, 318
rpmrc, 309-310
variable manipulation,
      308-309
verification, 319, 323-324

G

Garfinkel, Simson, 420
General Public License, *see*
   GPL
GIDs (%attr macro), 235
GIF - -queryformat tag, 378
global command options, 368
GNU licensing, 411-414
GPL (General Public License),
   409-410, 415-416
grep command, 57
group, 128
GROUP - -queryformat tag,
   378
Group attribute, 197
group descriptive tags, 168
group directive tags, 390
group file attribute, 400
group IDs, 196
group tag, 252
grouping packages, 14, 87,
   168-169
groups
   case sensitivity, 60
   file verificatoin, 82
   locating in databases, 314
   packages (queries), 59-60

H

hardware, 172, 338
   overriding verification, 35
   see also architecture
- -hash rpm -i command
   option, 18, 22, 370

- -hash rpm -U command
   option, 46, 371
header manipulation
   functions, 324-325
header structure, 342-343
header.h file, 306, 328
headerAddEntry( ) entry
   manipulation function, 326
headerCopy( ) header
   manipulation function, 325
headerDump( ) header
   manipulation function, 325
headerFree( ) header manipulation function, 325
headerFreeIterator( ) iterator
   function, 328
headerGetEntry( ) entry
   manipulation function, 326
headerInitIterator( ) iterator
   function, 327
headerIsEntry( ) entry
   manipulation function, 327
headerNew( ) header manipulation, 325
headerNextIterator( ) iterator
   function, 327
headerRead( ) function, 324
headers
   archives (compression), 349
   copying, 325
   creating, 325
   data, 343
   deallocation, 325
   decoding, 350
   entries, 326-327
   header structure, 342
   index entries, 343
   iterators, 327-329
   memory, 325
   packages, 308, 346-349
   printing, 325
   reading, 324
   store, 343
   tags, 347-348
   values, 343
   versions, 349
   writing, 324
headerSizeof( ) header
   manipulation function, 325
headerWrite( ) header
   manipulation function, 324

- -help option, 104
hierarchy (packages),
    displaying, 169

I

i386 architecture, 338
icon descriptive tag, 168, 389
ICON - -queryformat tag, 382
icons
    packages, 364
    software, 168
- -ignorearch rpm -i com-
    mand option, 18, 35, 370
- -ignorearch rpm -U
    command option, 46, 371
- -ignoreos rpm -i command
    option, 18, 35, 370
- -ignoreos rpm -U command
    option, 46, 371
ignoring spec file comment
    lines, 164
- -includedocs rpm -i
    command option, 18, 31,
    370
- -includedocs rpm -U
    command option, 46, 371
increasing verbosity, 322
index header structure, 342
index entries
    header structure, 342
    headers, 343
index sets (databases), 313
informational command
    options, 368
- -initdb command, 374
- -initdb option, 103
inputs
    patches, 120-121
    sources, 120
    spec files, 121-122
- -install command, *see* rpm -i
    command
install platform (detection),
    265
install scripts, 122, 181-182
    %post, 182, 256, 395
    %pre, 182, 256
    arguments, 181
    environmental variables, 181
install sections, 122

install% build-time script,
    180
installation, 20
    amanda, 279-280, 288-289
        %files list, 285
        build-time scripts, 284
        sources, 285
    binary files, 316
    binary packages, 406
    build roots, selecting,
        226-227
    config file, 221
    databases, locating, 34
    directories, 180
    files
        defaults, 33
        dependent, 29
        documentation, 30-31,
            157
        overwriting, 25-26
        replacing, 28-29
    forcing, 30
    from ftp sites, 406
    ftp port numbers, 34
    ftp proxy servers, 34
    ftp site files, 407
    installation, 6
    one-command, 9
    packages, 6, 11, 297, 370
        conflicts, 170
        queries, 57
        reinstallation, 24
        relocatable, 174, 222-223
        relocation, 31-32
        source, 160-162
        verification, 11, 85-86,
            117, 183, 369
    platforms, overriding, 268
    root directories, 33
    scripts, 297
        postinstall, 32
        preinstall, 32
    software
        configuration files, 19
        conflicts, 19
        dependency checks, 19
        files, 19
        postinstall tasks, 19
        preinstall tasks, 19
        root directory, 157
        status, 19

source files, 316
source package files,
    108-109
status, 22-23, 33
subpackages
    clients, 293, 298
    verification, 262
testing, 23-24
verification
    architecture, 35
    operating systems, 35
version checking, 105
installation scripts
    %pre, 395
    building packages, 300
    creating, 299
INSTALLPREFIX
- -queryformat tag, 384
INSTALLTIME
- -queryformat tag, 377
INSTALLTIME query tag, 71
INT16 header structure value,
    343
INT32 header structure value,
    343
INT64 header structure value,
    343
INT8 header structure value,
    343
integer data, 343
ISPs (Internet service
    providers), 34
iterator functions
    headerFreeIterator( ), 328
    headerInitIterator( ), 327
    headerNextIterator( ), 327
iterators, 329
    arrays, 71-72
    headers, 327
    resources, freeing, 328
    single-entry, 73

J–K

key encryption, 418
key pairs
    creating, 238-239
    random bits, 240
    user IDs, 239

L

labels (packages), 13, 85
  conventions, 13
  queries, 55-56
  releases, 13
  software names, 13
  software version, 13
leads (packages), 339-342
legal status (PGP), 420
libraries
  capability, 171
  packages (required), 213
  RPM routines, 11
  shared, 146, 207-208, 213
  sonames, 213
  tools directory, 349
  updating, 182
  version compatibility, 60
  see also rpmlib
licensing
  copying, 411
  distribution, 411
  General Public License, 416
  GNU, 411-414
  modifying, 411
  PGP, 421
  PGP software, 421
  source code, 411
Linux
  Bourne again shell, 43
  distribution, 9
  Elf-based (PGP), 422
  libraries, shared, 208
  technical support, 408
listing
  configuration files, 64
  database files, 66-67
  documentation files, 64
  files, 106
  package files, 62
  package (configuration files), 63
literal text, 69
locating
  database records, 330, 333
  databases, 34, 58, 90, 331
  files, 57-58, 291-293
  groups in databases, 314
  packages in databases, 314-315
  packages in databases, 313
  public keys, 95
  RPM on your system, 404
  source files, 175

M

m68k architecture, 338
macros, 130
  %attr, 233-235
  %patch, 286, 398
  %setup, 188-191, 396-397
  patch%, 191-194
mailing lists
  redhat-digest mailing list, 408
  redhat-list mailing list, 408
maintaining configuration files, 43
maj file attribute, 400
major number verification, 83
Major Number Attribute, 197
manual dependencies
  conflicts tags, 211
  provides tag, 212
  requires tag, 209-210
MD5 Checksum attribute, 197
MD5 checksums
  configuration files, 47-48
  current files, 48
  files, 48-49
  new files, 48
  original files, 48
  package files, 14
  upgrades, 47-49
  verification, 82
md5 file attribute, 400
memory
  availability, 216
  headers, 325
  package relocation, 216
message digest, *see* **MD5 checksum**
messagelevel entry, 362

messages
  help, 104
  warning, 21-22
min file attribute, 400
minor number verification, 83
Minor Number attribute, 197
mips architecture, 338
MIT PGP software, 421
Mode attribute, 197
mode file attribute, 400
modification time verification, 83
Modification Time attribute, 197
modifiers (query tags), 71
modifying
  software, 218, 411-413
  sources, 120
monitoring
  configuration files, 7
  files, 117
  packages, 6-7
MPILIB PGP international software, 421-422
mtime file attribute, 400
multiplatforms
  conditionals, 271-272
  optflags entry, 269
  package building troubleshooting, 273
  tags, 269-270

N

-n %setup macro option, 396
-n <string> subpackage, 201
-n option (% package directive), 401
name, 128
NAME - -queryformat tag, 376
name package naming tag, 165, 388
NAME query tag, 70, 73
naming
  directories, 185
  files, 13, 338
    architecture, 338
    names, 338
    package files, 14

release, 338
version, 338
naming tags, 165-166
nested conditionals, 271
net shared path files, 65
netsharedpath entry, 363
netsharedpath rpmrc files, 65
network entries, 298
new files, 48-49
- -**nodeps rpm -e command
   option, 38, 41, 372**
- -**nodeps rpm -i command
   option, 18, 29, 370**
- -**nodeps rpm -U command
   option, 46, 371**
- -**nodeps rpm -V command
   option, 87, 370**
- -**nofiles rpm -V command
   option, 88, 370**
non-commercial use
   PGP, 421
   PGP software, 421
non-PGP verification, 99
nonzero status, 24
**NOPATCH - -queryformat
   tag, 383**
nopatch tag, 177, 393
- -**nopgp command option
   (rpm -K), 94, 99**
- -**nopgp rpm -K command
   option, 374**
normal files, 64
- -**noscripts rpm -b command
   option, 372**
- -**noscripts rpm -e command
   option, 38, 41-42**
- -**noscripts rpm -i command
   option, 18, 32, 370**
- -**noscripts rpm -U command
   option, 46, 51-52, 371**
- -**noscripts rpm -V command
   option, 88, 370**
**NOSOURCE - -queryformat
   tag, 383**
nosource tag, 176, 393
**NULL header structure value,
   343**

O

offset (4-byte), 343
- -**oldpackage rpm -U
   command option, 46, 50-51,
   371**
one-command installation, 9
opening databases, 311
operating systems, 264, 354
   compatibility, 35, 310, 360
   confidential files, 201
   detection logic, overriding,
      152
   Linux technical support, 408
   multiple, 116
   name, 310
   package files, 35
   packages, building, 173
   RPM, locating, 404
   spec files, 203
   tags
      excludeos, 173, 392
      exclusiveos, 173, 392
   verification, overriding, 35
   see also platforms
optflags entry, 269, 363
options
   - -help, 104
   - -initdb, 103
   - -quiet, 104
   - -rebuilddb, 102
   - -version, 105
   rpm -K command
      - -nopgp, 94, 99
      -v, 94-97
**options.h configuration file,
   278**
original files, 48-49
OS - -queryformat tag, 379
os canon entry, 359
os compat entry, 360
output
   binary package files, 123
   commands, 159
   diagnostic verbosity, 322
   file(1) command, 351
   files, removing, 193
   package building, 133

packages, 349
   reducing, 104
   rpm -b command, 159
   rpm -K command, 96
   source package files, 123
      compressed tar files, 123
      patches, 123
      spec files, 123
   verbosity, 362
   verification, 96
      failure, 83-84
   viewing, 89
overriding
   architecture verification, 35
   buildroot tag, 174
   detection logic, 151-152
   hardware verification, 35
   operating system verifica-
      tion, 35
   platforms, 268
overwriting files, 25-26
owner attribute, 197
owner file attribute, 400
owners (package files), 14

P

-P %patch macro option, 398
**package building, 11-12,
   115-116, 134-136, 140,
   143-144, 303, 371-372**
   %build, 142
   %build section, 130
   %files list, 131, 146-148
   %install section, 130
   %prep, 141
   %prep script, 129
   architecture, 172-173
   binary files, 145
   build roots, 226-227, 229,
      231-232
   build trees, 142
   cross-platforms, 12
   date, 14
   dedicated systems, 226
   detection logic, 151-152
   directories, selecting,
      230-232
   directory structure, 126

directory trees, removing, 154
files
  cleaning, 132
  verification, 91
installation scripts, 298-300
length, 140
location, 230-232
macros, 130
multiplatforms, 273
multiple, 242
operating system, 173
output, 133
permissions, 142
platforms, overriding, 268
public keys, 95
relocatable, 219
root directory, 155-157
scripts
  installation, 297
  uninstallation, 300
shortcuts, 149-150
signatures, 152
source package files, 135
source packages, 146
sources, 127
spec file preamble, 127
status, 372
terminating, 132, 136
testing, 153-154
third-party, 114-115
time, 14
time options, 365
troubleshooting, 136
uninstallation scripts, 301-302
user IDs, 169
package data functions, 307-308
package files
binary, 108-109, 123
ftp port numbers, 34
hardware architecure verification, 35
operating systems, 35
source, 107-109
sources, 123
verification, 94

package labels
case sensitivity, 56
filenames, 13
name restrictions, 56
queries, 55-56
rpm -q command, 56
software, 55
package-naming tags, 388
packager, 129
PACKAGER - -queryformat tag, 378
packager descriptive tag, 169
packager directive tag, 390
packager entry, 363
packages
%files list, 218, 254
adding (dependency processing), 320
architectures (multiple), 8, 161
archives, 349
authentication, 14, 238
binary, 116, 289-291
  creating, 162
  installation, 316
capabilities
  provided, 206
  required, 206, 209
clients, 300
conditionals, 271-272
config file, 221
configuration, 114
configuration files, 7, 63
conflicts, 211, 315
conversion (cpio archives), 105
data, 307
  viewing, 7, 121
dependencies, 41, 60, 213
  requires tag, 210
dependency processing (automatic), 171
descriptions, 261
directories, 198-199
directory trees, removing, 154
displaying, 169, 368-369
erasing, 6, 38-40, 183, 318, 321, 371
  configuration files, 43
  older versions, 47

scripts, 41
testing, 40-41
file formats, 339
files
  attributes, 233-234
  binary, 108
  extracting, 106-107
  format, 349
  group specifications, 14
  installation, 14
  listing, 62, 106
  locating, 58
  MD5 checksums, 14
  names, 14
  net shared paths, 65
  netsharedpath rpmrc, 65
  normal, 64
  owners, 14
  permissions, 14
  restoring, 7
  size, 14
  source, 108
  status, 64-65
grouping, 14, 87, 168-169
headers, 308, 346-349
  decoding, 350
  store, 343
  tags, 347-348
icons, 364
installation, 6-8, 11, 297, 370
  conflicts, 170
  flags, 316
  reinstallation, 24
  relocatable, 174
  verification, 11, 85-86, 117
labels, 13, 85
leads, 339-342
libraries, 146
  shared, 213
  updating, 182
locating in databases, 313-315
memory, 216
monitoring, 6-7
optflags entry, 269
output, 349
patches, excluding, 177
path prefixes, 222

PGP signatures, 238-240
platforms, 270
postinstallation, 182
postuninstallation, 183
prefix tag, 221
preinstallation, 182
preuninstallation, 183
program references, 219
providing, 60, 65
queries, 8, 57, 117
  array iterators, 71-72
  binary, 62
  capabilities, 65-66
  compatibility, 60
  customizing, 68
  data, 61-62
  distribution, 62
  documentation, 63
  escape sequences, 69
  field width, 70
  files, 57-59, 64
  groups, 59-60
  justification, 70
  labels, 55-57
  literal text, 69
  readable data, 70-71
  scripts, 67-68
  single-entry tags, 73
  source RPM files, 62
  standard input, 59
  Summary, 62
  tags, 70, 73-74
  URLs, 59
  version, 61
README file, 221
rebuilding, 10, 102-103, 373
recompiling, 161
relocatable
  config file, 221
  installation, 222-223
  prefix tag, 216
  symlinks, 223
  testing, 222-223
relocation, 31-32, 216
  references, 219
  symlinks, 219
relocationprefix tag, 217
required, 65-66, 170, 213
requiring, 60

restoring, 43
RPM signatures, 240-241
scripts, 8
  presinstall, 32
  postsinstall, 32
  postuninstall, 39
  preuninstall, 39
serial numbers, 211
signatures, 97, 152, 238, 241-242, 324, 343-346, 349, 365
  adding, 152, 244, 373
  digital, 419
  identical, 245
  multiple, 244
  printing, 329
  replacing, 243, 373
  verification, 374
software, 5
  copyrights, 167
  icons, 168
  vendors, 168
sonames, 213
source, 160-162, 289-291
source files, excluding, 176
sources, pristine, 114-115
status, 307
subdirectories, excluding, 199
subpackages, 200
symlinks (absolute), 217
tags (exclusive.xxx), 270
testing, 137, 296
time limits, 158
uninstallation, 6-8, 11
upgrades, 6, 12
upgrading, 50, 320, 371
verification, 85-86, 100, 183, 221, 238, 319, 369
  clients, 303
  failure output, 83
  output failure, 84
  signatures, 323
versions, 115
  comparison operators, 210
  numbers, 210
viewing, 57, 74
virtual, 169, 212
writing o disks, 339
packet management system, *see* **PMS**

packet manipulation functions
  rpmNotifyFunction( ), 317
  rpmRemovePackage( ), 318
packet signatures, 241
parameters
  rpm -1, 18
  rpm -K command, 94
  rpm -U cmmand, 46
passphrases (secret keys), 239-240
PATCH - -queryformat tag, 379
patch % macros, 191
patch files
  compression, 194
  output files, removing, 193
patch tag, 176, 393
patch tags, 286
  nopatch, 177, 393
  patch, 176, 393
patch% macros, 193-194
patches, 120-121, 145, 283
  amanda, 281-283
  creating, 121
  excluding from packages, 177
  filenames, 177
  software, 176
  URLs, 177
patents
  PGP, 421
  software, 410
path prefixes, 223
paths
  binary files, 364
  databases, editing, 42
  directories, 241, 365-366
  filenames, 200
  prefixes, 221-222
  sharing, 363
  source files, 365
  spec files, 365
  symlinks, 58
  top-level directories, 366
- -percent rpm -i command option, 18, 33, 370
- -percent rpm -U command option, 46, 371
performance (RPM version 2), 10

Perl programming language (RPM), 9
permissions
  package files, 14
  packages, building, 142
PGP (pretty good privacy) software, 94, 364, 418, 421
  building, 422
  commercial use, 421
  decryption, 419
  digital signature, 419
  downloading, 421-422
  encryption, 418, 420
  ftp servers, 422
  key pairs
    creating, 238-239
    random bits, 240
  legal status, 420
  licensing, 421
  Linux (Elf-based), 422
  MIT, 421
  MPILIB, 421-422
  non-commercial use, 421
  package file verification, 94
  package signatures, 238-240
  patents, 421
  public keys, 95, 238, 363
  restrictions, 421
  RSAREF, 421
  secret keys, 238
  security (public key), 418
  verification (public keys), 97
  Web page, 421
pgp name entry, 241, 363
pgp path entry, 241, 364
pkg1...pkgN rpm
  -e command parameter, 38
  -q command option, 54
platform configuration files, 278
platform-dependent conditionals, 266
platform-dependent tags, 265, 269
platforms, 264
  build, 265
  build data, 267
  canonical names, 266
  canonical numbers, 266
  excluded, 270

  hardware, 172
  overriding, 268
  see also architecture;
    operating systems
PM, 9
PMS (packet management system), 7
  BOGUS distribution, 9
  creating, 7
  queries, 9
porting applications to multiple operating systems, 116
ports (ftp), 34, 362
post% install script, 182
POSTIN - -queryformat tag, 379
postinstall scripts, 68, 132
  installation, 32
  queries, 32
  servers, 300
  upgrades, 51-52
postinstall tasks, 19
postinstallation (packages), 182
POSTUN - -queryformat tag, 379
postun% erase-time script, 183
postuninstall scripts, 68, 132
  execution, preventing, 42
  packages, 39, 41
  rpm -e command, 39
postuninstallation (packages), 183
ppc architecture, 338
pre% install script, 182
preamble, 127
  %package directive, 250
  architecture tags, 392
  comment lines, 129
  copyright, 128
  dependency (autoreqprov), 391
  dependency tags, 390-391
  description, 129
  description tags, 389
  descriptive tags, 389-390
  directive tags, 390
  directory tags, 392

  distribution, 128
  GPL, 410
  group, 128
  name, 128
  operating system tags, 392
  package-naming tags, 388
  packager, 129
  patch tags, 393
  release, 128
  source, 128
  source tags, 393
  URLs, 128
  vendor, 129
  version, 128
preambles, 121
prefix directory tags, 174, 392
- -prefix <path> rpm -i command option, 18, 31-32
prefix relocation tag, 216-217
- -prefix rpm -i command option, 370
- -prefix <path> rpm -U command option, 46
- -prefix rpm -U command option, 371
prefix tag (%files list), 217
prefixes (paths), 221-223
PREIN - -queryformat tag, 379
preinstall scripts, 68, 132
  installation, 32
  queries, 32
  upgrades, 51-52
preinstall tasks (software installation), 19
preinstallation (packages), 182
premble (dependency tag conflicts), 391
prep sections, 121
prep% build-time script, 179
preprocessor directives, 422
Pretty Good Privacy, Inc., 421
Pretty Good Privacy, *see* PGP
PREUN - -queryformat tag, 379
preun% erase-time script, 183
preuninstall script, 132

preuninstall scripts, 68
    execution, preventing, 42
    packages, 39, 41
    rpm -e command, 39
preuninstallation (packages), 183
preventing
    postuninstall scripts, execution, 42
    preuninstall scripts , execution, 42
    scripts (execution), 51-52
printing
    headers, 325
    packages (signatures), 329
pristine sources, 8, 120
    BOGUS distribution, 9
    PM, 9
private key encryption, 418
processing
    dependency, 320, 171
    spec files (operating systems), 203
provided packages, 213
    capabilities, 65
provided capabilities, 206
PROVIDES - -queryformat tag, 383
provides dependency tag, 169, 390
- -provides rpm -q command option, 369
provides tag, 212
providing packages, 60
proxy servers, 362
    ftp, 34
    ISPs, 34
    security, 34
public key encryption, 418
public keys
    locating, 95
    PGP, 97, 238, 363

Q

queries, 117
    databases, 8, 10
    files, 57-59
    package labels, 55-56

    packages, 57
        array iterators, 71-72
        binary, 62
        capabilities, 65-66
        compatibility, 60
        customizing, 68
        data, 61-62
        distribution, 62
        documentation, 63
        escape sequences, 69
        field width, 70
        files, 57-59, 64
        groups, 59-60
        installed, 57
        justification, 70
        labels, 55-56
        literal text, 69
        readable data, 70-71
        scripts, 67-68
        single-entry tags, 73
        source RPM files, 62
        standard input, 59
        summary, 62
        tags, 70, 73-74
        URLs, 59
        version, 61
    PMS, 9
    scripts, 32
    tags, 73-74
- -query command, see rpm -q
- -queryformat rpm -q command option, 369
- -queryformat tags
    ARCH, 379
    ARCHIVESIZE, 382
    AUTOREQPROV, 385
    BUILDHOST, 377
    BUILDROOT, 384
    BUILDTIME, 377
    CHANGELOG, 378
    CONFLICTFLAGS, 384
    CONFLICTNAME, 384
    CONFLICTVERSION, 384
    COPYRIGHT, 378
    DEFAULTPREFIX, 384
    DESCRIPTION, 377
    DISTRIBUTION, 377
    EXCLUDE, 382
    EXCLUDEARCH, 385

    EXCLUDEOS, 385
    EXCLUSIVE, 382
    EXCLUSIVEARCH, 385
    EXCLUSIVEOS, 385
    FILEFLAGS, 381
    FILEGIDS, 380
    FILEGROUPNAME, 382
    FILELINKTOS, 381
    FILEMD5S, 381
    FILEMODES, 380
    FILEMTIMES, 381
    FILENAMES, 380
    FILERDEVS, 381
    FILESIZES, 380
    FILESTATES, 380
    FILEUIDS, 380
    FILEUSERNAME, 382
    FILEVERIFYFLAGS, 382
    GIF, 378
    GROUP, 378
    ICON, 382
    INSTALLPREFIX, 384
    INSTALLTIME, 377
    NAME, 376
    NOPATCH, 383
    NOSOURCE, 383
    OS, 379
    PACKAGER, 378
    PATCH, 379
    POSTIN, 379
    POSTUN, 379
    PREIN, 379
    PREUN, 379
    PROVIDES, 383
    RELEASE, 376
    REQUIREFLAGS, 383
    REQUIRENAME, 383
    REQUIREVERSION, 383
    ROOT, 381
    RPMVERSION, 385
    SERIAL, 376
    SIZE, 377
    SOURCE, 378
    SOURCERPM, 382
    SUMMARY, 377
    TIRGGERINDEX, 386
    TRIGGERFLAGS, 386
    TRIGGERNAME, 385
    TRIGGERSCRIPTS, 385
    TRIGGERVERSION, 386

URL, 379
VENDORS, 378
VERIFYSCRIPT, 386
VERSION, 376
XPM, 378
query options, 213
query tags
ARCH, 73
FILENAMES, 73
FILESIZES, 73
INSTALLTIME, 71
modifiers, 71
NAME, 70, 73
RELEASE, 70
RPMTAG, 73
RPMTAG ARCH, 73
RPMTAG
VERIFYSCRIPT, 73
VERSION, 70
- -quiet option, 104
**- -quiet rpm -b command
option, 159**
qzip, 194

R

.rhosts files, 300
.rpm files, *see* **packages**
**-root <path> rpm -U com-
mand option, 46**
random bits (key pairs), 240
- -rcfile <rcfile> rpm
-b command option, 160
-e command option, 38, 42
-i command option, 18, 33
-U command option, 46
**- -rcfile rpm -V command
option, 90**
**rcfile <rcfile> command
option, 94, 100**
**read/write access (amanda
backups), 298**
reading
files (disk devices), 298
headers, 324
README file (packages), 221
**- -rebuild build command,
161-162**
- -rebuild command, 373
- -rebuilddb command, 374

- -rebuilddb option, 102
rebuilding
databases, 312
packages, 10, 102-103, 373
**- -recompile build command,
160-161**
- -recompile command, 373
recompiling
packages, 161
software, 373
records (databases)
locating, 333
numbers, 312
Red Hat Package Manager,
see **RPM**
reducing output, 104
reinstallation (packages), 24
relative symlinks, 223
release, 128
files, naming, 338
naming tag, 166
software, 338
**RELEASE - -queryformat tag,
376**
**release package-naming tag,
388**
RELEASE query tag, 70
releases (package labels), 13
relocatable packages, 216
%files list, 218
installation, 174, 223
memory, 216
prefix tag, 216-217, 221
software references, 219
symlinks, 219, 223
testing, 222
relocation
packages, 31-32, 219
config file, 221
testing, 223
verification, 221
software, 217-219
**relocation tags (prefix),
216-217**
removing
%doc directive tag from
%files list, 220
directory trees, 154
output files, 193
- -replacefiles option, 137

- -replacefiles rpm
-i command option, 18,
25-29, 370
-U command option, 46,
371
- -replacepkgs rpm
-i command option, 18,
24-25, 370
-U command option, 46,
371
replacing
files (installation), 28-29
packages (signatures), 241,
243
signatures, 243, 373
**require distribution entry,
364**
require icon entry, 364
require vendor entry, 364
required
cabapilities, 65-66, 206, 209
packages, 170, 213
**REQUIREFLAGS
- -queryformat tag, 383**
**REQUIRENAME
- -queryformat tag, 383**
**requires dependency tag, 170,
390**
- -requires query option, 213
**- -requires rpm -q command
option, 369**
**requires tag (version require-
ments), 210**
**REQUIREVERSION
- -queryformat tag, 383**
requiring packages, 60
- -resign command, 373
**- -resign signature command
option, 243**
**resources (iterators), freeing,
328**
restores, 292
Bourne-again shell, 43
configuration files, 26-27
files, 7
packages, 43
restrictions
%files list, 218
package labels (names), 56
PGP software, 421

retrieving header entries, 326
- -**root <path> rpm**
  -e command option, 38, 42
  -i command option, 18, 33
- -**root rpm -V command
  option, 90**
**ROOT - -queryformat tag,
381**
**root directories, 33, 42, 74,
90, 361**
  alternate, 155-156
  build roots, 155
  databases, 74
  scripts, 33
  selecting, 226-227
  software (installation), 157
routines (libraries), 11
RPM
  discussion groups, 408
  locating on your system, 404
  mailing lists, 408
  packages (signatures),
  240-241
  Perl, 9
  technical support, 408
  Web site, 409
**rpm -b command options,
149, 159**
  - -buildarch, 151, 372
  - -buildos, 372
  buildos <os>, 152
  - -buildroot, 155-157, 372
  - -clean, 154-155, 372
  - -noscripts, 372
  output, 159
  - -quiet, 159
  - -rcfile <rcfile>, 160
  rpm -ba, 145-146
  rpm -bc, 142-143
  rpm -bi, 143
  rpm -bi, 144
  rpm -bl, 146-148
  rpm -bp, 141
  - -short-circuit, 149-150
  short-circuit, 372
  - -sign, 152, 372
  - -test, 153, 372
  - -timecheck, 158, 372
  -vv, 159
rpm -ba command, 145-146

rpm -bb command, 144
**rpm -bc command option,
142-143**
**rpm -bi command option,
143-144**
**rpm -bl command option,
146-148**
**rpm -bp command option,
141**
rpm -e command, 38, 43
  options
    - -*dbpath <path>, 38, 42*
    - -*nodeps, 38, 41*
    - -*noscripts, 38, 41-42*
    rcfile <rcfile>, 38, 42
    root <path>, 38, 42
    - -*test, 18, 38-41*
    - -*vv, 38-40*
  parameters (pkg1...pkgN),
  38
  postuninstall scripts, 39
  preuninstall scripts, 39
  syntax, 38
rpm -e command options, 372
rpm -i command options
  - -dbpath <path>, 18, 34
  - -excludedocs, 18, 30, 370
  - -force, 18, 30, 370
  - -ftpport <port>, 18, 34
  - -ftpproxy <host>, 18, 34
  - -hash, 18, 22, 370
  - -ignorearch, 18, 35, 370
  - -ignoreos, 18, 35, 370
  - -includedocs, 18, 31, 370
  - -nodeps, 18, 29, 370
  - -noscripts, 18, 32, 370
  - -percent, 18, 33, 370
  - -prefix <path>, 18, 31-32,
  370
  - -rcfile <rcfile>, 18, 33
  - -replacefiles, 18, 25-29,
  370
  - -replacepkgs, 18, 24-25,
  370
  - -root <path>, 18, 33
  - -test, 18, 23-24, 370
  -v, 18, 22
  -vv, 18, 23
**rpm -i parameters
  (file1.rpm...fileN.rpm), 18**

rpm -K command, 94-96
  - -nopgp, 374
  output, 96
rpm -q command, 54
  options, 369
  package labels, 56
  selections, 55
rpm -U command, 47, 50
  options
    - -*dbpath <path>, 46*
    - -*excludedocs, 46, 371*
    - -*force, 46, 51, 371*
    - -*ftpport <port>, 46*
    - -*ftpproxy <host>, 46*
    - -*hash, 46, 371*
    - -*ignorearch, 46, 371*
    - -*ignoreos, 46*
    - -*includedocs, 46, 371*
    - -*nodeps, 46, 371*
    - -*noscripts, 46, 51-52,
    371*
    - -*oldpackage, 16, 50-51,
    371*
    - -*percent, 46, 371*
    - -*prefix <path>, 46, 371*
    - -*rcfile <rcfile>, 46*
    - -*replacefiles, 46, 371*
    - -*replacepkgs, 46, 371*
    - -*root <path>, 46*
    - -*test, 46, 371*
    -*v, 46*
    -*vv, 46*
  parameters, 46
rpm -V command
  file groups, 82
  file mode, 82
  file ownership, 82
  file size, 82
  major number, 83
  MD5 checksum, 82
  minor number, 83
  modification time, 83
  options
    - -*dbpath, 90*
    - -*nodeps, 87, 370*
    - -*nofiles, 88, 370*
    - -*noscripts, 88, 370*
    - -*rcfile, 90*
    - -*root, 90*
    rpm -Va, 85

rpm -Vf, 86
rpm -Vg, 87
rpm -Vp, 86
rpm -Vv, 89
rpm -Vvv, 89
symlinks, 83
rpm -Va command option, 85
rpm -Vf command option, 86
rpm -Vg command option, 87
rpm -Vp command option, 86
rpm -Vv command option, 89
rpm -Vvv command option, 89
rpm -y command, 370
RPM ARCH
build-time variable, 394
environmental variable, 179
RPM BUILD DIR
build-time variable, 394
environmental variable, 179
RPM BUILD ROOT
build-time variable, 394
environmental variable, 179
RPM database, accessing, 42
RPM DOC DIR
build-time variable, 394
environmental variable, 179
RPM INSTALL PREFIX
environmental variable, 181
variable, 395
RPM OPT FLAGS
build-time variable, 394
environmental variable, 179
RPM OS
build-time variable, 394
environmental variable, 179
RPM PACKAGE NAME
build-time variable, 394
environmental variable, 179
RPM PACKAGE RELEASE
build-time variable, 394
environmental variable, 179
RPM PACKAGE VERSION
build-time variable, 394
environmental variable, 179
RPM ROOT DIR build-time variable, 394
RPM SOURCE DIR
build-time variable, 394
environmental variable, 179

RPM version 1, 9-10
configuration files (automatic handling), 9
databases, 10
file formats, 10
multiple architecture, 10
packages, rebuilding, 10
size requirements, 10
speed, 10
RPM version 2, 10
databases (queries), 10
performance, 10
rpm-b command options, 157
rpm-list mailing list, 408
rpm2cpio command, 105
rpmarchive tool, 349
rpmArchScore( ) rpmrc function, 310
rpmdbClose( ) database manipulation function, 311
rpmdbFindByConflict( ) database search function, 315
rpmdbFindByFile( ) database search function, 313
rpmdbFindByGroup( ) database search function, 314
rpmdbFindByProvides( ) database search function, 314
rpmdbFindByRequiredBy( ) database search function, 315
rpmdbFindPackage( ) database search function, 314
rpmdbFirstRecNum( ) database traversal functions, 312
rpmdbGetRecord( ) database traversal function, 312
rpmdbInit( ) database manipulation function, 311
rpmdbNextRecNum( ) database traversal function, 312
rpmdbOpen( ) database manipulation function, 311
rpmdbRebuild( ) database manipulation function, 312

rpmdepAddPackage( ) dependency functions, 320
rpmdepAvailable Package( )dependency function, 321
rpmdepCheck( ) dependency function, 321
rpmdepDependencies( ) dependency functions, 320
rpmdepDone( ) dependency function, 322
rpmdepFreeconflicts( ) dependency function, 321
rpmdepRemovePackage( ) dependency function, 321
rpmdepUpgradePackage( ) dependency function, 320
rpmdir entry, 364
rpmErrorCode( ) error handling function, 306
rpmErrorSetCallback( ) error handling function, 307
rpmErrorString( ) error handling function, 307
rpmGetArchName( ) rpmrc function, 310
rpmGetBooleanVar( ) variable manipulation function, 309
rpmGetOsName( ) rpmrc functions, 310
rpmGetVar( ) variable manipulation function, 308
rpmGetVerbosity( ) diagnostic control function, 322
rpmheader tool, 349
rpmIsDebug( ) diagnostic control function, 323
rpmIsVerbose( ) diagostic control functions, 322
rpmlead tool, 349
rpmlib
dependency, 320-322
diagnostic control, 322
error handling functions, 306-307
files, 306, 328
header manipulation functions, 324-325
headers, 329
iterator functions, 327-328
package data, 307-308, 316

rpmrc functions, 309-310
signature, 329
variable manipulation, 309
verification functions, 319
rpmlib library, 11
rpmlib.h file, 306, 328
rpmNotifyFunction( ) packet manipulation function, 317
rpmOsScore( ) rpmrc function, 310
rpmrc file, 309
   --showrc option, 354-355
   entries
     arch canon, 359
     arch compat, 360
     build xxx translate, 267
     buildarchtranslate, 359
     builddir, 361
     buildostranslate, 360
     buildroot, 361
     cpiobin, 361
     dbpath, 361
     defaultdocdir, 361
     distribution, 362
     excludedocs, 362
     ftpport, 362
     ftpproxy, 362
     messagelevel, 362
     netsharedpath, 363
     optflags, 269, 363
     os canon, 359
     os compat, 360
     packager, 363
     pgp name, 241, 363
     pgp path, 241, 364
     require distribution, 364
     require icon, 364
     require vendor, 364
     rpmdir, 364
     signature, 240, 365
     sourcedir, 365
     specdir, 365
     srcrpmdir, 365
     timecheck, 365
     tmpdir, 366
     topdir, 366
     vendor, 366
     xxx canon, 266
     xxx compat, 267
   locations
     - - rcfile option, 358
     /etc/rpmrc, 358

/usr/lib/rpmrc, 358
user login directory, 358
   locations;/usr/lib/rpmrc, 355
   syntax, 358
rpmrc functions, 309-310
rpmReadConfigFiles( ) rpmrc function, 309
rpmReadPackageHeader( ) function, 308
rpmReadPackageInfo( ) package data function, 307
rpmRemovePackage( ) packet manipulation function, 318
rpmSetVar( ) variable manipulation function, 309
rpmSetVerbosity( ) diagnostic control function, 322
rpmShowRC ( )rpmrc function, 310
rpmsignature tool, 349
RPMTAG ARCH query tag, 73
RPMTAG query tag, 73
RPMTAG VERIFYSCRIPT query tag, 73
rpmVerifyFile( ) verification function, 319
rpmVerifyScript( ) verification function, 319
rpmVerifySignature( ) functions, 323
RPMVERSION - - queryformat tag, 385
RPP, 8
RSAREF, 421
RSAREF software, 421-422

S

saving configuration files, 117
Schneier, Bruce, 420
- -scripts rpm -q command option, 369
scripts, 8, 154, 178, 298
   %build, 287-288
   %install, 288-289
   %pre, 262
   %prep, 129, 286
   arguments, 298
   build time, 178-180, 257, 284, 394-395

   execution, preventing, 51-52
   erase time, 181-183, 396
   execution, 122
   find-provides, 208
   find-requires, 207
   install, 122, 181-182, 395
   installation, 297-300
   packages (queries), 67-68
   PM, 9
   postinstall, 32, 39, 51-52, 68
   postuninstall, 39, 68
   preinstall, 32, 51-52, 68
   preuninstall, 39, 68
   testing, 303
   uninstallation, 122, 300-302
   verification
     %verifyscript, 396
     disabling, 88
   verification-time (%verifyscript), 183
   verify, 68, 122
   writing, 153
secret keys
   passphrases, 239-240
   PGP, 238
security
   passphrases, 239-240
   PGP, 418
   secret keys, 239-240
   servers (proxy), 34
selecting directories, 230-232
selecting build roots, 226
SERIAL - -queryformat tag, 376
serial dependency tags, 170, 391
serial numbers, 211
server subpackage, 249
servers
   %files list, 292-293, 304
   amanda, 284, 298-300
   backups, 276
   clients, 280
   ftp proxies, 34
   packages, 303
   proxy, 34, 362
   scripts (postinstall), 300
   subpackages, 250, 295

setup% macro
  directories, 185-188
  source files, 186-188
  spec files (multisource),
    188-190
  testing, 191
SGI architecture, 338
shared libraries, 182,
  207-208, 213
sharing
  files, 64
  paths, 363
- -short-circuit rpm -b
  command option, 149-150,
  372
- -showrc option rpmrc file,
  354-355
- -sign build command
  option, 241-242
- -sign rpm -b command
  option, 152, 372
signature command options,
  243-245
signature entry (rpmrc file),
  240, 365
signatures
  adding to packages, 373
  digitals, 14, 419
  packages, 97, 152, 238,
    241-242, 324, 343-346, 349
    adding, 241, 244
    build-time, 241
    identical, 245
    multiple, 244
    PGP, 238-240
    printing, 329
    replacing, 241-243
    RPM, 240-241
    verification, 323
  replacing, 243, 373
  signatures, 365
  verification, 374
site configuration files, 278
SIZE - -queryformat tag, 377
size file attribute, 197, 400
size requirements, 10
software, 145, 414
  architecture, 338
  comment lines, 129
  copying, 413

copyrights, 128, 167, 410
description, 129
distribution, 128, 413
downloading (disclaimers),
  415
encryption, 420
formats, 114
free, 410
group, 128
icons, 168
installation, 19, 157
licensing, 410
modifying, 218, 411-413
name, 128
names (package labels), 13
naming, 338
package labels, 55
package management,
  creating, 7
packager, 129
packages, 5
patches, 176-177
patents, 410
PGP, 421
recompiling, 373
references, 219
relative paths, 219
release, 128, 166, 338
relocation, 217-219
serial numbers, 171, 211
source, 128
upgrades, 116
URLs, 128
vendors, 129, 168, 364-366
verification, 196-197
versions, 55, 128, 165, 338
  compatibility, 341
  numbers, 210-211
  troubleshooting, 51
warranty information, 410
soname, 171
sonames, 60, 206-208, 213
SOURCE - -queryformat tag,
  378
source code, 12, 108
  distributing, 411
  upgrades, 12
source files, 145, 292
  %setup macro, 188-190
  archived, unpacking, 186

directories, 185-188, 190
directory paths, 365
excluding from packages,
  176-177
installation, 316
locating, 175
packages, rebuilding, 373
paths, 365
software, recompiling, 373
unpacking, 185-191
URLs, 175
source package files, 107-109,
  123, 135
  compressed tar files, 123
  installation, 108-109
  patches, 123
  spec files, 123
source packages, 108, 145,
  160, 162, 289-291, 340
source RPM files, 62
source tags, 175
  nosource, 176, 393
  source, 175, 393
source trees, comparing, 121
sourcedir entry, 365
SOURCERPM - -queryformat
  tag, 382
sources, 120
  amanda, unpacking, 277
  modifying, 120
  packages
    building, 127
    upgrades, 115
  patches, 121
  pristine, 8-9, 115, 120
  unpacking, 121, 285
sparc architecture, 338
spec file, 252-253, 283, 398
  %build, 142
  %build section, 130
  %clean section, 132
  %description tags, 252
  %files list, 131, 253-254,
    399
    adding, 285
    directives, 399
    file directives, 399-400
  %install section, 130
  %package directives, 401
  %prep script, 129

architecture tags, 172-173
binary package files, 109
build-time scripts, 178-180
comments, 164, 388
conditionals
   %else, 402
   %endif, 402
   %ifarch, 401
   %ifnarch, 402
   %ifnos, 402
   %ifos, 402
   size, 272
dependency tags, 169-171
descriptive (copyright), 167
descriptive tags, 167-169
directories, naming, 185
directory tags, 174
erase-time scripts, 181-183
install scripts, 181-182
macros, 130
   %patch, 286, 398
   %patch macro, 398
   %setup, 184-185, 396-397
naming tags, 165-166
operating system tags, 173
packages, erasing, 183
patch tags, 176-177
patches, 109, 283
preamble, 127, 249
   %package directive, 250
   architecture tags, 392
   comment lines, 129
   copyright, 128
   dependency tags, 390-391
   description, 129
   description tags, 389
   descriptive tags, 389-390
   directive tags, 390
   directory tags, 392
   distribution, 128
   group, 128
   name, 128
   operating system tags, 392
   packager, 129
   patch tags, 393
   release, 128
   source, 128
   source tags, 393
   tags, 388

   URLs, 128
   vendor, 129
   version, 128
premble (dependency tags), 391
scripts
   build time, 284, 394-395
   erase time, 396
   install, 395
   postinstall, 132
   postuninstall, 132
   preinstall, 132
   preuninstall, 132
   verification, 396
software, 109
source files (content), 177
source package files, 109
source packages, 109
source tags, 175-176
sources, unpacking, 285
subpackages, 257
tags (patch), 286
updating, 250
verification time
   (%verifyscript), 183
spec files, 121-122
%files list (directives), 194
%prep, 141
%setup macro, 188-191
architecture, 202
conditionals, 201-203
directives, 195-201
directories, 185
formats, 121-122
macros
   %patch, 191-194
   %setup, 184-191, 396
   patch%, 192
   setup, 397
operating systems, 203
packages, 140
paths, 365
source tags, 188
statements, 203
subpackages, 201
specdir entry, 365
speed (RPM version 1), 10
srcrpmdir entry, 365
standard input (packages), 59
statements (spec files), 203

status
   building packages, 372
   installation, 22-23, 33
   nonzero, 24
   packages, 64-65, 74, 307
   rpm -b command, 159
   software installation, 19
storing
   data, 342-343
   databases, 361
   header structures, 342
   headers, 343
STRING ARRAY header structure value, 343
string data, 343
STRING header structrue value, 343
structure (conditionals_, 271
subdirectories, 199
subpackages, 200, 248
   %description tags, 252
   %files list, 253-254
   %package directives, 250
   -n <string>, 201
   amanda, 284
   bazlib, 249
   building, 201, 259-260
   clients, 249-250, 293-295, 303
      directives, 293
      installation, 298
   erase-time scripts, 256
   erasing, 293
   install scripts, 256
   installation, 262, 293
   preamble, 249-250
   scripts
      %pre, 262
      build-time, 257
   servers, 249-250, 295, 303
   spec file, 257
   spec files, 201
   tags, 252
   testing, 260-261, 303
subscriptions
   redhat-digest mailing list, 408
   redhat-list mailing list, 408
   rpm-list mailing list, 408
Summary (packages), 62

SUMMARY - -queryformat tag, 377

summary descriptive tags, 167, 389

summary tag, 252

Symbolic Link String attribute, 197

symbolic links, 83
    see also symlinks

symlink file attribute, 400

symlinks, 58
    absolute, 217, 223
    paths, 58
    relative, 223
    relocatable packages, 219, 223
    verification, 83

syntax
    commands (build-related), 160
    rpm -e command, 38
    rpm -K command, 94
    rpmrc file, 358

T

-T %setup macro option, 397

tags, 70, 348
    %description tags, 252
    architecture
        excludearch, 172, 392
        exclusivearch, 173, 392
    autoreqprov, 209
    available, 73-74
    conflicts, 211
    dependency, 169-171, 390-391
    descriptive, 166-169, 389
    directive, 293-294
    directory, 174, 392
    exclude.xxx, 270
    exclusive.xxx, 270
    field width, 70
    headers, 347
    justification, 70
    naming, 165-166
    operating system, 173, 392
    package-naming, 388
    patch, 176-177, 286

platform-dependent, 265, 269

provides, 212

queries, 73-74
    ARCH, 73
    FILENAMES, 73
    FILESIZES, 73
    INSTALLTIME, 71
    NAME, 70, 73
    RELEASE, 70
    RPMTAG, 73
    RPMTAG ARCH, 73
    RPMTAG VERIFYSCRIPT, 73
    VERSION, 70

relocation (prefix), 216-217

requires, 209

single-entry, 73

source, 175-176

tar files (decompression), 121

technical support
    ftp sites, 404-406
    Linux, 408
    redhat-digest mailing list, 408
    redhat-list mailing list, 408
    RPM, 408
    rpm-list mailing list, 408
    Web site, 409

terminating
    build process, 136
    building packages, 132
    package building, 136

- -test rpm -b command option, 153, 372

- -test rpm -e command option, 18, 38-41

- -test rpm -i command option, 18, 23-24, 370

- -test rpm -U command option, 46, 371

testing
    %setup macro, 191
    amanda, 277, 303
    build roots (alternate), 227
    builds, 154
    installation, 23-24
    package erasing, 40-41

packages, 137, 296
    - -replacefiles option, 137
    relocatable, 222-223

scripts, 303

software (alternate build roots), 227

subpackages, 260-261, 303

third-party packages, building, 114-115

time (packages), building, 14

- -timecheck <secs> rpm -b command option, 158

- -timecheck rpm -b command, 372

timecheck entry, 365

tmpdir entry, 366

tools directory, 349

top-level directories, 190
    creating, 180
    paths, 366
    source files, 189

topdir entry, 366

TRIGGERFLAGS - - queryformat tag, 386

TRIGGERINDEX - - queryformat tag, 386

TRIGGERNAME - - queryformat tag, 385

TRIGGERSCRIPTS - - queryformat tag, 385

TRIGGERVERSION - - queryformat tag, 386

troubleshooting
    new software version, 51
    package building, 136, 273
    verification, 98-99
    warning messages, 21-22

U

/usr/local default path prefix, 222

UIDs (%attr macro), 235

uniform resource locators, see URLs

uninstallation
    amanda, 300-302
    one-command, 9
    packages, 6, 11

uninstallation scripts, 122, 300-302

unpacking
amanda sources, 277
source files, 185-191
sources, 121, 285
updating
libraries, 182
spec files, 250
upgrades, 47
applications, 116
configuration files, 47-49
forcing, 51
MD5 checksums, 47-49
packages, 6, 50, 320, 371
source code, 12
sources, 115
postinstall scripts, 51-52
preinstall scripts, 51-52
RPM, 10
software, 116
versions, older, 50-51
URL - -queryformat tag, 379
url descriptive tag, 168
url descriptive tags, 390
URLs (uniform resource locators), 20-21, 128, 168
packages (queries), 59
patches, 177
Red Hat Software Web site, 409
source files, 175
user IDs, 169, 196, 239

V

-v command option (rpm -K), 94-97
-v rpm
-i command option, 18, 22
-U command option, 46
-vv rpm
-b command option, 159
-i command option, 18, 23
-U command option, 46
values
Boolean, 309
header structure
BIN, 343
CHAR, 343
INT16, 343
INT32, 343

INT64, 343
INT8, 343
NULL, 343
STRING, 343
STRING ARRAY, 343
variables, 308-309
variable manipulation functions
rpmGetVar( ), 308
rpmSetVar( ), 309
variables
environmental, 394
values, 308-309
writing to files, 310
vendor descriptive tag, 168, 390
vendor entry, 366
vendors, 129, 168, 364-366
VENDORS - -queryformat tag, 378
verbosity
current, 322
increasing, 322
output, 362
verification
architecture, overriding, 35
configuration files, 81
dependency processing, disabling, 87
Emacs, 98
files, 86, 318-319
attributes, 91
defaults, 100
disabling, 88
file ownership, 82
groups, 82
major number, 83
MD5 checksum, 82
minor number, 83
modes, 82
modification time, 83
size, 82
symlinks, 83
hardware, overriding, 35
installation, 11
non-PGP, 99
operating systems, overriding, 35
output failure, 84, 96
package files, 94

package installation, 117
packages, 85-86, 100, 183, 319, 369
clients, 303
failure output, 83
grouping, 87
installation, 85-86
output failure, 84
relocation, 221
signatures, 97, 238, 323, 374
PGP (public keys), 97
scripts, disabling, 88
software, 196-197
subpackage (installation), 262
troubleshooting, 98-99
verification functions
rpmReadPackageInfo( ), 324
rpmVerifyFile( ), 319
rpmVerifyScript( ), 319
rpmVerifySignature( ), 323
verification scripts, 396
verification-time script (%verifyscript), 183
- -verify command, 80, 370
see also rpm -V; rpm -y command
verify scripts, 68, 122
VERIFYSCRIPT - - queryformat tag, 386
version, 128
files, naming, 338
package labels, 55
packages
erasing, 47
queries, 61
software, 51, 338
VERSION - -queryformat tags, 376
version naming tag, 165
- -version option, 105
version package-naming tag, 388
VERSION query tag, 70
versions
comparison operators, 210
file formats, 339
headers, 349
installation, checking, 105

libraries (compatibility), 60
numbers, 210
older (upgrades), 50-51
packages, 115, 349
serial numbers, 171
software, 13, 211
viewing
data for packages, 7
installation status, 22-23
packages, 57, 89
data, 121
status, 74
subpackages (spec file), 257
virtual packages, 169, 212

W

- -vv command option, 100
**- -vv rpm -e command option,
38-40**
warning messages, 21-22
**warranty information, 410,
414**
Web pages (PGP), 421
Web site (RPM), 409
**- -whatprovides rpm -q
command option, 369**
writing
headers, 324
packages to disks, 339
scripts, 153
variables, 310

X–Y–Z

XPM - -queryformat tag, 378
**xxx canon rpmrc file entry,
266**
**xxx compat rpmrc file entry,
267**

Slackware Linux Unleashed, Third Edition

—Timothy Parker, et al.

Slackware Linux is a 32-bit version of the popular UNIX operating system. In many ways, it enhances the performance of UNIX and UNIX-based applications. Slackware is a free operating system that can be downloaded from the Internet. And because it is free, there is very little existing documentation for the product. This book fills that void and provides Slackware Linux users with the information they need to effectively run the software on their computers or networks.

Price: $49.99 USA/$70.95 CDN   *User level: Accomplished—Expert*

ISBN: 0-672-31012-0   *1,300 pages*

Linux Unleashed, Second Edition

—Kamran Hussain, Timothy Parker, et al.

Readers will turn to this second edition for in-depth coverage of hot Linux topics—PPP's, networking, and site set-up and administration. This book is the only complete reference programmers, users, or system administrators will ever need.

Price: $49.99 USA/$67.99 CDN   *User level: Beginning—Intermediate*

ISBN: 0-672-30908-4   *1,224 pages*

UNIX Unleashed

—Various UNIX wizards

The power user's guide to UNIX! This book/CD-ROM set provides an in-depth examination of UNIX and its utilities. The CD-ROM contains shell scripts from the book and sample UNIX programs. This book includes definitions, practical information, tips, tricks, and examples.

Price: $49.99 USA/$67.99 CDN   *User level: New—Casual—Accomplished*

ISBN: 0-672-30402-3   *1,620 pages*

TCP/IP Blueprints

—Martin Bligh, Dennis Short, Thomas Lee, et al.

TCP/IP is the predominant network protocol in use today. *TCP/IP Blueprints* is a comprehensive, indispensable tutorial and reference for anyone working with TCP/IP using the new IP V6 standard. Using real-world, easy-to-understand examples, users will learn how to operate, maintain, debug, and troubleshoot TCP/IP.

Price: $39.99 USA/$56.95 CDN   *User level: Accomplished—Expert*

ISBN: 0-672-31055-4   *500 pages*

Add to Your Sams Library Today with the Best Books for Programming, Operating Systems, and New Technologies

The easiest way to order is to pick up the phone and call

1-800-428-5331

between 9:00 a.m. and 5:00 p.m. EST.

For faster service please have your credit card available.

ISBN	Quantity	Description of Item	Unit Cost	Total Cost
0-672-31012-0		Slackware Linux Unleashed, Third Edition	$49.99	
0-672-30908-4		Linux Unleashed, Second Edition	$49.99	
0-672-30402-3		UNIX Unleashed	$49.99	
0-672-31055-4		TCP/IP Blueprints	$39.99	
❏ 3 ½" Disk		Shipping and Handling: See information below.		
❏ 5 ¼" Disk		TOTAL		

Shipping and Handling: $4.00 for the first book, and $1.75 for each additional book. Floppy disk: add $1.75 for shipping and handling. If you need to have it NOW, we can ship product to you in 24 hours for an additional charge of approximately $18.00, and you will receive your item overnight or in two days. Overseas shipping and handling adds $2.00 per book and $8.00 for up to three disks. Prices subject to change. Call for availability and pricing information on latest editions.

201 W. 103rd Street, Indianapolis, Indiana 46290

1-800-428-5331 — Orders   1-800-835-3202 — FAX   1-800-858-7674 — Customer Service

Book ISBN 0-672-31105-4